Bridge for Beginners:

A Complete Course

Zia Mahmood

with Audrey Grant

Foreword by Omar Sharif

B T Batsford Ltd, *London*

To my brother Ali, to L.B.,
and to those we love who are no longer with us

First published in 1990 as three volumes:
Breakthrough Bridge: Bidding for Beginners
Breakthrough Bridge: Declarer Play for Beginners and
Breakthrough Bridge: Defence for Beginners
by Virgin Books, UK

Revised edition published in 1994 by
Collins Willow
an imprint of HarperCollins Publishers. London
Reprinted 1995

First Batsford edition 1998
Reprinted 2001

ISBN 0 7134 8359 8

Printed by The Bath Press, Bath
for the publishers,
B.T.Batsford Ltd,
9 Blenheim Court,
Brewery Road,
London N7 9NY

A member of the Chrysalis Group plc

A BATSFORD BRIDGE BOOK

Contents

Foreword

I think it was just before filming *Lawrence of Arabia* that I first discovered that 'finesse' didn't necessarily mean choosing the correct vintage of Dom Perignon. It was a discovery that changed my life, as this introduction to the game of bridge, which developed initially as a method of combating the frequent boredom of film making, changed to a passion and an involvement that are stronger today than ever. It would be difficult to count the hours of pleasure I have received from bridge, surely the most fascinating of games ever invented, and I hope that you too can derive the same joy after this introduction to the game.

Zia has long been a friend of mine and he is rated by many as the No 1 player in the world. In my opinion, however, his contribution has been much more than expertise because of the charisma and sense of fun that he brings with him to the game. He is the living proof that bridge is not a boring game for boring people but an exciting game that mixes all the most vital human qualities and emotions.

In *Bridge for Beginners*, Zia has combined his expertise and sense of humour with the talents of the internationally known teacher and author Audrey Grant to bring an introduction to the game that is essential for all beginners.

For once, you can learn the secrets of the game presented in a simple yet entertaining manner that is as much fun to read as to play. For once, you can actually listen to an expert as he talks you through his thoughts on every basic step and situation. Finally, once you have read this book, I hope you will take up the game of bridge as I once did, because I already know that its lure is irresistible once felt, its addiction heady and exciting, and I would to like share this knowledge.

Omar Sharif

PART ONE: BIDDING

CHAPTER 1

Introduction

It is generally accepted that contract bridge started in about 1925 when Harold Sterling Vanderbilt was cruising the Caribbean on the SS Finland. He picked up a pack of cards, shuffled them, and said 'Gentlemen, let me show you a new game. It may interest you.'

Bridge is said to be the Rolls-Royce of card games, and for good reason. It can be as comfortable as your favourite pair of shoes, and yet at the same time it can excite you as much after you have played for years as when you first experienced the game. Bridge can be a quiet source of pleasure when you play in familiar surroundings with friends you have known all your life, or a tool which introduces you to new people in new places. Tennis star Martina Navratilova once said that bridge meant a lot to her in her travels: 'No matter where I go,' she said, 'I can always make new friends at the bridge table'. Omar Sharif is said to have given up acting, horses and women for the game. For others, bridge is a great social activity. It is difficult to believe that bridge is good for us; to believe that something that brings so much joy is neither immoral, against the law nor bad for our health. If you are not yet familiar with the game, what have you been waiting for? If you have played for years, it's time to introduce you to some of the secrets of the experts, taught, we hope, with a mixture of fun and simplicity.

Getting started

All you need are three other people and a *pack* of cards. If you have a card table, four chairs and a pencil and paper to keep score, so much the better. Already you are as well-equipped as a world champion!

Bridge is a partnership game. Although you can play with a regular partner, it is common to *cut* for partners. To do this, take the cards and spread them face down on the table. Each player selects a card and turns it up. The cards are ranked as usual in this order: Ace (highest), King, Queen, Jack, 10, 9, 8, 7, 6, 5, 4, 3, 2 (lowest). The players choosing the two higher-ranking cards play together and those picking the two lower-ranking cards are partners. If the four cards turned over were an ace, a king, a jack and a 3, the players choosing the ace and king would play together and the players turning over the jack and 3 would be partners.

What if two players pick the same ranked card? Let's consider a most unusual case where all four players pick aces. It looks as if there is a four-way tie, but there is a method of breaking such a tie. The *suits* are ranked in alphabetical order with the clubs (♣) being the lowest ranked suit, then diamonds (◊), hearts (♡) and, at the top, the highest ranking suit, spades (♠). In the situation mentioned above, then, the players with the ace of spades (♠A) and ace of hearts (♡A) would play against the players holding the ace of diamonds (◊A) and ace of clubs (♣A).

The partners sit opposite one another. Bridge writers refer to the players not by name but by direction: North, East, South and West. Here, then, are the four players sitting round the table:

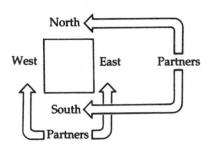

Introducing the play

Once everyone is sitting down and ready to play, the player who chose the highest card deals. The jokers are not used, so a bridge pack consists of 52 cards. Starting with the player on his left, the dealer deals one card at a time to each player, proceeding clockwise around the table, until the pack is exhausted and each player has 13 cards. If, during the deal, a card is accidentally turned face up, the deal must be restarted – the pack must be shuffled and cut, and the dealer tries again! Each player picks up his *hand* and sorts it into suits. It is easier to see your hand if you separate the black and red suits. Here is a sorted bridge hand:

In a book or newspaper, the above bridge hand is usually written out in the ranking order of the suits, with spades first, then hearts, diamonds and clubs as follows:

♠ A J 3
♡ K 9 7 4
♢ Q 8 2
♣ J 10 5

The objective during the play of the hand is for your partnership to try to take as many *tricks* as you can. A trick consists of four cards, one from each player, and the player contributing the highest card wins the trick for his side. The player who wins each trick *leads* the first card to the next trick face up on the table and the other three players play their cards, in turn, clockwise around the table. Everyone has to *follow suit* to the first card that is led, if they can. For example, let's suppose that West leads the king of spades. All the other players, in turn, have to follow suit by playing a spade, if they have one. Suppose North contributes the ace of spades, the

highest card in the suit, East plays the 3 of spades and South plays
the 2 of spades. North has won the trick for his side (North-South).
Here is the trick:

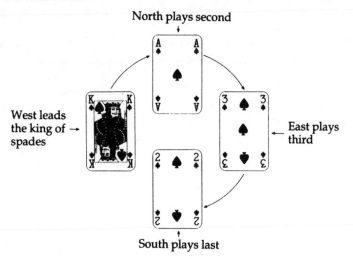

North plays second

West leads
the king of →
spades

East plays
third

↑
South plays last

North collects the four cards and puts them in a stack face down in
front of himself. Usually, one member of the partnership collects
all the tricks won for his side. At the end of the hand, thirteen tricks
will have been played and the table might look like this:

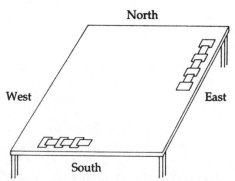

You can see that North-South took six tricks and East-West took
seven. The game can be played in one of two ways: with a trump

suit, or in no trumps. In no trumps, the highest card played in the suit led always wins the trick. If you cannot follow suit, you must play a card in another suit, but a card *discarded* in this way has no power to win the trick, even if it is higher-ranking than the card led. To take an unlikely example: West leads the two of clubs, on which North plays the ace of spades, East the ace of hearts and South the ace of diamonds. West is the winner of the trick, for his two was the highest – indeed the only – card played in the suit led. The winner of the trick, when playing in no trumps, is the person who played the highest card in the suit that was led.

The game can also be played in a *trump* suit where one suit becomes the most powerful suit for that hand. If you cannot follow suit you can play a trump and it will win the trick, provided a higher trump is not played on the same trick. For example, let's suppose that clubs have been designated as the trump suit. West leads the ◊A, North plays the ◊5, East plays the ◊3 and South plays the ♣2. The trick looks like this:

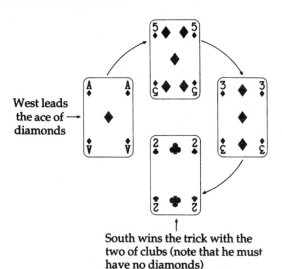

West leads the ace of diamonds →

South wins the trick with the two of clubs (note that he must have no diamonds)

Because clubs are trumps, the small club wins the trick. South, however, can only play the ♣2 if he has no diamonds left in his hand. Otherwise, he must follow suit by playing a diamond on the trick. South does not have to play a trump if he has no diamonds. Instead, he can discard a heart or spade and let West win the trick with the ◊A. It is permitted to lead trumps. If the trump suit is led, the highest trump played wins the trick. Let's summarise all these points about playing the cards:

Summary of play of the hand

1 You and your partner work together to take as many tricks as you can.
2 When one player leads a card to a trick, all other players must follow suit if they can. If a player cannot follow suit, he plays a card from another suit.
3 The player who wins the trick leads to the next trick. Each player follows clockwise in turn.
4 In no trumps, the highest card of the suit led wins the trick.
5 When playing with a trump suit, if a player cannot follow suit he can choose to play a trump. If more than one trump is played to a trick, the highest trump played wins the trick. This is the only exception to the cardinal rule of trick taking which is that the highest card played in the suit led always wins the trick.

Introducing the bidding

In some card games, the trump suit is decided by turning up a card, sometimes from another pack. In bridge, each player gets an opportunity to suggest that the longest suit in his hand be the trump suit. Suppose this is your hand:

♠ 3 2
♡ A K 7 5 2
◊ 7 3
♣ A K 7 3

Your longest suit is hearts and so you would suggest that hearts be trumps, by bidding hearts. Now let's look at your partner's hand:

♠ A 8 6 5 4
♡ 6
◊ 9 6 2
♣ Q J 8 6

The longest suit in your partner's hand is spades, so that would be his first choice, or bid. The bidding is simply a conversation that you have with your partner to reach a consensus about the trump suit. One drawback is that you have to reach this decision without seeing your partner's hand. That seems fair, doesn't it? Can you imagine how colourless the game would be if you could look at one another's hands? Another limitation is that you cannot mention the actual cards that you hold in a suit or the number of cards that you hold in each suit. It would take away the challenge if you could say to your partner that you have the ace, king, 7, 5 and 2 of hearts or that you have a four-card club suit headed by the ace and king.

Instead, the type of conversation you and your partner could have with the above hands would, possibly, go something like this:

You: I like hearts better than any other suit.
Partner: I like spades best; I don't have many hearts.
You: I don't like spades very much but what do you think about clubs?
Partner: I don't mind clubs.
You: So let's agree to choose clubs as our trump suit.
Partner: Seems reasonable.

This is the concept of bidding. It really is this simple, except for a very small catch we will come to shortly. You and your partner are having a conversation to tell each other as much as possible about your hands. How did you and your partner do in the above discussion? You found your longest combined suit, which is the idea of bidding. In either hearts or spades, on these hands, you have only seven combined cards in the suit. In clubs you and your partner have an eight-card *fit*, which means you have eight cards in the suit between the two hands. No matter how far you go in bridge, bidding should never be more complicated than the concept of a conversation between two friends.

The partnership, through the bidding, tries to uncover the suit in which it holds the most cards – the suit that would make the best trump suit. A good trump suit is usually one containing eight or more cards between the two hands. Since there are thirteen cards in a suit, if your side has eight, the opponents have only five cards and you hold the clear majority of the suit. If you can make your longest combined suit the trump suit, you will be able to use your small trump cards to help win tricks whenever you cannot follow suit, since they will then have more value than even the ace in a suit that is not trumps.

Now, about that catch! Let's take another look at the bidding. When you play a game of bridge, you are expected to use only the language and the vocabulary of the game. You cannot actually say 'I like hearts, how about you?' The good news, however, is that the bridge language is spoken world-wide and the vocabulary consists of only a handful of words: the numbers from one to seven; the names of the suits – clubs, diamonds, hearts and spades – or no trumps; and the words *pass* or *no bid*. These few simple words are all you need to describe your hand.

A bid is a combination of a number and a *denomination* (a suit or no trumps). A bid, for example, would be one heart (1♡), three spades (3♠), six no trumps (6NT) or seven clubs (7♣). You can envisage that, if you say one heart (1♡), it means you like hearts. The number refers to the number of tricks you are expected to take if you win the bid. One heart, however, does not refer to taking only one trick with hearts as trumps. Six tricks, referred to as your *book*, must be added to the number of the bid. If you say 'one heart', you and your partner would have to take seven (6 + 1 = 7) tricks if your bid for the trump suit is accepted. The idea behind this assumed book of six tricks in addition to the number that you actually bid is that you must commit yourselves to taking the majority of the thirteen tricks available if you want your suit to be the trump suit.

Bridge bidding is like an *auction*. The players try to outbid each other for the privilege of naming the trump suit. There is no auctioneer, however. Instead there is an agreed-upon, orderly way of conducting the bidding.

The dealer gets the first opportunity to open the bidding by suggesting a denomination (a trump suit or no trumps). If he does not want to commit his side to trying to take at least seven tricks – the minimum requirement for opening the bidding – he can say 'Pass' or 'No bid'. Each player, clockwise in turn, then gets a chance to make a bid or to pass. The auction continues round the table until a bid is followed by three passes, meaning that everyone is in agreement with the last bid, and no one wants to bid any further.

What if one player bids 1♠ and the next player wants to bid 1◊? Which bid is higher? There is an automatic tie-breaker built into the language of bridge. The suits are ranked, remember, in ascending alphabetical order (clubs, diamonds, hearts, spades). No trumps is considered to rank the highest of all, higher than spades. Since diamonds are lower-ranking than spades, a 1♠ bid outranks a 1◊ bid. If the next player wants to suggest diamonds as the trump suit, he will have to commit his side to taking more tricks by raising the level and bidding 2◊. On the other hand, if the next player wants to suggest no trumps, he can bid 1NT, since that outranks the 1♠ bid.

We can think of the possible bids as a series of steps leading from one level to the next as illustrated below:

The bidding steps

```
                              7♣ 7◊ 7♡ 7♠ 7NT
                           6♣ 6◊ 6♡ 6♠ 6NT
                        5♣ 5◊ 5♡ 5♠ 5NT
                     4♣ 4◊ 4♡ 4♠ 4NT
                  3♣ 3◊ 3♡ 3♠ 3NT
               2♣ 2◊ 2♡ 2♠ 2NT
            1♣ 1◊ 1♡ 1♠ 1NT
```

Each bid must be further up or further to the right on the bidding steps than the preceding bid. If a player starts the bidding at the one level (1♣, 1◊, 1♡, 1♠ or 1NT), contracting to take seven tricks, another player can make a bid in a higher-ranking denomination at the one level or must climb to the two level, contracting to take eight tricks, if he wants to make a bid in a lower-ranking denomination. If a player does not want to bid any higher, he will pass.

Hearts and spades are referred to as the *major* suits and, when you look at the bidding steps, you can see they are higher-ranking than clubs or diamonds which are referred to as the *minor* suits.

After there are three passes, the last bid determines the trump suit and the number of tricks that the side naming this trump suit must take to be successful. The final bid becomes the *contract*. Let's look at our two hands to see how they would be bid using the language of bridge. We will assume that the opponents do not wish to compete for the contract and choose to pass throughout the auction.

You	Partner
♠ 3 2	♠ A 8 6 5 4
♡ A K 7 5 2	♡ 6
◇ 7 3	◇ 9 6 2
♣ A K 7 3	♣ Q J 8 6

You: *One heart.*   (I like hearts and am contracting to take seven tricks with hearts as trumps.)

Partner: *One spade.*   (I would prefer spades as trumps. I can keep the bidding at the one level since spades rank higher than hearts.)

You   *Two clubs.*   (You don't seem to like my hearts. How about clubs? I have to move to the two level to show my second suit since clubs are lower-ranking than spades.)

Partner: *Pass*   (I like clubs much better than hearts and they should make a satisfactory trump suit. I do not want to go any higher up the bidding steps since we are already contracting to take eight tricks.)

Let's suppose you are sitting in the South position and your partner is North. This is the way the above auction would normally be written down, showing your opponents' passes as well as your bids:

South	West	North	East
1♡	Pass	1♠	Pass
2♣	Pass	Pass	Pass

West, North and East all have to say pass after the 2♣ bid in order to end the auction. North-South are said to have won the bid and the *final contract* is 2♣. What happens next?

Introducing the roles of each side

After the bidding is completed, one partnership has been successful in naming the trump suit and, in the process, has arrived at a
contract, which is a commitment to take a certain number of tricks.
In the example above, North-South arrived at a contract of 2♣ and,
in doing so, committed to take eight tricks with clubs as trumps. If
they take at least eight tricks with clubs as trump, they make their
contract. If they are not successful in collecting eight tricks, then
East-West defeat the contract. East-West are said to be the *defence*
and they are trying to prevent North-South from taking enough
tricks to fulfil the contract.

One player from the side who wins the contract is called the
declarer and that player is going to play both his and his partner's
hands. The other hand is referred to as the *dummy*. Which player is
the declarer and which player is the dummy? The player who first
mentioned the suit that ended up being the trump suit (or who-
ever bid no trumps first in a no-trump contract is the declarer and
his partner becomes the dummy. In the auction above, South is the
declarer since he was the first to mention the club suit and his partner, North, is the dummy. The player to the left of the declarer
makes the opening lead. In this case, it would be West and he
would choose a card and place it on the table. North's hand, the
dummy, is then placed face up on the table. The trump suit is put
on dummy's right – the declarer's left. Suppose the opening lead is
the ◊K. After the dummy is put down, the cards on the table might
look like this:

North
Declarer's partner (dummy)
●

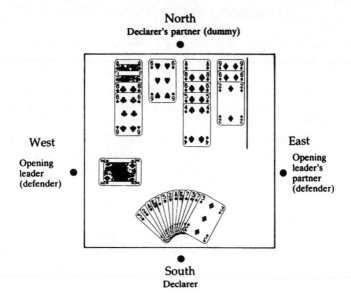

West   East

Opening   Opening
leader   leader's
(defender)   ●   ●   partner
                                                          (defender)

●
South
Declarer

In order to discuss the play from the declarer's viewpoint, the
hand is usually illustrated as follows:

Dummy
♠ A 8 6 5 4
♡ 6
◇ 9 6 2
♣ Q J 8 6

Opening Lead
◇ K

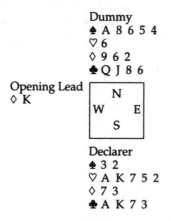

Declarer
♠ 3 2
♡ A K 7 5 2
◇ 7 3
♣ A K 7 3

The *defenders* (East-West) can take the first two diamond tricks but
you can trump the third round of diamonds with one of your

clubs. This is one of the advantages of playing this hand with clubs as the trump suit. It prevents the opponents from taking too many tricks with their diamond suit. You will learn how to play this hand as you read through the first part on declarer play.

Introducing the scoring

In the above hand, when you take the eight tricks to which you committed yourself in the auction, you are awarded a certain number of *points* for fulfilling the contract. The exact details of the scoring are contained in the appendix on p. 455. All that is important for now is that you have a general idea of how the game is scored. The partnership which earns the highest number of points from all the hands that are played wins the game. Points can be scored in three ways:

- If you *make* (fulfil) your contract, you are given a trick score for each trick you take beyond your book of six tricks.
- If you defeat the opponents' contract, by preventing them from taking the number of tricks to which they committed themselves, you gain points for each trick by which you defeat their contract. In effect, your opponents suffer a penalty when they *go down* (are defeated) in their contract.
- Points are awarded for reaching and making certain bonus level contracts.

Summary

The four players form two partnerships, with the partners sitting opposite each other across the table.

After the cards have been dealt out, the players, in clockwise rotation starting with the dealer, have an opportunity to suggest the denomination (trump suit or no trumps) in which they would like to play the hand.

Each bid must be higher on the bidding steps than the previous bid. If a player does not want to bid, he says pass or no bid.*

*Pass is commonly used in the USA, 'no bid' in Britain, but either is correct

The side willing to commit itself to the greater number of tricks for the privilege of naming the denomination wins the auction.

The last bid becomes the final contract.

The player who first suggested the denomination of the final contract becomes the declarer and his partner becomes the dummy.

The defender to the left of the declarer leads to the first trick and then the dummy's hand is placed face up on the table.

The declarer tries to take the number of tricks his side committed itself to in bidding the final contract. He plays the cards from both the dummy and his own hand on each trick.

The defenders try to take enough tricks to defeat the contract.

With this introduction, you are ready to play.

CHAPTER 2

Hand Valuation

The new game, contract bridge, not only interested those in the ship's stateroom, it caught the imagination of people around the world. The media caught the 'bridge bug' and bridge became front page news. The game became a popular pastime, with both men and women. Housewives, who had hitherto thought a dummy was a baby's pacifier, banded themselves together to the permanent ruin of their husbands' digestion.

Well, you are about to learn a foreign language. If you have ever tried this before, you know how difficult it can be – which is the bad news. The good news about learning the language of bridge is that the vocabulary consists of only a few words. The more fluent you become in using this new language, the better bidder you become. All you need to do is remember that the sole purpose of bidding is to describe the cards in your hand as clearly as possible to your partner, using the language of bridge. Using only two words – 'one spade', for example – you paint a picture of your hand. If you ever wanted to be a person of few words, bridge provides the opportunity!

Valuing a hand

A bid portrays something about both the *distribution* and *strength* of your hand. The distribution is the number of cards you hold in each suit. As we saw in the sample auction in Chapter 1, you start to describe your distribution through the denomination of your bid. If you open the bidding 1♡, for example, you are telling your partner that hearts is your longest suit – 'I like hearts'.

High card points

Before you can make a bid that starts to describe your distribution to your partner, however, you must have sufficient strength (trick-taking power) to enter the auction. After all, every time you make a bid you are committing your side to take a certain number of tricks. Since most tricks are taken with the high cards in each suit – aces, kings, queens and jacks – an estimate of the strength of your hand can be arrived at by giving a value to each of the high cards in your hand. Since the ace is the most valuable card in a suit, followed by the king, queen and jack, the following scale is used:

High card points

Ace	4 points
King	3 points
Queen	2 points
Jack	1 point

You add up the high card points (HCPs) for each of the high cards in your hand to arrive at a total value. For example, what do the following three hands have in common?

1	♠ A K Q 4	2	♠ A K Q 8 7	3	♠ A K Q 8 4 3 2
	♡ A 4 3		♡ A 7 6		♡ A 7 6 5 3
	◊ 9 8 2		◊ 6 5 3		◊ –
	♣ 6 4 2		♣ 9 2		♣ 7

They each contain 13 high card points (HCPs) – 4 for the ♠A, 3 for the ♠K, 2 for the ♠Q and 4 for the ♡A. That was easy; you are already halfway to becoming a bridge player.

Although all the hands contain exactly the same high cards, however, are they all of equal value? Which hand would you most like to have? If you chose the third hand, go to the top of the class! The trick-taking potential of the third hand is increased because of the long suits. If, for example, you can make spades the trump suit, you will take a lot of tricks with your small spades, in addition to the ♠A, ♠K and ♠Q. Likewise, the second hand is more valuable than the first. The total strength of a hand, therefore, is a combination of the strength and the *length* (distribution) of your suits.

Support points

When you are the dealer and have the first opportunity either to open the bidding or pass, you have no information about your partner's hand. Sometimes your partner is the dealer and you hear your partner's suggestion before you have to give your opinion. Consider this hand:

♠ –
♡ J 10 9 4
♢ A 9 4 3 2
♣ K 4 3 2

How would you feel about your hand if your partner opened the bidding 1♠? Compare this with the way you would feel if your partner opened 1♡. Most of us would feel that this particular hand is more valuable if our partner opens 1♡ since we can see that hearts would make a much more suitable trump suit than spades. To reflect the increased value of a hand in this type of situation, we use *support points*.

Support points are used when you are expecting to be the dummy, that is, when you are going to *support* (agree as trumps) your partner's suit. With the above hand, if your partner opens 1♠, you are not planning to support his suit. On the other hand, if partner opens the bidding 1♡, you want to agree to that suit as trumps. When you support your partner, you value your short suits: *voids* (no cards in a suit), *singletons* (one card in a suit) and *doubletons* (two cards in a suit) using the following scale:

Void	5 points
Singleton	3 points
Doubleton	1 point

In the above hand, then, if your partner opens 1♡, give yourself 8 HCPs and 5 points for the void in spades, for a total of 13 points. On the other hand, if your partner opens 1♠, you would not be supporting his suit so the hand would be worth only 8 points.

You can see from this that the value of your hand can change dramatically during the auction. To start with, before any player has made a bid, your hand is worth 9 points as explained. When your partner opens the bidding in spades, your hand is still worth only 9 points. But suppose you make a bid – we will see exactly what bid you might choose later, but say for the moment that you bid two diamonds – and your partner now bids two hearts. All of a sudden, your hand has become worth 13 points, because of the extra support points that you have if hearts are going to be trumps. It is the hallmark of the expert bidder that he can make mental adjustments to the initial value of his hand as the auction progresses.

Determining the hand pattern

In addition to focusing on the strength of your hand, you also want to take a look at the distribution or the shape. The fundamental thing to remember whenever you look at a hand is: does it belong to the family of *balanced* hands or the family of *unbalanced* hands? There is a strong family resemblance among balanced hands. There are no voids, no singletons and no more than one doubleton. It is a small family and has only three members:

1 X X X X	2 X X X X	3 X X X X X
X X X	X X X X	X X X
X X X	X X X	X X X
X X X	X X	X X
4–3–3–3	4–4–3–2	5–3–3–2

The numbers under each pattern refer to the number of cards in the four suits. For example, in the first hand, there are four cards in one suit and three in the other three suits (4–3–3–3). In the second hand, there are two four-card suits, a three-card suit and a doubleton (4–4–3–2). In the final pattern, there is a five-card suit, two three-card suits and a doubleton (5–3–3–2).

All other hand patterns are unbalanced. The possible combinations are now far greater. In an extreme case, a member of the unbalanced family of hands could have three voids and a thirteen-card suit. Here are three members of the unbalanced family:

1 X X X X X	2 X X	3 X
X X X X X	X X X X	X X X X X X
X X X	X X	X X X
None	X X X X X	X X X
5 – 5 – 3 – 0	5 – 4 – 2 – 2	6 – 3 – 3 – 1

The first hand qualifies as unbalanced because it has a void; the second because there are two doubletons; the third because there is a singleton.

Now that you are able to calculate the value of your hand and recognise its shape, you are ready to open the bidding.

Summary

Before you decide what to bid, value your hand using the following guidelines:

Hand value

High card points

Ace	4 points
King	3 points
Queen	2 points
Jack	1 point

Next, look at the shape of your hand and decide whether it is a member of the balanced or unbalanced family.

Hand families

Balanced	Unbalanced
• No void	• Could have a void
• No singleton	• Could have a singleton
• No more than one doubleton	• Could have more than one doubleton

If your partner has bid and you are planning to support the suit he bid, use support points, rather than length points, to value your hand.

Void	5 points
Singleton	3 points
Doubleton	1 point

Commonly asked questions

Zia: *Audrey, you work with a lot of students. What are some of the*
          questions they most frequently ask?

Audrey: Most of the questions at this point are about different
          methods of doing things which they have come across
          from other sources, such as books, newspapers, friends,
          relatives and even your television show, Zia. For exam-
          ple, they might wonder about giving points for length
          rather than shortness and whether they can play with a
          partner who values his hand by giving points for a void,
          a singleton or a doubleton when making an opening bid.
          They ask about valuing high cards in short suits – a sin-
          gleton ace or king, a doubleton queen or jack.

Zia: *Our answer, of course, would be to keep it simple.*

Audrey: That's right. There is no need to memorise a lot of
          material which you will rarely encounter. At the end of
          each chapter, we'll include a section on the most fre-
          quently asked questions – along with the answers, of
          course.

CHAPTER 3

One-level Opening Bids

At Wimbledon, when we got rained off, I spent my time playing bridge to keep me sharp and on my toes. An evening of bridge at home with family and friends is so much more enjoyable than sitting around watching TV, unless a good tennis match is on.

Martina Navratilova

You can start the auction if you are the dealer or if everyone in front of you has passed. Starting the auction is called *opening the bidding*. In order to consider opening the bidding, you need a hand of slightly more than average value. If you consider the value of all the high cards in the pack, there is a total of 40 high card points. An average hand, then, would be 10 points. Most players agree that 12 or 13 points is the minimum requirement to start the bidding at the one level. Your opening bid can be either in no trumps or in a suit.

Opening one no trump

When your hand belongs to the balanced family, a bid of no trumps should be on your mind. Whenever possible, a bridge player wants to give as much information about his hand as he can in a single bid. The opening bid of 1NT is very popular because it is so precise. Not only must it fall within one of the three balanced hand patterns but it must also be within a specific three-point range. You and your partner decide on the range you are going to use. Some players use a strong range of 15–17 points. In Britain, most players use the *Acol* system of bidding which is well-known for its *weak no trump* opening bid and so we suggest you use the following requirements for an opening bid of 1NT:

- A hand in the balanced family
- 12–14 points

Bids that describe the point count range within a few points are called *limit bids* and should be used at every opportunity. Look at each of the following hands and determine whether the dealer should start the bidding with 1NT:

1	♠ K53	2	♠ K109	3	♠ A4
	♡ AQ9		♡ QJ52		♡ A9852
	◊ A1098		◊ KJ75		◊ A1043
	♣ A83		♣ A3		♣ J4

The first hand is balanced, having no voids, no singletons and no more than one doubleton. However, there are 17 points, too many to open 1NT. To open 1NT you have to have 12, 13 or 14 points.

The second hand is balanced, having 4–4–3–2 distribution. It contains 14 points. Since it meets both requirements, you should open the bidding 1NT.

The third hand has 13 points but it is unbalanced, having two doubletons. It cannot be opened 1NT because it is not a member of the balanced family of hands.

As you can see, a hand has to be both balanced and contain 12, 13 or 14 points before it can be opened 1NT.

Opening one of a suit

Balanced hands containing more than 14 points and unbalanced hands of 12 or more points are opened at the one level with one of a suit (1♣, 1◊, 1♡ or 1♠). When opening with one of a suit, you bid your longest suit. There will always be at least one suit in your hand containing four or more cards. When you have a choice of two suits of equal length, there are some simple rules to help you decide.

Balanced hands

Hands which are balanced, yet have more than 14 points – too strong to open 1NT – are opened one of a suit. Consider the following hands:

1	♠ K Q 2	2	♠ A J 10	3	♠ A 10 7 6
	♡ A J 10 9 4		♡ K Q J		♡ K Q 3 2
	◊ Q J 8		◊ 10 9 7 4		◊ A J
	♣ A 7		♣ A 6 3		♣ Q 9 7

In the first example, with 17 HCPs, it seems straightforward to start with 1♡, the longest suit.

In the second example, with 15 HCPs, although the diamonds are the longest suit you may find it more difficult to open the bidding 1◊. You would like to have more diamonds, or at least a stronger looking four-card suit, but that is not what you were dealt. To feel more comfortable with such an opening bid, consider the alternatives. You do not want to pass since you have a much better than average hand and it is likely that your side can make a contract and score some points. To start with 1NT, however, would not be an accurate description of your hand. Your partner would think you had, at most, 14 points. Bid 1◊ and rest assured that it is the correct thing to do. The auction is not over yet. You are merely starting with the most descriptive bid within the limited language of bidding available to you.

In the third example, with 16 HCPs, you are again too strong to open 1NT. You want to start the bidding with one of a suit. In this case, you have a choice between two four-card suits. The general rule with two four-card suits is to bid the lower-ranking. Open the bidding 1♡. (The reason behind bidding the lower-ranking of two four-card suits is discussed in more detail on p. 38.)

Unbalanced hands

Usually it is very easy to know which suit to open when your hand is unbalanced. Choose the longest suit. If you have a choice of two five-card or six-card suits, you bid the higher-ranking suit. It would be easier if the rule for two five-card suits were the same as the rule for two four-card suits but the rules are designed to make the subsequent auction as economical as possible. (This is discussed more fully on p. 35.) Let's look at some examples:

1 ♠ 8	2 ♠ K Q 8 4 2	3 ♠ 3
♡ J 10 8 7 5 2	♡ A J 7 4 2	♡ A J 8 6 4 3
◇ A K 8 3	◇ K 4	◇ −
♣ A 4	♣ 3	♣ A K 7 5 4 2

With the first hand, open your longest suit, 1♡. On the second hand, you have an unbalanced hand with two five-card suits. Bid the higher-ranking, 1♠. The third hand contains two six-card suits. Again, start with the higher-ranking, 1♡.

There is one unbalanced pattern which we have not mentioned. You won't come across this pattern as often as the others we have mentioned but you may want to be aware of what to do when you have three four-card suits. The hand pattern is 4–4–4–1, such as the following:

♠ A J 10 3
♡ 7
◇ A 9 8 7
♣ A 10 9 4

If you do get a hand like this, open the bidding in the middle-ranking four-card suit, 1◇.

Over Zia's shoulder

Let's look over Zia's shoulder to see how he handles making an opening bid. These hands come from real tournaments where Zia was the dealer.

Audrey: *Zia, on this hand you opened 1NT, even though you have only two small spades. Weren't you worried that the opponents would take a lot of tricks in spades?*

♠ 8 7
♡ A 10 4 3
◇ A 4 2
♣ A J 9 8

Zia: Although that was a chance I was taking, I did have a partner who might be able to provide some help in spades. Also the opponents do not always do what you fear most. They might lead another suit. You should not be too cautious or put so many conditions on your bidding that it restricts you. There are pluses and minuses in everything you do, in every bid you make. The main idea is to describe the shape and strength of your hand. Open 1NT as often as you can, even with this weak doubleton.

Audrey: *You opened 1♡ with these cards:*

    ♠ A K J 2
    ♡ A 10 4 3 2
    ◊ A 8 7 4
    ♣ –

    The spades were so attractive. Did they tempt you, even a little?

Zia: Generally it is the length that you should focus on when considering your opening bid. Starting 1♡ worked out well on this hand. It was as if I had a magic wand when the lowest heart, the ♡2, took the opponents' ♣A. Open your longest, not your strongest suit.

Audrey: *You made another 1NT opening bid on this hand:*

    ♠ J 10
    ♡ A 9 8 4 2
    ◊ K Q 7
    ♣ Q 6 2

    Did you consider 1♡?

Zia: The problem on hands like this, if you avoid a no trump opening, is that you have chosen to give your partner a general picture of your hand rather than a specific picture. I want to tell my partner as much as I possibly can with one bid. If I open 1♡, I'm saying I have 12 or more points and a hand that is either balanced or unbalanced. When I open 1NT with these cards, I'm saying I have a

balanced hand and specifically 12, 13 or 14 points. That
should be very helpful to my partner.

Summary

When you have an opportunity to open the bidding, you can use
the following guidelines to decide what to do:

1 With fewer than 12 points, pass
2 Requirements for an opening bid of 1NT:
   • A balanced hand
   • 12, 13 or 14 points
3 Requirements for an opening bid of one in a suit:
   • With two four-card suits, open the lower-ranking
   • With two five-card suits, open the higher-ranking
   • With three four-card suits, open the middle-ranking
   • Otherwise, open the longest suit

Commonly asked questions

Q *Why do you open the bidding with the lower-ranking of two four-
   card suits?*
A To answer this, you have to consider how the auction is likely
   to proceed after your opening bid – a subject which we will be
   looking at in later chapters. For now, consider the following
   hand:

   ♠ A 10 7 6
   ♡ K Q 3 2
   ◊ A J
   ♣ Q 9 7

If you open the bidding 1♡ and your partner likes hearts, you
will have immediately found your trump fit. If your partner
does not like hearts, there is still room at the one level for him
to bid 1♠ and you will find your spade fit. If you were to open
the bidding 1♠, your partner would not be able to bid hearts
at the one level since they are a lower-ranking suit. If your
partner does not like spades and wants to bid hearts, he would
have to bid 2♡, going one level higher on the bidding steps. As

we will discuss later, your partner may not have enough strength to move to the two level, and it is possible that you will never find your best trump suit.

Q *Why do you open the lower-ranking of two four-card suits but the higher-ranking of two five-card or longer suits? Wouldn't it be easier to have only one rule to remember?*

A It would be nice to have only one rule but you must consider the difference in the shape of the two types of hands. When you have two four-card suits, your hand is balanced. You don't mind playing the contract in no trumps. On the other hand with two five-card suits, your hand is unbalanced and you want to mention both of your suits as inexpensively as possible. Look at this hand:

♠ 98
♡ A 10 9 8 7
◇ K Q 9 8 4
♣ A

You want to tell your partner as economically as possible about both the hearts and the diamonds. If you were to start with 1◇, the lower-ranking suit and your partner replied 1♠ you would have to bid 2♡ in order to show both of your suits. You have given your partner two choices, either diamonds or hearts. If your partner likes diamonds better, he has to bid 3◇ and you are at the three level, committed to taking nine tricks. Now, consider what would happen if you start the bidding with 1♡, the higher-ranking suit. Your partner bids 1♠ and you rebid 2◇. This time, the bidding can stay at a lower level. If your partner likes diamonds, he can pass; if he prefers hearts, he bids 2♡ and you are still at the two level.

Q *Do you suggest we open the suit below a singleton or doubleton?*

A Again, it isn't necessary to think about the suit below the short suit. Open the lower of two four-card suits, the higher of two five-card suits and the middle of three four-card suits. You don't need to be concerned about exceptions yet.

CHAPTER 4

Developing the Auction

Two bridge writers and players have dominated the game: Ely Culbertson and Charles Goren. In the 1930s, Culbertson went after the popular market. He staged tournaments challenging the best players of the day and this attracted media attention. Ely, however, did more than just this. He looked at his market and decided that his best chance to sell his books was to concentrate on ego, sex and fear.

Through the bidding, a partnership tries to exchange enough information to find the best denomination, either no trumps or a suit if there is a fit of eight or more cards between the two hands. In addition to this, the partnership wants to determine the best *zone* for the two combined hands in order to get the best possible score.

Introducing the bonus zones

There are three zones: the *slam zone*, the *game zone*, and the *partscore zone*. Since there are bonuses given for bidding and making slams and games, the partnership wants to know if there is enough combined strength to go for one of these bonus zones. This is very important, since the theme of determining the appropriate zone and denomination recurs at every level of the game. Let's look into this in more detail.

Slams

There are huge bonuses given for bidding and making a *grand slam*, which is a contract to take all of the tricks (see the appendix on p. 172 for the actual size of the bonuses). To be in a grand slam contract, consider the combined strength you and your partner would need to take all the tricks. If you were in a grand slam, you would want to be reasonably sure that the opponents didn't have the power to take even one trick. In other words, you want to be sure that the opponents don't have as much as an ace. Since an ace is worth 4 points, you want the opponents to have no more than 3 points. Since there are 40 high card points in the pack, to have a reasonable chance of making a grand slam the partnership wants to have 37 or more points in the combined hands so that the opponents have, at most, 3 points.

A *small slam* is a commitment to make all but one trick – in other words, to take twelve tricks. This time you can tolerate the opponents having one ace, but you would not want them to have two aces. The value of two aces is 8 points. To bid a small slam a partnership wants to have about 33–36 points. If a partnership bids a small slam with only 32 points, the opponents could have 8 points, which might be two aces – which would be embarrassing as well as unfortunate!

Although it is a delight to bid and make either a grand slam or a small slam, the experience does not come up that often, so the partnership usually satisfies itself with one of the game bonuses.

Games

There is a *game bonus* available in each suit. The minimum number of tricks you have to contract for in order to win one of the game bonuses is often within the reach of one of the partnerships on any given hand. There are three different game zones: one for no trumps; one for the major suits; one for the minor suits. The minimum contract on the bidding steps which receives the game bonus in each case is:

Game zones

No trumps:	3NT	(9 tricks)
The majors:	4♡ or 4♠	(10 tricks)
The minors:	5♣ or 5♢	(11 tricks)

Experience has shown that if your partnership has about 25 combined points, you can usually collect nine tricks in no trumps. When you are playing in a trump suit of eight or more combined cards, you can usually take one more trick than if you were playing in no trumps. So, if you have an eight-card or longer fit in hearts or spades, you also need about 25 points to make 4♡ or 4♠. If you are going to try to collect eleven tricks for the game bonus in clubs or diamonds, you need a little more, about 28 or 29 points.

Partscores

The partnership may find out through bidding that there are not enough combined points to consider bidding to one of the game zones. All is not lost, however. The partnership can settle on a partscore and still collect some points. If you discover that your partnership has fewer than 25 combined points, you should stop the auction in a partscore contract, keeping as low as possible on the bidding steps. There is no extra bonus for bidding and making a partscore contract of 2NT rather than a partscore contract of 1NT.

Partscore
No trumps: 1NT or 2NT
The majors: 1♡, 1♠, 2♡, 2♠, 3♡ or 3♠
The minors: 1♣, 1◇, 2♣, 2◇, 3♣, 3◇, 4♣ or 4◇

Since the focus is to aim for a game bonus whenever possible, the partnership's goal in the bidding can be thought of in this way:

- With 25 or more points, the partnership should reach a game contract.
- With less than 25 points, the partnership should stop in a partscore.

Working as a team

You have to work with your partner so that you can provide each other with enough information to know whether it is reasonable to bid to a game contract or whether to stop in a partscore. In order to be successful in this regard, it helps to have a clear picture of the role of each partner. This is one of the most overlooked strategies of the game and yet it is the most important. Knowing the role expected of each player will make your game much more relaxed.

First of all, let's suppose that your partner opens the bidding 1NT. Which player knows approximately how many combined points the partnership has? You do. Your partner, the person who opened 1NT, knows nothing about your hand but you know that your partner has specifically 12, 13 or 14 points. Not only that, you know that your partner has a balanced hand. You have a lot of information. As a matter of fact, when you add what you have in your own hand to what your partner has, you usually have enough information to *place* the contract (decide what the final contract should be). For that reason, your role is that of *captain*. On the other hand, your partner, the opener, is playing the role of *describer*, trying to paint an accurate picture of his hand so that you can make the appropriate decisions. It is wonderful when the opener makes a limit bid, such as 1NT, which with only one bid paints such a clear picture for the captain.

Acting the roles

During the bidding, the partnership is exchanging enough information to decide on both the appropriate zone and the appropriate denomination. Since those are two distinct decisions, the captain considers two questions:

- What is the best zone for the partnership?
- What is the best denomination for the partnership?

Deciding on the zone

When the opening bid is very specific, a 1NT opening, for example, the captain often has enough information to decide whether the partnership has the combined strength to go for the game bonus. It is a matter of adding up to 25. The captain adds his points to the point count range promised by his partner, mentally checking the total. For example, let's suppose your partner opens the bidding 1NT and you have exactly 13 points in your hand:

12 + 13 = 25   13 + 13 = 26   14 + 13 = 27

Whether your partner has 12, 13 or 14 points, the partnership has a combined total of at least 25 points, which should be sufficient to get to the game zone. So, if your partner opens the bidding 1NT, you, as captain, know that your side belongs in a game-zone contract whenever you hold 13 or more points.

On the other hand, suppose your partner opens the bidding 1NT and you have the following hand:

♠ A 8 7
♡ K 4 2
♢ Q J 10 3
♣ 5 3 2

You have only 10 points. Since your partner's 1NT opening bid describes a balanced hand with 12–14 points, you know that the most your partner could have is 14 points. The total, 24 combined points, is not enough for the game zone. So you, as captain, want to ensure that the partnership stays in the partscore zone, keeping as low as possible on the bidding steps. Whenever your partner opens the bidding 1NT and you have 10 or fewer points, stop the auction in the partscore zone.

If you know that the partnership belongs in the game zone when you have 13 or more points and belongs in the partscore zone when you have 10 or fewer points, what happens when you hold 11 or 12 points and your partner opens the bidding 1NT? You cannot be certain whether the partnership belongs in a game or a partscore. For example, suppose you have exactly 12 points. Knowing the range of the opening 1NT, you can do the following calculations:

Partner's points:	12	or	13	or	14
Your points:	12		12		12
Combined total:	24	or	25	or	26

If your partner has only 12 points, you belong in a partscore. If your partner has 13 or 14, you belong in a game. You, as captain, are in a position where you need more information about the opener's strength before you can make the final decision. In this situation, rather than decide immediately on the best game or partscore contract, you will have to make a bid that gets you more information about opener's hand. We will discuss that in more detail in the next chapter. For now, it is sufficient to know that when you have 11 or 12 points and your partner opens the bidding 1NT, the captain cannot make an immediate decision.

Deciding on the denomination

In addition to describing the strength of the hand, a 1NT opening bid tells the captain about the distribution of the hand. The opener is describing a balanced hand with two or more cards in each suit and no more than five in any suit. Again, it is a matter of addition for the captain to determine whether the partnership should be playing in a suit contract or in no trumps. Consider this hand:

♠ A K 5 4 3 2
♡ A 4 2
◇ Q J
♣ 7 3

With 14 HCPs there are enough points to decide that you want to be in the game zone. As captain, you now have to decide on one of the game zone contracts: 3NT, 4♡, 4♠, 5♣ or 5◇. Although you might consider 3NT, since it requires only nine tricks, there is a better choice. You know that your partner has at least two spades, giving you a combined total of eight cards in the suit. As we mentioned earlier, when you have an eight-card or longer major suit fit, you want to play there in preference to no trumps. With a trump suit, you will usually take at least one more trick than in no trumps since you will be able to trump the opponents' high cards when you have no cards left in a suit. On this hand, then, 4♠ is likely to be a better game zone contract than 3NT. Since you are the captain, that is the decision you should make. You bid 4♠. The bidding conversation would sound like this:

Partner: *One no trump.*   (I have a balanced hand with 12–14 points.)

You: *Four spades.*   (Thank you. That tells me all I need to decide that we belong in the game zone and that spades would be the best trump suit.)

Partner: *Pass.*   (You're the captain!)

If you and your partner are North-South, the complete auction would look like this:

North	East	South	West
(Partner)		(You)	
1NT	Pass	4♠	Pass
Pass	Pass		

Let's change your hand by removing some of the high cards:

♠ 10 8 7 4 3 2
♡ Q 8 7
◊ 4 3
♣ 7 3

Now, when your partner opens the bidding 1NT, you can see at a glance that the partnership does not have enough strength for the game zone. You have only 2 HCPs. Even if your partner has a maximum of 14 points, the total is only 16 points. You might think that all you have to do is to say 'Pass'. After all, you do not have a very good hand and 1NT is one of the partscore contracts. But remember, you are the captain. What do you really think is the best choice for the denomination, no trumps or spades?

Again, apply the principle that an eight-card fit in a major suit is better than playing in no trumps. You are likely to agree that spades is a better place to play. After all, if spades are trumps you can at least stop the opponents from taking too many diamond or club tricks by trumping the third round of either suit. If you are still not convinced, try making up a 1NT opening bid and putting this hand opposite it. Try to play the contract in no trumps and then with spades as trumps. We think you'll end up convinced that the best denomination is in spades. In order to put your conviction into practice, all you have to do is to bid 2♠. The conversation with your partner would go like this:

Partner:	*One no trump.*	(I have a balanced hand with 12–14 points.)
You:	*Two spades.*	(Thank you. That tells me all I need to decide that we belong in the partscore zone and that spades would be the best trump suit.)
Partner:	*Pass.*	(You're the captain!)

Deciding on the denomination won't always be this easy. Just as you are not always sure about whether or not you want to play in a game zone or partscore zone, there are times when you may be unsure of the denomination. For example, you might have a hand like this:

♠ A 9 8 7 6
♡ A 7 4
◊ 7 3
♣ A J 2

With 13 HCPs, you are satisfied that you want to move to the game zone. The best game contract might be 4♠, if your partner has three or four cards in spades, giving you the magic eight-card fit. But if your partner has only two spades, the best game contract is almost certainly 3NT. You are the captain, but you need some more information from your partner! To help make your decision, you would like to know how many spades your partner has. If he has three or more, you want to play in your eight-card fit. But, if your partner has only two, then playing in no trumps is likely to be the best decision. This is another case where you have some answers, but not all of them. So you want to suggest playing in spades but keep the option to play in no trumps if your partner has only a doubleton in spades. In the next chapter, we will see exactly how you conduct the bidding conversation to get the answer you require.

The general idea behind the captain's role is that, after your partner opens the bidding with a very specific bid like 1NT, you are in a position to decide on one of the following courses of action:

- To place the final contract in the game zone, either in a suit or in no trumps
- To place the final contract in the partscore zone, either in a suit or in no trumps
- To get more information about partner's strength or distribution before making the final decision

Bidding messages

During the auction, it is comforting to know whether your partner expects you to pass or to bid again. From the other side of the table, it is equally comforting to feel confident that your partner will pass or will bid again after you have made a certain bid. In other words, we have expectations of our partners. These expectations, or *bidding messages*, fall into three categories:

- We expect our partner to pass our last bid
- We don't mind if our partner passes or bids again
- We would like to insist that our partner bid again

We can't hide these expectations, nor should we want to. They are a vital part of the game. Partnership misunderstandings can best be solved if you know that each bid carries with it a message. To help you recognise the message, think of a traffic light:

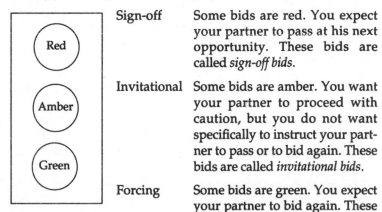

Sign-off   Some bids are red. You expect your partner to pass at his next opportunity. These bids are called *sign-off bids*.

Invitational   Some bids are amber. You want your partner to proceed with caution, but you do not want specifically to instruct your partner to pass or to bid again. These bids are called *invitational bids*.

Forcing   Some bids are green. You expect your partner to bid again. These are called *forcing bids*.

Over Zia's shoulder

Audrey: *Zia, you are known as one of the most imaginative players in the world. When your partner opens the bidding – more specifically, Zia, when your partner opens the bidding 1NT – do you go through the addition steps to figure out if there is a game and then do you ask yourself about the denomination?*

Zia: No matter how imaginative you are, or how much experience you have, you have to go through the process. After a while, it becomes so quick that it may seem as if you are making the decisions without thinking which, of course, is not true. For example, here is a hand I held after my partner opened the bidding 1NT:

♠ 4 3
♥ A 4
♦ K 10 8 4 3 2
♣ K Q 4

I knew I wanted our partnership to be in the game zone. I have 12 HCPs and I take into consideration the length in the diamond suit. Since my partner has at least 12 points, that adds up to a total of at least 24, plus the diamond suit. My next decision is to consider the denomination. Here my decision is based on the fact that I want to move the partnership to a game contract. The choice of contract, then, is between 5◊ and 3NT.

Audrey: *What did you decide?*

Zia: Like most people, I like to play the hands and by bidding 5◊ I would be the declarer. But sometimes you must look for the best result possible. It seemed that we were less likely to have the point count to make eleven tricks in 5◊ but had a fair chance of making nine tricks in 3NT. I bid 3NT. Although my little diamonds would have value if diamonds were trumps, they would also be very likely to have value in no trumps. Remember that in no trumps, the highest card of the suit led wins the trick. So, if my partner could lead small diamonds from my hand when neither of the opponents had diamonds, they would all win tricks just as if they were trumps. It is important always to consider that a long suit can have value at a no trump contract, as well as a contract where a suit is trumps.

Audrey: *Give us another hand which you held after your partner opened the bidding 1NT.*

Zia: Here is a hand where I have HCPs and a long heart suit, so I know I am in the game zone.

     ♠ A 4 2
     ♡ J 9 8 4 2
     ◊ K Q J
     ♣ J 4

My next question would be the same as a player who is just learning the game. Since, as captain, I have decided to lead the partnership to game, I ask myself what game? Two choices come to mind, either 4♡ or 3NT. After years of mixed experiences, I know that getting along with my partner is a most important aspect of the game so instead of taking a guess, I'm going to ask my partner what he thinks.

Audrey: *And how will you do that?*

Zia: We will look at the specific bid in the next chapter, but the important thing is that, if I ask myself what zone and what denomination the partnership should be in, I know what message I would like my bid to convey. With this hand, I want my bid to ask my partner for more information about the denomination, not about the zone, since I already have that answer. That is what determines the course I must take.

Audrey: *Have you ever been tempted to ignore the bidding message that your partner is sending you?*

Zia: Very rarely. For example, with the following hand I held the other day, I opened 1NT. Nothing too challenging at that point. Then my partner bid 2♡ and our partnership understanding was that this was a sign-off bid. This was my hand:

♠ 8 4 3
♡ A K Q 4
◊ A J 2
♣ 9 4 2

I knew my partner was asking me to pass. Now, I could have looked at my hearts longingly and thought that this was the time to bid again, in spite of my partner's request. But you have to ask yourself, why has my partner asked me to pass? My partner, the captain, had decided from the very specific picture that I gave by bidding 1NT that the best spot was a partscore in hearts. I had no reason to object. This is what my partner had:

♠ 9 5 2
♡ J 10 9 5 3 2
◊ K 10
♣ Q J

You can see that if we went any higher, even though we have a strong trump suit, we would be in trouble. On the actual hand the opponents took three tricks in spades and two club tricks before we had a chance to take the lead. My partner had made a good decision and I was glad that I had respected his message.

Summary

When your partner opens the bidding, he is playing the role of describer, trying to paint a picture of his hand. If he makes a bid which describes his hand within narrow limits, such as 1NT, that puts you in the role of captain, trying to determine the contract in which the partnership belongs. After your partner's opening bid, you need to consider two questions:

• What zone would it be best for us to play in?
• What denomination would it be best for us to play in?

Your decision about the zone is answered by adding together
the range of strength promised by the opener to the exact strength
which you can see in your own hand. Once you come up with the
possible combined total, you can set your sights on the appropriate zone using the following guidelines:

Zone	Points required
Grand slam	37 or more
Small slam	33 or more
Game	25 or more
Partscore	Less than 25

The decision about the denomination is guided by the number of
cards you have in each suit combined with the number of cards
that the opener has promised through his description of the hand.
With eight or more combined cards in a major suit, always choose
a contract in hearts or spades. With eight or more combined cards
in a minor suit, choose a contract in clubs or diamonds unless you
think you have a better chance at a game bonus in no trumps; then
choose no trumps.

Bidding messages

Each bid carries one of three messages:

- Sign-off   (Red – STOP)
- Invitational   (Amber – PROCEED WITH CAUTION)
- Forcing   (Green – GO)

As we move to the next chapter and look at responses to opening
bids of one in a suit, we will consider the message given by each
response. It is so much easier to come up with a bid if you understand the message that your partner is sending.

Commonly asked questions

Q   *When you have eight or more combined cards in a minor suit and
enough combined points for the game zone, would you ever take the
risk of playing in 3NT when you have a small singleton or doubleton
in another suit?*

A   If you have only 25 or 26 combined points and a fit in a minor suit, you have three choices: you can decide to be conservative and play for a partscore in the minor suit; you can decide to be aggressive and play for a game in the minor suit, even though that normally requires 28 or 29 points; or you can decide to take a chance that your 25 or 26 combined points will be enough to let you take nine tricks in a 3NT contract, despite your shortness in some suits. Each choice has its advantages and disadvantages, but most players prefer to take a chance on 3NT. There is no perfect solution for hands like these. Sometimes, you may have such shortness in one or more suits, or the opponents may have bid a suit for which you have no protection, that you decide to play in a minor suit in either the game or partscore zone. Zia personally uses the maxim: 'When in doubt bid 3NT.' At least, he says, he has lots of fun taking the risk and going for the game bonus.

Q *Is it always the partner of the opening bidder who is the captain?*

A After an opening bid of 1NT, because the opening bidder's partner knows so much, he is the captain. After an opening bid of one of a suit, there are times, as we shall see, when the opener may become the captain. To keep things simple, however, you should consider that the opener's partner is always the captain, although he may need to ask the opener's help when making a decision.

CHAPTER 5

Responding to an Opening Bid of One No-trump

We appealed to women, to their natural inferiority complex. Bridge was an opportunity for them to gain intellectual parity with their husbands. We worked on their fear instincts. We made it almost tantamount to shame not to play contract.

Ely Culbertson describing some of the methods he and his wife Josephine (thought by many to be the better player) used to get public interest.

When your partner opens the bidding, you are in the position of *responder* since you are responding to the opening bid. When the opener starts the bidding with a limit bid, such as 1NT, he clearly describes the strength and shape of his hand. As we saw in the previous chapter, the responder now plays the role of captain and can often decide quickly on the final contract. The responder can think about the final contract through considering the following questions:

What is the best zone for our partnership?

- Do we have 25 or more combined points? If so, the partnership belongs in a game contract
- Do we have fewer than 25 combined points? If so, the partnership belongs in a partscore contract

What is the best denomination for our partnership?

* Do we have an eight-card or longer fit? If we are going to play in the game zone, we want to play in 4♡ or 4♠ if we have an eight-card or longer major suit fit, otherwise, in 3NT. If we are going to play in the partscore zone, we want to play in any eight-card or longer fit, otherwise, in no trumps.

Remember the assumption that if you are in the game zone you would rather play in 3NT than climb all the way to 5♣ or 5◇ when you have a minor suit fit. On the other hand, if you have decided on a partscore, you may decide to play in a minor suit since you are not going for a bonus level and can play safely at a low level.

Let's see how the responder, the captain, can apply these principles when his partner opens the bidding 1NT. The simplest approach is to divide the responder's hand into three categories, according to his point count:

* 13 or more points (the responder wants to be in a game contract)
* 10 or fewer points (the responder wants to be in a partscore contract)
* 11 or 12 points (the responder is not sure whether to be in a game or partscore contract)

Responding with 13 or more points

With 13 or more points, the responder knows the partnership should be in the game zone since there are at least 25 combined points. The only decision is the denomination: no trumps or a major suit (occasionally a minor suit). Let's look at some examples. Your partner opens the bidding 1NT. What would you respond with each of the following hands?

	1		2		3	
♠	8 7 4	♠	A 10 9 6 4 3	♠	K 7
♡	A 4 2	♡	K J 10	♡	K J 10
◇	K Q 8 4 3	◇	Q J	◇	Q J
♣	A 10	♣	K 7	♣	A 10 9 6 4 3

With the first hand, you have a balanced hand and know that your partner also has a balanced hand. Since there are enough

combined points for a game, bid 3NT. Even if there is an eight-card
or longer fit in diamonds, it will be much easier to take nine tricks
in no trumps than eleven tricks in diamonds.

In the second example, you also want to be in a game contract,
but would prefer to play with spades as trumps. Since your partner's hand is balanced, you know he has at least two spades to go
along with your six-card suit. Make the decision to play in a major
suit game contract and bid 4♠.

In the last example, we have interchanged the spades and clubs.
This makes a difference. This time, even though you are certain to
have at least an eight-card club fit, you should prefer to play in
3NT rather than 5♣. Respond 3NT.

In all three examples, you, as responder, were immediately able
to make a decision on the final contract. You jumped directly to a
game contract. Since you are the captain, the opener is expected to
pass your response in this situation. A bid which your partner is
expected to pass is called a *sign-off bid*.

Responding with 0–10 points

We are going to look next at the lower end of the scale for the
responder, 0–10 points, because, as with the upper range of 13 or
more points, the responder can make a decision without any more
information from his partner. Even when the responder has as
many as 10 points, the partnership has at most 24 combined points
(14 + 10 = 24) and the decision, should be to play in a partscore
contract. Having made that decision the responder need only
decide on the denomination. Let's look at some examples when
your partner opens 1NT:

1	♠ J 10 4	2	♠ J 10 4	3	♠ J 10 4
	♡ Q 8 7 6		♡ Q 8 7 6 5 3		♡ 10 9
	◇ 10 9 5 3		◇ 10 9		◇ Q 8 7 6 5 3
	♣ J 2		♣ J 2		♣ J 2

In the first hand, with only 4 HCPs and a balanced hand, you are
satisfied with the contract and would decide to pass. There is no
obvious eight-card or longer fit and you do not want to get any
higher on the bidding steps trying to find one. By passing, the

partnership stops in the partscore of 1NT. You may not make the seven tricks you need for your contract – after all, the opponents have more points than you do, so may well take more tricks! – but there is nothing you can do about that. 1NT is your side's safest resting place at this point in time.

The next hand has the same number of high card points, but you would rather play in hearts than in no trumps since you know there are at least eight hearts in the combined hands. The decision you would make is to bid 2♡, the cheapest available partscore in hearts.

In the third hand, we have exchanged the hearts and diamonds. Since you are not going for a game bonus, there is no need to prefer to play in a no-trump contract rather than a minor suit. Bid 2♢. Remember, when you know you have an eight-card fit and are in the partscore zone, you want to play with that suit as trumps. It is only when you are in the game zone that you prefer playing in no trumps to clubs or diamonds.

As with the jumps to game when responder has 13 or more points, the response of 2♡ in the second example and 2♢ in the third example are both sign-off bids and the opener is expected to pass. (If you pass 1NT, as in the first example, the opener will have no choice!) The opening 1NT bidder has described his hand so well with the first bid that, when the responder decides on a final contract at the game zone or a partscore, the opener has nothing further to add.

Responding with 11–12 points

The responses with 11–12 points were left until last because, when the responder is in this range, he cannot make a decision without getting more information from the opener. As we saw in the last chapter, if the responder has 12 points, this is what happens when he does his addition:

Partner's points:	12	or	13	or	14
Responder's points:	12		12		12
Combined total:	24	or	25	or	26

If the opener has minimum values for the 1NT opening bid, only 12 points, there is not enough combined strength for the game zone and the partnership should stop in partscore. If the opener is at the top of his range, 13 or 14 points, there is enough combined strength to expect to make a game. Although the responder could just make his best guess, there is a way in which he can ask his partner for more information about his strength. He does this by bidding 2NT. He moves toward a game without actually bidding it.

The response of 2NT differs from the response of a suit at the two level or a jump to the game level. It is inviting the opener either to bid again or to pass. Not surprisingly it is called an *invitational bid*. If the opener has a maximum hand of 13 or 14 points, he accepts the invitation by bidding 3NT. If he has only the minimum of his range, 12 points, he declines the invitation by passing and the partnership stops in the partscore of 2NT.

Since the opener will usually accept the 2NT invitation if he has 13 points, the responder may want to be a little more cautious when he has only 11 points. This is what his addition tells him:

Partner's points:	12	or	13	or	14
Responder's points:	11		11		11
	—		—		—
Combined total:	23	or	24	or	25

Only when the opening bidder has 14 points will the partnership have the required 25 combined points. If the responder invites by bidding 2NT with 11 points and the opener accepts by bidding 3NT with 13 points, the partnership is at the game zone with only 24 combined points. However, the limited language of bidding does not allow you to be 100 per cent accurate and it is usually best to be aggressive when you have 11 points and offer the invitation.

Deciding the denomination

While the responder is usually in a position to determine the denomination after hearing the 1NT opening bid, there are times when he needs more information from the opener.

A typical situation of this type is when the responder knows that the partnership belongs in the game zone but is not sure whether the final contract should be a game in a major suit or in no trumps. This occurs when responder has a five-card major suit and 13 or more points. He knows that he would like to play in the major suit if there is an eight-card or longer fit, but is not sure if there is one. Consider this hand:

♠ A 9 8 4 3
♡ A 10 9
◊ K J 8
♣ Q 10

The responder has enough strength to want to play in a game. He could guess about whether it should be in spades or no trumps or he can ask the opener for more information. To do this he bids 3♠. This is a *forcing bid*. The opener is not expected to pass but must bid again. He has two choices, either 4♠ or 3NT. If he has only two spades, he chooses 3NT. On the other hand, if he has three or more spades, he chooses 4♠.

Sometimes the responder has only four hearts or four spades and would like to know whether the opener also has four cards in the major suit. In such situations, the *Stayman Convention* can be used. This is a special response that is discussed in Chapter 13.

Over Zia's shoulder

Audrey: *Zia's partner has opened 1NT and he holds this hand:*

♠ 5 3
♡ A 4 2
◊ K Q J 4 3 2
♣ J 10

Our eyes are fixed on the great diamond suit. It seems natural to bid them, but no, Zia bids 3NT. Why?

Zia: It shouldn't seem that natural to bid the diamonds. My partner has opened 1NT promising 12–14 points. There are only 11 high card points in my hand but we have to consider the length in diamonds. I know the diamonds are tempting, and I hope to take five or six tricks with them when I bid 3NT. I would rather risk taking nine tricks in no trumps than moving all the way to 5◇, where I would need more points between the two hands – remember, when in doubt bid 3NT.

Audrey: *The next hand is the kind we would like to pass automatically.*

♠ 9 8 7 6 5 4
♡ 5
◇ 5 4 3
♣ 8 7 3

Zia: It is important to think beyond how many points you have in a hand, and consider what you are trying to do – that is, to take the number of tricks for which your partnership contracted. After my partner opens 1NT, I know he is going to have difficulty taking seven tricks in no trumps. My hand offers no tricks for him. On the other hand, if spades are trumps, there may be four tricks from this hand. After the opponents take the first heart trick my small spades are as big as an ace. With this kind of hand, put the final contract where you know it should be, in a partscore in spades. Bid 2♠. Remember the eight-card fit rule.

Summary

When your partner opens the bidding 1NT, you are the responder, or captain. Use the following guidelines to help you decide what to bid:

Responding to an opening bid of 1NT

With 0–10 points, stop in the partscore zone:

- Bid 2◇, 2♡, or 2♠ with a six-card suit, or with a five-card suit and an unbalanced hand. You may wonder why you can't bid 2♣ also with a weak hand and a long club suit. Be patient, please, until Chapter 13 when all will be revealed!
- Otherwise, pass

With 11–12 points, invite your partner to the game zone:
• Bid 2NT

With 13 or more points, bid to the game zone:
• Bid 4♡ or 4♠ with a six-card or longer suit
• Bid 3♡ or 3♠ with a five-card suit (asking your partner for more information)
• Otherwise, bid 3NT

Commonly asked questions

Q *When your partner opens the bidding 1NT, do you ever want to bid higher than the game zone?*

A Since you need about 33 or more combined points for the slam zone, you would need 19 or more points to consider bidding a slam. With less, you should stop safely in the game zone. We will take a look at bidding slams in Chapter 15.

Q *Since 2◇, 2♡ and 2♠ are all sign-off bids in response to a 1NT opening bid, why isn't 2♣ included in the list?*

A Although some players use 2♣ as a sign-off bid, most players have adopted the Stayman Convention, which reserves the 2♣ response to have a special meaning. This bid is discussed in Chapter 16, the chapter on conventions.

Q *What is the message given by my partner's opening bid? Do I have to say something?*

A All the opening bids at the one level are amber, invitational. You do not have to bid when you know the partnership belongs in a partscore. If your partner were unwilling that you should pass in response to his opening bid, he would start the auction with a forcing bid. We will be discussing forcing opening bids in Chapter 15.

CHAPTER 6

Responding to an Opening Bid of One Heart or One Spade

When Ely Culbertson staged a bridge match between his American team and Great Britain, he had actors in Madison Square Garden dress up as playing cards and duplicate the plays made before a packed crowd of spectators. I wonder what he would be doing today with all the advances made in technology?

When your partner opens the bidding 1NT, you can often make an immediate decision about the zone and the denomination. After all, you know not only that the opener has specifically 12, 13 or 14 points, but also that he has at least two cards, and no more than five cards, in every suit. That gives you a very clear picture indeed.

When the opening bid is one of a suit, you simply don't have enough information to make a final decision right away. For example, when the opener bids 1♡, the value of his hand could be as weak as 12 points or as strong as 20 points. The shape could be balanced – the opener could have a balanced hand and yet too many points to start with 1NT – or unbalanced. Consider what you do know. Your partner has a better than average hand of at least 12 points and the suit he is bidding is his longest, which means he has at least four cards in it.

Supporting partner's major suit

Suppose your partner opens a major suit, either 1♡ or 1♠. Since your partner has at least four cards in the suit, whenever you have four or more cards in the suit – *support* – you know the partnership has at least an eight-card fit. If you have support for your partner's major suit, the Acol system is one of the most logical systems in the world. You simply show your support by *raising* (bidding the same suit) to the appropriate level – meaning: the stronger your hand the more you bid.

To decide the appropriate level, the responder thinks of his hand as small, medium or large. When the responder has 13 or more points, he knows that even if the opener has a minimum count of 12 or 13 points, there should be enough combined strength for a game. Think of hands in this range as *large*. With 10–12 points, the responder knows a game is a possibility, and would like to move toward this zone without possibly getting too high. Think of hands in this range as *medium*. With 6–9 points, the responder wants to bid only to keep the auction going in case the opener has a lot of additional strength for his opening bid. After all, the opener could have as many as 20 points. Hands in the 6-9 points range are *small*. Raise your partner to the appropriate level using this chart:

Raising partner's major suit

0–5 points	Pass
6–9 points	Raise to the two level
10–12 points	Raise to the three level
13 or more points	Raise to the four level

Using this scale, you will not get too high on the bidding steps if your partner has a minimum strength hand for his opening bid. On the other hand, if your partner has some extra strength he will be able to tell you about it with his next bid.

Let's put the idea of supporting your partner's major suit into practice. Suppose your partner opens the bidding 1♠. What would you do, as responder, on the following hands?

1	♠ A K J 2	2	♠ Q J 10 9	3	♠ A 7 6 4
	♡ 9 4 3		♡ 10 9 2		♡ 10 9 5
	◊ 4 3 2		◊ A K 3		◊ A 10 4
	♣ 10 6 2		♣ J 10 4		♣ A Q 2

In the first example, you have excellent support but your hand is 'small', with only 8 HCPs, so it is appropriate to raise your partner's suit only to the two level. Respond 2♠.

The second hand falls into the 'medium' category since you have 11 HCPs. So it is appropriate to show this strength by jumping a level. Raise to 3♠.

The last hand is of the 'large' variety, with 14 HCPs. You can move even further up the bidding steps, all the way to a game. You know your partner has at least 12 points and you have 14. Surely your partner will thank you for such a fine dummy. Raise directly to 4♠.

What could be simpler and more beautiful! Acol does have a way of getting straight to the point, just like English.

Of course you don't always have a hand with which you can support your partner. On many hands you have to come up with another bid. Keep the purpose of the bidding in mind. The partnership is looking for the answer to the two questions:

- What zone should we be in?
- What denomination should we be in?

The partnership is hoping to discover enough combined strength for one of the bonus levels, either a game or a slam. The best game contract, providing the partnership has an eight-card fit, is either 4♡ or 4♠. A fit isn't always available and so the next choice is to look for a game in 3NT.

It has to be remembered that there isn't enough combined strength in every hand for a game. In the search for the best denomination, the partnership has to be careful not to get too high, since every bid moves the partnership up the bidding steps.

Responding in no trumps

With a balanced hand (and no interest in the other major) you can make a limit response in no trumps. The stronger your hand, the higher you can bid. To respond in no trumps, use the following chart:

Responding in no trumps to partner's major suit

0–5 points	Pass
6–9 points	Respond 1NT
10–12 points	Respond 2NT
13 or more points	Respond 3NT

Here are some examples. Your partner opens the bidding 1♠. What would you bid with each of the following hands?

1	♠ 6 4	2	♠ 6 4	3	♠ 6 4
	♡ A K 2		♡ A K 2		♡ A K 2
	◊ J 8 7 3		◊ K J 10 3		◊ K J 10 4
	♣ 9 8 4 2		♣ 9 8 4 2		♣ K 7 5 3

In the first example you have a balanced hand and 8 points, so respond 1NT. In the second hand, with 11 HCPs, you want to move to the next level and bid 2NT. Finally, in the third example, with 14 points, you know there is at least enough combined strength for the game zone, so you can respond 3NT.

Bidding a new suit

There are times when you cannot support your partner's major suit and you don't have a balanced hand. In such cases, you want to bid a new suit, looking for the best denomination. However, you do not want to get too high on the bidding steps while searching for the best contract, so there are a couple of guidelines to consider:

Responding in a new suit to partner's major suit

0–5 points	Pass
6–9 points	Bid a new suit only if you can do so at the one level. Otherwise, bid 1NT
10 or more points	Bid a new suit (even if it is at the two level)

It might seem quite straightforward to use these guidelines but let's take a moment to look at one kind of hand which might appear troublesome. Your partner opens the bidding 1♠ and this is your hand:

♠ A 8
♡ J 9 8
◊ J 10 9 8 7 6
♣ 8 3

You cannot support your partner's spades and your hand is not balanced. Your next choice is to bid a new suit. The diamonds have sufficient length and it might be tempting to bid 2◊ but there is another consideration. In order to bid a new suit at the two level, the guideline suggests that you need 10 or more points. This hand has 6 HCPs, not enough to venture up the bidding steps to the two level. If your partner has only 12 points, your opponents will have as much, or more, strength than your side. If you bid 2◊ you would be contracting to take at least 8 of the 13 tricks and you have not yet even finished deciding the denomination in which you are going to play – your partner may not like diamonds as a trump suit! What can you do?

The guideline suggests that you should respond 1NT. You have too many points to pass – the opener might have as many as 20 points and you would miss the opportunity for a game bonus. You cannot support your partner's suit with only two cards – he could have only a four-card suit. You do not have the 10 or more points needed to venture into a new suit at the two level. That leaves the 'catch-all' response of 1NT.

This is a good time to mention that one of the most common errors made by a responder is to bid a new suit at a higher level without sufficient strength. With the above hand, it may seem strange not to be able to mention the diamond suit right at the start of your bidding conversation. The auction is not over, however, and you may get the opportunity to show your suit later. By then the opener will know that your hand was too weak to bid a new suit at the two level and he won't be tempted to move too high up the bidding steps.

If you take another look at the requirements for bidding a new suit, you can see that a suit can be bid at the one level with 6 or more points. Look at the following three hands and decide what they have in common and how they differ. Then decide what you would respond if partner has opened the bidding 1◊.

1 ♠ J984	2 ♠ AJ987	3 ♠ KJ8765
♡ A42	♡ AK4	♡ 87
◊ Q109	◊ K53	◊ QJ10
♣ 842	♣ 32	♣ 98

On each hand, you would respond 1♠. The difference is clear to see. The first hand has only four spades and 7 HCPs. The second hand has five spades and 15 HCPs. The third hand has six spades, and 7 HCPs. You might wonder how the opener will ever have a picture of your hand when you start out with the same response, 1♠, to describe three such different hands.

First of all, the responder usually takes on the role of the captain. By bidding 1♠, the responder is in a position to hear another bid from the opener. The opener, the describer, will give a clearer picture of his hand and then, the responder can make a final decision. For example, suppose the opener next bids 2♠. With the first hand, you could pass, satisfied with a partscore. In the second hand, you have enough points to want to be in a game contract. After all, your partner has shown at least 12 points and you have 15. Since the opener's second bid has told you that he has support for your spade suit, in addition to his diamond suit, you could choose a final contract of 4♠. In the last example, you would want to push towards a game without actually bidding it, and could make an invitational bid of 3♠ at your next opportunity. So, your response of 1♠ is only commencing the dialogue between you and your partner. At this first stage, you are saying: 'I want to respond to your opening bid and I have at least four spades. Later I will tell you more'.

When you support your partner's major suit right away, you have settled the question of which denomination to play in and are only concerned with determining the zone in which you belong. When you respond in a new suit, you are still exploring for both the best denomination and the best zone. You want to take your time and keep as much room as you can available on the bidding steps, rather than jumping the level of the bidding. You are merely making a suggestion to your partner that you would prefer another suit. You and your partner may have some talking to do before you arrive at your final destination. For this reason, the response of a new suit is *forcing* and the opener must bid again. So, you can bid a new suit with as few as 6 points or as many as 13 without being afraid that the opener will pass and leave you in the wrong zone.

Before we leave the subject of bidding a new suit, let's consider two very similar hands. You are the responder and your partner has opened the bidding 1♡:

1	♠ A 10 9 8 4 2	2	♠ 10 9
	♡ 8 6		♡ 8 6
	◇ Q 4 3		◇ Q 4 3
	♣ 10 9		♣ A 10 9 8 4 2

On the first hand, you have a new suit which you can mention at the one level, so respond 1♠.

On the second hand, we have exchanged the spades and clubs to see the difference. Although you would like to show the clubs, you cannot bid a new suit at the two level without promising 10 or more points. You don't want to pass, so you will have to use the catch-all response of 1NT.

Using the bidding messages

Sign-off bids

There are no sign-off bids that the responder can make, since the opener could have a very strong hand. The responder isn't signing off even when he jumps to the game zone of 4♠ after an opening 1♠ bid. He is merely suggesting that if the opener has a minimum hand, 4♠ is a reasonable contract. If the opener has more than minimum values, the partnership can head towards a slam. More about this in Chapter 12.

Invitational bids

There are two kinds of invitational bids by the responder:

- A raise of the opener's suit to the two, three or four level
- A response of 1NT, 2NT or 3NT

The opener can pass any of these bids since each one limits the responder's hand to a specific strength and the responder is prepared to be left in the denomination. For example, when the responder raises the opener's suit, a fit has been found. The responder is satisfied with the denomination. Similarly, when the responder bids no trumps, he is content to play in that denomination. The invitation is for the opener to continue to bid again with extra strength and to pass with a minimum hand.

Forcing bids

There is one type of forcing bid that the responder can make:

* A new suit

The opener must bid again because the responder's range is very wide and he could have as few as 6 points or as many as 13. The responder may not be content to be left in either the denomination or the level.

Over Zia's shoulder

Let's look over Zia's shoulder. Here are two hands which Zia held after his partner opened 1♠. Let's see how he responded.

1 ♠ 8764   2 ♠ A4
   ♡ –   ♡ J109876
   ◊ A1065   ◊ 872
   ♣ Q10973   ♣ J5

Audrey: *On the first hand, you bid 3♠, overlooking the clubs and jumping a level. This seems aggressive with only 6 HCPs.*

Zia: This is a perfect hand to illustrate the importance of counting support points (see Chapter 2) rather than length points when you plan to support your partner's major suit. I gave myself 5 points for the void in hearts. This hand then values at 11 total points, enough to make a limit jump raise. The 3♠ bid proved to be the winning call, getting our side to an excellent contract, and all that was necessary to arrive at it was to follow our rules.

Audrey: *In the next example, it might be tempting for our readers to bid the heart suit.*

Zia: This is a temptation but one to which you shouldn't
            yield. I responded 1NT. Remember that the responder's
            bid of 1NT simply shows a hand with 6–9 points and no
            support for the opener's suit. This hand fits the descrip-
            tion exactly, whereas a bid of 2♥ would have shown at
            least 10 points.

Summary

When your partner opens either 1♥ or 1♠ and you have four-card
or longer support, your first priority is to raise your partner's suit
to the appropriate level:

Raising partner's major suit

0–5	Pass
6–9 points	Raise to the two level
10–12 points	Raise to the three level
13 or more points	Raise to the four level

With a balanced hand (and if you cannot bid 1♠ over 1♥) make a
limit raise in no trumps:

Responding in no trumps to partner's major suit

0–5 points	Pass
6–9 points	Respond 1NT
10–12 points	Respond 2NT
13 or more points	Respond 3NT

When you don't have support for your partner's major suit and
have an unbalanced hand, bid a new suit at the appropriate level:

Responding in a new suit to partner's major suit

0–5 points	Pass
6–9 points	Bid a new suit only if you can do so at the one level. Otherwise, bid 1NT
10 or more points	Bid a new suit (even if it is at the two level)

An opening bid of 1♥ or 1♠ is an invitational bid. The responder
can't make a sign-off bid since he doesn't know the limit of the
opener's hand. He can only make a limited or forcing bid.

Responder's bidding messages

Sign-off bids	None
Invitational bids	Raising your partner's major suit
	Bidding no trumps
Forcing bids	A new suit

Commonly asked questions

Q *Suppose my partner opens 1♡ and I have the following hand:*

♠ J 9 8 7
♡ 4 3
◇ A Q
♣ K Q 8 7 4

Should I respond 1♠, the suit I can bid at the one level, or my longer suit, 2♣, even though I have to bid it at the two level?

A There are two schools of thought. Many players would respond 1♠ since you are more interested in finding a major suit fit than a minor suit fit – time enough for the club suit later. Others prefer to start with their longer suit, planning to show the spades at their next opportunity. Either bid could work out best on the actual hand, but sticking to our rule of keeping it simple, we would recommend bidding 2♣, your longest suit.

CHAPTER 7

Responding to an Opening Bid of One Club or One Diamond

Both Culbertson and Goren made some impact in the United Kingdom. From the beginning, however, the British market was unique. It held a distaste for the new bidding gadgets introduced by the Americans. Even when auction bridge, the predecessor to contract bridge, was popular, the British fought the new ideas which came from America. They wanted to keep it simple.

You might wonder why there is one chapter on responding to a major suit opening bid and a separate chapter on responding to a minor suit opening bid. After all, you might say, they are all opening bids of one of a suit. But as in any conversation (remember bidding is a language) different starts sometimes evoke different responses. Let's consider the difference.

If you have more than 6 points, enough to respond to an opening bid of one of a suit, you have only three choices. You can:

- Support your partner's suit
- Bid a new suit
- Bid no trumps

Once you choose an option, you must then decide how high to bid. When your partner opens 1♡ or 1♠, your first priority is to support his major suit if you can. You don't look first for another suit to bid or bid no trumps. This is because a major suit game requires the same number of points (25–26 points) as a no-trump game. A game in a minor suit, however, requires considerably more points (about 28–29 points). So when your partner opens 1♣ or 1♢, supporting your partner's minor suit is not necessarily your first priority.

Bidding a new suit

Look at both your partner's hand and your own in this example:

Partner's hand	*Your hand*
♠ A K 8 7	♠ Q J 10 9
♡ 6 5 3	♡ 9 8 2
♢ A Q J 5	♢ K 10 4 3 2
♣ K 5	♣ A

With too much to open the bidding 1NT, your partner starts the auction by bidding the lower-ranking of his two four-card suits, 1♢. You have great support for your partner's diamonds and may be tempted to raise them to the appropriate level. Since you have 10 HCPs and 3 for the singleton club, that would be 3♢. Your partner knows the side belongs in the game zone since you are showing 10–12 points and he has 17 points. Which game will he choose? Either 3NT or 5♢ would seem reasonable to him. At this stage, he has no reason to consider a contract of 4♠. And yet, if you look at the two hands, this is the game contract most likely to succeed. In 5♢ the opponents could defeat your contract by taking the first three heart tricks before you can stop them. In 3NT, the opponents might be able to defeat you by taking the first five heart tricks, since you do not have a trump suit to stop them. In 4♠, on the other hand, you can afford to lose the first three heart tricks and still take the next ten tricks, enough to make the contract.

Therefore, when your partner opens a minor suit, your first priority is to bid a new suit, even if you have support for his suit. Let's look again at your hand:

♠ Q J 10 9
♡ 9 8 2
♢ K 10 4 3 2
♣ A

If your partner opens 1◊, before automatically raising diamonds to the appropriate level, see if you can bid a new suit. In this hand you have four reasonable spades and can bid 1♠. Since your partner also has spades, the partnership will now find its way to the major suit game.

The guidelines for bidding a new suit when your partner opens the bidding 1♣ or 1◊ are almost the same as those used when responding to a 1♡ or 1♠ opening bid:

Responding in a new suit to a partner's minor

0–5 points	Pass
6–9 points	Bid a new suit if you can do so at the one level. Otherwise, raise your partner's suit or bid 1NT.
10 or more points	Bid a new suit (even if it is at the two level)

If your partner opens 1♣, you can afford to bid any new suit, diamonds, hearts, or spades, at the one level. If the opening bid is 1◊, you can still bid either of the major suits at the one level, but would have to move to the two level to mention the club suit. To do this, you require 10 or more points. If you don't have the strength to suggest a new suit at the two level, you have to return to considering your other choices: either support your partner's diamonds or bid 1NT.

Let's look at some examples. Your partner opens the bidding 1◊. What would you respond with each of the following hands?

1	♠ 5 3	2	♠ 6 5 2	3	♠ J 10
	♡ 8 4		♡ K 8 7		♡ J 8 4
	◊ J 10 4 2		◊ 4 3		◊ A 8
	♣ K Q 10 8 2		♣ A J 7 4 2		♣ K Q 8 4 3 2

On the first hand, with only 6 HCPs, you do not have enough strength to bid your club suit at the two level. Instead, you can support your partner's diamonds, so respond 2◊. On the next hand, you still lack sufficient points to bid a new suit at the two level. Without four-card support for your partner's minor, respond 1NT since you do not have a suit you can bid at the one level. In the third example, you have enough strength to bid a new suit, even if you have to go to the two level. Respond 2♣.

After your partner bids a minor suit, although you still have the same choices as after a major suit opening – to support your partner, to bid a new suit or to bid no trumps – the priorities have changed. The first priority is to bid a new suit, especially a major suit. Only when you cannot bid a new suit do you consider supporting your partner's minor suit or bidding no trumps.

Supporting partner's minor suit

Suppose your partner opens 1♣ and you have no new suit to bid but you do have good support for your partner's clubs. The limit raises are almost the same as those for responding to an opening major suit bid. Do you remember the ranges? Let's review the major suit raises:

0–5 points	Pass
6–9	Raise to the two level
10–12 points	Raise to the three level
13 or more points	Raise to the four level

There is one difference when you are raising your partner's minor suit. Can you work it out? Suppose your partner opens 1♣ and you have one of the following hands:

1 ♠ 42	2 ♠ K84	3 ♠ K108
♡ QJ9	♡ 109	♡ AJ2
◊ K107	◊ 86	◊ K7
♣ J6432	♣ KQJ765	♣ K9862

In the first example, you have 7 points (including support points) and would raise to the two level by bidding 2♣. With the second hand, you have 9 HCPs and 2 support points for a total of 11 points. You would make a limit raise to the three level, showing 10–12 points, by responding 3♣. On the third hand, you have 14 HCPs and 1 point for the doubleton diamond suit. Here is where the difference occurs. Raising to the 4 level – bidding 4♣ – would take you past 3NT, which may be the only game contract you can make. Yet, jumping to 5♣ seems too ambitious since you might not have the 28–29 combined points needed to take 11 tricks. Instead, respond 3NT to give the partnership the best chance of collecting a game bonus.

So the guidelines when you have support for your partner's minor suit and cannot bid a new suit is this:

Raising a partner's minor suit

0–5 points	Pass
6–9 points	Raise to the two level
10–12 points	Raise to the three level
13 or more points	Bid 3NT if your hand is fairly balanced. With a wildly unbalanced hand, either bid a new suit if you can or raise the minor suit all the way to game.

Bidding no trumps

We now come to the final option when your partner opens a minor suit, either 1♣ or 1◊. As the responder, you want to keep your eye on no-trump contracts. The guidelines for responding in no trumps are identical to those after a major suit opening:

Responding in no trumps to partner's minor suit

0–5 points	Pass
6–9 points	Respond 1NT with no four-card or longer suit to bid at the one-level
10–12 points	Respond 2NT
13 or more points	Respond 3NT

For example, suppose your partner opens the bidding 1◊. What would you respond with each of the following hands?

1 ♠ A64	2 ♠ A84	3 ♠ KJ7
♡ QJ2	♡ A75	♡ Q102
◊ 983	◊ QJ10	◊ 1042
♣ Q432	♣ K432	♣ AJ82

In the first hand, you have 9 HCPs and a balanced hand. This is an ideal hand on which to respond 1NT. As we have seen earlier, you do not have the option of bidding your club suit since you do not have enough strength to bid a new suit at the two level.

With the second hand, you know that you belong in the game zone since the partnership must have at least 26 combined points.

You have enough to bid a new suit at the two level, 2♣, but, with a balanced hand, that is not as attractive as no trumps. The best choice is to bid no trumps at the appropriate level by responding 3NT.

On the third hand, you again have the choice of mentioning your club suit or bidding no trumps. With a balanced hand of 11 HCPs, the invitational response of 2NT is the best way to describe the shape and strength of your hand. This limits your hand to 10–12 points and the opener should be able to make decision as to whether or not to bid on to the game zone.

Over Zia's shoulder

Audrey: *Zia, do you remember any interesting hands which you held after your partner opened the bidding with a minor suit?*

Zia: Yes, here is a hand which illustrates the difference in your thinking after a minor suit opening bid. My partner opened 1◊ and this was my hand:

♠ J 8 7
♡ A 10
◊ A K 8 7 4 3
♣ Q 3

In spite of my unbalanced hand and great support for diamonds, my partner's suit, I thought it was likely to be easier to try for nine tricks in no trumps than eleven in diamonds where there could easily be three losers. I therefore bid 3NT.

Sometimes you have to take a chance. Here is another interesting hand. This time my partner opened 1♣.

♠ 5 4 3 2
♡ A K
◊ J 10 4
♣ A J 9 3

As you can see, I couldn't have been dealt poorer spades. You might wonder whether bidding 1♠, a new suit, is advisable. I like to find my eight-card major suit fits and this seemed like the best step in that direction, so I responded 1♠. My partner's next bid was 2♠. Now I was satisfied that we had enough points for a game and an eight-card fit in spades and so I went to 4♠ – a great success! The moral – don't be afraid to bid any four-card suit. The strength doesn't usually matter.

Summary

Use the following guidelines when responding to an opening bid of 1♣ or 1◇:

Responding in a new suit to partner's minor suit

0–5 points	Pass
6–9 points	Bid a new suit if you can do so at the one level. Otherwise, raise partner's suit or bid 1NT
10 or more points	Bid a new suit (even if it is at the two level)

Raising partner's minor suit

0–5 points	Pass
6–9 points	Raise to the two level
10–12 points	Raise to the three level
13 or more points	Bid 3NT if your hand is fairly balanced. With a wildly unbalanced hand, either bid a new suit if you can or raise the minor suit all the way to game.

Responding in no trumps to a partner's minor suit

0–5 points	Pass
6–9 points	Respond 1NT
10–12 points	Respond 2NT
13 or more points	Respond 3NT

Remember that when your partner opens the bidding in a minor suit, bidding a new suit or looking for a no-trump contract has priority over raising your partner's suit. This is the opposite to the priority when your partner opens a major suit.

Commonly asked questions

Q *Why is the first priority a major suit game when a minor suit game only requires one more trick? After all, a major suit game requires one more trick than 3NT.*

A You could think of it as the straw that broke the camel's back. You can usually take one more trick in a suit contract than you can in no trumps if you have an eight-card or longer fit. That means you prefer a game in the major suits, even though they are one trick more expensive. On the other hand, you usually cannot take two tricks more in a suit contract. That is why 3NT is preferred over a game in a minor suit which would be two tricks more expensive.

CHAPTER 8

Rebids by the Opener

There are many systems of bidding just as there are many languages; the language you choose may be a product of your culture, your location and your taste. It is not a matter of one language being universally better than another.

In this chapter we are going to take a look at the opener's second bid, or *rebid* after opening with one of a suit. After both the opener and the responder have had their initial chance to bid, the partnership is moving towards a decision on the zone and the denomination. At such times one member of the partnership becomes captain, listening to information that his partner, the describer, passes on. Generally, the opener takes on the role of describer, providing the responder, the captain, with enough information to decide on the best final contract. There are times, however, when the responder passes this responsibility back to the opener. This happens when the responder has painted a very clear picture of his hand by making a limit or invitational bid. When the responder makes such a bid he is inviting the opener either to pass or to bid on.

Rebidding after a limit (invitational) response

When you, as responder, make an invitational or limit bid, you must be willing to accept your partner's decision and be prepared to play in the contract you bid if partner passes.

Which of the responder's bids are invitational?

Responder's invitational bids
- A raise of opener's suit to the two, three or game level
- A response of 1NT, 2NT or 3NT

Opener's rebid after the responder raises

Suppose you open the bidding 1♠ and your partner, the responder, raises to 2♠, a limit bid showing 6–9 points. You are now in a position to add up the partnership assets and to make one of three decisions. If you are satisfied to be in the partscore zone, you can pass 2♠; if you want to be in the game zone, you can bid 4♠; if you are uncertain, you can move towards the game zone by bidding 3♠.

Notice that the decision has only to do with the zone. The denomination has already been decided – the partnership is playing in spades. In general terms, the key to deciding the zone is that the more strength you have, as opener, the more you should bid. Let's look at this in practice. What is your decision with each of the following hands after you open 1♠ and your partner raises to 2♠?

1	♠ A 10 8 4 2	2	♠ Q J 10 8 6 2	3	♠ K Q J 9 4 2
	♡ A 8		♡ A K		♡ 9 5
	◇ A 5 4 3		◇ A K J 4		◇ A J 2
	♣ J 10		♣ 8		♣ K J

On the first hand, you have 13 HCPs. Even if your partner has the maximum for his limit raise to 2♠ – 9 points, giving a total of 22 points – there are not enough combined points to want to be in the game zone which requires at least 25 points. You would pass when it is your next turn to bid.

With the second hand, you know that, even if partner has only the minimum of his range, 6 points, you want to be in the game zone. You have 18 HCPs and a good six-card suit. Added to partner's potential minimum, it still gives you at least 24 combined points and a good trump fit. You would rebid 4♠.

On the last hand you have some doubt. You have 15 HCPs and a good six-card spade suit. If your partner has the top of his range, 8 or 9 points, then you want to be in the game zone. On the other hand, if your partner has the minimum of his range, 6 or 7 points, you would like to stop in a partscore. Even though your partner has passed the decision to you, you do not have quite enough information. You would rebid 3♠. By moving to the three level, you are showing a hand with about 16–18 points and passing the final decision back to the responder. Responder can pass, if he has the minimum of what he has promised, or bid on to 4♠, if he has the maximum of his promised range.

In summary, when your partner raises your opening bid of one of a suit to the two level, the more strength you have, the more you bid. The general guidelines are:

Opener's rebid after the responder raises to the two level
12–15 points   Pass
16–18 points   Move to the three level inviting game
19 or more points   Bid game

When you open the bidding in a suit at the one level, your partner may raise you to the three level, rather than the two level. This shows 10–12 points. As when your partner raises to the two level, take what you know about your partner's hand and add it to your values to decide on the zone. Remember, the denomination has already been decided. For example, you open the bidding 1♡ and your partner raises to 3♡. Let's see what you do with each of these hands:

```
1  ♠ A 10            2  ♠ A K 4
   ♡ K Q 8 4 2          ♡ K J 8 4
   ◇ J 4               ◇ K J 10 2
   ♣ J 10 3 2          ♣ 10 4
```

In the first example, you should be satisfied with a partscore and pass as your rebid. You have only 11 HCPs. Even if your partner has 12 points, your combined total is only 23 points. 3♡ should be high enough.

In the second example, adding your 15 HCPs to your partner's minimum, 10 points, gives you a combined total of 25 points. Move to the game zone by rebidding 4♡.

When the responder raises the opener's suit to the three level, it is merely a matter of adding up the combined points to see if there is a total of 25 or more points. In fact, 24 points will often be enough if the trump fit is very good.

Opener's rebid after the responder raises to the three level

12–14 points	Pass
15 or more points	Bid game

If the responder jumps right to the game level, showing 13–15 points, you will usually pass since you will be getting the game bonus if you make the contract. There will be times when you might want to move to the slam zone and those hands are discussed in more detail in Chapter 12. For now, be satisfied with the game contract your partner has bid.

Opener's rebid after the responder bids no trumps

When your partner responds in no trumps, there are still two decisions to make. Although it could be correct to play in no trumps, there may be a better denomination if the opener has an unbalanced hand. The opener may want to mention another suit, or rebid his original suit. Basically, even though the responder is limiting his hand by bidding no trumps at an appropriate level, the opener is still in the role of the describer and needs to play his part in determining the final contract. With his rebid the opener wants to finish describing the strength and distribution of his hand.

Let's look first at what the opener does when he holds an unbalanced hand. Suppose you open the bidding 1♡ and your partner responds 1NT, a limit bid showing 6–9 points. What should you rebid with the following hands?

1	♠ Q84	2	♠ 72	3	♠ A10
	♡ KQJ32		♡ AJ10842		♡ AK843
	◊ AJ87		◊ KQ8		◊ AQ74
	♣ 4		♣ A9		♣ K5

On the first hand, you only have 13 HCPs and so you want to stop in a partscore. However, you are not happy with a 1NT contract since you have a singleton club. Since your partner did not support your hearts, you should mention your second suit, giving him a choice of playing in either hearts or diamonds. Rebid 2◊. If the responder prefers hearts, he can bid 2♡; if he prefers diamonds, he can pass.

When you opened the bidding 1♡ with the second hand, you

were promising only a four-card heart suit. Your partner's 1NT
response could well be based on a hand including two or three
hearts. He would only raise your suit if he had four-card support.
Since you have a much longer suit than you have shown, you want
to bid the suit again to describe your hand more accurately.
There's more to it than that. You have an intermediate strength
hand of 14 HCPs and a good heart suit – so you also want to
describe your extra strength with your rebid. Instead of rebidding
2♡, which is what you would do with a minimum strength hand,
you rebid 3♡ to give your partner an accurate description of both
your strength and distribution.

With the third hand, you again have another suit you can bid to
give the responder a choice of contracts. Your hand is very strong,
however, and you would like to pass this information to your partner. Instead of bidding your second suit at the cheapest available
level, you can jump to 3◊ to show your enormous strength.

There is another way in which you can show strength after you
have opened the bidding and partner has responded. This is to
make a bid in another suit which is *higher-ranking* than your first
suit. For example:

♠ K 3
♡ A
◊ A Q 9 3
♣ K Q 9 7 6 5

If you open 1♣ and your partner responds 1NT, you can show
your second suit and extra strength by bidding 2◊. You need extra
strength to do this because, if responder wishes to give *preference*
to your first suit, he has to go to the three level in order to do this.
A bid which compels partner to go a step higher on the bidding
ladder in order to give preference to your first suit is called a
reverse. We will discuss reverses in more detail later.

You can use the following guidelines when a partner responds
1NT and you have an unbalanced hand:

Rebidding with an unbalanced hand after a 1NT response

12–15 points   Bid a new suit or rebid your original suit at
                        the two level

16–18 points	Bid a higher-ranking suit at the two level (a reverse), or bid a lower-ranking suit with a jump to the three level, or rebid your original suit with a jump to the three level.
19 or more points	Bid a lower-ranking suit by jumping to the three level or rebid your original suit by jumping to the game level, or bid a higher-ranking suit at the two level (a reverse)

Now let's turn our attention to balanced hands. There are times when the opener's hand is balanced, but he did not start with 1NT because he had too many points. When his partner responds 1NT, the opener uses the following guidelines:

Rebidding with a balanced hand after a 1NT response

15–16 points	Pass
17–18 points	Raise to 2NT
19 or more points	Raise to 3NT

Here are some examples. You have opened the bidding 1◊ and your partner has responded 1NT. What is your rebid with each of the following hands?

1 ♠ Q J 8 2	2 ♠ K J 4 2	3 ♠ K Q 4
♡ A 8	♡ Q J 10	♡ A 8 4
◊ A 9 6 3	◊ A Q 8 3	◊ A Q J 3
♣ A 9 6	♣ A 5	♣ A 7 6

With 15 HCPs, the first hand is not strong enough to want to advance past the partscore zone. Your partner has at most 9 points for the 1NT response. You would pass and play in the partscore of 1NT.

With 17 HCPs on the second hand, there is a possible game if your partner has 8 or 9 points. On the other hand, you want to be in a partscore if your partner has only 6 or 7 points. Rebid 2NT, moving towards a game but allowing the responder to pass if he is at the bottom end of his promised range.

On the last hand, you have 20 points. That should be enough for the game zone, even if the responder has only 6 points. Jump to the game level, 3NT.

The responder may have bid 2NT, showing 10–12 points and a

balanced hand, or 3NT, showing 13–15 points and a balanced
hand. The same principles apply as in rebidding after a 1NT
response. The opener can calculate the combined partnership
assets and usually decide on the best zone and denomination.

For example, you have opened the bidding 1♣, and your partner jumps to 2NT. Let's see what you would rebid with the following hands:

1 ♠ Q 9 8 4	2 ♠ 7	3 ♠ A 4
♡ A 9	♡ 10 7 2	♡ K 9 4
◇ K 8 4	◇ K Q 3	◇ 8 3
♣ A Q 9 7	♣ A Q 10 8 4 2	♣ A K J 8 4 2

On the first hand, you know that your partner is unlikely to have
any interest in your second suit, spades, because he had a chance
to bid spades at the one level and chose to bid no trumps instead.
With your 15 HCPs and your partner's 10–12 points, there is
enough combined strength for the game zone. Rebid 3NT.

On the second hand, with only 11 HCPs, you should be satisfied
to stop in a partscore. With an unbalanced hand, you can simply
rebid your suit at the cheapest available level, 3♣, telling the
responder you would rather play there than in 2NT.

In the last example, you know there is enough strength to be in
the game zone. Your partner is showing a balanced hand so you
should probably risk the game in no trumps rather than moving to
clubs at the five level. Rebid 3NT.

Rebidding after a forcing response

The responder does not always make a limit bid. There are times
when he holds on to his role as captain and needs the opening bidder to further describe his hand. At times like this, the responder
insists that the opener bid again by making a forcing bid, and
ensuring that the opener cannot pass. It helps to be able to recognise a responder's forcing responses.

Responder's forcing bids: a new suit bid at any level

After responder's forcing bid, opener cannot pass and must decide on the best rebid. The search is still on for a major suit fit. If the responder's new suit is a major, and the opener has support for it, that becomes the opener's first priority. As usual, the opener supports the responder's suit at the appropriate level. Remember, when the responder bids a major which the opener can support, the opener can count support points, giving 5 points for a void, 3 for a singleton and 1 for a doubleton. Let's see how this works. You have started the bidding with 1◇ and your partner responds 1♡. What is your rebid with each of the following hands?

1 ♠ 7	2 ♠ 7 2	3 ♠ –
♡ A Q 7 2	♡ K J 8 7	♡ K Q 7 6
◇ A 8 4 3 2	◇ K Q 10 4 3	◇ A Q 8 4 3
♣ K Q 3	♣ A 2	♣ A Q 10 4

You have 18 total points on the first hand, counting 15 HCPs and 3 points for the singleton spade. This is more than a minimum strength hand, so jump to 3♡, rather than raising only to the cheapest available level.

On the second hand, you also have support for the responder's heart suit. This time, however, your hand is of minimum strength. You cannot pass, because the responder's bid of a new suit is forcing. So rebid 2♡, raising the responder's suit to the cheapest available level.

The last hand is full of wonderful news. Even if the responder has only 6 points, you want to be in a game. You have 17 HCPs and 5 points for the void in spades. Rebid 4♡. You are describing a very fine hand in support of hearts.

Of course the responder will not always bid a new suit which you want to support. Since you cannot pass, and you cannot support the responder's suit, you have only a limited number of choices:

- Bidding a new suit
- Rebidding your original suit
- Bidding no trumps

With an unbalanced hand, you cannot rebid no trumps but you can use the same guidelines as when rebidding with an unbalanced hand after a 1NT response.

Rebidding with an unbalanced hand after a new suit response

12–15 points   Bid a new suit or rebid your original suit at the two level

16–18 points   Bid a higher-ranking suit at the two level (a reverse), or bid a lower-ranking suit with a jump to the three level, or rebid your original suit with a jump to the three level.

19 or more points   Rebid your original suit by jumping to the game level, bid a higher-ranking suit at the two level (a reverse), or bid a lower-ranking suit with a jump to the three level.

Generally, the more strength you have, the more vigorous your rebid. There are some precautions to go along with each option. For example, if you want to rebid your own suit, you should usually have a six-card or longer suit. Remember, the first time you bid the suit, partner didn't show any interest. Here are some examples of unbalanced hands where you have opened the bidding 1♡ and your partner has responded 1♠:

```
1  ♠ K 4            2  ♠ J 2            3  ♠ 5
   ♡ A Q J 7 6 2       ♡ K Q 10 8 3       ♡ A K J 9 6 3
   ◊ 8 4               ◊ 7 4              ◊ A 10 5
   ♣ Q 5 2            ♣ A K 10 6          ♣ K J 3
```

On the first hand, with no support for your partner's suit, an unbalanced hand and no second suit to bid, rebid your six-card suit. With a minimum strength hand, you rebid at the cheapest available level, 2♡. By rebidding your suit, you are telling the responder that you have more than four cards in the suit. The responder will now be able to support your suit if he has only two or three hearts.

In the next example, you have a second suit you can show. Rebid 2♣, giving the responder a choice of hearts or clubs as the trump suit.

In the last hand, you have no second suit to show so you should rebid your first suit. With 16 HCPs and 2 points for the six-card suit, you have enough to jump to 3♡, describing both your distribution and strength to the responder.

There are some further considerations when you want to bid a new suit. If you have a new suit to bid which could possibly push the partnership up to the three level, you may have to satisfy yourself with another choice when you have a minimum strength hand. This is best seen with an example:

♠ 9
♡ Q 10 8 4
◇ A Q J 5 2
♣ K 8 7

You have opened 1◇ and your partner has responded 1♠. Since this is a forcing bid, you must find a suitable rebid. It seems easy enough to bid your second suit, 2♡, to give the responder a choice between diamonds and hearts, but you must keep an eye on how high you are getting on the bidding steps. If your partner prefers diamonds to hearts as a trump suit, he will have to tell you by bidding them at the three level, 3◇. If he has only 6 or 7 points, the partnership will be contracting for nine tricks with less than half the total high card strength in the pack. Another reason to avoid rebidding 2♡ is that if your partner were interested in hearts as a trump suit, he would probably have bid them at the one level. Remember, the responder bids the lower-ranking of two four-card suits when he has a choice. With your unbalanced hand, what is the alternative? Although it is not perfect, you can rebid your diamonds, 2◇, ignoring the heart suit. This will keep the partnership from getting too high when the responder has a minimum hand. If the responder has a strong hand with five or more spades and four or more hearts, he will be able to bid again and you can still find your heart fit.

Let's change the hearts and diamonds in the above example:

♠ 9
♡ A Q J 5 2
◇ Q 10 8 4
♣ K 8 7

You open your longest suit, 1♡, and your partner again responds 1♠. This time your second suit, diamonds, is lower-ranking than hearts. Look at the difference when you bid this suit at the two level, 2◊. If the responder prefers diamonds to hearts, he can pass. If he prefers hearts, he can bid 2♡. In either case, the auction remains at the two level. Now let us make the hand stronger:

♠ 9
♡ A Q 8 4
◊ A K J 5 2
♣ K 8 7

This time you have 17 points. When partner responds 1♠ to your opening 1◊, you have enough extra strength to rebid 2♡ because even if your partner has to go to the three level to support diamonds, your extra high cards should ensure that this will be safe enough. Always bear in mind that your side is trying to arrive at a final contract that it can make! Every time you make a bid, you risk having to increase the level of the contract in order to play in the best denomination, so proceed with care!

Rebidding with a balanced hand after a new suit response

15–16 points	Rebid no trumps at the cheapest available level
17–18 points	Rebid no trumps, jumping one level
19 or more points	Rebid no trumps, jumping to 3NT

When a responder bids a new suit and opener has a balanced hand without support for his partner's suit, the opener can rebid in no trumps at the appropriate level, using the above guidelines.

Let's look at some examples. You have opened the bidding 1◊ and your partner bids 1♡. What is your rebid on each of the following hands?

1	♠ Q 10 9	2	♠ A K 9	3	♠ A K 9
	♡ J 8 2		♡ A 8 7		♡ J 8
	◊ A K 3 2		◊ K Q J 4		◊ A Q J 4 3
	♣ A J 8		♣ J 8 2		♣ A 8 7

With the first example, you have a balanced hand with 15 HCPs, too much strength to open the bidding 1NT so you start with 1◊.

After your partner's 1♥ response, you can describe your hand by rebidding no trumps at the cheapest available level, 1NT. Had your partner responded 2♣, you would have had to rebid 2NT, which would be the cheapest available level.

In the second example, your hand is also balanced but this time you have 18 HCPs. After your partner's 1♥ response, you again want to describe your balanced pattern and strength. This time, you paint the picture by jumping a level to 2NT.

The last balanced hand contains 19 HCPs and so you jump two levels when rebidding no trumps and end up bidding 3NT.

Over Zia's shoulder

Audrey: *By the time both opener and responder have made their first bids the auction can have proceeded in a number of different directions. How do you deal with all the possibilities?*

Zia: The choice of the opener's rebid is important. I keep in mind that the partnership is trying to zero in on the final contract and that the opener's role in the team effort is to try to describe his hand, both the strength and distribution. You might be interested in this hand:

♠ K 5
♥ 10 8 4 3
◇ A Q 6
♣ A K 9 2

With 16 HCPs and a balanced hand, I opened the bidding 1♣. I was intending to describe a balanced hand by rebidding no trumps at my next opportunity. I had visions of being declarer – and I love to play the hands. But my partner responded 1♥ and, since I had four-card support for his suit, I knew my first priority was to describe my hand and show my partner that we had an eight-card fit in hearts. Before raising my partner's suit, I stopped to consider how I might also describe the strength of my hand. I had more than a minimum strength hand but not enough to take my partner all the way to the game zone, since he could have only 6 points

Bidding

for his 1♡ response. I raised my partner to 3♡, showing a medium strength hand and leaving the final decision up to him. He actually had 10 points, and used the information I had given him to carry on to an excellent contract of 4♡.

Audrey: *After responder's initial bid, an opener still wants to give his partner as much information about his hand as possible. The difficult decisions come about when the responder bids a new suit and the opener cannot afford to give all the information he would like because it moves the partnership too far up the bidding steps. Zia, let's see how you describe the following hand with your rebid.*

♠ K 3
♡ 8
♢ A Q 7 2
♣ K 10 9 6 5 2

Zia: I started the bidding 1♣ and my partner responded 1♡. At this point, I wanted to tell my partner about my diamonds so that he could choose one of my suits as trumps. But, before rebidding 2♢, I stopped to consider whether or not I might be pushing the auction too high. If my partner had four diamonds, he would have bid them in response to my 1♣ bid unless he had five or more hearts. If I bid diamonds now, my partner would probably prefer to put me back in the club suit. To do this, he would have to bid 3♣ and even I might not be able to take nine tricks if we both had minimum hands. Instead, I settled for rebidding my first suit, 2♣. My partner had only 6 points and two little cards in each minor suit, so he passed and we were in our best contract. If I had bid my higher-ranking suit at the two level, we would have been too high.

Summary

On the rebid, the opener wants to describe both the shape and strength of his hand. He can think of his hand as small, medium, or large using the following ranges:

- 12–15 points   Small
- 16–18 points   Medium
- 19–20 points   Large

Generally, the more strength the opener has, the more he wants to bid.

Rebidding after responder raises to the two level

12–15 points	Pass
16–18 points	Move to the three level
19 or more points	Bid game

Rebidding after responder raises to the three level

12–14 points	Pass
15 or more points	Bid game

Rebidding with an unbalanced hand after a 1NT response

12–15 points	Bid a lower-ranking suit or rebid your original suit at the two level
16–18 points	Bid a higher-ranking suit at the two level (a reverse), or bid a lower-ranking suit with a jump to the three level, or rebid your original suit with a jump to the three level.
19 or more points	Bid a lower-ranking suit by jumping to the three level or a higher-ranking suit at the two level or rebid your original suit by jumping to the game level

Rebidding with a balanced hand after a 1NT response

15–16 points	Pass
17–18 points	Raise to 2NT
19 or more points	Raise to 3NT

Rebidding with an unbalanced hand after a new suit response

12–15 points	Bid a higher-ranking suit at the two level (a reverse), or bid a lower-ranking suit with a jump to the three level, or rebid your original suit with a jump to the three level.

| 16–18 points | Bid a new suit at the two level or rebid your original suit by jumping to the three level |
| 19 or more points | Bid a lower-ranking suit by jumping to the three level or a higher-ranking suit at the two level or rebid your original suit by jumping to the game level |

Rebidding with a balanced hand after a new suit response

15–16 points	Rebid no trumps at the cheapest available level
17–18 points	Rebid no trump, jumping one level
19 or more points	Rebid no trumps, jumping to 3NT

Commonly asked questions

Q *A new suit bid by a responder is always forcing. Is a new suit bid by an opener forcing? Sometimes my partner expects me to pass when he rebids a new suit and, at other times, he expects me to bid. How do I know what to do when the bidding messages appear to change?*

A It is more of a challenge to understand the bidding message of a new suit bid by an opener than a new suit bid by a responder. As you have correctly said, a response in a new suit is always forcing. Your partner is also correct in that the message of a rebid in a new suit by an opener can either be invitational or forcing. Here are some guidelines:

- If responder has bid a new suit at the one level, a new suit by an opener is only forcing if the opener jumps a level or if his second suit is bid at the two level and is higher-ranking than his first suit
- If responder has bid a new suit at the two level or higher, any new suit by the opener is forcing

Q *When I open one no-trump, the responder has several sign-off bids he can make, telling me to pass. What sign-off bids can responder make when I open one of a suit?*

A There are no sign-off bids that responder can make after an opening bid in a suit. How can there be when opener could have as many as 20 points? A responder must either make an invitational (limit) response or the forcing response of a new suit.

CHAPTER 9

Rebids by the Responder

Luck is where preparation meets opportunity.

By the time the responder is in the position of making his second bid, the *responder's rebid*, he has heard two bids from the opener and should have a much clearer picture of the opener's hand. The responder takes what he knows about the shape and strength of the opener's hand and asks himself two questions:

- What is the best zone for the partnership
- What is the best denomination

Much of the time the responder's rebid will be able to place the final contract. When the partnership has already arrived at the answer to one of the two questions, all the responder has to do is to answer the other to decide on the final contract. Let's look at how straightforward this can be.

Rebidding after the opener shows a minimum strength hand

An opener can show a minimum strength hand in a number of ways:

- Raising the responder's suit to the cheapest available level
- Rebidding his own suit at the cheapest available level
- Rebidding no trumps at the cheapest available level
- Bidding a new suit at the cheapest available level

Opener raises the responder's suit

Consider how much information responder has after the bidding has progressed as follows:

Opener	*Responder*
1♡	1♠
2♠	?

First, the opener has described a hand that has four or more hearts, the suit he first mentioned. Secondly, he has four spades, since he supported your spade suit. Thirdly, his hand has minimum strength, 12–15 points, since he only raised to the two level. You, as responder, are in a good position to decide on the zone of the final contract. The denomination was already decided once the opener supported your spade suit. Let's see what you would rebid after the above auction with each of the following hands:

	1	♠ J 10 9 8		2	♠ K 8 6 5 3		3	♠ Q 10 4 3 2
		♡ A 4			♡ A 7			♡ A 4
		◊ 9 7 4 3			◊ K 9			◊ A 9 3
		♣ J 5 3			♣ 9 8 5 3			♣ A 7 2

On the first hand, you would pass. The partnership should remain in the partscore zone. The opener has shown minimum values by supporting your suit at the cheapest level and you only have 6 points.

On the second hand, you have 10 HCPs and 2 points for the doubletons. Game is still possible even though the opener has shown a minimum strength hand of 12–15 points. If the opener has only 12 or 13 points, you want to remain in the partscore zone. If the opener is at the top of his range, 14 or 15 points, you want to be in the game zone. To find out the information you need, move towards the game zone by rebidding 3♠, inviting the opener to carry on. The opener will accept your invitation with the top of his range, but decline if he has the bottom of his range, leaving the contract in the partscore.

On the third hand, you do not need any more information from the opener to decide to rebid 4♠. Since you have 14 HCPs plus 1 for the doubleton heart and the opener has promised at least 12 points with his opening bid, there is enough combined strength for the game zone.

The general guidelines when an opener's rebid has shown a minimum strength hand is the following:

6–9 points	Stop in the partscore zone
10–12 points	Make a move towards the game zone
13 or more points	Get to the game zone

Opener rebids his own suit

Suppose the auction goes as follows:

Opener	Responder
1♡	1♠
2♡	?

The opener is again showing a minimum hand of 12–15 points, but without support for the responder's suit. Since the opener did not rebid no trumps or show a second suit, he must have an unbalanced hand, probably with a six-card or longer suit. The responder can use the same guidelines as when the opener raises the responder's suit. Let's see what you would do with each of the following hands after the above auction.

1 ♠ K 10 8 5 2	2 ♠ A 9 8 5 3	3 ♠ A J 9 5 2
♡ J 4	♡ K 8 2	♡ A 7 3
◊ Q 7 5	◊ 9 3	◊ A 4
♣ J 9 5	♣ K 7 5	♣ 10 9 5

On the first hand, you have only 7 HCPs. Opposite the opener's minimum hand, you want to remain in the partscore zone. Since your partner has an unbalanced hand with a long heart suit, the best partscore appears to be 2♡. Pass and let your partner get on with playing the hand.

In the second example, you have 10 HCPs. Since you are in the 10–12 point range, you want to move towards the game zone. Now that your partner has rebid his suit, you know there is an eight-card or longer fit in hearts. Make an invitational raise to 3♡. The opener will decline the invitation with the bottom of his minimum range, but will accept if he is at the top of the range.

With the last hand, you have enough strength to want to be in the game zone. You want to play in the eight-card or longer suit fit, so raise the opener to game, 4♡.

Opener rebids in no trumps

Suppose the auction goes as follows:

Opener	Responder
1♢	1♠
1NT	?

The opener has told the responder a lot about his hand. He has a balanced hand with 15–16 points, too many points to open the bidding 1NT but too few to jump to 2NT on the rebid. The opener has also shown a four-card, or possibly five-card, diamond suit and fewer than four spades, since he did not raise the responder's suit. With all this information the responder should be able to decide the zone and denomination on each of the following hands:

1 ♠ J109432	2 ♠ AQJ742	3 ♠ K743
♡ Q6	♡ 72	♡ K104
♢ K42	♢ K6	♢ A842
♣ 87	♣ J98	♣ K2

On the first hand, the responder has 6 HCPs and 2 points for the six-card suit, a total of 8 points. Since the opener has shown 15–16 points, the responder knows the partnership should stay in a partscore. If the responder had a balanced hand, he could pass and leave opener in 1NT. However, the opener has shown a balanced hand and must have at least two spades, giving the partnership an eight-card fit. The responder can sign-off in 2♠.

With the second hand, the responder has 11 HCPs and 2 points for the six-card suit. Combined with the opener's promised 15–16 points, the partnership belongs in the game zone. As on the previous hand, the denomination should be spades, so the responder jumps to game, 4♠.

On the final hand, you also belong in the game zone. Since your partner has not supported your spades, the best game contract should be 3NT. The responder can ignore the diamond fit since 3NT should be easier to make than 5♢.

Opener bids a new suit

When the opener's rebid is in a new suit, he is giving the responder a choice of trump suits. The responder should keep in mind that the opener always starts the bidding in his longest suit, so the opener's first bid suit will be as long, or longer, than his second suit. With equal support for both suits, the responder should prefer to play in the opener's first suit. Of course, the responder may not like either of the opener's suits and may want to rebid his own suit or bid no trumps.

In deciding on the zone, the responder should assume that the opener has a minimum hand of 12–15 points. In some situations, the responder could have more than a minimum, since the opener only jumps in a new suit when he has a maximum strength hand of 19 or more points. The opener will have to show any extra strength at his next opportunity, if the auction is still going. Assuming the opener has a minimum, the responder can follow the guidelines of stopping in a partscore with 6–9 points, moving towards a game with 10–12 points, and getting to the game zone with 13 or more points. For example, suppose the auction starts this way:

Opener	Responder
1♡	1♠
2♣	?

1	♠ QJ 10 4	2	♠ AJ 9 3	3	♠ KQ 10 8
	♡ Q 8 7		♡ 4 3		♡ Q 8
	◊ J 4 3		◊ 9 5 2		◊ K 10 9 8
	♣ Q 8 7		♣ AQ 10 9		♣ A 3 2

You have only 8 HCPs on the first hand, so it looks as though the partnership belongs in the partscore zone. Your partner has not supported your spades but has given you a choice between hearts and clubs. With equal length support for both suits, remember that your partner bid his longest suit first. Give preference to your partner's first suit by rebidding 2♡.

With 11 HCPs on the second hand, you want to move towards the game zone. Since you prefer your partner's second suit, you can raise to the three level, 3♣. With only 12 or 13 points, your

partner can pass the invitation and stop in a partscore. If your partner has 14 or more points, he can accept your invitation by bidding
to a game contract.

On the last hand, you have 14 HCPs, enough to put the partnership in the game zone. With no particular preference for either of
partner's suits, rebid 3NT, putting the partnership in the most
appropriate game contract.

Rebidding after the opener shows a medium strength hand

Suppose the auction has proceeded:

Opener	Responder
1♡	1♠
3♡	?

By jumping to 3♡, rather than rebidding 2♡, the opener is showing
an unbalanced hand of more than minimum strength, about 16–18
points, with a six-card or longer heart suit. Let's see what you
would rebid with the following hands:

1 ♠ K 9 8 7	2 ♠ K 10 8 5 2	3 ♠ K J 7 6
♡ 10 8	♡ K 9 6	♡ 4
◊ Q J 5 4	◊ A 9	◊ A J 4 2
♣ 9 7 3	♣ 7 4 2	♣ Q 10 7 6

You only have 6 HCPs on the first hand. The opener's jump to 3♡
is highly invitational but not forcing. Since the opener has at most
18 points and could have as few as 16, you should decline the invitation and pass.

With 10 HCPs you have enough strength to want to be in the
game zone, even if the opener only has 16 points. Since the opener
has promised a long heart suit, accept by raising to 4♡.

Your 11 HCPs on the last hand are enough to put the partnership in the game zone. Since you do not care for your partner's
heart suit, rebid 3NT, the most likely game contract.

The opener would also be showing a medium strength hand in
the following auctions:

Opener	*Responder*
1♡	1♠
3♣	?

Opener	*Responder*
1♡	1♠
2NT	?

In general, use the following guidelines when the opener's rebid shows a medium strength hand:

6–7 points	Stop in the partscore zone
8 or more points	Get to the game zone

Rebidding after the opener shows a maximum strength hand

When an opener makes a rebid that shows a maximum strength hand – either by jumping in a new suit or jumping two levels when rebidding no trumps – he is promising 19 or more points. Even if the responder has only 6 points, there are at least 25 combined points, so the partnership always belongs in the game zone.

For example, suppose the auction starts off this way:

Opener	*Responder*
1♠	1NT
3♡	?

The opener's jump shift to 3♡ shows an unbalanced hand of 19 or more points with both spades and hearts. The spades will be as long, or longer, than the hearts since the opener bid spades first. Let's see what the responder rebids with each of the following hands:

1	♠ J9 ♡ 10972 ◊ A52 ♣ J1083	2	♠ 85 ♡ 62 ◊ KQ753 ♣ Q1092	3	♠ Q93 ♡ J42 ◊ K953 ♣ 1072

Although you have only 6 HCPs on the first hand, you cannot pass the opener's 3♡ rebid. The partnership is committed to the game zone. With four-card support, raise the opener's second suit to game, 4♡.

On the second hand, you do not have support for either of the opener's suits. Since you belong in the game zone, rebid 3NT. That appears to be the best contract from your side of the table. If your partner has a very unbalanced hand, he can always override your decision and rebid one of his suits.

On the last hand, you can put your partner in a game in his first suit by rebidding 4♠. It might seem strange to raise his spade suit when he has only bid it once but, remember, he opened the bidding 1♠. If he had a four-card spade suit and a four-card heart suit, he would have opened the lower-ranking of two four-card suits, 1♡. Since he opened 1♠, you can assume that he must have at least five spades. This is the type of inference you can learn to draw from the opener's bidding to help you select the best contract.

Over Zia's shoulder

Audrey: *By the time the responder makes his rebid, a lot of bidding has gone on. The responder usually knows the zone and denomination of the final contract. Show us a hand demonstrating how you arrived at a decision when you were the responder and had to make your rebid.*

Zia: You have to imagine what your partner has in order to decide on the final contract. Here is a hand I recently held:

♠ Q 10 8 6
♡ K 4 3
◇ K J 7
♣ A 4 2

My partner, the dealer, bid 1♡. The opponents passed throughout the auction. I responded 1♠ and my partner rebid 2◇. Look closely at the auction so far:

North	East	South	West
(Partner)		(Zia)	
1♡	Pass	1♠	Pass
2◇	Pass	?	

Before you decide on the rebid, think about what your partner is telling you about his hand. He started with hearts and rebid diamonds. When an opener bids two suits in this fashion, his first suit must be five cards or longer in length, otherwise he would have opened 1◊. So my partner has described a hand with five hearts and I have three hearts. We have found a major suit fit. Now I think about the zone. My partner has 12 or more points and I have 13. That's enough for a game. I know I want to be in a game in hearts so my rebid is 4♡.

I had another hand where my partner bid two suits, neither of which I particularly liked. This was my hand:

♠ A Q 8 7 6 5
♡ J 4 3 2
◊ K Q
♣ J

My partner opened 1◊ and I responded 1♠. My partner rebid 2♣. I had to find a rebid. Look again at the auction:

North	East	South	West
(Partner)		(Zia)	
1◊	Pass	1♠	Pass
2♣	Pass	?	

I wanted to be in a game. My partner had shown at least five diamonds and at least four clubs. Since that totals nine cards, the most my partner had in both hearts and spades was four cards. I wondered how they were divided. I wanted to be in 4♠ if my partner had two or three spades, otherwise, in 3NT. I rebid 2♡. Remember, a new suit bid by the responder is forcing so my partner had to bid again. He had already told me about his diamonds and clubs and knew I wanted more information about his spades or hearts.

Audrey: *Don't leave us in the dark. How did the auction continue?*

Zia: My partner bid 2♠, showing some spade support and I decided on the spade game. On my third bid as responder the final contract was decided. I rebid 4♠. When the auction carries on for that long, there is always a chance for misunderstanding. However, my partner remembered that a new suit by responder is forcing and so he co-operated to help find the best contract.

Summary

By the time the responder makes his second bid, he has heard two bids from the opener. He considers the strength and distribution that the opener has described and looks at his own hand to answer two questions:

- What is the best zone for the partnership?
- What is the best denomination?

In making his decision, responder can use the following guidelines:

Responder's rebid when opener has a minimum strength hand

6–9 points	Stop in the partscore zone
10–12 points	Make a move towards the game zone
13 or more points	Get to the game zone

Responder's rebid when opener has a medium strength hand

6–7 points	Stop in the partscore zone
8 or more points	Get to the game zone

Responder's rebid when opener has a maximum strength hand

6 or more points	Get to the game zone

Commonly asked questions

Q   *I have heard that the responder can only make one bid with fewer than 10 points. Is this true?*

A   The responder is usually in the position of being the captain and has the responsibility of putting the partnership in the best final contract. This may mean making two bids with as few as 6 HCPs. For example, suppose the auction has proceeded:

Opener	Responder
1♡	1♠
1NT	?

This is the responder's hand:

♠ J 10 9 8 7 6
♡ A 4
◊ J 7 3
♣ 3 2

The responder knows that the opener has at least two spades, since the opener is showing a balanced hand. There is no need to play in a partscore in no trumps with an eight-card spade fit. The responder, as captain, rebids 2♠. His focus should not only be on his point count but also on the best final contract.

CHAPTER 10

Strong Two Opening Bids

At the top level, women do not play as well as men, although at a social level, they are thought to be the better players.

From time to time, you pick up your cards and see a hand that is so strong you would be very disappointed if your partner passed your opening bid and left you in the partscore zone. Remember, you never want to put your partner in the position of being able to disappoint you so, if you want your partner to respond to your bid, you have to make a forcing bid.

Opening the bidding at the two level

If you feel that your hand is so powerful that you do not want your partner to pass, even if he has 0–5 points, you can start the bidding at the two level, rather than at the one level. The Acol system uses a variety of strong opening bids at the two level:

- An opening bid of 2♣ is an *artificial opening bid*, showing either a very powerful balanced or unbalanced hand of 23 or more HCPs. It does *not* show a club suit! The opener will describe the type of hand when he makes his rebid. If the opener's rebid shows a balanced hand, the responder does not have to bid again if he is happy with the contract. On the other hand, if the opener shows an unbalanced hand, the responder must keep bidding until the partnership is in the game zone. In this case, the opening 2♣ bid is said to be *forcing to game*.

- An opening bid of 2◊, 2♡ or 2♠ is called an *Acol Two Bid* and shows a slightly less powerful hand than an opening bid of 2♣. However, responder must bid at least once. An Acol Two Bid is said to be *forcing for one round* (of bidding)
- An opening bid of 2NT shows a balanced hand of 20–22 HCPs. It is an invitational bid only and the responder can pass if he has a balanced hand of about 0–3 points

Let's take a closer look at each of these opening bids.

Opening 2♣ bid

An opening bid of 2♣ is a strong, artificial, forcing bid. It is strong because it shows a hand containing 23 or more points, or the equivalent in trick-taking power. It is artificial because it says nothing about the club suit – in fact, it could even be a hand containing no clubs at all! It is forcing because the responder cannot pass. Here are some examples:

1	♠ 9	2	♠ A K 9	3	♠ A K Q 10 9 8 7
	♡ A K Q 9 4		♡ K Q 8		♡ A 8
	◊ A K Q J 4		◊ A Q J 9		◊ A K 6 2
	♣ A 3		♣ A J 6		♣ –

If you were to open at the one level with the first hand, you would be very disappointed if the responder passed, even if he had no points at all. You have enough strength to make a game contract all by yourself. On the other hand, you don't want to open the bidding 4♡, for example, since that does not leave much room to explore other contracts or the possibility of a slam. Instead, you want to start with a forcing bid, which commits the partnership to a game, and then you can take your time describing the hand and finding the best denomination and zone. You open the bidding with an artificial 2♣. On your subsequent bids, you will describe the hand by bidding your heart suit and, probably, your diamond suit as well. Having opened 2♣, you have no fear that your partner will pass before you reach at least the game zone.

On the second hand, you have a strong balanced hand of 24 HCPs. This is too much to open the bidding 2NT, which would show only 20–22 HCPs (see later). Instead, you open the bidding with an artificial 2♣, planning to rebid no trumps after your partner's response to describe his type of hand.

On the last hand, you have only 20 HCPs but you have a lot of trick-taking power. You should be able to take ten tricks – seven spade tricks, one heart trick and two diamond tricks – even if your partner has nothing but small cards. Open 2♣, since you want to end up at least at the game zone, and there may be a slam if your partner has some high cards. Notice that you do not need any clubs at all to open 2♣. You are not planning to play in clubs and your partner cannot pass your forcing bid. You will tell him about your spades when making your rebid.

Opening an Acol Two Bid

An opening bid of 2◊, 2♡ or 2♠ is forcing, but only for one round. It is used for unbalanced hands that are not quite strong enough to open 2♣ but with which you expect to be able to take at least eight tricks. The opening bid is *natural*, not artificial, since it shows the suit that you have. Unfortunately, since the opening bid of 2♣ is reserved as an artificial bid for the very strong hands, you can only open an Acol Two Bid in diamonds, hearts or spades. If your suit is clubs, you will have to choose between opening 1♣ and opening an artificial 2♣, planning to rebid 3♣ to show your suit.

The following hands are examples leading to an opening Acol Two Bid:

1	♠ A K Q J 10 8	2	♠ A K 7	3	♠ 9
	♡ A		♡ 9 8		♡ A K Q 9 8
	◊ A 7 3		◊ A Q J 10 8 6 2		◊ A K J 8 7
	♣ J 6 3		♣ 3		♣ J 4

With the first hand, you expect to take at least six spade tricks to go with the ♡A and ◊A. With eight tricks all of your own, open the bidding 2♠. If your partner turns out to have a very weak hand, you can stop in the partscore zone since he is only forced to bid once.

The second hand is similar. You expect to take about six diamond tricks, even if the opponents have the ◊K, as well as your two spade tricks. Open with an Acol 2◊ bid to let your partner know you do not need too much help to get to the game zone.

The last hand contains two strong five-card suits. While it is not quite as evident where your eight tricks might come from, powerful two-suited hands are usually opened with an Acol Two Bid. You intend to bid both your suits and it is quite likely that your partner will like at least one of them as a trump suit. With a choice of five-card suits, open the higher-ranking, 2♡, planning to rebid 3◊ after your partner's response.

Opening 2NT

With a balanced hand of 20–22 points, you open the bidding 2NT to describe your hand. For example:

♠ K J 8
♡ A J
◊ K Q 7 2
♣ A Q 5 2

Since you have described the strength of your hand within a narrow range, the responder can pass your 2NT opening bid if he has a weak balanced hand of 0–3 points. The responder will know that there is not likely to be enough combined strength for the game zone.

Putting this bid together with all our earlier opening bids to describe balanced hands, you now know what to open with any balanced hand that you pick up, no matter how many points:

Opening balanced hands

12–14 points	Open 1NT
15–16 points	Open one of a suit, planning to rebid 1NT
17–19 points	Open one of a suit, planning to jump in no trumps
20–22 points	Open 2NT
23–24 points	Open 2♣, planning to rebid 2NT
25–27 points	Open 2♣, planning to rebid 3NT

Responding to opening two bids

Responding to 2♣

Since the opening bid of 2♣ is forcing, you are expected to bid
again even if you have no points. You might wonder what to do
with a hand like this:

♠ 9 7
♡ 8 6 3 2
♢ 8 4 3
♣ J 9 4 2

What an unhappy collection. Surely you are not expected to bid
with only 1 point? But just think what will happen if you pass.
Your partner will be playing in a contract of 2♣ and he might have
no clubs at all since 2♣ is an artificial bid. You have to respond in
order to give your partner a chance to describe his hand. So, you
want to have some way of saying to your partner, 'I have a weak
hand.'

As with the artificial 2♣ opening, an artificial response of 2♢ is
used when you have a weak hand. This artificial, or conventional,
bid has nothing to do with the diamond suit but, instead, gives
your partner the message that you have 0–7 points. Now the opener has a chance to describe his hand. For example, the auction
might start off this way:

North	East	South	West
(Partner)		(You)	
2♣	Pass	2♢	Pass
2♠	Pass	?	

What next? Remember, when the opener starts with 2♣ and then
describes an unbalanced hand, the partnership must keep bidding
until it is in the game zone. Since you have already given a weak,
or *negative*, response, the opener is not expecting anything much
from you, only to help him find the best contract in the game zone.
If you really do not like your partner's suit and do not have a good
suit of your own to bid, as in the above hand, you can make a
second negative, or discouraging, bid of 2NT. The opener will con-

tinue to describe his hand, looking for the best contract. For example, with you holding the previously mentioned hand, the complete auction might be:

North	East	South	West
(Partner)		(You)	
2♣	Pass	2◊	Pass
2♠	Pass	2NT	Pass
3♡	Pass	4♡	Pass
Pass	Pass		

When your partner shows that he has a heart suit, in addition to his spades, you have found a suitable fit. You cannot pass the 3♡ bid, since the auction is still forcing to the game zone, so you can raise to 4♡. The opener, knowing you may have no points at all, can now pass, having given up any aspirations of a slam contract.

If the responder has a hand with about 8 or more points, he can make a *positive* response over 2♣, rather than the negative response of 2◊. The responder can bid a good five-card suit of his own or bid 2NT with a balanced hand. Of course, if he wants to make a positive response with a diamond suit, the responder will have to jump to 3◊, since 2◊ shows a weak hand. Here are some examples of responding to an opening bid of 2♣:

1	♠ K Q 10 8 5	2	♠ Q 9 7	3	♠ 8 2
	♡ K 9 2		♡ Q 10 4		♡ 10 5
	◊ 7 5		◊ K 8 5		◊ A Q J 8 4 2
	♣ 10 8 4		♣ Q 10 6 3		♣ 9 4 3

On the first hand, you have 8 HCPs and a good five-card spade suit. You would make a positive response of 2♠. This tells your partner you do not have a weak hand, so there is the possibility of reaching a slam contract.

With a balanced hand and 9 HCPs in the second example, make a positive response of 2NT. This will describe your hand and pave the way to a possible slam contract once you have found the appropriate denomination. For example, if the opener rebids 3♡, describing an unbalanced hand with a long heart suit, you can raise to 4♡ and your partner will know if there is enough combined strength to move toward the slam zone.

You have only 7 HCPs on the last hand but can add 2 points for
the six-card suit, giving you enough to make a positive response.
Since your suit is diamonds, however, you have to respond 3◊,
avoiding the artificial 2◊ response.

Responding to 2◊, 2♡ or 2♠

If your partner opens with an Acol Two Bid, you again have to
respond, even with a very weak hand. There is no room left to use
2◊ as the negative response so a response of 2NT is used instead to
show a weak hand of about 0–7 points. Any other bid is a positive
response, showing about 8 or more points. The difference between
an Acol Two Bid and the stronger opening bid of 2♣ is that the
responder only has to bid once when the opener starts with 2◊, 2♡
or 2♠. If the responder shows a weak hand by responding 2NT, he
can then pass the opener's rebid of his first suit or of a second,
lower-ranking suit. Here are some examples of responding to an
opening bid of 2♡:

1 ♠ J 7 5	2 ♠ 8 5 3	3 ♠ K J 10 8 5 2
♡ 8 6	♡ Q 7 2	♡ 3
◊ J 8 7 4 2	◊ A 9 5 2	◊ K Q 8 2
♣ 10 8 5	♣ Q 6 2	♣ 7 3

With only 2 HCPs, you would make the negative response of 2NT
with the first hand. Remember, 2NT is an artificial response, it
does not express any desire to play in that contract. Your partner is
unlikely to want to play in no trumps since he is showing an
unbalanced hand. If he rebids 3♡, for example, you can now pass,
since the Acol Two Bid is not forcing to game. If he had a strong
enough hand to want to be in a game when you have as little as
this, he would have started with 2♣.

With the second hand, you have enough to make a positive
response. Since your partner is showing an unbalanced hand with
at least a five-card heart suit, you only need three-card support to
raise. Respond 3♡. Once you give a positive response, the partnership must have enough combined strength for a contract in the
game zone. You only raise to 3♡ to leave plenty of room on the bidding steps to explore the possibility of a slam contract now that
you have found a suitable denomination.

With the third hand, you do not have support for the opener's suit but you have enough strength to make a positive response by bidding a suit of your own, 2♠. Again, the positive response commits you to the game zone, but you will have to explore to find the best denomination.

Responding to 2NT

An opening bid of 2NT shows a balanced hand of 20–22 points. Since the upper limit is 22 points, the responder can pass with a balanced hand of about 0–3 points since there is not enough combined strength for game. Otherwise, the responder can raise to 3NT, with a balanced hand, bid 4♡ or 4♠ with a six-card or longer major suit, or bid 3♡ or 3♠ with a five-card major suit, asking the opener to choose between 3NT and game in the major suit. Suppose the opener bids 2NT, here are some examples of responding:

1	♠ 1085	2	♠ QJ8742	3	♠ 75
	♡ J73		♡ 8		♡ KJ642
	◊ 10642		◊ Q93		◊ 85
	♣ J62		♣ 642		♣ Q642

With only 2 HCPs on the first hand, pass and hope your partner can scramble home with eight tricks. With the six-card major suit on the next hand, you know there is a combined eight-card fit opposite the opener's balanced hand. Jump right to 4♠. On the last hand, you can bid 3♡. This is similar to a response of 3♡ to an opening 1NT bid. It asks the opener to raise to 4♡ with three-card or longer support, otherwise bid 3NT.

The situation is similar if the auction starts this way:

North	East	South	West
(Partner)		(You)	
2♣	Pass	2◊	Pass
2NT	Pass	?	

Only, this time, your partner is showing a balanced hand with 23–24 points. Now you only need two or three points to want to be in the game zone.

Over Zia's shoulder

Audrey: *Zia, opening strong two bids is an exciting topic. You must
         have some interesting auctions for us.*

Zia: It is important to recognise that, even when you open the
         bidding at the two level, you and your partner are still
         conducting a conversation to try to reach the best con-
         tract. You get quite excited when you pick up a big hand,
         with visions of a slam dancing through your head, but
         you must first hear what your partner has to say.

> ♠ A K Q 7 6 4
> ♡ K Q J
> ◇ A K
> ♣ Q 8

I was certainly pleased to have been dealt the above
hand. With 24 HCPs and a six-card suit, I had enough for
the game zone all by myself and could smell the potential for an even bigger bonus if my partner had some
high cards. But, first things first. Since I did not want my
partner to pass before we reached the game zone, I started the bidding 2♣. My partner cooled my ardour somewhat by bidding 2◇, the negative response. I continued
to describe my hand by bidding 2♠ and heard my partner bid 3♡. Holding the ♡K, ♡Q and ♡J, the thought of a
slam bonus briefly passed through my mind again but,
remembering I had already promised a big hand and
that my partner could have very little, I just showed my
support by raising to 4♡. My partner passed and this was
his hand:

> ♠ 5
> ♡ 1 0 8 7 5 4 2
> ◇ 9 6 3
> ♣ 9 7 2

It was certainly fortunate that we did not get any higher
since the opponents took the first three tricks. My
partner made the rest of the tricks, however, and we got

our game bonus. My partner bid the hand very well, first bidding 2◊ to tell me he had a weak hand and then showing his long heart suit with his rebid. We could not have made 4♠, since one of the opponents held four spades, so we reached the best contract.

Summary

With a very powerful hand, you have a choice of the following opening bids:

Opening the bidding at the two level

2♣	A very powerful balanced or unbalanced hand of 23 or more points which will be described on the rebid
2◊, 2♡ or 2♠	An *Acol Two Bid* showing a slightly less powerful hand than an opening bid of 2♣, worth about eight tricks
2NT	A balanced hand of 20–22 HCPs

An opening bid of 2♣ is forcing to the game zone unless the opener rebids 2NT, showing a balanced hand of 23–24 HCPs. The responder uses the following guidelines:

Responding to a 2♣ opening

0–7 points	Bid 2◊, the negative response
8 or more points	Bid a good five-card or longer suit (3◊ with diamonds), otherwise 2NT

An *Acol Two Bid* is forcing for one round only. If the responder has a weak hand, he can pass the opener's rebid. The responder uses the following guidelines:

Responding to an Acol Two Bid

0–7 points	Bid 2NT, the negative response
8 or more points	Raise with three-card or longer support, otherwise, bid a new suit

Commonly asked questions

Q   *What would I open with the following hand? It is not balanced and I
do not have a five-card suit:*

♠ A Q 8 4
♡ A
◇ K Q J 3
♣ A Q 10 5

A   Strong hands with a 4–4–4–1 pattern are always difficult to
bid. Some players prefer to open at the one level – with the
middle-ranking of three four-card suits – hoping that their
partner will have enough to respond and that they can show
the strength of the hand with their rebid. With so many HCPs,
however, most players prefer to open at the two level. If your
singleton is a high card, as in the above hand, you can open
2NT, treating the hand as though it were balanced. If your singleton is a small card, you would probably pick one of your
four-card suits and treat it as though it were a five-card suit. If
your partner raises with three-card support, too bad!

CHAPTER 11

Pre-emptive Opening Bids

Omar Sharif says that bridge has helped him to stay sane. He says most actors have nothing to do in their spare time so they worry about their next picture and fret because the phone doesn't ring; they notice wrinkles that indicate they're getting older. Not so with him, says Omar.

Just when it seems as if you know all about opening the bidding with and without competition from the opponents, you pick up a hand like this:

♠ 9
♡ 4 3
◊ A K 10 9 8 7 3
♣ 5 4 3

If you recall the guidelines we developed for opening the bidding at the one level, you can see that you cannot open the bidding 1◊. With 7 HCPs and 3 points for the length in the diamond suit, the hand does not meet the strength requirements for an opening bid of 1◊. And yet, you probably don't feel like passing with this hand, do you? It is likely that you could take six or seven tricks all by yourself if diamonds were the trump suit.

Another way of looking at the situation is that there are 33 HCPs among the other three hands. There is a good chance that the opponents have the majority of the missing strength and may be able to make a partscore or, more likely, a game contract in either hearts or spades. If that is the case, you would like to make it as difficult as possible for the opponents to reach their game contract. After all, you want to give the opponents every chance to make a mistake when they are likely to buy the contract.

Opening with a pre-empt

With these thoughts in mind, many players like to make what is called a *pre-emptive opening bid* (*pre-empt*) with hands like the one mentioned earlier. A pre-emptive opening bid is made at the three level, so you would open 3◊ with the previous hand. By opening at the three level you are hoping to make it difficult for the opponents to enter the auction. When the bidding starts at the three level, they are not going to be sure whether to let you play the contract and try to defeat you, or to bid to a contract of their own. If they do decide to let you play in your contract, you will probably take a lot of tricks, thanks to your long suit. Even if you are defeated, the penalty you suffer is likely to be less than the value of the partscore or game the opponents could make.

Requirements for a pre-emptive opening bid

- A good seven-card or longer suit
- Less than the strength for an opening bid at the one level

It is important to remember that the reason for pre-empting is to make it difficult for the opponents, not for your side. If you have an opening bid, even though you have a seven-card suit, start the bidding at the one level. There are other reasons why you might decide not to make a pre-emptive opening bid even when your hand meets the above requirements. For example, if you have a four-card major suit, it is best to avoid starting the bidding at the three level as it will make it difficult for your side to find its fit if your partner also has four or more cards in the major suit. Let's look at some examples. You are the opener. What would you bid with each of the following hands?

1	♠ A K 9 8 7 6 5	2	♠ A	3	♠ 10 3
	♡ A 8		♡ Q J 8 7		♡ 4
	◊ 9 8		◊ 9 8 7 6 4 3 2		◊ J 9 8
	♣ J 3		♣ 8		♣ K Q 10 8 7 6 5

With 12 HCPs and a seven-card suit, the first hand is too strong to open with a pre-empt of 3♠. Make the normal opening bid of 1♠. Your side, not the opponents', has the best chance of reaching the game zone on this hand. By starting too high, you could interfere with your side's orderly exchange of information.

Although you have a seven-card diamond suit and less than the values for an opening bid at the one level, the second hand is also not the right type of hand for an opening pre-emptive bid. Your suit is too weak, with your high cards in other suits. You also have a four-card major suit. It would be difficult to find out if your side has a fit in hearts if you start the bidding with 3◊. Instead, pass with this hand.

The third hand meets the requirements for an opening pre-empt. You have a good seven-card suit without enough strength to open the bidding at the one level. Start the auction with 3♣.

Responding to a pre-emptive opening bid

This time, it is your partner who has started the bidding at the three level. How do you respond to such a bid? You can assume that your partner has about 9 points on average. If you have 16 or more, you probably want to bid on with the intention of reaching a suitable contract in the game zone. If you have fewer than 16 points, you should usually pass and be satisfied that your partner has disrupted the opponents' bidding.

Here are some examples. Your partner starts the bidding 3♣ and the opponent on your right says pass. What do you respond with each of the following hands?

1	♠ Q98	2	♠ K752	3	♠ AKJ952
	♡ KQJ1098		♡ KQ32		♡ AK98
	◊ K76		◊ AQ8		◊ 5
	♣ 2		♣ A8		♣ 72

Although you have a reasonable hand and would prefer to be playing in a contract of 3♡, rather than 3♣, with the first hand, you should pass. If you, as responder, bid a new suit at the three level, it is a forcing bid and your partner will have to bid again. You will end up getting too high. Since your partner has less than the values for an opening bid, pass and leave well enough alone.

With 18 HCPs on the second hand, it is likely that you belong in the game zone even though your partner has a weak hand. Since he has seven or more clubs, it is unlikely that he has four hearts or four spades, so it is not worth looking for a fit in one of those suits. Instead, respond 3NT. It will be easier to try to take nine tricks in a no-trump contract than eleven tricks in 5♣.

On the third hand, you have 15 HCPs and 2 points for the six-card spade suit. With this much strength, it is worth looking for a contract in the game zone. You can respond 3♠, a new suit. Since you are not yet at the game zone, a new suit by the responder is forcing and your partner's next bid will help you decide on the best contract.

Rebidding by the pre-emptor

The basic reason for making a pre-emptive opening bid is to inter-fere with the opponents' auction, not to get your side to a contract which it cannot make. An opening bid at the three level is very descriptive. It tells your partner you have a seven-card suit and less than opening points. Your partner is now the captain so let him decide what to do next. Suppose you are North and the bid-ding progresses as follows:

North	East	South	West
(You)		(Partner)	
3♡	3♠	Pass	4♠
?			

You started at the three level to make it difficult for the opponents but they still reached a contract of 4♠. What do you do now? Pass. We don't even have to look at your hand. We know you have a seven-card or longer suit and less than opening points. Leave the decision up to your partner, who can either pass or move to 5♡. Remember, after you have made a pre-emptive opening bid, you have passed the captaincy to your partner.

If your partner bids a new suit below the game level, it is forc-ing and you must bid again. Suppose you started with a pre-emp-tive opening bid of 3◊ and your partner responds 3♡. Let's consider what you would do with this hand:

♠ 2
♡ 4 3 2
◊ K Q J 9 8 7 6
♣ 10 2

Your partner is interested in finding the best contract in the game zone and will have a five-card or longer heart suit. With support for his suit, raise to 4♡. Had the responder bid 3♠, you would rebid 4◊, showing no interest in the spade suit. Your partner will take it from there.

Over Zia's shoulder

Audrey: *Zia, you are a very flamboyant player. You must have some interesting stories about pre-emptive bidding. I have a feeling you like to start the bidding at the three level.*

Zia: I'm afraid that my ideas about pre-empting are X-rated and not fit for printing. Suffice to say that I am a strong supporter of pre-empting whenever and wherever possible. It is not easy to play well when you are under pressure and pre-empts certainly put the opponents under pressure. Since I never seem to get my fair share of the high cards, the pre-emptive opening bid is one way I can have some fun in the auction even when I don't have the best hand at the table. I don't like to let my opponents have the auction all to themselves. Too often they get to the right contract. Here is a hand I held playing against very good opponents:

   ♠ 8 7
   ♡ 9 4
   ◊ Q J 9 8 7 6 4 2
   ♣ 3

Although I only had 3 HCPs, I did have an eight-card suit, so I started the auction with 3◊. The opponents did come into the auction but they misjudged the zone in which they belonged. They ended up playing in a game contract when they could actually make a grand slam! Even the best players in the world can make mistakes when you put them under pressure.

Audrey: *Part of the skill in making pre-emptive opening bids is to know when to avoid opening the bidding at the three level.*

Zia: That's true. You want to avoid opening every hand that has a seven-card or longer suit with a pre-empt. What would you do if you held this hand?

♠ K Q 8 7
♡ 4
◊ A K 9 5 4 3 2
♣ 3

I hope that you would start with 1◊. Starting at the three level with this hand would only prevent you from getting to your best spot. After I started the bidding with 1◊, my partner responded 1♡ and I now showed the four-card spade suit by bidding 1♠. My partner jumped to 4♠ and we made the contract. It would have been very difficult for us to find the major suit game if I'd started the auction at the three level. My partner would have passed and we would have missed our game bonus.

Summary

When you have a seven-card or longer suit and not enough strength to open the bidding at the one level, you can consider making a pre-emptive opening bid at the three level.

Requirements for a pre-emptive opening bid
- A good seven-card or longer suit
- Less than the strength for an opening bid at the one level

Keep the following points in mind when pre-empting:

- Avoid pre-empting with a long suit when you have enough strength to open the bidding at the one level
- Avoid pre-empting with a four-card or longer major suit in addition to your long suit

- After you have pre-empted, the responder is the captain. Don't bid again unless the responder makes a forcing bid
- If the responder bids a new suit, you have to bid again

If your partner opens the bidding with a pre-empt at the three level, you should generally pass unless you have about 16 or more points.

If your opponent opens the bidding with a pre-empt, you can compete with an overcall or takeout double if your hand is suitable. Since you are entering the auction at the three level or higher, you should have more strength than a minimum opening bid.

Commonly asked questions

Q *Do all pre-emptive opening bids start at the three level?*

A No. Any opening bid in a suit at the three level or higher is a pre-emptive opening bid. The longer and stronger your suit is, the higher you can start with your pre-empt. However, there is no point in bidding beyond the game zone since you do not want to lose the game bonus if your side has the balance of strength. For example, suppose you have the following hand:

♠ A K J 10 6 4 3 2
♡ 3
♢ 9 7
♣ 3 2

With a good eight-card spade suit, you could open the bidding 4♠. This will work out well if your partner has some strength, since you are likely to make your contract. It is also likely to work well if the opponents have the majority of the strength, since they will have a difficult time entering the auction.

CHAPTER 12

Slam Bidding

If the partnership has 33 or more combined points, it wants to reach the slam zone and pick up one of the large bonuses for bidding and making a slam contract. With 37 or more points, the partnership wants to find a grand slam contract, if possible. The partnership will often be considering the slam zone after a strong opening bid at the two level but there is also the possibility of a slam after an opening bid at the one level.

Considering slam after a strong opening two bid

An opening bid of 2♣ shows a hand of about 23 or more points and, if a responder makes a positive response, showing about 8 or more points, the combined partnership strength is at least 31 points. If either partner has anything extra, he will want to move the partnership into the slam zone.

The first priority, of course, is to find the denomination in which the partnership belongs. Once that has been decided, the partner with the extra strength can simply bid a slam contract. If he is uncertain about whether or not the partnership belongs in the slam zone, he can invite a slam by bidding a new suit or raising beyond the game zone. In the next chapter, we will discuss the Blackwood Convention which can be useful when exploring for a slam, but here we will keep things simple.

For example, suppose you are South and the auction starts off this way:

North	East	South	West
(Partner)		(You)	
2♣	Pass	2♡	Pass
3♡	Pass	?	

Let's look at what you would do with each of the following hands:

1	♠ 7 4	2	♠ 7 4	3	♠ 7 4
	♡ K J 6 4 2		♡ K Q 6 4 2		♡ K Q J 6 4 2
	◊ Q 9 8 2		◊ K 9 8 2		◊ 1 0 8 2
	♣ J 5		♣ Q 5		♣ J 5

With 7 HCPs and 1 point for the five-card heart suit, you have just enough for your positive response of 2♡. When your partner raises to 3♡, settling the denomination, you have nothing extra and can simply bid 4♡. If your partner is still interested in a slam, he can bid again.

On the second hand, you have 10 HCPs plus a point for the five-card suit. Since your partner should have 23 or more points, there is enough combined strength for a slam and you can jump to 6♡.

On the last hand, you have only 7 HCPs but 2 more points for the six-card suit. This is not quite enough to be in the slam zone if your partner has only 23 points, but you would like to be there if he has anything extra. You can invite slam by bidding 5♡, going one level beyond the game zone but leaving room to stop below the slam zone if your partner has nothing extra.

Considering a slam after an opening bid at the one level

Even after an opening bid at the one level, there are times when one partner may discover that there is enough combined strength to be in the slam zone. For example, suppose the bidding has progressed this way:

North	East	South	West
(Partner)		(You)	
1♣	Pass	1♠	Pass
2NT	Pass	?	

Your partner's jump rebid to 2NT describes a balanced hand with about 17 or 18 points. Suppose this is your hand:

♠ A Q 9 8
♡ K 10 3
◊ A Q 10
♣ J 8 7

Since you have 16 HCPs, the partnership's combined total is at least 33 points and you should be headed into the slam zone. Your partner has shown a balanced hand without four-card support for your spade suit, so the best denomination is no trumps. Make sure the partnership arrives in the slam zone by bidding 6NT.

Let's look at another example. You start the bidding 1♡ and your partner jumps to 4♡, showing a hand worth at least 13 points. This is your hand:

♠ A J 9
♡ A Q 10 8 6 2
◊ A J 4
♣ Q

With 18 HCPs (and, assuming you are counting length, 2 points for the six-card suit), the partnership should have the required 33 combined points needed for the slam zone. Rebid 6♡. With slightly less strength, you could invite your partner to bid a slam by bidding 5♡.

When you are considering the slam zone, you work with your partner to find out if the combined strength is 33 or more points. The idea is the same as considering whether or not there are enough points for the game zone. In both cases, it is basically a matter of addition.

Over Zia's shoulder

Audrey: *Tell us about a hand where you and your partner arrived at a slam contract.*

Zia: I opened 1♣ with a hand that didn't, at first, seem to me to have much slam potential.

♠ K J 9 8
♡ –
◊ K J 10 9
♣ A 10 8 7 6

When my partner responded 1♠, however, my ears pricked up. This was a lot better than hearing 1♡. I gave myself 5 support points for the void in hearts and my hand was now worth 17 points in total. This was enough to rebid 3♠, rather than 2♠. This encouraged my partner who now bid 5♠, inviting me to a slam. I had promised about 16–18 points, so I was not at the bottom of my range and, never one to be shy, I accepted the invitation and bid 6♠. Although the opponents had the ♡A and the ♡K they didn't take a trick and we made the slam.

Commonly asked questions

Q *When I opened the bidding 1NT, my partner raised to 4NT. What should I have done?*

A Partner's raise beyond the game zone, without bidding a slam, is an invitational, or *quantitative*, raise inviting you to bid a slam. Since you have promised 12–14 points with your opening bid of 1NT, you should decline the invitation, by passing, if you only have 12 points. With 14 points, you should accept and bid 6NT. With 13 points, your guess is as good as mine! It is similar to the situation when partner raises to 2NT, inviting you to bid a game.

CHAPTER 13

Conventional Bids

Learn from the mistakes of others. You won't live long enough to make them all yourself.

Alfred Sheinwold

It is most comfortable when the bidding consists of *natural bids*, that is, each bid describes a possible denomination for the contract. If your partner bids clubs, he has clubs and if he bids hearts, he has hearts and so on. As we have seen in the previous chapter, however, some artificial, or *conventional*, bids can be quite useful. For example, the opening bid of 2♣ says nothing about clubs, merely that the opener has a very powerful hand of 23 or more points. Similarly, the response of 2◇ to the 2♣ opening has nothing to do with diamonds. Instead, it conveys the message that the responder has a weak hand.

Our recommendation is that you use as few conventional bids as possible. Having said that, there are some conventional bids which are quite commonly used. You may not want to use them, but you should probably know about them in case your partner expects you to be familiar with them or your opponents use one of them during the auction. These two conventions are the Stayman Convention and the Blackwood Convention.

Introducing the Stayman Convention

The *Stayman Convention* is used only after an opening bid of 1NT or 2NT. The convention is named after Sam Stayman from New

York. Let's look at why Mr Stayman, and some of his associates, found it necessary to employ such a convention and why it became so popular. Look at these two hands:

Opener	*Responder*
♠ A J 9 4	♠ K Q 8 7
♡ K 9 8	♡ A 10 3
◊ 4 2	◊ J 10
♣ A Q 5 3	♣ K J 10 6

The opener, with a balanced hand and 14 points, starts with 1NT. The responder has enough points for a game and, without knowing that the opener has exactly four spades, might choose 3NT with his balanced hand. As you can see, the diamond suit is unprotected and the defence could take the first five tricks or more, defeating the contract. On the other hand, the defenders would only be able to take two diamond tricks if the contract were 4♠. How can the responder find out about the spade fit? There is no natural bid available. In response to a 1NT opening bid, 2♠ is a sign-off bid asking the 1NT opener to pass; 3♠ is a forcing bid showing a five-card spade suit and asking the opener to bid 3NT with two spades and 4♠ with three or more spades; 4♠ is a sign-off bid showing a six-card spade suit. What is the solution? Mr Stayman decided to take the response of 2♣ and use it as an artificial bid carrying the message, 'Do you have a four-card major suit?' This bid became known as the Stayman Convention.

Responding to the Stayman Convention

In response to the 2♣ bid, the 1NT opener bids a four-card major suit if he has one. If the opener does not have a four-card major, he bids 2◊, which is an artificial response, saying nothing about the diamond suit. This is similar to the 2◊ negative response to an opening bid of 2♣. Let's see what you would rebid with the following hands after you have opened the bidding 1NT and your partner has used the Stayman Convention by responding 2♣:

1 ♠ A 8 7 3	2 ♠ A 8 4 2	3 ♠ A 8 4
♡ J 10 4	♡ K J 10 4	♡ A 10 6
◊ A 9 8 6	◊ J 8 6	◊ K 8 7
♣ A J	♣ K 6	♣ Q 10 9 4

In the first example, you have a four-card spade suit, and so you would rebid 2♠ in response to the 2♣ bid. In the second example, you have four hearts and four spades. Bid the lower-ranking of your two four-card major suits first, 2♡. In the last example, with no four-card major, rebid 2◊. This has nothing to do with the diamond suit, it merely says you do not have a four-card major suit.

Responding to Stayman (2♣ response to 1NT)

2◊   No four-card major suit
2♡   A four-card heart suit
2♠   A four-card spade suit

Using the Stayman Convention

Let's look at how the responder makes use of the Stayman Convention with various types of hands.

With 13 or more points

Suppose your partner opens 1NT and this is your hand:

♠ J 9 8
♡ A 8 7 6
◊ A 4
♣ K J 5 3

You want to play in the game zone and your choice is between no trumps and hearts. To find out if your partner is interested in hearts, you use the Stayman Convention and bid 2♣. Suppose your partner responds 2♡. What now? Since you know your partner has at least 12 points and four hearts, you are prepared to make the decision to play a game in a major suit. Bid 4♡. Suppose, instead, your partner responds 2◊, showing no four-card major? Now you are satisfied to play in no trumps and can rebid 3NT. Similarly, if partner rebids 2♠, showing a four-card spade suit, you would be satisfied to play in 3NT since no heart fit has been found.

With 11–12 points

There are times when you have a hand in which you are sure of neither the zone nor the denomination after your partner opens 1NT. For example:

♠ 10 9 8
♡ A 6 5 2
◊ A 2
♣ K 8 3 2

With only 11 HCPs, you need to know if the opener has the top or bottom of his range to decide whether or not the partnership belongs in the game zone. You could invite to a game by raising to 2NT but you also want to investigate the possibility of playing in hearts rather than no trumps. To get the information you need, start out by bidding 2♣, the Stayman Convention. Suppose the opener answers 2♡. You still need to know whether there are enough combined points for the game zone. Invite the opener to bid a game with maximum values by moving towards game with a raise to 3♡. The opener can pass if he has the minimum of his range and accept, by bidding 4♡, if he is at the top of his range.

Suppose the opener bids 2◊, showing a hand with no four-card major suit, or bids 2♠ to show a four-card spade suit. Now, you can bid 2NT, again inviting the opener to a game if he has the top of his range.

Typically, a responder uses the Stayman Convention with hands which he thinks have a possibility of being played at the game level in a major suit. The Stayman Convention uncovers the information that responder needs: whether or not his partner has a four-card major suit. Having found the necessary information to determine the denomination, a responder can bid to the game zone with 13 or more points or make an invitational bid with 11–12 points.

If the opening bid is 2NT, the Stayman Convention can be used by responding 3♣. If the opener has a four-card major suit, he bids it at the three level. Otherwise, the opener rebids 3◊.

Using the Blackwood Convention

The *Blackwood Convention* was named after its inventor, Easley Blackwood of Indianapolis. The convention rapidly attained worldwide popularity. It is used when you feel there are enough combined points for a slam but want to make sure that the opponents do not have enough aces to defeat the contract right away. For example, consider the following hands:

Opener	*Responder*
♠ A 10 9 5 4 2	♠ K Q 8 7 3
♡ K Q	♡ 3
◊ K 2	◊ Q J 10 6
♣ A Q 5	♣ K J 6

The opener bids 1♠ and the responder, with 12 HCPs and 3 support points for the singleton, raises to 4♠. Opener has 18 HCPs and 2 points for the six-card spade suit, giving him a total of 20 points. It looks as though there is enough combined strength for a slam but, if the opener now bids 6♠, he will be disappointed when the opponents take the first two tricks with the ♡A and ◊A. What went wrong? The partnership has enough combined points for the slam zone, but they are the wrong points. If the opener held the ♡A – 4 HCPs – instead of the ♡K and ♡Q – 5 HCPs – he would be able to make the 6♠ contract. When you enter the slam zone, aces become very important.

When bidding a small slam, the partnership does not want to be missing two aces. When bidding a grand slam, the partnership cannot afford to be missing even one ace. The Blackwood Convention is used to find out how many aces the partnership has when it is considering bidding a slam contract.

This is how the Blackwood Convention works. Once a suit has been agreed upon, a bid of 4NT by either partner asks his partner to show how many aces he holds using the following responses:

Responding to Blackwood (4NT)

5♣	No aces (or all four aces)
5◇	1 ace
5♡	2 aces
5♠	3 aces

So, in the above hand, the opener could bid 4NT after the responder's 4♠ bid asking responder how many aces he has. The responder would bid 5♣, showing no aces, and the opener would know to stop in 5♠, since there are two aces missing. The complete auction might go like this:

North	East	South	West
(Opener)		(Responder)	
1♠	Pass	4♠	Pass
4NT	Pass	5♣	Pass
5♠	Pass	Pass	Pass

The responder would pass the opener's 5♠ bid since, by using the Blackwood Convention, the opener took over the captaincy and is in the best position to decide on the final contract. Had the responder bid 5◇, showing one ace, the opener would know there was only one ace missing and could safely bid 6♠.

If the responder had bid 5♡, showing two aces, the opener would know that there were no aces missing and might become interested in the possibility of a grand slam. If the opener is interested in a grand slam and has found out that the partnership has all the aces, he can use an extension of the Blackwood Convention by bidding 5NT to ask his partner how many kings he has. It is unlikely that you want to be in a grand slam if you are missing a king in one of your suits. His partner responds in the same fashion: bidding 6♣ with no kings, 6◇ with one king, and so on.

You need to be careful when using the Blackwood Convention. Remember, it only tells you how many aces partner has, not which aces. If you need to know exactly which ace(s) partner has, you will have to use other methods, which are beyond the scope of this book – or take your chances and just bid the slam. Also, the Blackwood Convention is only used after a trump suit has been agreed. For example, if your partner opens the bidding 1NT, you cannot use a response of 4NT to ask for aces. As mentioned in the previous chapter, a raise to 4NT would be an invitation to slam, which could be passed.

Over Zia's shoulder

Audrey: *Zia, do you ever use the Stayman Convention?*

Zia: It is not always necessary but, since I prefer to play in an eight-card major suit fit whenever possible, rather than no trumps, it does come in useful at times. Here is a typical hand:

♠ K J 8 2
♡ A Q 8 3
◊ 8
♣ K 7 4 2

My partner opened 1NT and I certainly did not like the idea of raising to 3NT with a singleton diamond. Instead, I bid 2♣, asking my partner for a major suit. He bid 2♡ and I happily raised to 4♡. Had he bid 2♠, I would have been just as happy to bid 4♠. Of course, if he had rebid 2◊, showing no four-card major suit, I would still have been a little nervous bidding my 3NT game but at least I would know that it was unlikely that there was a better game contract. If my partner didn't have four hearts or four spades, there is a good chance he had something in diamonds.

Audrey: *Do you get much use out of the Blackwood Convention?*

Zia: As you know, I rarely get dealt good enough hands to get to the slam zone. It's my opponents who always hold all the high cards! However, Blackwood can be very useful when the opportunity to use it does arrive.

I remember holding this hand:

♠ K 4
♡ A K J 9 7 5 2
◊ A K Q
♣ 4

With such a strong hand, I opened the bidding 2♣ and was pleased to hear my partner make a positive response of 2♠. I bid 3♡ and was even more pleased to hear my partner raise to 4♡. Now that I knew we had a place to play the contract, I turned my attention to the slam zone. I bid 4NT to ask my partner how many aces he had and he responded 5♡. Counting on my fingers, I worked out that this showed two aces, obviously the ♠A and ♣A. Now I was really ecstatic. Looking at my hand, I couldn't see any way that I could lose a trick, so I took the plunge to a grand slam contract. As soon as partner put down his two aces and heart support, I was able to show everyone my hand and claim all the tricks.

Summary

The Stayman Convention can be very useful when your partner opens the bidding 1NT and you have a four-card major suit and enough strength to invite or bid to the game zone. To find out if the opener has four cards in the same major suit, respond 2♣, the Stayman Convention. The opener responds as follows:

Responding to Stayman (2♣ response to 1NT)

2♢	No four-card major suit
2♡	A four-card heart suit
2♠	A four-card spade suit

The Blackwood Convention is used when you have determined the trump suit and are considering a slam contract. You can find out how many aces partner has by bidding 4NT. Your partner responds as follows:

Responding to Blackwood (4NT)

5♣	No aces (or all four aces)
5♢	1 ace
5♡	2 aces
5♠	3 aces

You can add the number of aces your partner shows to those that you have and determine whether or not you are missing too many aces to be in the slam zone.

Commonly asked questions

Q   *Why does the opener respond 2◊ to the Stayman Convention to show
a hand with no four-card major suit? Wouldn't it be simpler to rebid
2NT? The response of 2◊ is artificial, since it doesn't necessarily
show diamonds, and I thought we should be using as few artificial
bids as possible.*

A   There is only so much room available on the bidding steps for
each partner to describe his hand. If your partner uses the
Stayman Convention by bidding 2♣ after your 1NT opening
bid, you can give the information that you have a four-card
major suit by bidding 2♡ or 2♠ or that you don't have a major
suit by bidding 2◊. The information the responder asked for
can be given with one of these three bids.

When you bid 2◊, showing no major suit, the responder can
now make use of the 2NT bid to show a hand of invitational
strength, asking you to pass with a minimum or bid 3NT with
a maximum. If you, as opener, were to use 2NT as the
response to show no major suit, the responder would have no
way of inviting you to a game once he had searched for the
major suit fit and not found it. Most conventional bids are
designed in this manner, to make the maximum use of the
available space on the bidding steps.

Q   *Some players bid 4♣, not 4NT, to ask partner for aces. Is this also the
Blackwood Convention?*

A   The use of a 4♣ bid to ask for aces is similar to the Blackwood
Convention but it has a different name. It is called the *Gerber
Convention*. It is normally used over an opening bid of 1NT or
2NT, where a response of 4NT is a quantitative raise – inviting
you to bid slam with the top of your range – rather than the
Blackwood Convention which is only used when a suit has
been agreed upon.

The responses follow a similar pattern to those used for the
Blackwood Convention. The next cheapest bid, 4◊, shows no
aces (or all four); 4♡ shows 1 ace; 4♠ shows 2 aces; and 4NT
shows three aces. If the partnership holds all the aces, 5♣ can
now be used to ask for the number of kings held.

As with any conventional bid, you need to discuss it carefully with your partner before using it to make sure that you both have the same understanding of how it works and when it applies. Until you become very familiar with the game, our recommendation is that you keep your bidding simple, using as few conventional bids as possible.

CHAPTER 14

Overcalls and Responses

Bids should be made in the same tone and tempo. An opening bid of 1♡ with 13 points should be said with the same enthusiasm as an opening bid of 1♡ with 20 points.

In the preceding chapters we have assumed that the opponents have not interfered in our auction. Sadly, they are not always so kind. Since every bid, whether by your side or by the opponents', takes the auction higher up the bidding steps, a competitive auction will have an impact on the amount of information you can exchange with your partner. In the next few chapters, we will be looking at what happens when both sides are trying to bid on the same deal.

Making an overcall

Suppose you pick up the following hand:

♠ A K J 10 8
♡ 10 8
◊ K 8 7 6
♣ J 2

With 12 HCPs and a good spade suit, you are planning to open the bidding 1♠. However, if the opponent on your right is the dealer, he might start the auction off by bidding 1♡. What now? The opponent's opening bid does not prevent you from bidding 1♠ but you are no longer opening the bidding. If you bid 1♠, you are said to be making an *overcall*, competing to name the trump suit. Is there any difference between overcalling and opening the bidding? Let's consider what you would do with the following hands after the opponent on your right opens the bidding 1◊:

1	♠ Q 4	2	♠ Q 4	3	♠ Q 4
	♡ A Q J 7 5		♡ K 8		♡ K 8
	◊ 9 8 3 2		◊ 9 8 4 2		◊ A J 7 4 2
	♣ K 8		♣ A Q J 7 5		♣ Q 9 7 5

On the first hand, the opponent's opening 1◊ bid has not taken away much room on the bidding steps and you can make an overcall of 1♡, bidding as though the opponent had said pass.

On the second hand, however, you planned to open the bidding 1♣. After the 1◊ bid, you will have to overcall 2♣ to show your suit. This shows one of the differences between opening bids and overcalls; you may have to start the auction for your side at the two level when making an overcall if there is no room left at the one level.

On the last hand, your opponent has bid the suit you were planning to bid. It does not make much sense to overcall 2◊, competing in the same suit as your opponent! After all, if the opponents want to make diamonds the trump suit, you are happy enough. What about overcalling your other suit, 2♣? This also does not appear to be a sound decision. You would need to start the bidding for your side at the two level, contracting to take eight tricks, with only a four-card suit – and not a very strong suit at that! The best decision is to pass and await developments. There is nothing in the rules that says you must bid whenever you have 12 or more points. In this case, silence may well be golden. If the opponents end up playing in a diamond contract, you should have a good chance of defeating them.

In general, when the opponents open the bidding, you have the option of making an overcall to enter the auction for your side. To do so, you should have a good five-card or longer suit. We shall see later on how you can compete when you do not have a good five-card suit with which to make an overcall.

In our earlier discussions on opening the bidding, one of the requirements for an opening bid at the one level was a slightly better than average hand of 12 or more points. Is the same strength required when making an overcall? Before answering this question, let's consider some of the reasons why you would want to enter the auction after the opponents have opened the bidding:

• There is a reasonable chance that you might be able to buy the contract, making the suit you prefer the trump suit, rather than leaving the choice to the opponents. Although the opening bid warns you that the opponents have some of the high cards, there is no reason why your side cannot make a contract in the partscore zone, or even the game zone, if you have a share of the strength.

• By competing for the contract, you may push the opponents higher on the bidding steps than they would like to go. The higher they get, the better your chance of defeating their contract.

• By bidding, you are giving your partner some information about your hand. Even if the opponents win the auction, the information you exchange may help your partnership defeat their contract.

• Your bidding may take up valuable room on the bidding steps, interfering with the opponents' auction. They might not be able to exchange all the information they would like and end up in the wrong contract as a result.

Because of all the advantages, the strength requirements for an overcall are somewhat lower than for opening the bidding. An overcall in a suit at the one level can usually be made with 8–15 HCPs. An overcall at the two level can be made with about 10–15 HCPs. The less strength you have, the more powerful your five-card suit should be. Let's look at some examples. The bidding has been opened 1♡ by the opponent on your right.

1	♠ A K 10 9 2	2	♠ Q 7 4	3	♠ 2
	♡ 8 7 6		♡ 8 7 6		♡ Q 3
	♢ Q 7 4		♢ A K 10 9 2		♢ A Q J 9 8
	♣ 8 3		♣ 8 3		♣ A Q 9 7 3

In the first example, although your hand is only worth 9 HCPs, you do have a powerful five-card suit and you have room to bid it at the one level. Overcall 1♠. Even if you do not succeed in buying the contract, you might interfere with the opponents' auction or help your partner find the best opening lead against their contract.

On the second hand, you again have a good suit but this time you would have to go to the two level to bid it. With only 9 HCPs, this would be a very risky venture, since the opponents might be able to defeat your contract by several tricks. You should pass. Don't forget, the auction is not over yet. If your partner has some strength, he may well be able to enter the auction when it is his turn to bid.

On the last hand, you have more than enough strength to compete. With a choice of suits, use the old guideline of bidding the higher-ranking of two five-card suits and overcall 2◊.

Requirements for an overcall in a suit

- A good five-card or longer suit
- 8–15 HCPs for an overcall at the one level
- 10–15 HCPs for an overcall at the two level

Responding to overcalls

To keep things uncomplicated after your partner has overcalled, you can respond in almost the same fashion as if he has made an opening bid, remembering, however, that your partner has shown a five-card suit. This means that you need only three-card support to raise your partner's suit. Let's see how this works. Suppose you are in the West seat and the opponent on your left bids 1◊, your partner overcalls 1♡ and the opponent on your right says 'Pass.' It is your bid after the following auction:

North	East	South	West
	(Partner)		(You)
1◊	1♡	Pass	?

Let's see how you respond to your partner's overcall with each of the following hands:

1	♠ 1087	2	♠ A107	3	♠ A7
	♡ A43		♡ AJ32		♡ A43
	◊ A96		◊ A9		◊ K987
	♣ J1043		♣ J1043		♣ 10963

On the first hand, you have support for your partner's heart suit since he is showing a five-card or longer suit with his overcall. With 9 points, you have enough to raise to the two level. Respond 2♡.

On the second hand you have 14 HCPs plus 1 support point for the doubleton diamond. This should be sufficient to take your partner all the way to the game zone with a response of 4♡. Although your partner could have as few as 8 HCPs, he has promised a good suit and should have a reasonable chance to make a game even if the combined strength is a little less than 25 points. Without complicating the responses, this is about as accurate as you can get in a competitive auction.

The last hand has 11 HCPs and 1 support point for the doubleton spade, a total of 12 points. Make an invitational raise to 3♡, just as you would over an opening bid of 1♡. Remember, you only need three-card support to raise your partner's overcall.

After your partner has overcalled, you may not have support for his suit and yet have enough points to want to bid a suit of your own or to bid no trumps. For example, suppose you are West and the auction has again started in this fashion:

North	East	South	West
	(Partner)		(You)
1◊	1♡	Pass	?

Let's see what you respond with each of these hands:

1	♠ KQ10943	2	♠ Q43	3	♠ K42
	♡ 102		♡ 102		♡ 10
	◊ A42		◊ KQ9		◊ Q532
	♣ J3		♣ J10973		♣ AKJ94

In the first example, you do not have support for your partner's suit but you do have a suit which you can bid at the one level. Respond 1♠.

On the second hand, you have only 8 HCPs and 1 point for the fifth club, not enough to bid a new suit at the two level. Without support for your partner's suit, if you decide to bid, the best choice would be to respond 1NT to describe your hand. But on balance, it is probably best to pass. Your side will have a maximum of 23 points, so there is no game for you, and may have as few as 16, in which case you would far rather be in 1♡ – where at least your partner will be able to take some trump tricks – than 1NT.

With the last hand, you have enough strength to bid a new suit at the two level and can respond 2♣.

Since the overcaller could have less than the values for an opening bid, many partnerships do not play the response of a new suit as forcing. There is some further discussion of this at the end of the chapter, but, to keep things simple, the most straightforward approach is to treat the responses to overcalls in the same manner as responses to opening bids.

Making other types of overcalls

An overcall in a suit at the cheapest available level is called a *simple overcall*. There are other types of overcalls you might want to consider making when you wish to compete.

The one no-trump overcall

Although the Acol system uses a weak no-trump range of 12–14 points for an opening 1NT bid, a stronger range of 16–18 points is used when making an overcall of 1NT. The reason for the stronger range is that it is more dangerous to enter the auction when the opponents have opened the bidding. They have promised some strength and already exchanged some information, so they will have an easy time defeating your contract if your side has too little combined strength. Let's take a look at some examples after the opponent on your right has started the bidding with 1♡:

1	♠ Q87	2	♠ A87	3	♠ AJ
	♡ AQ10		♡ 1053		♡ KQ10
	◇ KQ109		◇ KJ9		◇ K108
	♣ A84		♣ KQ84		♣ Q10972

With 17 HCPs and a balanced hand, the first example is an ideal hand to overcall 1NT. With nearly half the high card points in the pack, you should stand a good chance of making your contract even if your partner does not have a very good hand.

Although you would have opened the second hand 1NT with your 13 HCPs, it is dangerous to overcall 1NT when the opponents have opened the bidding. They are likely to hold the balance of power and the opponent on your left already knows that his partner's longest suit is hearts. They should have no trouble defeating your contract. With no good five-card suit to overcall, pass and wait to see how the auction develops. You do not have to bid just because you hold 13 points.

On the last hand, you have only 15 HCPs (but can add 1 point for the five-card club suit if counting length). This makes the hand strong enough to overcall 1NT and is probably a better choice than overcalling 2♣ with such a weak suit.

Requirements for an overcall of 1NT

- A balanced hand
- 16–18 points

If your partner overcalls 1NT, you can respond using the same principles as when your partner opens the bidding 1NT. The only difference is that your partner is showing 16–18 points rather than 12–14. You are the captain, so add your points to those promised by your partner to determine whether you belong in the partscore or game zone. Look at your distribution to decide whether or not you have an eight-card or longer fit and decide on the denomination accordingly.

Jump overcalls

When you have about 16–19 points and a six-card (or very strong five-card) suit, you are too strong to make a simple overcall since that has an upper range of about 15 points. Instead, you can jump one level to show your powerful hand. This is not a forcing bid, but it is a very strong invitation for your partner to carry on to the game zone if he has a few points. For example, suppose your opponent opens the bidding 1♣ and you have the following hand:

♠ A K Q 4 3 2
♡ 9 8
◊ A Q 2
♣ J 10

With 16 HCPs and a good six-card suit, jump to 2♠, rather than overcalling 1♠. This type of bid is called an *intermediate jump overcall*. Your partner needs only 6 or 7 points to raise you to the three level and, with 8 or more points, will normally take you to the game zone.

Requirements for an intermediate jump overcall

- A six-card or longer suit
- 16–19 points

Higher jump overcalls

Surprisingly, an overcall which skips two levels on the bidding steps is used to show a weak hand with a long suit, rather than a very strong hand. This is called a *pre-emptive jump overcall*. Over an opening bid of 1◊, you might make a pre-emptive jump overcall of 3♡ – skipping two levels – with this type of hand:

♠ 8
♡ K Q J 9 8 6 4
◊ J 8 3
♣ 10 5

This type of bid is a defensive measure, designed to take a lot of bidding room away from the opponents, making it difficult for them to find their best contract. The theory behind pre-emptive bidding will be discussed in more detail in Chapter 14. For now, it is only important to know that a double jump, or higher jump, shows a weak hand, not a strong hand.

Requirements for a pre-emptive jump overcall

- A seven-card or longer suit
- 6–10 HCPs

Over Zia's shoulder

Audrey: *Zia, I have noticed that there is a variety of opinion among the experts concerning the range of strength used for overcalls and how to handle responses to overcalls.*

Zia: That's quite true. It is really a matter of partnership style. Many players like to compete in the auction at every chance they get and are not afraid to overcall with very few points and a poor suit. Others prefer having a good suit and the approximate values for an opening bid. I like to be somewhere in the middle. I always like to have a good suit but, if the conditions are right, I might have less than the strength for an opening bid. For example, I held the following hand:

♠ 8 3
♡ K Q J 7 5
◇ K 6 2
♣ 9 5 2

The opponent on my right opened the bidding 1◇ and I had to decide whether or not to make an overcall. Even though I only held 9 HCPs, I really wanted to tell my partner about my heart suit. Since I could bid it at the one level, I decided to overcall 1♡. The opponents ended up playing in a 3NT contract and my partner, who had listened to my overcall, led a heart against their contract. This helped defeat the contract. They would have made the contract if my partner had chosen any other lead.

Audrey: *The important thing is that your partner understands what your bids mean.*

Zia: Yes, you need to agree on your approach. For example, it is important to decide whether or not a response in a new suit is forcing. The other day, I was playing with an unfamiliar partner and picked up the following hand:

♠ A K J 8 5 2
♡ 7 2
◇ 8 5
♣ A J 3

The opponent on my left bid 1◊ and my partner overcalled 1♡. After the opponent on my right passed, I was nervous about responding 1♠ with this hand in case my partner passed when we belonged in the game zone. Fortunately, he had a good hand and bid again so we reached our game contract. I'm still not sure whether he would have left me in 1♠ if he had a minimum hand for his overcall! When I'm playing with a new partner, I like to keep things simple and treat a new suit bid by the responder as forcing just as over an opening bid. If the overcaller has a weak hand, he will have to make a minimum rebid and then I'll tread cautiously in case he has stretched to get into the auction.

Summary

When the opponents have opened the bidding, you can compete for the contract by making an overcall. Use the following guidelines:

Requirements for an overcall in a suit

- A good five-card or longer suit
- 8–15 HCPs for an overcall at the one level
- 10–15 HCPs for an overcall at the two level

Requirements for an overcall of 1NT

- A balanced hand
- 16–18 points

Requirements for an intermediate jump overcall

- A six-card or longer suit
- 16–19 points

Requirements for a pre-emptive jump overcall

- A seven-card or longer suit
- 6–10 HCPs

Commonly asked questions

Q　*When responding to an overcall, I've heard some players talk about using a cue bid response. What is a cue bid? You don't seem to have mentioned this.*

A　First of all, let's clarify what a cue bid means in the context of responding to overcalls. A *cue bid* is a bid of the same suit as your opponent. For example, suppose the auction starts this way:

North	*East*	*South*	*West*
1◊	1♡	Pass	2◊

West's 2◊ response to his partner's 1♡ overcall is a cue bid of the opponent's suit. What does it mean? It is unlikely that West wants to play with diamonds as the trump suit since the opponents were considering playing in that suit. Instead, it is more useful to assign some special artificial meaning to the bid of the opponent's suit. The common agreement is that it is merely a forcing bid, asking a partner for more information about his hand.

A cue bid response to an overcall is useful, for example, if the partnership does not play a new suit by the responder as forcing after an overcall. Now the cue bid can be used if the responder wants to force the overcaller to bid again. The reason this treatment has not been mentioned is that you do not need to concern yourself with such complexities if you take the straightforward approach of treating responses to overcalls in the same manner as responses to opening bids. You can use the responder's bid of a new suit as forcing and you do not need to use the cue bid. As your experience with competitive bidding grows, you and your partner may want to incorporate the cue bid into your bidding repertoire.

CHAPTER 15

Doubles

Bridge is not owned by any class or any nationality.

Have you ever been tempted to bid higher than the opponents on the bidding steps, not with the intention of making your bid, but to prevent the opponents from playing their contract which you feel they can easily make? Suppose your opponents have reached a contract of 4♡, and you bid 4♠. You don't make your contract; in fact you fall three tricks short. Is this better than letting the opponents play in their 4♡ contract?

Making a penalty double

Since you have not made your contract, the opponents get a bonus which is referred to as a *penalty*. The bonus they collect depends, in part, on the number of tricks by which you are defeated. The more tricks you are defeated by, the bigger the penalty. The actual size of the penalty is explained in more detail in the Appendix on scoring on p. 455, but, unless you are defeated by a large number of tricks, it is less than the bonus the opponents would get for making their game contract. This hardly seems fair! You have robbed them of their chance for a game bonus and suffered only a small penalty in return. To even things out, the opponents can make a *penalty double* of your contract if they think you are not going to make it. This substantially increases the size of the penalty if your contract is defeated. Of course, it also increases the reward if you make the contract.

The term *double* is a new word to add to your bidding vocabulary. Here are some guidelines on using the double:

- Like any other bid, you can only say double when it is your turn to bid
- You can only double an opponent's contract, not your partner's contract
- The double has to be followed by three passes before the auction is over. For example, if you double and one of the opponents, or your partner, makes a bid, the double is no longer in effect

Suppose you are sitting East. Here is how the double might look in an auction:

North	East	South	West
	(You)		(Partner)
1♡	1♠	3♡	3♠
4♡	4♠	Double	Pass
Pass	Pass		

Your final contract of 4♠ has been doubled. If you are defeated by a sufficient number of tricks, the penalty bonus the opponents receive will be larger, perhaps much larger, than the value of their game bonus. This is what stops one side or the other bidding too wildly in the auction, trying to prevent the opponents from getting the contract.

If you make your 4♠ doubled contract, you will receive more than the normal score for making your contract, especially if you take more than the number of tricks for which you contracted. In general, you should only double the opponents' contract for penalties if you are quite certain that you can defeat it and that they cannot escape to a better contract. It is particularly risky to double a partscore contract because, if the opponents make their contract, they are likely to receive a score worth as much as, or more than, making a game zone contract (see scoring tables at back of book). For this reason, a double of a partscore contract is often used for reasons other than penalising the opponents, as we shall see in the next chapter.

Let's look at one example of making a penalty double. Suppose you are North and open the bidding 1♡ with the following hand:

♠ 10 7
♡ A J 9 8 5
◊ K J 10
♣ A Q 2

and the auction proceeds as follows:

North	East	South	West
(You)		(Partner)	
1♡	2◊	3♡	4◊
4♡	5◊	Pass	Pass
?			

You bid 4♡, expecting to make your contract and receive a game bonus. When East bids 5◊, you have two choices. You can bid on to 5♡, hoping that you can take eleven tricks and still receive the game bonus, or you can try and defeat the opponents' contract by taking three or more tricks. It will be a lot easier to take three tricks rather than eleven with this hand, especially since some of your high cards are in the opponents' suit. Since you expect to defeat the contract by at least one trick – likely several tricks – you should double to try to get a large enough penalty to compensate for the game bonus you would have received.

Redoubling

If you have been doubled in a contract and feel that you have every chance of making it, you can say *redouble*. This is the last word you need to learn to complete your bidding vocabulary – there are no re-redoubles! The redouble increases the bonuses for making or defeating the contract still further. As with the double, you can only redouble when it is your turn to bid. You can only redouble after an opponent has doubled the contract and the final contract is only redoubled if it is followed by three passes.

In the previous auction, a redouble would look like this:

North	East	South	West
(You)		(Partner)	
1♡	2◇	3♡	4◇
4♡	5◇	Pass	Pass
Double	Redouble	Pass	Pass
Pass			

The final contract is 5◇ redoubled and one side is going to be very happy when the hand is over, while the other side is likely to regret its decision.

Over Zia's shoulder

Audrey: *I have heard that you love to play or defend a hand when the stakes are very high. Does this mean we could often expect to be doubled by you?*

Zia: Doubling is a way of increasing the excitement of any hand. There are precautions, however, which even I take. Remember that, after you double, each of the opponents has another chance to bid. You might feel like doubling when the opponents have obviously arrived at the wrong contract. However, once you say the word double, you give them a chance to find a better contract. You have to consider, therefore, not only the contract you are doubling but what contract the opponents could find if you scare them away. Here is a hand I held when playing for rather high stakes in a bridge club:

♠ 4 3 2
♡ 8 3
◇ 10 9 2
♣ A K Q J 10

This is how the auction went:

North	East	South	West
			(Zia)
1♡	Pass	2◇	Pass
3♡	Pass	3NT	?

I was on lead against the contract of 3NT and knew I could take the first five tricks, defeating the contract. However, I passed quietly and 3NT ended up being the final contract, which I defeated by one trick. It may seem as though I passed up a good chance to make a penalty double but, if I had doubled, the opponents might have retreated to a better contract. On the actual hand, they could make 4♡. This was a time when silence was golden.

Audrey: *So, knowing when not to double is as important as knowing when to double?*

Zia: You have to be very careful and to look ahead. However, when the opponents have nowhere to run, I like to bring down the axe. Here is another hand from that same game:

♠ 7 4
♡ Q J 10 9
◊ A K 3
♣ A 8 6 4

I was West and the bidding went this way:

North	East	South	West (Zia)
1♡	Pass	2♡	Pass
4♡	Pass	Pass	?

This time, I was quick to double. The opponents had not bid badly. If the trumps had been evenly divided, the declarer could have made the contract. As it was, I was able to defeat the contract by two tricks and collect a nice profit on the hand.

Summary

The double is a bid which can be used to increase the penalty bonus for defeating the opponents' contract. If your contract has been doubled for penalties and you think you are going to make it, you can redouble to increase the bonuses further.

Commonly asked questions

Q *If you have two aces, should you always double the opponents' if they reach a slam contract? It is unlikely that they can take twelve of the thirteen tricks.*

A Not necessarily. If the opponents have arrived at the slam zone in a trump suit they may well have a void in one of the suits and one of your aces won't take a trick.

Takeout Doubles and Responses

Suppose you sort your hand, and this is what you see:

♠ A 9 8 4
♡ 3
♢ K Q 4 3
♣ A J 9 8

You are planning to open the bidding 1◊, the middle-ranking of your three four-card suits, but unfortunately you are not the dealer. Instead, the opponent on your right opens the bidding 1♡. You would like to compete, but you do not have a five-card suit to overcall. Is there anything you can do?

Making a takeout double

You don't have one suit to overcall but what you would like to do is to bid all three of your suits at once and have your partner choose whichever one he liked best as the trump suit. There is a way to do this and that is to use our new word from the last chapter – double – to send this message to your partner. When you are in the partscore zone, this is generally a more worthwhile use of the double than trying to obtain a large penalty from the opponents' contract. It does not take up any room on the bidding steps and, used in this context as a *takeout double*, it says: 'Bid your best suit, partner. When you have a choice, bid an unbid major suit.

In order to send your partner the message to bid his best suit, you need a certain kind of hand. In the hand mentioned earlier, since the opener bid hearts, you had support for the *unbid suits*:

clubs, diamonds and spades. You also had 14 HCPs, the values for an opening bid. This is a classical takeout double. Suppose we change the hand:

♠ A876
♡ 9
♢ Q543
♣ AJ82

You again have support for the unbid suits but you have only 11 HCPs. Do you still feel like competing with this hand? Most players would like to compete but would like to have enough strength that they would be pleased to put the hand down as the dummy when partner bids his best suit. They don't want their partner to say 'You only have 11 points, how could you double?' There is a way to value your hand so that you come up with an opening bid, and that is to count support points. When you make a takeout double, you expect to provide the support since you are asking your partner to pick the suit. When you are planning to make a takeout double, value your hand by adding together your HCPs and support points. On the above hand, you can add 3 points for the singleton heart, arriving at 14 total points, enough to make a takeout double. In summary:

Requirements for a takeout double

- Support for the unbid suits
- The values for an opening bid, counting support points

Let's clarify the meaning of support for the unbid suits by changing the hand again:

♠ A987
♡ 75
♢ KQ92
♣ AJ3

With 14 HCPs and 1 support point for the doubleton heart, you still want to compete after your opponent opens the bidding 1♡. Again, you cannot overcall because you do not have a five-card suit. What is it that worries you about making a takeout double?

You are promising your partner support for the unbid suits and, ideally, you would like to have at least four cards in each suit, in case your partner has only four cards in the suit he picks. On this hand you have only three clubs. However, look on the positive side. You have enough strength to open the bidding and you have four spades, the suit your partner will probably pick if he has a choice. Take an optimistic attitude and double. The worst that can happen is that you end up playing with clubs as the trump suit – and your partner may have five or more clubs.

If we change the hand again, you have a choice between an overcall and a double:

♠ A975
♡ –
♦ KJ84
♣ AJ642

After the opponent's 1♡ bid, you could overcall 2♣ since you have a five-card suit. You could also double since you have an opening bid and support for the unbid suits. Which should you choose? The partnership objective is still to look for major suit fits whenever possible. If you overcall in clubs, it is unlikely that you will later be able to find a fit in spades, if there is one. The takeout double is more flexible and gives the partnership the greater chance of finding the best denomination.

Some hands don't qualify for a takeout double. Consider this hand:

♠ K984
♡ A1043
♦ 9
♣ AQ72

If the opponents' opening bid is 1♦, you have a perfect hand for a takeout double: the strength for an opening bid and support for the unbid suits. But suppose the opening bid is 1♡. You can no longer afford to double since you do not have support for the unbid suits. If you double, your partner might pick diamonds and then you would feel uncomfortable about putting down the dummy. With a hand like this, you have to pass for now, since you cannot overcall or make a takeout double. Let's look at some more examples after your opponent opens the bidding 1♠:

1 ♠ 8
  ♡ A 8 7 6
  ◊ K Q 9 8
  ♣ Q 10 9 8

2 ♠ K Q 8 4
  ♡ 3
  ◊ K Q 9 8
  ♣ Q 10 9 8

3 ♠ 3
  ♡ A 8 4 3
  ◊ A Q 7 5 4
  ♣ K 7 4

In the first example, although you have only 11 HCPs, you have a singleton spade which is worth 3 support points. The total value of the hand is 14 points, enough to make a takeout double since you also have support for the unbid suits.

With the second hand, you have the point count for a takeout double, but you don't have support for all the unbid suits. Instead, you have to pass.

On the last hand, you have a choice between an overcall of 2◊ or a takeout double. Since your priority is to try to locate the major suits, a double is a better choice than overcalling your minor suit. Your partner may have a four-card heart suit and you would have found a major suit fit. If he bids clubs, at least you have three-card support.

Responding to a takeout double

You are West. The opponent on your left opens the bidding 1♡, your partner doubles and the opponent on your right passes. It is your bid after the auction has gone:

North	East	South	West
	(Partner)		(You)
1♡	Double	Pass	?

It is important to realise that the takeout double is a forcing bid. Your partner is not giving you the choice of either passing or bidding. His takeout double is a request or, more appropriately, a demand, that you bid. At times, this will not be a difficult decision:

♠ J 10 8 7
♡ 4 3 2
◊ K 4
♣ K 8 6 4

You have two suits which you could choose, either clubs or spades. After a takeout double, prefer the major suit when you have a choice. Your response to your partner's takeout double would be 1♠. Now, let's keep the same number of cards in each suit but take away the points:

♠ 9873
♡ 642
◊ 98
♣ 5432

This is the kind of hand which might tempt you to say pass. After all, you have not a single point. Can any reasonable partner expect you to bid? The answer is, yes. The takeout double is forcing and you are being asked to reply – if the opponent on your right does not bid – regardless of the strength of your hand. Bid 1♠. You are not promising any strength, but merely following instructions. Your partner said, 'pick a suit' and that is exactly what you have done.

Let's put some points back in the hand. As a matter of fact, let's give you 13 HCPs:

♠ K8542
♡ KQ8
◊ 32
♣ AJ10

Since your partner has shown an opening bid and support for the unbid suits, you can be reasonably sure the partnership belongs in the game zone and the best denomination is likely to be spades. Bid 4♠.

If your hand is not quite this strong, you want to make an invitational bid, moving towards a game by jumping a level when responding to the takeout double. When you have decided on the suit you are going to bid, use the following guidelines to decide how high you should go on the bidding steps when responding to a takeout double:

0–9 points	Bid your suit as cheaply as possible
10–12 points	Bid your suit jumping one level
13 or more points	Bid to the game zone

Some partnerships prefer a more aggressive approach, lowering the range so you are bidding at the cheapest level with 0–8 and jumping a level with 9–12.

Although we have discussed the importance of trying for a game in no trumps in preference to a minor suit, the takeout double tells you that your partner probably does not have much strength or length in the suit bid by the opponents. Because of this, beware of bidding no-trump games. You should only bid no trumps if you have considerable strength in the opponents' suit. Otherwise, you should go ahead and bid your minor suit.

Rebidding by the takeout doubler

Since the player making a takeout double has essentially opened the bidding for his side, he can think of his rebid in the same terms as when rebidding after an opening bid of one of a suit. He can classify his hand as small (12–15 points), medium (16–18 points) or large (19 or more points). With the bottom range of 12–15 points, you should pass when a responder shows a weak hand by bidding at the cheapest available level. With a medium strength hand of 16–18 points, you can move toward the game zone by raising the responder's suit. A responder could have up to 9 points when he bids at the cheapest available level. Of course, if a responder shows an invitational hand of 10–12 points by jumping a level, you will accept the invitation when you have a medium strength hand or stronger. With a strong hand of 19 or more points, you can make a jump raise when the responder bids at the cheapest available level. There is no need to jump right to the game zone since the responder could have as few as zero points. Remember, *you forced your partner to respond*.

Suppose the opponent on your right bids 1◊ and you make a takeout double. Your partner responds 1♡, a bid at the cheapest available level. You have forced your partner to bid so this shows a hand with anything from 0–9 points. Let's look at what you would do with each of the following hands:

1 ♠ K964	2 ♠ K964	3 ♠ A964
♡ A J 5 2	♡ A J 5 2	♡ A Q 5 2
◊ 7	◊ 7	◊ 7
♣ K 10 7 5	♣ A Q 7 5	♣ A Q 7 5

With only 11 HCPs and 3 support points for the singleton diamond, the first hand is at the bottom of the range for a takeout double. You've done enough by getting into the auction. Pass your partner's minimum response.

On the second hand, you have 14 HCPs to go along with the 3 support points, putting you in the medium category. There is still a chance you belong in the game zone if your partner has 8 or 9 points. Raise gently to 2♡. You do not want to get too high in case your partner has nothing.

On the final hand, your 16 HCPs and 3 support points give you a total of 19 points, putting you at the top of the range. Jump to 3♡, strongly inviting your partner to carry on to the game zone if he has any strength at all. You want to leave him a little leeway in case he has a very weak hand. The more you have, the less your partner is likely to have.

In summary:

Rebidding after a minimum response from your partner

12–15 points	Pass
16–19 points	Raise one level
19 or more points	Jump one level

Showing a strong overcall

Suppose you hold the following hand and the opponent on your right opens the bidding 1◊:

♠ A K J 9 6
♡ A Q 4
◊ 8 4 2
♣ A 5

With 18 HCPs and a five-card spade suit, you are too strong to make a simple overcall of 1♠. Neither can you jump to 2♠ since this shows a 6-card suit. Most partnerships assume that the upper range for a simple overcall is about 15 HCPs. Your hand is not suitable for a classic takeout double since you do not have support for clubs and you have only fair support for hearts. Nonetheless, the takeout double is usually used with this type of hand – a hand too strong for a simple overcall.

The idea is that you can start with a takeout double and your partner will dutifully bid his best suit. Now, you can reveal the true nature of your hand by bidding your own suit. For example, if your partner responds 2♣, you will bid 2♠, showing a hand too strong to make a simple overcall of 1♠. This fits in well with the general guidelines for rebidding after making a takeout double since, as we discussed above, you would pass after your partner made a minimum response unless you have 16 or more points.

Telling the doubles apart

As we have now seen, there are two different meanings that can be given to the word 'double' in the auction. In the previous chapter, it was used as a penalty double, to increase the size of the score for defeating the opponents' contract. In this chapter, it is used as a takeout double, asking your partner to bid his best suit. Since you can only use the one word, double, in both situations, how are you going to know if a double is for penalty or takeout? Here are some simple guidelines:

Penalty versus takeout doubles

A double is for penalty if:
• Your partner has already made a bid or
• The opponents are in the game zone

A double is for takeout if:
• Your partner has not already made a bid and
• The opponents are in the partscore zone

Here a 'bid' does not include a pass – even if your partner has already passed and both opponents have bid, you may still want to make a takeout double if they are below the game zone. See the fourth example at the top of p.159. Now consider the following auctions:

North	East	South	West
(You)		(Partner)	
1♡	2♣	Double	Pass
?			

Since you have already bid, your partner's double is for penalty. That makes sense, doesn't it? A takeout double is a request to bid your suit. Since you opened the bidding 1♡, your partner already knows that is the suit you like best.

North	East	South	West
(You)		(Partner)	
Pass	1♣	Double	Pass
?			

In this example, you have not bid – a pass doesn't count – and the opponents are still in the partscore zone. Your partner's double is for takeout, asking you to bid your best suit. Again, this seems reasonable. It is unlikely that your partner would have enough strength to defeat East's 1♣ contract and, if he did, his best action would be to pass, rather than frighten the opponents into a better contract.

North	East	South	West
(You)		(Partner)	
Pass	1♠	Pass	4♠
Pass	Pass	Double	Pass
?			

In this example, you have not bid but the contract is in the game zone. You can assume that your partner is doubling for penalties and is not interested in hearing about your best suit starting at the five level! If your partner wanted to make a takeout double, he could have done so at his first opportunity, when East bid 1♠. Finally, consider this auction:

North	East	South	West
(You)		(Partner)	
			1♡
Pass	2♡	Double	Pass
?			

Despite your original pass, your partner is still doubling for take-out and wants you to bid your best suit. He probably has a hand like:

♠ A Q 10 3
♡ 4
◊ A K 6 2
♣ Q 10 9 8

with good support for you, even if you have to bid at the three level.

Over Zia's shoulder

Audrey: *I have heard that competitive bidding is a favourite part of your game, so you probably have some hands to share.*

Zia: Competitive bidding provides a lot of opportunity for imagination. Here is a hand you might find interesting:

♠ K Q 10 7
♡ Q J 3 2
◊ –
♣ Q 10 8 5 3

If I were the dealer, I would pass. I didn't get that opportunity, however, since the opponent on my right started the bidding with 1◊. He actually did me a favour. Now, I had an opportunity to tell my partner about the shape of my hand. Since I could double and show three suits at once, the value of my hand increased. I counted 5 support points for the diamond void and came to enough strength to make a takeout double. My partner bid 1♡, showing 0–9 points and I passed. We were allowed to play the contract in the partscore and my partner made it. This was a lot better than defending the

opponents' partscore in diamonds which we could not
have defeated.

In this hand, my opponent actually helped both my partner and myself through opening the bidding. I was able
to give a clear picture of my hand with the takeout double and my partner knew where most of the missing
high cards were when he played the hand.

Audrey: *Do you have another hand for us?*

Zia: When it comes to competitive bidding, I have many
hands. This time take a look at the hand I held after the
opponent on my left had opened 1♠ and my partner had
made a takeout double:

    ♠ 9 8 7
    ♡ 4 3
    ◇ 9 4 3 2
    ♣ J 10 4 3

This is the kind of hand that can make you very uncomfortable but it doesn't need to. My partner had asked me
to bid and I never like to refuse my partner's request. I
calmly responded 2♣. Don't be uneasy on hands like
this. Your partner isn't expecting anything of you, except
that you bid something. My partner did not want to hear
me pass. As it turned out, the opponents carried on bidding to their own partscore and I never did have to play
the hand.

Summary

The double is a dual purpose bid. It can be used to increase the
penalty for defeating the opponents' contract or as a takeout double, asking your partner to bid his best suit. You can use the following guideline to decide which type of double is which:

Penalty versus takeout doubles

A double is for penalty if:

• Your partner has already made a bid or

• The opponents are in the game zone

A double is for takeout if:
• Your partner has not already made a bid and
• The opponents are in the partscore zone

You can start with a takeout double when you have a hand too strong for a simple overcall (16 or more HCPs) but a normal take-out double meets the following requirements:

Requirements for a takeout double

• Support for the unbid suits
• The values for an opening bid, counting support points

The takeout double is a forcing bid and you should not pass unless the opponent on your right bids rather than passes. When responding, use the following guidelines:

Responding to a takeout double

0–9 points	Bid your suit as cheaply as possible
10–12 points	Bid your suit jumping one level
13 or more points	Bid to the game zone

When you have made a takeout double, you should be very careful about bidding again when your partner makes a minimum response showing 0–9 points:

Rebidding after a minimum response from partner

12–15 points	Pass
16–19 points	Raise one level
19 or more points	Jump one level

Commonly asked questions

Q *Do you have to have support for the unbid suits when making a take-out double? Some players say you only need support for the major suits. The opponent on my right started with 1◊ and this was my hand:*

♠ A K 4 2
♡ A Q 7 6
◊ J 10 8
♣ 8 7

I had enough strength to consider competing. I didn't want to pass.
The hand would be fine for a takeout double except for the clubs.
What should I do?

A   This is a matter of partnership style. Many players would risk
    a takeout double with this hand, being eager to compete. It
    will work out fine if their partner chooses hearts or spades. If
    your partner bids clubs, you can always put your dummy
    down rather sheepishly, explaining that you thought a
    couple of your diamonds were clubs! Other players might
    choose to overcall one of their strong four-card suits, treating
    it as though it were a five-card suit. Neither action is ideal.
    However, your alternative is to pass, leaving the auction
    to your opponents. That is a very conservative approach.
    Remember, there are not many bids that fit exactly with the
    textbook examples when you sit down at the table to play. You
    have to use the guidelines and adapt them as best you can to
    the hand you have been dealt.

Q   *Can I ever pass my partner's takeout double? What do I do if my best*
    suit is the one bid by my opponents?

A   When you have a weak hand, you can pass your partner's
    takeout double if the opponent on your right makes a bid. For
    example:

North	East	South	West
	(Partner)		(You)
1♡	Double	2♡	?

South's bid has let you off the hook. The contract is no longer
doubled so you can pass with a weak hand. If you have some
points, however, you want to try and find a bid. After all, your
partner invited you into the auction.

 If South had passed, you would have to bid unless you
wanted to end up defending a 1♡ doubled contract. This
would generally be a bad idea since your partner has

expressed willingness to play with any trump suit other than hearts. However, you might decide to pass with this type of hand:

♠ 7
♡ Q J 10 9 7 6
♢ A 8 3
♣ K 4 2

With such a good heart suit, you can expect to defeat the 1♡ contract so you could pass, converting your partner's takeout double into a penalty double. This is the only exception to the guideline that a partner's takeout double is a forcing bid.

PART TWO: DECLARER PLAY

CHAPTER 16

General Principles

'Lady Coote and Gerald Wade were amiable and discursive and the young man never failed to say at the conclusion of each hand, "I say, partner, you played that simply splendidly," in tones of simple admiration which Lady Coote found both novel and extremely soothing. They also held very good cards.'

From *The Seven Dials Mystery* by Agatha Christie

The play of the hand can be a high point in the game of bridge and many of us, like Lady Coote, find it extremely soothing when our partner notices that we played a hand well. After all, we are representing the partnership as the declarer when trying to take the number of tricks that we committed to in the auction. Taking tricks is what the game is all about. If the declarer takes enough tricks to fulfil the contract, his side collects points and if he is not successful, the opponents collect points. The play of the hand, or *declarer play*, is the focus of this book. We'll let you in on some of the secrets of the experts and show you the methods they use to get the most from the cards.

Making a plan

Since the declarer is responsible for both his own hand and the *dummy*'s hand, we will focus on his decisions. In this book, the declarer will always be sitting in the South position and the dummy will be in the North position. Before we get any further, though, we want to ask you a question. Since this is a book on play, let's get right to the point. You are playing in a contract of 2NT. This means that you have to take eight tricks to make your contract, and there is no trump suit. The opening lead is the ♠J from West, who would lead this card from a suit headed by ♠J10 or ♠KJ10. Which card would you play from the dummy on the first trick: the ♠A or the ♠Q? Here are the combined hands:

Dummy
♠ A Q 2
♡ 8 6 4
◊ K J 3
♣ Q 10 6 3

Opening Lead
♠ J

Your Hand (Declarer)
♠ 8 6 4 3
♡ 10 5
◊ A Q 7
♣ A K J 8

More important than whether you decide to play the ♠A or the ♠Q is the way you arrive at your decision. Before you choose the particular card to play in a specific suit, whether it is your first hand or whether you are a world-class player, you have to take a look at the big picture. *You have to make a plan.*

There are many different aspects to making a plan and many considerations. Most important is the concept that you have to stop and take a moment to decide how you are going to make your contract. The letters S T O P can be used to help remember the steps you go through on nearly every hand you play.

S – stop to consider your goal
T – tally your winners
O – organize your plan
P – put your plan into operation

Stop to consider your goal

The first step in playing a hand is to consider your goal. In other words, how many tricks do you need to take to make your contract? Does this sound too simple? It is the only way you can decide whether to play the ♠A or the ♠Q in the hand above. You are in 2NT and so have set your sights on taking eight tricks.

Tally your winners

After you have stopped to consider your goal, the next step is to discover how close you are to getting there. Tally your winners. A winner, or a *sure trick*, is one you can take without giving up the lead to the opponents. Here are two examples to illustrate the point:

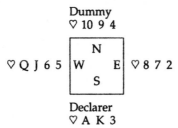

You have two tricks in this suit, one with the ♡A and another with the ♡K. You can take both of these tricks without giving up the lead to the opponents.

Now, how many sure tricks are there in this suit?

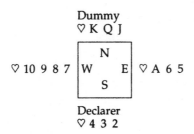

After the ♡A is *driven out* – that is, after East has played the ♡A in order to capture one of dummy's high cards – the declarer will be able to take two tricks. However, there are no sure tricks since, by definition, sure tricks refer to those you can take without giving up the lead to the opponents.

Three more ideas about sure tricks are worth noting. First, the declarer does not need to have all of the *high cards* in one hand. Each of the following examples has three sure tricks: one with the ace, one with the king and one with the queen.

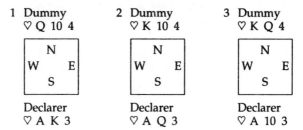

1 Dummy
   ♡ Q 10 4

   Declarer
   ♡ A K 3

2 Dummy
   ♡ K 10 4

   Declarer
   ♡ A Q 3

3 Dummy
   ♡ K Q 4

   Declarer
   ♡ A 10 3

Secondly, you cannot take any more sure tricks than the number of cards in the hand with the greater number of cards in the suit.

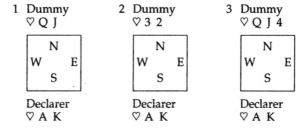

1 Dummy
   ♡ Q J

   Declarer
   ♡ A K

2 Dummy
   ♡ 3 2

   Declarer
   ♡ A K

3 Dummy
   ♡ Q J 4

   Declarer
   ♡ A K

In the first example, although you have the top four high cards, you can take only two sure tricks since both the declarer and the dummy each has only two cards in the suit. In the next example, although you have only two of the high cards, you still take two sure tricks. Those extra high cards in the first example – the ♡QJ in dummy instead of the ♡32 – did not do you any good, because of the rule which says that declarer has to play a card from both hands to each trick! When you play the ♡A from the South hand, you must follow suit with the ♡J from the North hand, and when you next play the ♡K from South you must follow with the ♡Q from North. In the final example, you have the four top cards, but can take at most three winners, since you have only a three-card suit in the dummy. In fact, you may not even be able to take three winners – after cashing the ♡A and the ♡K, the lead will be in the South hand. If you cannot get to dummy in another suit to cash the ♡Q, you will never make a trick with it! (Note: to *cash* a card means to play a sure winner and take the trick with it.)

Another consideration is that when the cards are unevenly divided between your hand and the dummy, you may have to play the cards in a certain order to enable you to collect all of your sure tricks. Take this example:

Dummy
◊ K 4

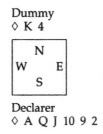

Declarer
◊ A Q J 10 9 2

You have the six top cards: the ace, king, queen, jack, ten and nine. You have a six-card suit in your hand, so you can expect to take six tricks. The order in which you play the cards, however, can be important. If you play the ◊A and then a small diamond to the ◊K, you are in the dummy. You have no more diamonds left to get back to your hand. If you can get there in another suit, fine, but this is not always the case.

Play the suit again. This time play a small diamond to the ◊K in the dummy. Next, play a low diamond to the high cards in your hand. Now you can easily take all six tricks. The idea is to get to your *long side*. You want to get rid of the high card, the ◊K in the dummy, on the first trick so that it does not get in the way of your getting back to your hand. This is referred to as playing the high card from the *short side*.

Another example:

Dummy
◊ Q J 7 2

Declarer
◊ A K 3

You have the top four cards, and dummy has a four-card suit, so you should have four sure tricks. In order to take them, though, you must be careful to follow the rule and play your high cards from the *short side* first. You must cash the ◊A, playing dummy's ◊2, then the ◊K playing dummy's ◊7. Next lead the ◊3 to dummy's ◊J, and you will be in the right hand to cash the ◊Q. Work out for yourself what might happen if you lead the ◊3 on either the first or the second round of the suit.

Organize your plan

You want to look at the choices you have. If you have enough sure tricks to make your contract, then you should consider whether there are any special considerations – such as playing high cards from the short side first – that you need to be careful about when taking your tricks. If you do not have enough sure tricks to make your contract, then you should consider various ways to generate extra tricks. Let us go back to our example hand at the beginning of the chapter.

Dummy
♠ A Q 2
♡ 8 6 4
◊ K J 3
♣ Q 10 6 3

Opening Lead
♠ J

Your Hand (Declarer)
♠ 8 6 4 3
♡ 10 5
◊ A Q 7
♣ A K J 8

You have the option of playing either the ♠A or the ♠Q on the first trick. If you needed an extra winner apart from your sure tricks to make your contract of 2NT, then you would think about playing the ♠Q. But the first two steps of your plan should tell you that you don't need any extra winners to make your contract. Your goal is to take eight tricks and you have the eight sure tricks that you need. On this hand, you don't need to plan to consider ways of developing extra tricks.

Put your plan into operation

Only after you have gone through the first three steps of your plan are you ready to play a card to the first trick. Let's return to our original question: should you play the ♠A or the ♠Q on the first trick?

Stop to consider your goal

You are in a contract of 2NT and so need to take eight tricks. Simple as that! Your goal is to take eight tricks.

Tally your winners

Remember that a winner is a trick that you take without giving up the lead to the opponents. Looking at the cards you hold in each suit, count your sure tricks as follows:

Spades	1 sure trick with the ♠A
Hearts	0 sure tricks
Diamonds	3 sure tricks with the ◊A, ◊K and ◊Q
Clubs	4 sure tricks with the ♣A, ♣K, ♣Q and ♣J

The total is eight tricks. You have enough tricks to reach your goal.

Organize your plan

You have the option to play either the ♠Q or the ♠A on the first trick. Having gone through the first two steps, you know that you have the tricks you need. Therefore, you should take them. Your priority is to take enough tricks to make your contract. By playing the ♠A you can do this. If you were to play the ♠Q, you might get an extra trick but you may also put the contract, unnecessarily, in jeopardy.

Put your plan into operation

Play the ♠A, not the ♠Q on the first trick, and then take your sure tricks.

Let's look at the entire hand:

Contract: 2NT

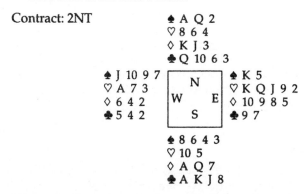

```
              ♠ A Q 2
              ♡ 8 6 4
              ◊ K J 3
              ♣ Q 10 6 3
♠ J 10 9 7              ♠ K 5
♡ A 7 3         N        ♡ K Q J 9 2
◊ 6 4 2      W   E       ◊ 10 9 8 5
♣ 5 4 2         S        ♣ 9 7
              ♠ 8 6 4 3
              ♡ 10 5
              ◊ A Q 7
              ♣ A K J 8
```

If you play the ♠Q on the first trick, East will win the trick with the ♠K and lead back a heart. The defenders can take one spade trick and five heart tricks to defeat your contract.

Let's look at this same hand again, making one small change. This time, you are in a contract of 3 NT. The lead is again the ♠J.

The question remains the same: What do you play on the first trick: the ♠A or the ♠Q?

Dummy
♠ A Q 2
♡ 8 6 4
◊ K J 3
♣ Q 10 6 3

Opening Lead
♠ J

Your Hand (Declarer)
♠ 8 6 4 3
♡ 10 5
◊ A Q 7
♣ A K J 8

STOP

Stop to consider your goal

This time, in a contract of 3NT, you need nine tricks.

Tally your winners

You still have eight winners.

Organize your plan

You need one more trick to make the contract. If you play the ♠A on the first trick, as you did in the first hand, you will take eight tricks, not enough to make 3NT. Where can you develop an extra trick? None of the other suits provides an opportunity to get the extra winner you need. Your best chance to develop an extra trick is to play the ♠Q on the first trick and hope that East does not have the ♠K.

Put your plan into operation

Having gone through your plan, you can see that the only way of getting an extra trick is in spades. Play the ♠Q. This time, let's see what the opponents hold:

Contract: 3NT

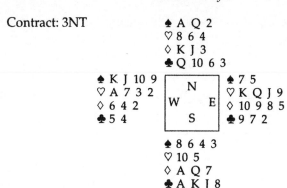

♠ A Q 2
♡ 8 6 4
◇ K J 3
♣ Q 10 6 3

♠ K J 10 9
♡ A 7 3 2
◇ 6 4 2
♣ 5 4

♠ 7 5
♡ K Q J 9
◇ 10 9 8 5
♣ 9 7 2

♠ 8 6 4 3
♡ 10 5
◇ A Q 7
♣ A K J 8

The way the cards lie this time, by playing the ♠Q on the first trick you are able to take two spade tricks, three diamond tricks and four club tricks for a total of nine tricks. You meet your goal. Of course, you might have ended up taking only seven tricks if the opponents' cards were located as they were in the first hand, but you had no choice in a contract of 3NT. You needed to take nine tricks. You are not risking your contract by playing the ♠Q because, if you don't take that chance, you can't take nine tricks. The point is that you don't want to take any unnecessary chances. In the first hand, you had enough tricks to make your contract and there was no need to jeopardize that by trying for an extra trick.

Summary

Before you decide what card to play on any particular trick, **S**top to consider the total picture. What is your goal? **T**ally your winners: how close are you to reaching your goal? **O**rganize your plan: either to take your winners if you have enough to make the contract, or to develop a way of getting the extra winners you need. Finally, **P**ut the plan into operation. Only after you have gone through all the steps of the plan should you play a card to the first trick.

Over Zia's shoulder

Let's watch Zia in action to see how even a world-class player has to STOP and make a plan before deciding on what card to play in a specific suit. At the end of each chapter, Zia will play three hands with you. Zia is always sitting in the South position so that you can look over his shoulder.

On each hand, we will give the auction first, along with Zia's comments. Then you can see the opening lead and both your hand and the dummy. Examine the hand to see how you would plan to play it and then turn the page to see how Zia tackles the hand.

Here's our first hand:

Hand 1 Dealer: South

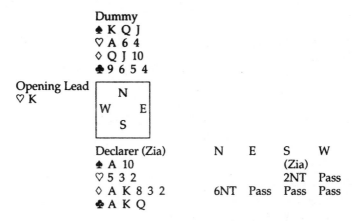

Dummy
♠ K Q J
♡ A 6 4
◇ Q J 10
♣ 9 6 5 4

Opening Lead
♡ K

Declarer (Zia)	N	E	S	W
♠ A 10			(Zia)	
♡ 5 3 2			2NT	Pass
◇ A K 8 3 2	6NT	Pass	Pass	Pass
♣ A K Q				

On this first deal, I have dealt myself an attractive hand and we have ended up in my second favourite contract. I am sure you know my favourite?, Yes, 7NT!

After an opening lead of the ♡K, I am pleased to see my partner's dummy and I am certainly planning to go through our S T O P procedure in such an important contract. How are we going to make our slam contract?

Solution to Hand 1:

Contract: 6NT

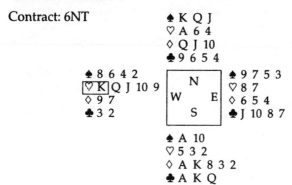

                         ♠ K Q J
                         ♡ A 6 4
                         ◊ Q J 10
                         ♣ 9 6 5 4

♠ 8 6 4 2   ♠ 9 7 5 3
♡ K Q J 10 9   N   ♡ 8 7
◊ 9 7   W   E   ◊ 6 5 4
♣ 3 2   S   ♣ J 10 8 7

                         ♠ A 10
                         ♡ 5 3 2
                         ◊ A K 8 3 2
                         ♣ A K Q

S   Stop to consider the goal.
     We need twelve tricks.

T   Tally the winners.
     This is a most enjoyable pastime:

Spades	3 winners:	♠A, ♠K, ♠Q
Hearts	1 winner:	♡A
Diamonds	5 winners:	◊A, ◊K, ◊Q, ◊J, ◊10
Clubs	3 winners:	♣A, ♣K, ♣Q

O   Organize the plan
     Well, it looks as if we don't need to develop extra tricks. As often does happen, we plan to take our sure tricks and make the contract.

P   Put the plan into operation.
     This time it is simple – but there is one important rule that we should not overlook! We have two suits that are unevenly divided – spades and diamonds. We must remember to play the high cards from the *short side first* in these two suits. The sequence of plays should be:

     Win trick 1 with the ♡A. Cash the ♠A, lead the ♠10 to the ♠Q and cash the ♠K.

     Next cash dummy's ◊Q, ◊J and ◊10.

     Return to the ♣Q and cash our remaining winners in the minor suits for twelve tricks. Note that I did not play a card to the first trick until I had gone through the whole S T O P procedure in my mind.

Things are going well. We've made a slam, and we've only just started playing!

Hand 2 Dealer: North

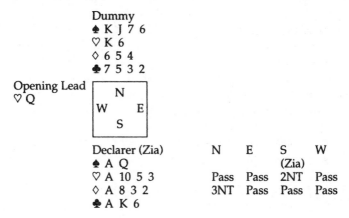

Dummy
♠ K J 7 6
♡ K 6
◊ 6 5 4
♣ 7 5 3 2

Opening Lead
♡ Q

		N		
	W		E	
		S		

Declarer (Zia)
♠ A Q
♡ A 10 5 3
◊ A 8 3 2
♣ A K 6

N	E	S	W
		(Zia)	
Pass	Pass	2NT	Pass
3NT	Pass	Pass	Pass

It often happens that you get two powerful hands in a row. Can we make two contracts in succession?

Solution to Hand 2:

Contract: 3NT

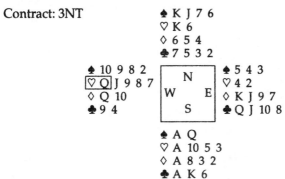

```
              ♠ K J 7 6
              ♡ K 6
              ◊ 6 5 4
              ♣ 7 5 3 2
 ♠ 10 9 8 2              ♠ 5 4 3
 ♡ Q J 9 8 7   N         ♡ 4 2
 ◊ Q 10      W   E       ◊ K J 9 7
 ♣ 9 4         S         ♣ Q J 10 8
              ♠ A Q
              ♡ A 10 5 3
              ◊ A 8 3 2
              ♣ A K 6
```

This is a very good hand to play together because it often catches those who don't remember to STOP before playing the first card.

S We need nine tricks.

T We tally our sure tricks.

Spades	4 winners:	the four top cards
Hearts	2 winners:	the ♡A and ♡K
Diamonds	1 winner:	the ◊A
Clubs	2 winners:	the ♣A and ♣K

O We organize our plan.

Since we have nine tricks, enough to make the contract provided we don't make any careless mistakes, we don't need to look for extra tricks. High cards in a suit are of no use unless we can get to them. The ♡K in the dummy is the way we can get to our good spades after we have played the two high cards from our hand. So, on the first trick, we can't play the ♡K. Instead we win the trick in our hand with the ♡A and play the two top spades. Now we use the ♡K to get over to the two good spades in the dummy.

P We put the plan into operation.

We play the ♡A on the first trick. Then we play the ♠A and the ♠Q. Now we get to the dummy with the ♡K and cash our two spade winners. We then take the rest of our sure tricks to make the contract.

Hand 3 Dealer: West

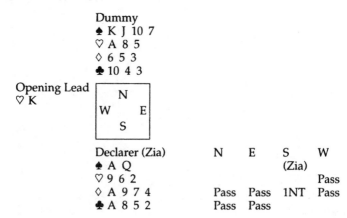

```
                    Dummy
                    ♠ K J 10 7
                    ♡ A 8 5
                    ◊ 6 5 3
                    ♣ 10 4 3
Opening Lead    ┌─────────┐
♡ K             │    N    │
                │  W    E │
                │    S    │
                └─────────┘
                    Declarer (Zia)      N      E      S      W
                    ♠ A Q                            (Zia)
                    ♡ 9 6 2                                  Pass
                    ◊ A 9 7 4          Pass   Pass   1NT    Pass
                    ♣ A 8 5 2          Pass   Pass
```

A quiet auction to a quiet contract. Nonetheless, we mustn't lose sight of our goal. Even a little hand like this can require some careful planning.

Solution to Hand 3:

Contract: 1NT

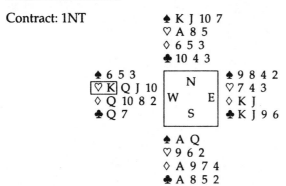

♠ K J 10 7
♡ A 8 5
◊ 6 5 3
♣ 10 4 3

♠ 6 5 3
♡ K Q J 10
◊ Q 10 8 2
♣ Q 7

♠ 9 8 4 2
♡ 7 4 3
◊ K J
♣ K J 9 6

♠ A Q
♡ 9 6 2
◊ A 9 7 4
♣ A 8 5 2

S Stop to consider the goal.

To make 1NT, we need seven tricks.

T Tally the winners.

Spades	4 winners:	♠A, ♠K, ♠Q, ♠J
Hearts	1 winner:	♡A
Diamonds	1 winner:	◊A
Clubs	1 winner:	♣A

O Organize the plan.

We only require seven tricks this time and we appear to have the tricks we need. However, the lead of the ♡K has made our task more difficult. After we win a trick with the dummy's ♡A, it will not be so easy to take our four spade tricks. If we take the ♠A and ♠Q in our hand, how are we going to get across to dummy to take the ♠K and ♠J? Can you see what we have to do? The dummy's ♠10 gives us a way to end up taking four spade tricks. After playing the ♠A, we play the ♠Q and *overtake* it with the dummy's ♠K. It may seem wasteful to play two of our high cards on one trick but, on this hand, it is the only way we can get to the dummy. Now, we can take two more spade tricks, with the ♠J and ♠10.

P Put the plan into operation.

Win the ♡A, play the ♠A and then the ♠Q, overtaking with the
dummy's ♠K. Take the dummy's ♠J and ♠10 and then your ◊A
and ♣A – and it's on to the next chapter. Well, if you made all
three hands, you're well on your way to becoming a good
declarer.

CHAPTER 17

Promoting High Cards

Unsolicited advice at the bridge table should be avoided.

Sometimes you have the number of tricks you need and all you have to do is take them. Most of the time, however, when you compare your goal with the number of sure tricks you have, you find that in order to make your contract you have to develop extra tricks. One of the most untroubled options for finding extra tricks is through *promotion*.

Promoting winners

You can *promote* winners in a suit when you have a series, or *sequence*, of high cards. Consider this suit:

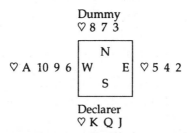

Dummy
♡ 8 7 3

♡ A 10 9 6   ♡ 5 4 2

Declarer
♡ K Q J

You have no sure tricks. Remember, a sure trick is one you can take without giving up the lead to the opponents. The suit does have potential for developing tricks, however. After you have played the suit and given the opponents the ace, you have promoted two winners. With this suit, you had only to give up the lead once. To take two tricks in this suit, you don't need to be concerned about how the opponents' cards are *divided* or which of your opponents holds the ♡A. They could be divided like this:

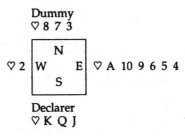

You would still be able to collect two tricks in the suit by giving up a trick to the opponents. We are assuming, of course, that there are no trumps, so that West cannot trump either of the winners that you have promoted. We will not discuss trump contracts until Chapter 20. If you want to promote two tricks from this suit, all you have to do is drive out the ace. Let's look at another example:

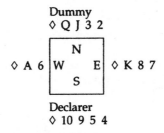

Again, you have two potential winners. Only, this time, you have to give the lead up twice before you can enjoy them. Notice that the cards in the sequence do not all need to be in one hand. In the example above, the ◊Q and ◊J are in the dummy and the ◊10 and ◊9 are in declarer's hand.

There are times when you may have to give the lead up three times in order to promote your winners. Here is another layout:

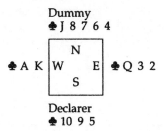

Dummy
♣ J 8 7 6 4

♣ A K | N W E S | ♣ Q 3 2

Declarer
♣ 10 9 5

There are two potential tricks in this suit, even though you would have to give the lead up three times in order to promote them. This time, not only are the cards in the sequence divided between your hand and the dummy, but the suit is unevenly divided since the dummy has more cards than the declarer in the suit.

Getting to your winners

When the suit you are promoting is unevenly divided and there are more cards on one side of the table than the other, it is important to keep your eye on the long suit. Promoted winners are of no value unless you can get to them. Although you can't call a taxi, with a little care you can provide yourself with the transport you need to get from one side of the table to the other. A means of getting from one side of the table to the other is called an *entry*. We'll be looking at entries throughout the book.

Promoting your winners in the correct order

When taking sure winners, it is important to play the high card from the short side so that a small card is left to get over to winners on your long side. When promoting winners you also need to play the cards in the right order. For example, you would like to promote five winners in this diamond suit:

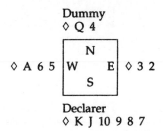

Dummy
◊ Q 4

◊ A 6 5   N W E S   ◊ 3 2

Declarer
◊ K J 10 9 8 7

Suppose you play the ◊K from your hand first and West does not play his ◊A. Next, you play a small diamond over to the ◊Q in the dummy. West still does not play his ◊A. You are in the dummy and need an *entry* to get back into your hand. You may have one entry in another suit. Suppose you use it to get back to your hand. Let's consider what has happened so far. Because West did not play his ◊A on either the first or second trick, you have taken two diamond tricks and have used one entry to your hand. You play a third round of the suit. West takes his ◊A. Diamonds have been played three times; you have taken two tricks and the defenders have taken one. Two more winners have been promoted in the suit – if you can get to them. You need another high card to get back into your hand and you may not have one. You will never take the tricks you spent time promoting.

Play the suit again. This time, on the first trick play a small diamond from your hand toward the ◊Q in the dummy. West plays low. Lead a diamond to a high card in your hand. Again, West plays low. You have now taken two diamond tricks and can lead a third diamond. This time West takes the ◊A. You have not used your one outside entry to play the diamonds so far and you have promoted three winners in your hand. Instead of needing two entries you need only the one to enjoy your promoted diamond winners.

Putting it into practice

It is important to watch your high cards in other suits. Keep the high cards with your long side of the suit in which you have to promote winners. After all, a winner is of no value unless you have some way to get to it. Let's look at a complete hand. The contract is 3NT and the opening lead is the ♣Q:

Contract: 3NT

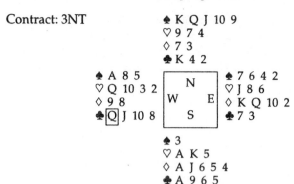

♠ K Q J 10 9
♡ 9 7 4
♢ 7 3
♣ K 4 2

♠ A 8 5   ♠ 7 6 4 2
♡ Q 10 3 2   ♡ J 8 6
♢ 9 8   ♢ K Q 10 2
♣ Q J 10 8   ♣ 7 3

♠ 3
♡ A K 5
♢ A J 6 5 4
♣ A 9 6 5

What is your plan? Your goal is to take nine tricks. Your sure winners are two heart tricks, one diamond trick and two club tricks – a total of five tricks. Organize your plan. You need to increase the number of winners by four so that you have enough to make the contract. The four winners you need are available in the spade suit, after the ♠A has been driven out. You need that precious ♣K to stay in the dummy until your spades are established. Don't play it carelessly on the first trick. Your priority is to keep that entry with the long suit you are planning to promote.

When you are seeking to promote extra tricks for your contract, you should play first of all on the suit or suits where the extra tricks are needed. Do *not* make the mistake of cashing your sure winners first! If you do that, you will find that by the time you come to play on the suit where you need extra tricks, you will have promoted enough winners for the opponents, for them to beat you.

You put your plan into action by taking the first trick in your hand with the ♣A and then playing your ♠3. Keep playing spades until the opponents take their ace. On this hand, West has to take it on the third round of the suit. The opponents lead another card. You don't care what it is. Suppose the opponents continue with the club suit. Take the trick with the ♣K in the dummy and enjoy your promoted spades.

It is horrible to contemplate, but what if you had played the ♣K on the first trick? You could play your spades and the opponents would win the trick with the ♠A. Now you would have no way of getting over to your promoted winners. Remember, you have two methods to help get your promoted winners. First, you can play the high card from the short side in the suit that you are promoting. Second, you can keep an entry in another suit – in this case it was the ♣K – on the same side of the table that has the length in the suit.

Summary

Extra tricks can be promoted when you have a sequence of cards in a suit by giving up the lead to the opponents and driving out the cards they hold which are higher than yours. This is a comfortable way of getting extra tricks. You don't need to be concerned about how the opponents' cards are divided. Your thoughts should focus on:

- Knowing how many times you have to give up the lead to promote your winners.
- Playing the high card from the short side when the cards in the suit are unevenly divided to give yourself every chance to get to your promoted winners.
- Observing the other suits so that you try to keep high cards with the long suit that you want to promote.

Over Zia's shoulder

Hand 1 Dealer: North

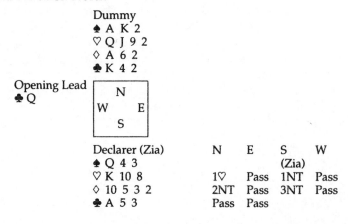

Dummy
♠ A K 2
♡ Q J 9 2
◇ A 6 2
♣ K 4 2

Opening Lead
♣ Q

	N	
W		E
	S	

Declarer (Zia)		N	E	S	W
♠ Q 4 3				(Zia)	
♡ K 10 8		1♡	Pass	1NT	Pass
◇ 10 5 3 2		2NT	Pass	3NT	Pass
♣ A 5 3		Pass	Pass		

How should you and I proceed on this hand? I STOP – and so do you – to make my plan.

Solution to Hand 1:

Contract: 3NT

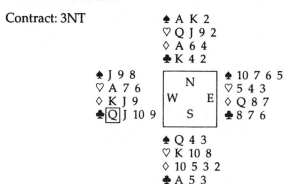

♠ A K 2
♡ Q J 9 2
◇ A 6 4
♣ K 4 2

♠ J 9 8   ♠ 10 7 6 5
♡ A 7 6   ♡ 5 4 3
◇ K J 9   ◇ Q 8 7
♣ Q J 10 9   ♣ 8 7 6

♠ Q 4 3
♡ K 10 8
◇ 10 5 3 2
♣ A 5 3

S Our goal is to take nine tricks.
T Let's tally our sure winners:

Spades	3 winners
Hearts	0 winners
Diamonds	1 winner
Clubs	2 winners

O We organize our plan.

We need three more tricks and hearts seems a reasonable place to get them. By driving out the ♡A, we would make three heart tricks. We have enough high cards in the dummy to be able to get to our promoted heart winners.

P Put the plan into operation.

Now, and only now, can we play to the first trick. We win the ♣Q with the ♣A. Next we play the ♡K. No matter when West takes the ♡A, we end up with nine tricks.

Hand 2 Dealer: South

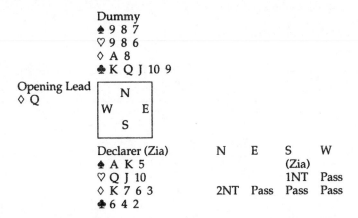

Dummy
♠ 9 8 7
♡ 9 8 6
◊ A 8
♣ K Q J 10 9

Opening Lead
◊ Q

Declarer (Zia)
♠ A K 5
♡ Q J 10
◊ K 7 6 3
♣ 6 4 2

	N	E	S	W
			(Zia)	
			1NT	Pass
	2NT	Pass	Pass	Pass

Our partner has tempted us to get dangerously high. We might have bid 3NT. But we have conservatively passed in a part-score contract. Thank you, partner. Nice clubs.

Solution to Hand 2:

Contract: 2NT

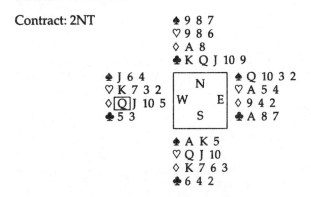

♠ 9 8 7
♡ 9 8 6
◊ A 8
♣ K Q J 10 9

♠ J 6 4
♡ K 7 3 2
◊ Q J 10 5
♣ 5 3

♠ Q 10 3 2
♡ A 5 4
◊ 9 4 2
♣ A 8 7

♠ A K 5
♡ Q J 10
◊ K 7 6 3
♣ 6 4 2

S We need eight tricks to make our contract.
T We have only four sure tricks: two spades and two diamonds.
O We need four more tricks, and they certainly seem to be available in clubs. We could win the ◊A and play the ♣K. East could put on the ♣A and our suit would be promoted. But, the defenders aren't usually that kind. East may not play the ♣A

until the third round. We will have taken two club tricks, but we have two more to take and we can't get to them. Fortunately we have the ◊K in our hand. So let's plan to win the first trick in our hand, leaving the ◊A in the dummy.

P Having won the first trick with the ◊K, we can then play a club. Suppose East waits until the third round to take the ♣A. Although we have no clubs left in our hand to get over to the winners in the dummy, we do have that carefully preserved ◊A which will get us to the dummy and the promoted winners.

Hand 3 Dealer: East

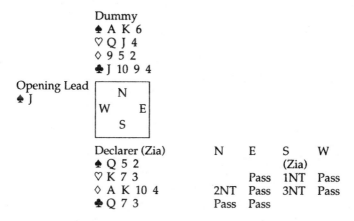

Dummy
♠ A K 6
♡ Q J 4
◊ 9 5 2
♣ J 10 9 4

Opening Lead
♠ J

Declarer (Zia)
♠ Q 5 2
♡ K 7 3
◊ A K 10 4
♣ Q 7 3

	N	E	S	W
			(Zia)	
		Pass	1NT	Pass
	2NT	Pass	3NT	Pass
	Pass	Pass		

This time, we have enough to accept our partner's invitation to a game. If you do not understand this auction, then refer back to 'Responding with 11-12 points' on p. 53. Having bid a game, we still have to make it. It looks as though there is a lot of work to do. Where do we start?

Solution to Hand 3:

Contract: 3NT

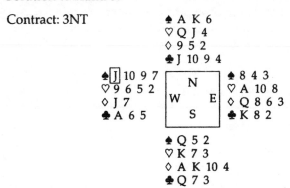

♠ A K 6
♡ Q J 4
◊ 9 5 2
♣ J 10 9 4

♠ J 10 9 7
♡ 9 6 5 2
◊ J 7
♣ A 6 5

♠ 8 4 3
♡ A 10 8
◊ Q 8 6 3
♣ K 8 2

♠ Q 5 2
♡ K 7 3
◊ A K 10 4
♣ Q 7 3

S We'll need nine tricks to make our contract of 3NT.

T We only have five sure tricks to start with: the three top spades and the two top diamonds.

O With four more tricks to develop, we'll have to look at all our resources. In the heart suit, we can promote two extra tricks by driving out the ♡A. In the club suit, we can also develop two extra tricks but we'll have to drive out two of the opponents' high cards, the ♣A and ♣K. Where do we start? When there's a lot to do, it is usually best to start with the suit that requires the most work to develop – in this case, the clubs.

P Win the first spade trick in either hand and play the ♣Q, starting with the high card from the short side. Assuming the opponents win the ♣K and lead another spade, win the trick – this time, it is best to make sure that our remaining high spade is in dummy, keeping the high card in the hand with the length in clubs. Lead clubs again, driving out the opponents' ♣A and promoting two club winners. If the opponents lead another spade, we can win it and take our established club tricks. Now, it's time to go to work on the heart suit. Once we've driven out the ♡A, we'll have all the tricks we need to make the contract.

Hard work, but worthwhile – as we score up our game bonus.

CHAPTER 18

Establishing Small Cards

In Toronto, a National Tournament was held in 1986 in which there were over 23,000 tables of bridge in play over a ten-day period.

Since there are only four face cards in each suit – the ace, king, queen and jack – it is important to develop techniques for turning small cards into winners. Does this sound like a magic trick? It can be done. Once the opponents have no cards left to play and cannot follow suit, a card as seemingly insignificant as a two can be as powerful as an ace.

Establishing tricks in long suits

Consider this suit:

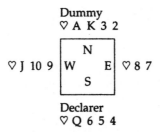

You expect to take your three high cards, the ace, king and queen. By playing the suit three times, however, you have exhausted the opponents' supply of cards in the suit. Your ♡4 also becomes a winner. Look at the suit again. This time we'll change the *distribution*, or *division*, of the opponents' cards:

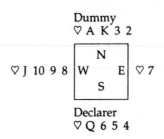

Dummy
♡ A K 3 2

♡ J 10 9 8   W   E   ♡ 7

Declarer
♡ Q 6 5 4

Your three top hearts are still winners. However, after you have played the suit three times, West still has a card left and it is higher than your ♡4. When the suit is divided like this, you are unable to develop an extra winner with your small card.

When you were promoting tricks through the force of your high cards, as we saw in the last chapter, you didn't need to consider how the opponents' cards were divided. Now, however, the division of the defenders' cards is important. You want to be able to predict how the opponents' cards are likely to be divided in order to feel comfortable trying to get extra tricks from small cards in a suit. What can you expect on most hands? Is the suit more likely to be divided the way it was in the first layout or the second layout?

Considering the division of the opponents' cards

If the opponents have an odd number of cards in a suit, as they do when they hold five cards between them, the suit is likely to be divided as evenly as possible – that is, the way it was in the first example. When they are divided with three cards in one opponent's hand and two cards in the other opponent's hand, it is referred to as 3–2 distribution.

Now, suppose this is your suit:

Dummy
♡ A K 3 2

Declarer
♡ Q 6 5

You have seven cards in the suit and the opponents have six cards, an even number. When the opponents have an even number of cards, they are likely to be divided unevenly. What does this mean? The six cards held by the defenders are likely to be divided so that there are four on one side and two on the other: 4–2 distribution, rather than 3–3. Look at two possible layouts:

1

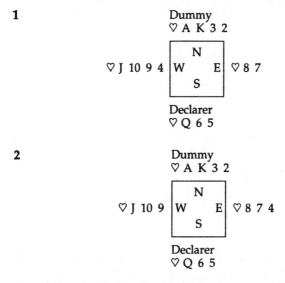

Dummy
♡ A K 3 2

♡ J 10 9 4   ♡ 8 7

Declarer
♡ Q 6 5

2

Dummy
♡ A K 3 2

♡ J 10 9   ♡ 8 7 4

Declarer
♡ Q 6 5

Although you would like the cards to be divided as they are in the second example, 3–3, you cannot expect this to be the case. It is more likely that they will be divided 4–2 as in the first layout. Notice that we don't expect them to be divided very unevenly, 5–1 or 6–0, too frequently. Here is a chart of what you can expect:

Expected division of opponents' cards

Number of cards held	Most likely distribution
3	2–1
4	3–1
5	3–2
6	4–2
7	4–3
8	5–3

You don't need to memorise the chart. It is enough to notice the general concept: an even number of cards tends to divide unevenly, an uneven number of cards tends to divide evenly.

Getting to your winners

This time, we have a delightful suit to consider:

Dummy
♠ A K Q 7 6

```
        N
    W       E
        S
```

Declarer
♠ 4 3 2

You have eight spades and can expect the opponents' five cards, an odd number, to be divided 3–2. That means that if you play the suit three times, neither one of your opponents will have any cards left in the suit. You, on the other hand, will have two spades left in the dummy, which are winners. With this suit, then, you can expect to take five tricks. Let's look at the suit again and this time, we are going to make the layout more realistic. After all, you can't always wait to have such strength and length in a suit before you try to establish tricks with your small cards.

Dummy
♠ A 9 8 7 6

```
    N
W       E
    S
```

Declarer
♠ K 3 2

After playing the suit three times, you still expect the opponents will have no cards left and that your remaining two small spades in the dummy will be winners. This time, however, you have to do a little work to get to this point. You play the suit three times, expecting to win two tricks – one with the ace in the dummy, the other with the king in your hand – and to lose one trick to the opponents. You have to lose one trick before your small cards are *established* as winners. Does it matter whether you take your two high cards and lose the third trick or whether you lose the first trick and then take your two high cards? It might well matter!

Winners which have been established in a suit are of no use unless you can get to them. If your only high card in the dummy is the ♠A, then you had better save it until you are in a position to take your established winners. Consider what would happen if you won the first two tricks with the ace and king and gave up a trick. After the defenders take the third spade trick, you have two good spades in the dummy, but no way to get to them.

Now, try giving up the first trick to the opponents. The next time you get the lead, be careful. Play the high card from the short side, your ♠K, and then a small card over to your ♠A in the dummy. You are now in a position to enjoy the last two winners in the suit.

Putting it into practice

Let's look at the concept of developing tricks from small cards in a complete hand. The contract is 3NT and the opening lead is the ♣Q.

Declarer Play

Contract: 3NT

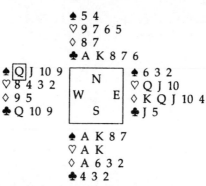

```
                    ♠ 5 4
                    ♡ 9 7 6 5
                    ◊ 8 7
                    ♣ A K 8 7 6
    ♠ Q J 10 9              ♠ 6 3 2
    ♡ 8 4 3 2      N        ♡ Q J 10
    ◊ 9 5      W       E    ◊ K Q J 10 4
    ♣ Q 10 9       S        ♣ J 5
                    ♠ A K 8 7
                    ♡ A K
                    ◊ A 6 3 2
                    ♣ 4 3 2
```

Plan the play. You need nine tricks and have seven sure winners: two spades, two hearts, one diamond and two clubs. The two more tricks you need can best be developed in the club suit. You can expect the opponents' five cards in the suit to be divided 3–2 which means that after you play the suit three times, your two small clubs in the dummy will be winners.

Remember, you have to have transport to get to your winners. This would seem to be no problem at all. After all, you have both the ♣A and ♣K in the dummy. You do, however, have to play the suit three times, not twice, before those winners are established. If you play the ♣A and ♣K first, and then a third round of clubs, the defenders would take their trick. True, you have now exhausted their supply of clubs and have two winners in the dummy but you also have no way to get to them.

Instead, lose the first (or second) club trick. Now when you get the lead, you can play a small card to your ♣A and ♣K and are in a position to take the next four tricks. In a contract of 3NT, you have to take nine tricks – but there is no law that says they have to be the *first* nine tricks! As a matter of fact, one of the most important factors in the play of the hand at no trumps is to take your losses early. Remember, if you have a suit in which you need to lose tricks in order to promote winners, play on that suit immediately! Do *not* take your sure tricks first – if you do, you will be promoting winners not for yourself, but for your opponents!

Giving up the lead

Before we leave the subject of long suits, it is important to notice
that you might have to give up the lead not once, not twice but
three times to establish a winner from your small cards:

Dummy
◊ 8 7 6 4

Declarer
◊ 9 5 3 2

Is there any sense in giving a suit like this a second glance? The
opponents have five cards in the suit, which you expect to be
divided 3–2. If you could afford to give the lead up three times,
you could eventually establish a winner in the suit. Let's hope you
don't have to resort to this too often, but it is worth noticing that it
could be done.

Summary

- When you have a suit with eight or more combined cards, you
  should look to that suit as a source of tricks with your small
  cards, even if the suit is not headed by a bevy of honours.
- Consider how you are going to get to your established winners.
  It might require giving up the lead early once or twice in order
  to preserve an ace until the small cards have been established.
- Be prepared to give up the lead once, twice or even three times
  in order to establish a winner with a small card.
- Expect that an odd number of cards held by the opponents, five
  for example, will be divided evenly – 3–2 rather than 4–1.
  Similarly, expect an even number of cards held by the opponents, six for example, to be divided unevenly – 4–2 rather than
  3–3. When you have a suit or suits in which extra winners need
  to be developed, play on those suits first. Do not cash your sure
  winners before playing on suits where you need extra tricks.

Over Zia's shoulder

Hand 1 Dealer: East

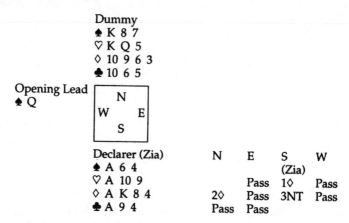

Dummy
♠ K 8 7
♡ K Q 5
◊ 10 9 6 3
♣ 10 6 5

Opening Lead
♠ Q

	N	
W		E
	S	

Declarer (Zia)
♠ A 6 4
♡ A 10 9
◊ A K 8 4
♣ A 9 4

N	E	S	W
		(Zia)	
	Pass	1◊	Pass
2◊	Pass	3NT	Pass
Pass	Pass		

We are in the most frequently played contract in bridge, 3NT, and not for the last time. Let's go through our steps again.

Solution to Hand 1:

Contract: 3NT

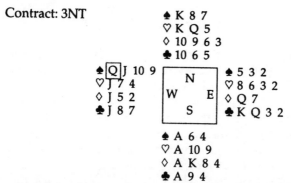

♠ K 8 7
♡ K Q 5
◊ 10 9 6 3
♣ 10 6 5

♠ Q J 10 9
♡ J 7 4
◊ J 5 2
♣ J 8 7

	N	
W		E
	S	

♠ 5 3 2
♡ 8 6 3 2
◊ Q 7
♣ K Q 3 2

♠ A 6 4
♡ A 10 9
◊ A K 8 4
♣ A 9 4

S We have to take nine tricks. This should not be too much of a problem, but let's take a look.

T Our tally gives us the following information. Our sure tricks are:

Spades	2 winners
Hearts	3 winners
Diamonds	2 winners
Clubs	1 winner

We have eight sure tricks and need one more to make our contract.

O Organize a plan.

The most obvious place for the extra trick is from our diamond suit. We can play the ◊A and ◊K and another diamond. We assume the suit breaks reasonably, 3–2 (which it does), and we can establish an extra diamond winner with our last small diamond.

P Put the plan into operation.

We'll take the first trick with the ♠A in our hand or the ♠K in dummy and play the two top diamonds and a third diamond, which we lose. When we regain the lead, the small diamond is established for the ninth trick. Note that after winning the first trick, we immediately go after the diamond suit – we do not take any of our sure tricks until we have established the extra trick that we need.

Hand 2 Dealer: North

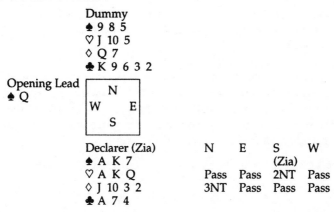

Dummy
♠ 9 8 5
♡ J 10 5
◊ Q 7
♣ K 9 6 3 2

Opening Lead
♠ Q

Declarer (Zia)
♠ A K 7
♡ A K Q
◊ J 10 3 2
♣ A 7 4

N	E	S	W
		(Zia)	
Pass	Pass	2NT	Pass
3NT	Pass	Pass	Pass

You can never really explain the pleasurable feeling of picking up a hand like the one we have on this deal. It may be luck, but it still feels great. Well, once we are over the euphoria, how do we continue?

Solution to Hand 2:

Contract: 3NT

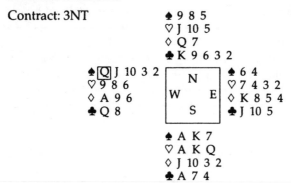

```
                    ♠ 9 8 5
                    ♡ J 10 5
                    ◊ Q 7
                    ♣ K 9 6 3 2
    ♠ Q J 10 3 2                      ♠ 6 4
    ♡ 9 8 6           N               ♡ 7 4 3 2
    ◊ A 9 6      W         E          ◊ K 8 5 4
    ♣ Q 8             S               ♣ J 10 5
                    ♠ A K 7
                    ♡ A K Q
                    ◊ J 10 3 2
                    ♣ A 7 4
```

S Stopping to consider our goal tells us we need nine tricks. The opponents have started attacking spades which is ominous. The opponents have goals too!

T Tallying our winners gets us to a total of seven sure tricks: two spades, three hearts and two clubs.

O Our natural instinct tells us the best place to go for tricks is in the club suit. If, however, we were to play the ♣A and the ♣K and another, even though the clubs would be set up, we would have no entry to enjoy them. So, we need to watch our entry carefully.

P After taking the opening spade lead with one of our high spades, we play the ♣A. Then we *duck* a club, playing low from both hands and letting the opponents have a club trick. Now, when we regain the lead, we hope – as you can see in the actual layout – that all of our remaining clubs are winners. We have a small club left in our hand to get to them.

Did you decide this by using your plan? If so, well done.

Hand 3 Dealer: North

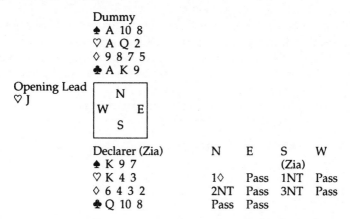

Dummy
♠ A 10 8
♡ A Q 2
◇ 9 8 7 5
♣ A K 9

Opening Lead
♡ J

Declarer (Zia)
♠ K 9 7
♡ K 4 3
◇ 6 4 3 2
♣ Q 10 8

	N	E	S	W
			(Zia)	
	1◇	Pass	1NT	Pass
	2NT	Pass	3NT	Pass
	Pass	Pass		

We have some way to go before we can make this contract – or do we?

Solution to Hand 3:

Contract: 3NT

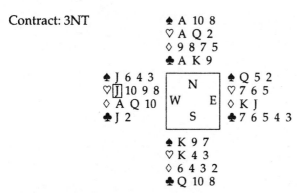

♠ A 10 8
♡ A Q 2
◇ 9 8 7 5
♣ A K 9

♠ J 6 4 3
♡ J 10 9 8
◇ A Q 10
♣ J 2

♠ Q 5 2
♡ 7 6 5
◇ K J
♣ 7 6 5 4 3

♠ K 9 7
♡ K 4 3
◇ 6 4 3 2
♣ Q 10 8

S Our goal is to take nine tricks.

T Eight seem to be easily available: two spades, three hearts and three clubs. We need to concentrate on finding just one trick.

O We have lots of strength in each suit and can afford to give up some tricks in order to create winners – how about that diamond suit? Even though we have no high honour cards in the suit, if we keep plugging away at it, we can finally get a trick from a small diamond. We have to hope that the diamonds *break* – divide –reasonably.

P We win the first heart trick and lead a diamond. The opponents win and, let's say, they lead another heart. We lead another diamond. They win and lead a heart. We win and lead diamonds once more. West wins with the last high diamond and can take his established heart trick – after all, he worked hard to get it! But, whatever he leads next, we win and can take a trick with our established diamond winner.

More power to establishing those small cards!

CHAPTER 19

The Finesse

The vision of bridge, a cigar and a column of smoke curling up to a low-hung lamp is yesterday's picture. Many of the major bridge tournaments around the world are non-smoking.

Finesse is described in the dictionary as 'delicate manipulation'. Let's consider the meaning of the finesse as it applies to bridge and see how we can delicately manipulate the cards to take more tricks. A *finesse* refers to taking a trick with a card when the opponents hold a higher card. We say that you finesse *against* the higher card that the opponents hold.

Finessing against the ace

Here are some card combinations which illustrate the concept of the finesse. We'll assume that no cards have yet been played in the suit.

Dummy
◇ K 4 3

```
    N
 W     E
    S
```

Declarer
◇ 6 5 2

In spite of the fact that the opponents have the ◇A, you can try to take a trick with the ◇K by finessing against the ace. Your next question probably is, how are you going to try to take a trick with the king when the opponents have a higher card in the suit, the ace? If you were to play the ◇K, obviously your opponents would put on the ◇A. Therefore, in this example, the method of winning a trick with the king cannot be to lead the ◇K. Instead, play towards the king. Play a small diamond from your hand toward the ◇K in the dummy.

In bridge, this type of finesse is successful only half of the time. You are going to lead from your hand towards the king. The missing ace could be in one of two places:

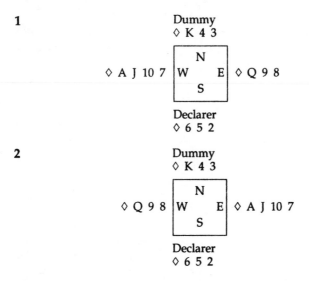

1   Dummy
                              ◇ K 4 3

◇ A J 10 7   W   E   ◇ Q 9 8

                              Declarer
                              ◇ 6 5 2

2   Dummy
                              ◇ K 4 3

◇ Q 9 8   W   E   ◇ A J 10 7

                              Declarer
                              ◇ 6 5 2

If the ◇A is held by West, as in the first layout, your finesse will be successful. Play a small card from your hand. If West plays the ◇A, your ◇K will be good on the next round of the suit. If West does not play the ◇A, your ◇K will win the trick on this round. On the other hand, in the second layout, when you play a small card, West plays a small card, you play your ◇K and East's ◇A wins the trick.

You are hoping that the missing ace will be in the position it is in the first example, with West. Isn't a 50 per cent chance of winning better than nothing? After all, if you were to lead the king, you are guaranteed to get no tricks in the suit.

Finessing against the king

By using the idea of the finesse, you can sometimes hope to take a trick with a queen when the opponents have the king. Consider this example:

Dummy
♠ A Q 2

Declarer
♠ 8 6 4 3

Does this suit look familiar? It is the spade suit from the very first example hand in the book. We saw then that we have a sure trick with the ♠A, but sometimes we need also to take a trick with the ♠Q. The general concept is that you lead towards the card you hope will win a trick – you can only hope, because you know that the opponents have the king. It is interesting that, when you were promoting winners, you were not concerned with the number of cards held by either opponent. When you were developing tricks with the small cards in your long suits, you were concerned with the division of the opponents' cards. This time you are interested in the *location* of the opponents' king. There are two possibilities. It is either held by East or West. Let's suppose West has it:

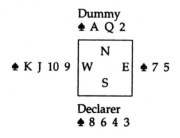

Dummy
♠ A Q 2

♠ K J 10 9

♠ 7 5

Declarer
♠ 8 6 4 3

Play a small card toward the ace-queen combination in the dummy. If West plays the ♠K, take it with your ♠A and the ♠Q is a winner on the next trick. If West plays small, finesse the ♠Q and it wins the trick. Of course, if East held the ♠K, you would not be successful in winning a trick with the ♠Q. A finesse like this is only successful half of the time.

The ace and queen do not have to be on the same side of the table:

Dummy
♠ A 5 4

Declarer
♠ Q 3 2

You still hope the ♠Q will win a trick, so lead from the dummy towards the ♠Q in your hand. You are hoping that this is the layout of the opponents' cards:

Dummy
♠ A 5 4

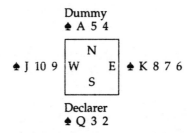

♠ J 10 9   ♠ K 8 7 6

Declarer
♠ Q 3 2

Now, if East plays the ♠K when you play small from the dummy, your ♠Q is good on the next trick. If East plays low, your ♠Q will win this trick.

Leading the high card

There are times when you play a high card in the process of taking a finesse. Look at this example:

Dummy
♣ A 9 8

Declarer
♣ Q J 10

The opponents have the ♣K, a higher card than the ♣Q, and yet you are hoping to finesse successfully against the ♣K and take a trick with the ♣Q. You would also like to take a trick with the ♣J or ♣10, making a total of three tricks in this suit. You want to prevent the opponents from winning a trick with their ♣K while you get your three tricks. The objective is to try to *trap* the opponents' ♣K. If that is your aim, let's consider how you would go about accomplishing it. Here is the entire layout you are hoping for:

Dummy
♣ A 9 8

♣ K 6 5 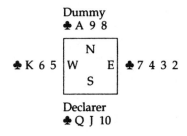 ♣ 7 4 3 2

Declarer
♣ Q J 10

In the previous examples, if you wanted to take a trick with a card when the opponents held a higher card, you played towards the card you hoped would take a trick. In this case, to trap the opponent's ♣K, you must lead one of your high cards. In order to distinguish when you can and when you cannot play a high card, ask yourself this question: how would I feel if the next opponent *covered* with a higher card? In the above example, play the ♣Q from your hand. How would you feel if West played the ♣K? That would be fine. You would take it with the ♣A and now your ♣J and ♣10 have been promoted into winners. If West did not cover your ♣Q with the ♣K, you would next lead the ♣J. Eventually, you would get three tricks in the suit, without losing any.

Do not confuse the example above with this situation.

Dummy
♣ A 9 8

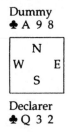

Declarer
♣ Q 3 2

Suppose you were to play the ♣Q and the opponent on your left covered with the ♣K. You could take the trick with the ♣A, but you would be no better off than if you had simply played the ♣A and put the ♣Q on the trick. You have promoted no extra winners, as you did in the previous example where you also held the ♣J and ♣10. By playing the ♣Q, you have given up a trick regardless of where the ♣K is located. If East rather than West has the ♣K, then he will take the trick with it when it is his turn to play. Either way, you do not get a trick with the ♣Q. Instead, play a small card from dummy towards the ♣Q. If the cards are located like this, your finesse will have been successful:

Dummy
♣ A 9 8

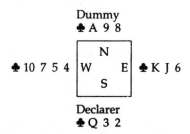

♣ 10 7 5 4   ♣ K J 6

Declarer
♣ Q 3 2

If East plays the ♣K, then your ♣Q is a winner on the next round. If East does not play the ♣K, then your ♣Q wins the first trick.

How can you decide when to play towards the high card you would like to win a trick and when to lead the high card? Look to the next trick. Ask yourself what will happen if your opponent covers your high card. Will you have gained anything? When you had the queen, jack and ten, you would gain something if the queen were covered. You would have promoted two winners, one with the jack and one with the ten. In the second example, where you have nothing to promote, you would gain nothing by leading the queen and would, in fact, have given up a chance to take a trick with it, since by leading towards it, you might have executed a successful finesse against the king.

Finessing against the queen

There are times when you want to take a trick with the jack when the opponents have the queen.

Dummy
♡ A K J

```
    N
W       E
    S
```

Declarer
♡ 4 3 2

The idea is the same. Lead towards the card you hope will take a trick, the ♡J. Notice that you already have two sure tricks in the suit, the ♡A and ♡K. You hope that the layout of the opponents' cards is like this:

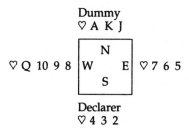

Dummy
♡ A K J

♡ Q 10 9 8
```
    N
W       E
    S
```
♡ 7 6 5

Declarer
♡ 4 3 2

Both of the high honours, the ace and king, do not need to be on the same side of the table. For example, the layout could be like this:

Dummy
♡ A 4 3

Declarer
♡ K J 2

Now you are hoping that East holds the ♡Q. You would lead small from the dummy towards the ♡J in your hand; towards the card you hope will take a trick.

Repeating a finesse

There are times when you have more than one card you hope will take a trick. Consider this layout:

Dummy
◊ K Q 4

Declarer
◊ 7 3 2

You might need to get two tricks from this suit, hoping to take tricks with both the ◊K and ◊Q. Lead towards the card or, in this case, cards which you hope will take tricks. The cards may be divided like this:

Dummy
◊ K Q 4

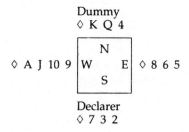

Declarer
◊ 7 3 2

Lead towards your king-queen combination in the dummy. If West plays the ◊A, your ◊K and ◊Q will be winners on the next two tricks. If West plays low, you can win the first trick with one of your high cards and repeat the finesse against the ace. To do this, you would have to come back to your hand with a high card in another suit and then again lead low towards the honour you have left in the dummy. For example, suppose you played the ◊K on the first trick. This is what is left in the suit:

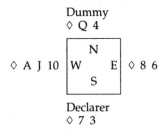

Dummy
◊ Q 4

◊ A J 10   ◊ 8 6

Declarer
◊ 7 3

Come back to your hand and lead another low card towards the ◊Q. If West plays the ◊A, your ◊Q is good on the next trick. If West plays low, your ◊Q will win this trick.

Putting it into practice

What opportunities for the finesse do you see in the following hand? The final contract is 3NT and the opening lead is ◊2.

Contract: 3NT

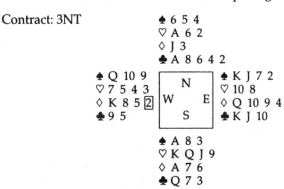

♠ 6 5 4
♡ A 6 2
◊ J 3
♣ A 8 6 4 2

♠ Q 10 9   ♠ K J 7 2
♡ 7 5 4 3   ♡ 10 8
◊ K 8 5 2   ◊ Q 10 9 4
♣ 9 5   ♣ K J 10

♠ A 8 3
♡ K Q J 9
◊ A 7 6
♣ Q 7 3

Your goal is to take nine tricks. There is one sure spade trick, four hearts, one diamond and one club for a total of seven winners. Two more need to be developed. The opening lead is a diamond and you have the ◊A in your hand and ◊J in the dummy. You would like to win a trick with the ◊J but when you are missing both the king and the queen this is unlikely. Is there any possibility to develop extra tricks by finessing? Look at the clubs. You could hope to take a trick with the ♣Q by leading from the dummy toward your hand. Since you can see the opponents' cards, you can see that this is successful. You can develop one extra trick by finessing against the ♣K.

The other extra trick can be developed through the length in the club suit. This is what we talked about in the last chapter. You expect the opponents' five clubs to be divided 3–2. After you have played the suit three times, then, you have established two winners in the dummy. You still need to be able to get to your winners and the ♡A can be used as the entry you need.

Having organized your plan, it is time to put it into operation. After you win a trick with the ◊A, lead a small club to the ♣A in the dummy and then play a club from dummy towards the ♣Q in your hand. Suppose East plays low and you win the trick with the ♣Q. You have played the suit twice and won the first two tricks. Lead the suit again, giving East a trick with his ♣K and establishing your remaining two small clubs in the dummy as winners. The opponents can now take the three diamond tricks they have established but, when you regain the lead there are enough winners to make the contract.

Summary

- A finesse is an attempt to win a trick with a card when the opponents hold a higher card in the suit. In order to do this, you usually lead towards the card you believe could win the trick. You will be successful in your efforts about half of the time.
- There are times when you have sufficient strength in the suit to plan to lead one of your high cards towards a higher card in the other hand in an attempt to trap one of the opponents' intervening high cards. You can tell whether or not leading the high card

is a good idea by imagining how you would feel if your high card was covered by an opponent's higher card. If you don't mind, then go ahead and play the high card. If you can see that you have sacrificed a trick by playing a high card then the better idea would be to lead towards it.

• There are times when you need to repeat a finesse, leading twice or more towards the cards which you hope will take tricks.

Over Zia's shoulder

Hand 1 Dealer: East

Dummy
♠ 4 3 2
♡ 7 6 3
◇ 6 5 4 3
♣ A 9 5

Opening Lead
♣ K

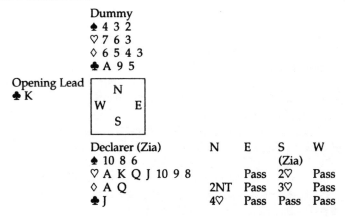

Declarer (Zia)	N	E	S	W
♠ 10 8 6			(Zia)	
♡ A K Q J 10 9 8		Pass	2♡	Pass
◇ A Q	2NT	Pass	3♡	Pass
♣ J	4♡	Pass	Pass	Pass

I can open with a strong bid at the two level to show about eight playing tricks. This has encouraged my partner to bid on to a game with his ace and three-card trump support. I hope we can make the contract. Let's plan it together.

Solution to Hand 1:

Contract: 4♡

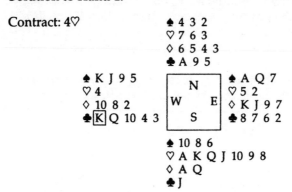

```
                        ♠ 4 3 2
                        ♡ 7 6 3
                        ◊ 6 5 4 3
                        ♣ A 9 5
        ♠ K J 9 5                      ♠ A Q 7
        ♡ 4            ┌─────────┐     ♡ 5 2
        ◊ 10 8 2       │    N    │     ◊ K J 9 7
        ♣ K Q 10 4 3   │ W     E │     ♣ 8 7 6 2
                       │    S    │
                       └─────────┘
                        ♠ 10 8 6
                        ♡ A K Q J 10 9 8
                        ◊ A Q
                        ♣ J
```

S Our goal is to take ten tricks.

T We have seven heart tricks to go with the ◊A and ♣A, for a total of nine tricks.

O The best chance for the extra trick we need is the diamond suit. If East has the ◊K, we should be able to get a trick with the ◊Q with the help of a finesse.

P It looks normal to win the ♣A, draw trumps and then try the diamond finesse but, if I look closely as opposed to casually – which with my lazy nature is not so easy to do – I can see that I cannot get to the dummy in the heart suit because my hearts are too good. What will we do to get back to the dummy after the ♣A has been played on the first trick?

This is the kind of hand where we have to delay taking our trumps and try the finesse immediately, when we are in the dummy after winning the first trick. We use this opportunity to lead a small diamond and, when East plays a small diamond, play the ◊Q. As you can see in the full layout, this works and we chalk up another game.

Hand 2 Dealer: South

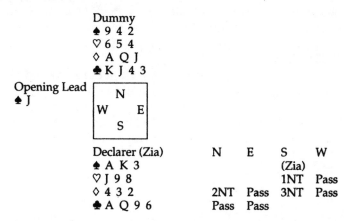

Dummy
♠ 9 4 2
♡ 6 5 4
◊ A Q J
♣ K J 4 3

Opening Lead
♠ J

Declarer (Zia)	N	E	S	W
♠ A K 3			(Zia)	
♡ J 9 8			1NT	Pass
◊ 4 3 2	2NT	Pass	3NT	Pass
♣ A Q 9 6	Pass	Pass		

For once West has not attacked our main weakness, the heart suit, but I am superstitious about feeling happy about anything until the hand is over. Let's make our plan.

Solution to Hand 2:

Contract: 3NT

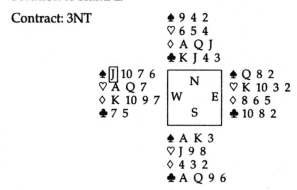

♠ 9 4 2
♡ 6 5 4
◊ A Q J
♣ K J 4 3

♠ J 10 7 6
♡ A Q 7
◊ K 10 9 7
♣ 7 5

♠ Q 8 2
♡ K 10 3 2
◊ 8 6 5
♣ 10 8 2

♠ A K 3
♡ J 9 8
◊ 4 3 2
♣ A Q 9 6

S We need to take nine tricks.

T Our sure trick count brings us to seven top tricks: two spades, one diamond and four clubs.

O The diamond holding looks really tempting and should be good for an extra trick or two. We can see that if West has the ◊K, by leading up to the ace-queen-jack combination, we can take three tricks. Whereas, leading the ace first and then playing the queen would promote one extra trick but would give the lead away unnecessarily whenever West does have the ◊K. It is always enjoyable to take a winning finesse and that is the answer here.

P We win the opening lead with our ♠K in our hand and play a low diamond toward the dummy. If West plays the ◊K, we take the trick with the ◊A, and the ◊Q and ◊J are promoted into winners. If West plays low, we win the first trick with the ◊Q or ◊J. Now we come back to our hand to repeat the finesse.

Hand 3 Dealer: East

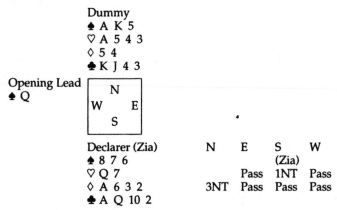

Dummy
♠ A K 5
♡ A 5 4 3
◊ 5 4
♣ K J 4 3

Opening Lead
♠ Q

Declarer (Zia)
♠ 8 7 6
♡ Q 7
◊ A 6 3 2
♣ A Q 10 2

N	E	S	W
		(Zia)	
	Pass	1NT	Pass
3NT	Pass	Pass	Pass

My reputation in the bridge world for overbidding is well known, and in real life I get into a lot of dicey contracts.

Solution to Hand 3:

Contract: 3NT

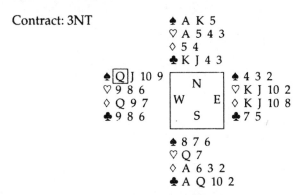

```
                    ♠ A K 5
                    ♡ A 5 4 3
                    ◊ 5 4
                    ♣ K J 4 3
      ♠ Q J 10 9                    ♠ 4 3 2
      ♡ 9 8 6          N            ♡ K J 10 2
      ◊ Q 9 7      W       E        ◊ K J 10 8
      ♣ 9 8 6          S            ♣ 7 5
                    ♠ 8 7 6
                    ♡ Q 7
                    ◊ A 6 3 2
                    ♣ A Q 10 2
```

S We need nine tricks to make 3NT.

T We have eight winners: two spades, one heart, one diamond and four clubs. Only one more trick needs to be developed.

O There is a finesse against the ♡K although it doesn't look the same as those in the earlier hands. This time, the ace and the queen are in two different hands. Nevertheless, when we are in the dummy, we plan to lead a small heart towards the ♡Q, the card which we hope will take a trick. If East has the ♡K then we will get a trick with the ♡Q. Otherwise, too bad! There is nothing better to do on this hand.

P So here goes. We win the first trick in dummy and lead a small heart. Whether East plays his ♡K on this trick or not, we have two heart tricks and nine in all.

CHAPTER 20

The Power of High Cards

It is never too early or too late to learn to play bridge.

When playing a hand, you often look to the four honours in each suit – the ace, king, queen and jack – to take tricks. If, however, you see these cards only in the light of their ability to take a single trick, you are underestimating their importance. Let's first consider the ace. Certainly it is usually good for taking a trick. But did you know that it has the power to prevent the opponents from taking their winners? Or to enable you, the declarer, to be in the right place at the right time in order to take winners. The ace, and your other high cards, are valuable members of your team.

Using high cards to prevent the opponents from taking winners

A high card in a suit only wins a trick if you manage to play it. Taking winners consists not only of developing the winners in the first place but also of being in the right place at the right time. Consider this layout of the diamond suit. You are in a no-trump contract and West leads the ◊K.

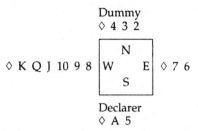

Dummy
◇ 4 3 2

◇ K Q J 10 9 8   ◇ 7 6

Declarer
◇ A 5

It looks as if you have only one trick in the suit, which you can win with the ◇A. The opponents, on the other hand, have established five winners after your ◇A is played. At first glance, there may seem to be nothing you can do about the situation. But remember, winners are only good if you have a way to get to them. It is true that your ace has the power to take only one trick. Another way of looking at the situation, however, is to consider not only the trick-taking power of the card but the way it can control a suit. Played at the right time, it may prevent the opponents from taking all five of their diamond tricks. Timing is everything.

Suppose you play your ◇A on the ◇K. Unless you can immediately take enough tricks to make your contract, you will have to give the lead to the opponents while you are developing the winners you need. If West gets the lead, he will take his diamond winners. If East gets the lead, he will be able to lead his remaining small diamond to West's promoted winners. Either way, the opponents take five diamond tricks. What can you do to prevent this?

Suppose you don't play your ◇A until the second trick. The defenders will have collected one diamond trick. What has changed? You still may have to give up the lead to the opponents. This time, however, if it is East who gets the lead, he will have no diamonds left to lead back to West's winners. Of course, West may have an entry in another suit, or it may be West that gets the lead when you are developing the winners you need. Too bad. At least you gave yourself the best chance. By holding up your ace until the second round, you may hold the opponents to only one trick in the diamond suit.

Let's look at this idea in a complete hand. You are in 3NT and the opening lead is the ◇K.

Contract: 3NT

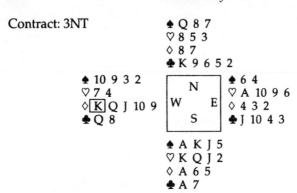

```
                    ♠ Q 8 7
                    ♡ 8 5 3
                    ◊ 8 7
                    ♣ K 9 6 5 2
  ♠ 10 9 3 2                        ♠ 6 4
  ♡ 7 4            N                ♡ A 10 9 6
  ◊ K Q J 10 9   W   E              ◊ 4 3 2
  ♣ Q 8            S                ♣ J 10 4 3
                    ♠ A K J 5
                    ♡ K Q J 2
                    ◊ A 6 5
                    ♣ A 7
```

You need to take nine tricks to make your contract of 3NT. Count
your winners: four spades, one diamond and two clubs, a total of
seven. Two more winners need to be developed and the heart suit
offers a good opportunity to promote the winners you need.
Organize your plan. If you plan to take the ◊A on the first trick and
try to develop your heart winners, whichever defender wins the
♡A will be able to lead a diamond and the defenders can take all
their diamond winners. On the actual hand, West has four promoted winners and the defenders defeat your contract.

We need to organize a plan with more chance of success. This
time, let West win the first two diamond tricks, and take the third
round of diamonds with the ◊A. After three rounds of diamonds
have been played you have lost only two tricks. Now, try to promote your heart winners. East takes the trick with the ♡A, you
can't prevent that. However, on the actual hand, East has no diamonds left to get back into West's hand and has to lead another
suit. Whether East chooses spades, hearts or clubs, you are ready
to take your nine tricks.

Are we just lucky that East has the ♡A and no diamonds left?
Not really. The opponents have eight cards in the diamond suit
and you would expect them to be divided 5–3. If East had a diamond left to lead back when he won the ♡A, they would have
originally been divided 4–4 and the opponents would only end up
with three diamond tricks and one heart trick. You would still
make the contract. At any rate, if West holds the ♡A along with a
five-card diamond suit, there is nothing you can do to make your

contract. You gave it the best chance.

When you choose to play low on a trick when you could win it, it is called a *holdup play*. The ace is not the only card you can use when making a holdup play. After the ace has been played, the king, the next highest card, takes over the ace's position and its importance. In the previous example, we saw that, by holding up the ace, you can prevent the defenders from getting to their promoted winners. When the ace has been played, holding up the king can have the same effect. Consider this layout. You are in 3NT and West leads a small diamond, the ◊7:

Dummy
◊ 4 3

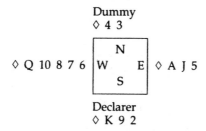

◊ Q 10 8 7 6   W   E   ◊ A J 5

Declarer
◊ K 9 2

You play a small card from the dummy, East takes the first trick with the ◊A, and leads another diamond. After the ◊A has been played, your ◊K is the highest outstanding card in the suit. If you take it on the second round, diamonds will have been played twice, with one trick won by the defenders and one trick by you. The layout of the suit would now be the following:

Dummy
◊ –

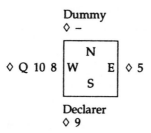

◊ Q 10 8   W   E   ◊ 5

Declarer
◊ 9

You have the lead and, unless you are taking the next eight tricks, enough to make your contract, you will have to give the lead to the opponents while developing the extra winners you need. Whether East or West gets the lead, the defenders are ready to take three diamond tricks.

Suppose, on the second round of the suit, you hold up your ◊K. East can play the suit again and, on the third round, you take ◊K. Now diamonds have been played three times. You have taken one trick with the ◊K and the opponents have taken two tricks. The layout of the suit is now:

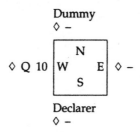

Although West has two established winners, they are of no value if East gets the lead. He has to lead another suit and with luck, you are then in a position to take enough tricks to make your contract. This isn't a guaranteed method of making your contract, but it does give you some chance.

Notice the difference between the above situation and this layout:

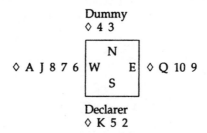

If West leads a small diamond and East puts on the ◊Q, your ◊K does not have the power of the ace because the ◊A has not been played. This is not the time to hold up your king. You will have to take it – to avoid the possibility of losing the first five diamond tricks – and hope you can develop the tricks you need without giving up the lead to the opponents.

Using high cards as entries

High cards can provide a means of transport from one side of the table to another. Why is this important? Not only do you need entries to get to your promoted or established winners, you also need them to be able to try finesses. In order to lead towards the card you hope will take a trick, you have to be in the hand opposite the high card – and that requires an entry. You also need to be on the right side of the table to trump losers in the dummy or to throw away a loser in the declarer's hand on the dummy's extra strength.

High cards as entries to small cards in long suits

Long suits provide an excellent opportunity to develop the extra tricks to make your contract. When a small card is part of a long suit, it can be developed into a winner. Usually, your long suits have one or two honour cards and these have to be carefully handled, being played at the right time in order to take best advantage of them. Let's first consider a suit which has length in the dummy but no outside card to get to any established winners. That means that the dummy's high card in the suit has to be carefully handled.

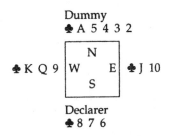

Dummy
♣ A 5 4 3 2

♣ K Q 9   N   ♣ J 10
          W   E
          S

Declarer
♣ 8 7 6

The ♣A will take one trick in the club suit. You want to be more ambitious than expecting only one trick from this suit, however. You are hoping the five cards that the opponents have are distributed as in the layout, 3–2. You can get one trick with the ♣A, lose two tricks to the opponents and thereby establish the two remaining clubs in the dummy as winners – provided you can get to them. The ♣A provides not only a trick, but also your means of transport to the established winners. If you play the ♣A on the first or second trick, you have no way of getting the winners. On the other hand, if you lose two tricks and then take your ♣A on the third round, you are not only winning the trick you expected with the ♣A, but you have taken it at the right time, after your small cards are established. In total, you take three tricks in the suit.

High cards as entries to promoted winners

When you are promoting winners in one suit, you often need an entry in another suit to get to the promoted winners. Sometimes, when you have both an ace and a king in a side suit, you might think that the order in which you play these high cards doesn't matter. Nothing could be further from the truth. The order is usually very important. In order to emphasize this point, let's consider an entire hand. Your are in a contract of 3NT and West leads the ◊Q. Since you have both the ◊A and the ◊K, you have a choice of which card you play on the first trick. Which honour would you use to take the first trick?

Contract: 3NT

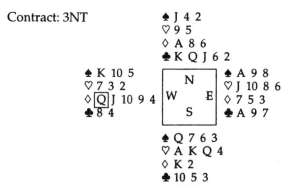

You need nine tricks to make the contract. You have three sure heart tricks, and two diamonds, a total of five tricks. Four more need to be developed and the club suit offers excellent potential. After the ♣A is driven out, you will have promoted the four tricks you need to make your contract. East will probably make things as difficult as possible by holding up the ♣A until the third round.

You will have taken two tricks in the suit, and will have lost one. Your two clubs in the dummy are promoted as winners. All you have to do is get to them. Which diamond did you play on the first trick? Let's hope you played the ◊K from your hand, leaving the ◊A in the dummy as an entry to your promoted clubs. You can see on this hand that the diamonds not only took two tricks but provided the potential for two extra tricks in another suit.

Using your high cards to take a finesse

Take a look at this layout:

Dummy
♠ 8 7

Declarer
♠ A Q

The ♠A and ♠Q will take only one trick overall if you lead them from your hand. On the other hand, if you lead a low spade from the dummy towards the ace-queen combination, there is the potential for two tricks in the suit: one with the ♠A and one with the ♠Q. It isn't a 100 per cent chance, but it is a 50 per cent chance and that is worth trying if that is the only way of getting the extra trick you need. In order to take a trick with the ♠Q you have to start from the dummy. You therefore need an entry to the dummy.

We will discuss the play of trump contracts in detail in the next section of the book, but here are some examples of the power of high cards in trump contracts.

The following hand shows how carefully your entries have to be used. The contract is 4 ♡ and the opening lead is the ◊2:

Contract: 4♡

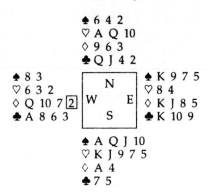

♠ 6 4 2
♡ A Q 10
◇ 9 6 3
♣ Q J 4 2

♠ 8 3   ♠ K 9 7 5
♡ 6 3 2   ♡ 8 4
◇ Q 10 7 2   ◇ K J 8 5
♣ A 8 6 3   ♣ K 10 9

♠ A Q J 10
♡ K J 9 7 5
◇ A 4
♣ 7 5

You can afford only three losers and it looks as though you will
have to lose a diamond trick and two club tricks. So you cannot
afford to lose a spade trick, even though you are missing the ♠K.
You will have to hope that East has the ♠K and you can take
repeated finesses through him to avoid losing a spade trick. What
are you going to use for entries to the dummy? Only the trump suit
will provide the entries you need. Since you may have to repeat
the finesse three times, you will have to combine carefully drawing trumps with leading spades from the dummy at every opportunity.

After winning the first diamond trick, play a heart to one of the
dummy's high cards and lead a small spade towards your hand.
Assuming East follows with a small spade, finesse the ♠10 (or ♠J or
♠Q). When this wins, cross back to the dummy with another heart
and lead another low spade, repeating the finesse. As you cross to
the dummy for a third time, you draw the last trump and end up
in the right place to lead your final small spade from the dummy
and take one more finesse. Only by careful use of each of the
dummy's high hearts can you make the contract.

Using high cards as entries for getting rid of losers

Let's see how important our high cards are in helping to be in the
right hand when trumping losers in the dummy. The contract is
6♠ and the lead is the ♠3:

Contract: 6♠

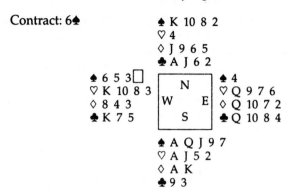

```
              ♠ K 10 8 2
              ♡ 4
              ◊ J 9 6 5
              ♣ A J 6 2
♠ 6 5 3                          ♠ 4
♡ K 10 8 3      N                ♡ Q 9 7 6
◊ 8 4 3      W     E              ◊ Q 10 7 2
♣ K 7 5         S                ♣ Q 10 8 4
              ♠ A Q J 9 7
              ♡ A J 5 2
              ◊ A K
              ♣ 9 3
```

To make your slam, you can only afford one loser. There are three heart losers and a club loser to worry about and, since there is not much you can do about the club loser, you plan to trump the heart losers in the dummy. West's trump lead, removing one of the dummy's trumps, has not helped your cause. You cannot afford to use your trumps as entries or let the opponents in to lead another trump, as that would leave you with too few trumps in the dummy. Instead, win the trump lead and immediately play the ♡A and trump a heart in the dummy. Cross to the ◊A and trump another heart in the dummy. Come back to the ◊K and trump your last heart in the dummy. The only loser you are left with is a club and you end up making the contract.

Finally, let's look at a hand where you need to discard a loser:

Contract: 4♠

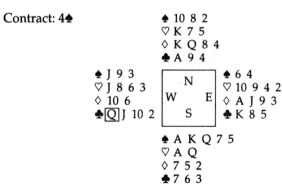

```
              ♠ 10 8 2
              ♡ K 7 5
              ◊ K Q 8 4
              ♣ A 9 4
♠ J 9 3                          ♠ 6 4
♡ J 8 6 3       N                ♡ 10 9 4 2
◊ 10 6       W     E             ◊ A J 9 3
♣ Q J 10 2      S                ♣ K 8 5
              ♠ A K Q 7 5
              ♡ A Q
              ◊ 7 5 2
              ♣ 7 6 3
```

In 4 ♠, you can afford three losers. Provided the missing trumps are divided 3–2, you will not have to lose a spade trick, but you will have two losers in diamonds and in clubs. If West has the ◇A, you can lead twice towards the dummy's ◇K and ◇Q to lose only one diamond trick. But, if the ◇A is with East, you will have to find another way to take care of your second diamond loser. The heart suit provides an opportunity to discard one of your losers, but you will have to plan the play carefully since the club lead has driven out the dummy's only quick entry. Win the ♣A, draw trumps, and then play the ♡A and ♡Q. Now you can lead a diamond to create an entry to the dummy's ♡K. Once you get to the dummy with the ◇K or ◇Q, discard your remaining diamond loser on the ♡K.

Your high cards are important not only for the tricks they can take but for the influence they have in enabling you to take the tricks you have worked to develop and to prevent the opponents from taking the tricks they have developed.

Summary

The high cards in the deck are a good source for taking tricks. They have other powers. By using the holdup play, you can prevent the opponents from taking good tricks because your holdup has prevented them from getting to their winners. When you have the tricks you need, you have to get to them and the high cards provide a means of transport to get from one side of the table to another. This is important not only in taking your high cards but in developing the extra tricks you need through promotion, length in a suit and the finesse which can be used in either no-trump or suit contracts. The high cards are also important entries when you are getting rid of your losers by either trumping in the dummy or throwing away losers on the dummy's extra strength.

Over Zia's shoulder

Hand 1 Dealer: North

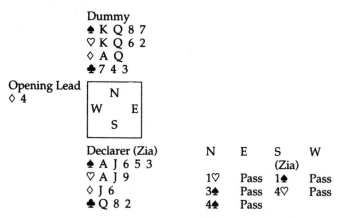

Dummy
♠ K Q 8 7
♡ K Q 6 2
◇ A Q
♣ 7 4 3

Opening Lead
◇ 4

	N	E	S	W
Declarer (Zia)			(Zia)	
♠ A J 6 5 3				
♡ A J 9	1♡	Pass	1♠	Pass
◇ J 6	3♠	Pass	4♡	Pass
♣ Q 8 2	4♠	Pass		

What should we play on the first diamond trick? It is always tempting to take a finesse when we have been given the opportunity to take use of our high cards in this fashion. However, our high cards can be useful in other ways as well. Let's go through the plan before making our decision.

Solution to Hand 1:

Contract: 4♠

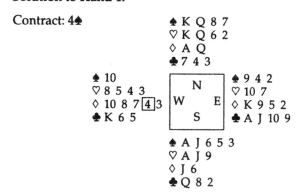

♠ K Q 8 7
♡ K Q 6 2
◇ A Q
♣ 7 4 3

♠ 10
♡ 8 5 4 3
◇ 10 8 7 4 3
♣ K 6 5

♠ 9 4 2
♡ 10 7
◇ K 9 5 2
♣ A J 10 9

♠ A J 6 5 3
♡ A J 9
◇ J 6
♣ Q 8 2

S We can afford only three losers in our contract of 4 ♠.
T We have a diamond loser and three club losers.

O We could try the diamond finesse, getting rid of our diamond loser if West holds the ◊K. Is there anything else? We have an extra heart winner in the dummy and we could use it to discard one of our club losers. Is there any danger in trying the finesse first and, if it does not work, later discarding one of our club losers? There certainly is! If the finesse loses, East will probably not be kind enough to give us the opportunity to discard a club loser. He will switch to clubs and the opponents will take their three club winners, defeating the contract.

P One of the extra powers of an ace is its ability to give us control of a suit by taking a trick at the right time. On this hand, we must take the ◊A right away, rather than yielding to the temptation of the finesse – which, as the cards lie, doesn't work out. We then draw the opponents' trumps and play our heart suit, eventually discarding one of our losers. Playing this way, we guarantee success, no matter which defender holds the ◊K.

Hand 2 Dealer: East

Dummy
♠ Q J 7
♡ 9 5
◊ K 10 8 7 5
♣ A K 8

Opening Lead
♡ 4

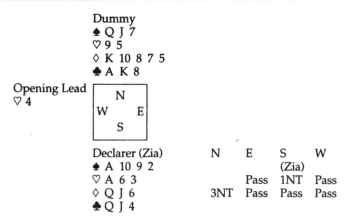

Declarer (Zia)
♠ A 10 9 2
♡ A 6 3
◊ Q J 6
♣ Q J 4

N	E	S	W
		(Zia)	
	Pass	1NT	Pass
3NT	Pass	Pass	Pass

It looks as though we have a choice of taking a spade finesse or driving out the ◊A to develop the extra tricks we need. Are there any other considerations?

Solution to Hand 2:

Contract: 3NT

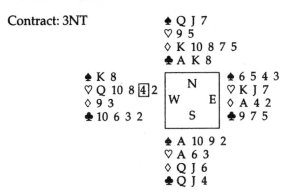

♠ Q J 7
♡ 9 5
◊ K 10 8 7 5
♣ A K 8

♠ K 8
♡ Q 10 8 4 2
◊ 9 3
♣ 10 6 3 2

♠ 6 5 4 3
♡ K J 7
◊ A 4 2
♣ 9 7 5

♠ A 10 9 2
♡ A 6 3
◊ Q J 6
♣ Q J 4

S We need to come up with nine tricks to make this contract.

T We have one sure spade trick, one heart trick and three club tricks, for a total of five.

O We need four more tricks. We could try leading the ♠Q or ♠J from the dummy, hoping to trap the ♠K in the East hand. That would give us three more tricks. Even if the finesse loses, we will have promoted two extra winners. The diamond suit, however, offers the opportunity to develop all four extra tricks, once the ◊A has been driven out. Is there anything else to worry about? West has attacked our weakness. Once our ♡A is gone, the opponents may be able to take enough heart tricks to defeat the contract when they get the lead with the ◊A. We had better make use of the holdup play.

P We let the opponents win the first heart trick, and the second heart trick. Only when they lead the third round of hearts do we win the trick with our ♡A. Now we lead the ◊Q and continue leading high diamonds until the ◊A is driven out. Luckily for us, it is East who holds the ◊A and, thanks to our holdup play, he has no hearts left to lead. If he leads a spade, we quickly take the ♠A and run for home with our nine tricks. There is no point in risking the spade finesse. If it loses, we would let West – the opponent with the established heart winners – get the lead. We'll take our sure profit. On the actual layout, we would be defeated if we played the hand any other way.

Hand 3 Dealer: West

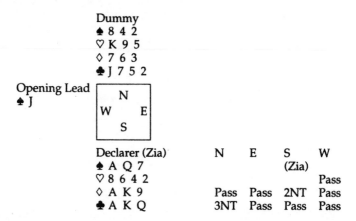

Dummy
♠ 8 4 2
♡ K 9 5
♢ 7 6 3
♣ J 7 5 2

Opening Lead
♠ J

Declarer (Zia)	N	E	S	W
♠ A Q 7			(Zia)	
♡ 8 6 4 2				Pass
♢ A K 9	Pass	Pass	2NT	Pass
♣ A K Q	3NT	Pass	Pass	Pass

It looks as though we may have some difficulty coming to nine tricks with these cards. West's opening lead has simplified things a little, since we are now assured of getting two spade tricks, whichever player has the ♠K. What's our plan?

Solution to Hand 3:

Contract: 3NT

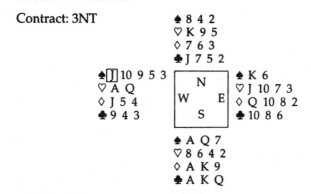

♠ 8 4 2
♡ K 9 5
♢ 7 6 3
♣ J 7 5 2

♠ J 10 9 5 3
♡ A Q
♢ J 5 4
♣ 9 4 3

♠ K 6
♡ J 10 7 3
♢ Q 10 8 2
♣ 10 8 6

♠ A Q 7
♡ 8 6 4 2
♢ A K 9
♣ A K Q

S We need to find nine winners.

T We have two sure spade tricks, the ♠A and ♠Q, since West has led a spade. We also have two sure diamond tricks and four sure club tricks. That's eight tricks to start with.

O The best place for a ninth trick is the heart suit. If West has the

♡A, we can get a trick by leading towards the dummy's ♡K. Are there any other problems? We are counting on four club tricks but we have to get to the dummy in order to take our fourth club trick and the dummy has no sure entry. We will have to make the ♡K do double work. Not only will it have to provide our ninth trick but it will also have to be our entry to the dummy. That means we will have to be careful about the order in which we play our cards.

P After winning the first spade trick, we'll have to play the ♣A, ♣K and ♣Q. Now we lead a small heart towards the dummy and hope. When West turns out to have the ♡A, our problems are over. We will get to the dummy with the ♡K and, while we are there, we can take a trick with the ♣J. Careful play lands us nine tricks.

CHAPTER 21

Principles of the Trump Suit

If you can't play well, play fast. You will never be short of partners if you follow this advice.

Playing in a suit contract is, in many ways, similar to playing in a no-trump contract. The first step is to make a plan before playing a card to the first trick. When you compare your goal and your assets you may find you have all the tricks you need; all you have to do is to take them. As we saw in the first chapter, you still have to consider the best way of taking what you deserve. You may have to play a suit with more cards on one side than the other in the right order – the high card from the short side. You may have to remind yourself of your goal so that you are not tempted to jeopardize the contract in an attempt to get an extra trick which you don't need to make the contract. Other than that, it is quite straightforward. If you don't have the number of tricks you need, you could try to develop extra tricks by promoting winners in your solid sequences, by establishing the small cards in long suits, or by finessing against higher cards than you hold in a suit.

Playing in a suit contract, you also look to these tactics to develop extra tricks. Why then, you might ask, is there a separate section on play in a suit contract? We have seen that there are similarities between playing in no-trump and suit contracts. Let's now consider the differences.

Playing with a trump suit

The trump suit does have an effect on your priorities. You may have all the tricks you need, for example, and yet, if you don't play the trump suit first, you find one of your sure tricks might disappear to an opponent's small trump card. Here is an example. You are in a contract of 4 ♠ and the lead is the ♡K.

Contract: 4♣

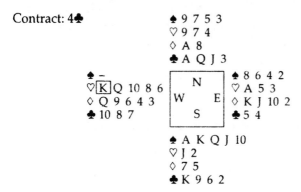

```
                    ♠ 9 7 5 3
                    ♡ 9 7 4
                    ◊ A 8
                    ♣ A Q J 3
   ♠ -                            ♠ 8 6 4 2
   ♡ K Q 10 8 6      N            ♡ A 5 3
   ◊ Q 9 6 4 3    W     E         ◊ K J 10 2
   ♣ 10 8 7          S            ♣ 5 4

                    ♠ A K Q J 10
                    ♡ J 2
                    ◊ 7 5
                    ♣ K 9 6 2
```

You need ten tricks to make your 4 ♠ contract. You have five tricks in spades, one in diamonds and four in clubs, enough to make the contract. All you have to do is to take your tricks. Consider your priorities, however, taking into consideration the power of the trump suit. You will lose the first two heart tricks, but can take the third trick by trumping the third round of hearts with the ♠10. What do you play next? If you decide to play the clubs, East can win the third round of clubs by trumping with a small spade. You had counted on taking all four clubs. You have given the opponents a chance to take a trick they didn't deserve. Now they can take the two hearts they started with, a diamond (after your ace is gone) and the small trump used to trump the third round of clubs.

If you have the number of tricks you need, you should *draw* the trumps first, by playing the trump suit until the opponents have none left. Don't give the opponents a chance to trump one of your winners. The trump suit does have an effect on the order in which you play the cards. In every hand you play in a trump contract, your first consideration is whether to play the trumps first or to delay playing trumps. We will go into this topic in more detail in Chapter 22.

Changing your point of view

The trump suit, as well as having an effect on the order in which you play your cards, affects the way you look at your hand. Before we consider the mechanics of tallying our losers, it is important to remember this difference between the way we plan trump contracts and the way we plan no-trump contracts. In no trumps, we count winners and look at ways to develop extra winners. In trumps, we count losers and look for ways to eliminate losers. It's all a matter of perspective.

Planning the play in a suit contract

Let's see how we use the letters S T O P to plan the play in a suit contract.

Stop to consider your goal

The first step in playing a hand in a trump contract is to consider your goal. How many losers can you afford and still make your contract? If you are in a contract of 4 ♡, you can afford three losers. In a contract of 6 ♢, you can afford only one loser.

Tally your losers

After you have stopped to consider your goal, the next step is to discover how close you are to getting there. Tally your losers. Focus on the declarer's hand and glance at the dummy to see if there is any help. At this point, you are not considering how to get rid of losers, only how to tally them. Consider this suit:

Dummy
♡ 8 4 3 2

```
      N
 W         E
      S
```

Declarer
♡ A K

How many losers do you have? None. Remember, you count losers from the *declarer's* point of view. Let's move the suit around:

Dummy
♡ A K

```
      N
 W         E
      S
```

Declarer
♡ 8 4 3 2

You appear to have four losers when you first look at your hand. By glancing at the dummy, however, you can see that the ♡A and the ♡K can take care of two of your losers. You are left with two losers in this suit. Now, consider this suit:

Dummy
♠ K Q 3

```
      N
 W         E
      S
```

Declarer
♠ J 10 2

You have three losers when you look only at your hand. Looking over at the dummy, and seeing the king and queen, you can see that you have only one loser, to your opponents' ♠A.

Organize your plan

It is an advantage to count losers against a suit contract because you can use the benefit of the trump suit to help get rid of some of your losers. When you compare the number of losers you can afford with the number you have and find that you have too many losers, you want to organize a way to get rid of your extra losers.

There are two methods of getting rid of your losers in a suit contract that are not available in a no-trump contract. These methods are developed in more detail in the next two chapters, but here is the general idea.

One way of getting rid of losers in your hand is to trump them in the dummy. Consider, for a moment, the spade and heart suits in the two hands below. Spades are the trump suit and the hearts are a *side suit*. The clubs and diamonds are represented by Xs since we are not focusing on them for the moment.

Dummy
♠ 4 3 2
♡ –
♢ x x x x x
♣ x x x x x

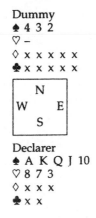

Declarer
♠ A K Q J 10
♡ 8 7 3
♢ x x x
♣ x x

If you were to count your winners in spades and hearts you would have five spade winners and no heart winners for a total of five tricks. Now let's look at the hand from the point of view of how many losers you have in each suit. Focus on the declarer's hand. You have no losers in the spade suit and three losers in the heart suit.

There would be no advantage in counting losers if there was nothing you could do about them. But you have a way of getting rid of your heart losers. You can use the three trump cards in the dummy to trump each of the heart losers in your hand and end up with eight tricks, or no losers. We will look further at this idea in the next chapter but, for now, you can see that by focusing on your losers in the above hand, you may be able to find a way to eliminate them to help make your contract.

If you were to focus on your losers in a no-trump contract – although you would not want to be playing in no trumps with the void in hearts on the above hand – there would be nothing you could do about your three heart losers. Not only that, but you might lose a lot more than three tricks in the suit since the opponents have ten hearts between them.

The second way that the declarer can get rid of the losers in his hand is to throw them on the dummy's extra winners. Again, you are looking for an unevenly divided side suit but, this time, instead of having fewer cards in the dummy than in your hand, you want to have more cards in the dummy than in your hand. Look at these hands where spades are the trump suit. This time, we'll focus on the clubs and diamonds:

Dummy
♠ x x x
♡ x x x x
◊ K 8 7
♣ A K Q

Declarer
♠ x x x x x
♡ x x x
◊ A 4 2
♣ 9 5

There is one diamond loser and no club losers. The clubs are unevenly divided between your hand and the dummy. On the third round of clubs you will have no clubs left to play and can discard another suit. You can throw away your diamond loser. Now, on the third round of diamonds, instead of giving the trick to the opponents, you can trump it, eliminating your loser.

Put your plan into operation

Once you have considered the number of losers you can afford,
the number you have, and what you can do to diminish the losers
you cannot afford, you are ready to play the hand. As in a no-
trump contract, you never play your first card until you have gone
through the steps of the plan.

Putting it into practice

Let's use the plan on the following hand. The contract is 4 ♡ and
the opening lead is the ♣K:

Contract: 4♡

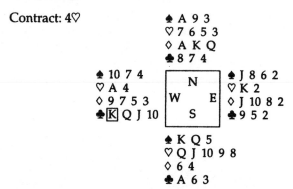

Before playing your first card, go through the plan. Since the final
contract is 4 ♡, the goal is to lose no more than three tricks. Next,
total the number of losers you have. There are two heart losers, the
♡A and ♡K and, after the ♣A is played, you have two club losers
left in your hand. That's four in total, one more than you can
afford. If you were playing in a contract of 3NT and were counting
losers, there would be nothing you could do to get rid of them.
You would have to lose the ♡A and ♡K along with three club tricks
after your ♣A has been driven out, a total of five tricks for the
defenders.

It is different in a trump contract. Because of the trump suit,
there are ways of getting rid of the losers. Taking this hand as an
example, focus on the club suit. You have three clubs on each side
of the table. If you could get rid of one of the clubs on either side,

you could trump the third round of clubs. There is extra help in the dummy in the diamond suit. On this hand, you could play your diamonds and, on the third round, throw a small club from your hand. Now, when the opponents try to take their club winners, you can trump the third round and lose only one club trick.

Timing is very important here. If you play the trumps first, the opponents will get the lead and take their two club tricks to go along with their two top hearts to defeat the contract. Therefore, you have to get rid of the club loser on the extra diamond winner in the dummy before you give up the lead to the opponents. Once the club loser is eliminated, then you can play trumps.

You can see that the decision to draw the trumps right away or to wait until later in the hand depends upon your plan. You have to know how many losers you have and, more than that, you have to know the character of your losers. Are they immediate or slow? In the hand we just looked at, your losers were immediate and you had to get rid of them before you gave the lead up to the opponents. Since drawing trumps would have given them the lead, that had to take second priority.

How can you know, then, when to draw trumps right away and when to delay drawing trumps? We will look in more detail at your options in Chapter 22 but, for now, make your plan before playing the first card so that you know the number of losers you can afford and the number that you actually have. If you have too many losers, you may be able to get rid of one on an extra winner in the dummy, as we saw on this hand.

Summary

The trump suit has an effect on the way you play a hand of bridge. Because of this, when you make your plan, focus on losers rather than winners. Stop to consider how many losers you can afford; that is your goal. Tally your losers, telling you how close you are to reaching your goal. Organize your plan. If you have the number of losers you can afford, start by drawing the opponents' trumps. If you have too many losers, plan how to get rid of them and whether or not you can afford to draw trumps first. In a suit contract, in addition to all the techniques available in no trumps, you can trump losers in the dummy or throw them away on extra winners in the dummy. Finally, having decided on your plan, Put it into operation.

Over Zia's shoulder

Hand 1 Dealer: West

Dummy
♠ A 8 6
♡ J 10 3 2
◇ 10 9 6
♣ J 6 5

Opening Lead
♠ 9

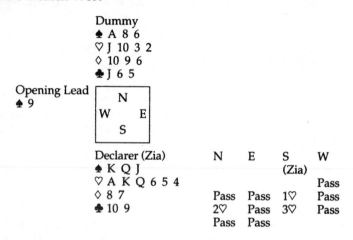

Declarer (Zia)
♠ K Q J
♡ A K Q 6 5 4
◇ 8 7
♣ 10 9

N	E	S (Zia)	W
			Pass
Pass	Pass	1♡	Pass
2♡	Pass	3♡	Pass
Pass	Pass		

Oops! I hope we haven't got too high by trying for a game. Well, we're playing a trump contract this time. We'll have to change our focus and look at the hand from the point of view of our losers.

Solution to Hand 1:

Contract: 3♡

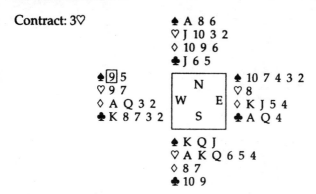

```
            ♠ A 8 6
            ♡ J 10 3 2
            ◊ 10 9 6
            ♣ J 6 5
  ♠ 9 5                      ♠ 10 7 4 3 2
  ♡ 9 7           N          ♡ 8
  ◊ A Q 3 2   W     E        ◊ K J 5 4
  ♣ K 8 7 3 2     S          ♣ A Q 4
            ♠ K Q J
            ♡ A K Q 6 5 4
            ◊ 8 7
            ♣ 10 9
```

S In a contract of 3 ♡, we can afford four losers.

T Our tally tells us that we have no losers in either spades or hearts, two in diamonds and two in clubs. That is exactly what we can afford.

O All we need to do is win the first trick and draw the opponents' trumps before they can trump any of our winners.

P Bridge is an easy game, isn't it? Did you notice how we still went through the steps of our plan before playing our first card?

Hand 2 Dealer: East

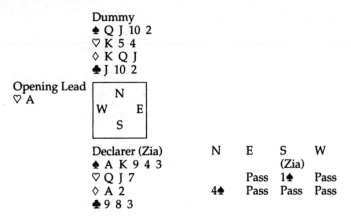

Dummy
♠ Q J 10 2
♡ K 5 4
◊ K Q J
♣ J 10 2

Opening Lead
♡ A

Declarer (Zia)
♠ A K 9 4 3
♡ Q J 7
◊ A 2
♣ 9 8 3

N	E	S	W
		(Zia)	
	Pass	1♠	Pass
4♠	Pass	Pass	Pass

West leads the ♡A and another heart. What's happened here? West seems to have made a mistake. It looks as if we had three clubs and one heart loser but now we have a chance. How do we continue?

Solution to Hand 2:

Contract: 4♠

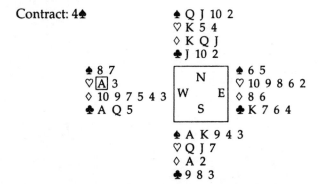

♠ Q J 10 2
♡ K 5 4
◊ K Q J
♣ J 10 2

♠ 8 7
♡ A 3
◊ 10 9 7 5 4 3
♣ A Q 5

♠ 6 5
♡ 10 9 8 6 2
◊ 8 6
♣ K 7 6 4

♠ A K 9 4 3
♡ Q J 7
◊ A 2
♣ 9 8 3

It is tempting to start to play immediately, having had a reprieve, to get rid of those losing clubs before the defence change their mind and decide to take their winners. But let's pause and look at our plan.

S We can afford three losers.

T We have one heart loser and three club losers, one too many.

O When we plan how to eliminate a loser we see that we have an opportunity to get rid of a club loser on one of the extra diamond tricks in the dummy. When you are in a trump contract, unless the trumps are needed for some other purpose, the number one priority is to draw the trumps. You don't have to give up the lead to draw trumps on this hand, so it is safe to do so. After you have drawn the trumps, then you can discard your club loser.

P Only after making your complete plan do you put it into operation. Notice that, if we had tried to play the diamonds first, East would have trumped the third round of diamonds. West was also waiting to trump the third round of hearts. By drawing trumps first, you didn't give the opponents the chance to take tricks with their small trump cards.

Hand 3 Dealer: North

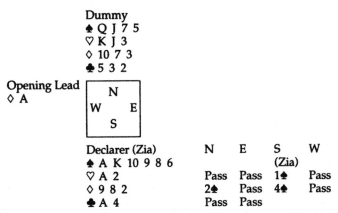

```
                    Dummy
                    ♠ Q J 7 5
                    ♡ K J 3
                    ◇ 10 7 3
                    ♣ 5 3 2

Opening Lead    ┌─────────┐
◇ A             │    N    │
                │ W     E │
                │    S    │
                └─────────┘

                    Declarer (Zia)      N      E      S       W
                    ♠ A K 10 9 8 6                   (Zia)
                    ♡ A 2               Pass   Pass   1♠      Pass
                    ◇ 9 8 2             2♠     Pass   4♠      Pass
                    ♣ A 4              Pass   Pass
```

It looks as if we have our work cut out for us on this hand since the opponents are about to take the first three diamond tricks and we still have a club loser. Is there any hope?

Solution to Hand 3:

Contract: 4♠

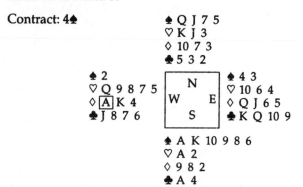

       ♠ Q J 7 5
       ♡ K J 3
       ◊ 10 7 3
       ♣ 5 3 2

♠ 2   ♠ 4 3
♡ Q 9 8 7 5   ♡ 10 6 4
◊ A K 4   ◊ Q J 6 5
♣ J 8 7 6   ♣ K Q 10 9

       ♠ A K 10 9 8 6
       ♡ A 2
       ◊ 9 8 2
       ♣ A 4

S   In 4 ♠, we can only afford to lose three tricks.

T   The opponents take the first three diamond tricks and we might yet lose another trick, a club. That would be one too many.

O   What can we do about our club loser? We can't trump it in dummy since the dummy has more clubs than we do. How about discarding it on an extra winner in the dummy? At the moment, there is no extra winner in the dummy but the hearts do offer some possibility. There is a 50 per cent chance that either opponent has a particular outstanding card and, if West has the ♡Q on this hand, we can get an extra trick by leading towards the dummy and finessing the ♡J. That would give us three heart tricks and we could dispose of our club loser. If the ♡Q is held by East, we won't make our contract. In fact, we'll probably be defeated by two tricks. But it is a small price to pay with a game on the line. They say you only live once.

P   After the opponents take their three diamond tricks, suppose they lead a club. Win the ♣A and draw the outstanding trumps. Note that you can afford to draw the trumps first because you do not have to give up the lead while doing so. Now, it's time for the ♡A and the ♡2 towards the dummy. When West follows with a small heart, we play the dummy's ♡J and keep our fingers crossed.

CHAPTER 22

Trumping Losers

Remember that your partner is on your side.

The delightful aspect of counting losers is that there is a chance to get rid of them. In this chapter, we will focus on using the trumps in the dummy to get rid of losers in the declarer's hand. You can go through four simple steps when planning to get rid of losers in your hand by trumping them in the dummy. First, you have to recognize the hand patterns where the opportunity exists. Second, the trumps in the dummy have to be carefully handled. Third, you have to know that you might have to play the suit more than once, perhaps giving up the lead while doing it. Finally, you have to arrange transport, or entries, to your hand so that you are in a position to put the plan into action. Let's look at each of these steps in turn.

Recognising hand patterns

It is important to spot the characteristics in your hand and the dummy that offer the opportunity to trump losers in the dummy. The first step is to select a side suit in which there are more cards in your hand than there are in the dummy. Consider this hand. You are in a contract of 4 ♠ and the lead is the ♣Q:

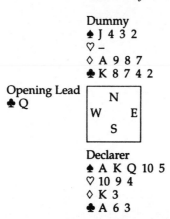

Dummy
♠ J 4 3 2
♡ –
◊ A 9 8 7
♣ K 8 7 4 2

Opening Lead
♣ Q

N
W   E
S

Declarer
♠ A K Q 10 5
♡ 10 9 4
◊ K 3
♣ A 6 3

There are more hearts in your hand than there are in the dummy
and so the heart suit offers a chance to get rid of losers by trumping them in the dummy. You can play a heart from your hand and,
since the dummy is void, you can trump it. Then you can come
back to your hand in another suit and again lead a heart, which
you trump in dummy. If you come back to your hand a third time
and play your final heart which you trump in the dummy, you will
have disposed of all of your heart losers in your hand by trumping
them in the dummy. The sequence of plays would be:
Win the first trick with the ♣A. Lead the ♡4 and trump with the ♠2.
Play a diamond to your ◊K. Trump the ♡9 with the ♠3. Play a
spade to your ♠10. Trump the ♡10 with the ♠J. Cash the ◊A and
trump a diamond. Now – and only now – are you in a position to
draw trumps! It is an important principle that if you intend to
trump losers in the dummy, you must have enough trumps to do
this, which may mean that you have to put off the drawing of
trumps until quite late in the hand.

Here are three other possible layouts for the heart suit. Which
ones offer a chance to trump a loser in the dummy?

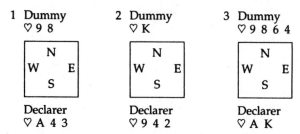

1 Dummy
♡ 9 8

2 Dummy
♡ K

3 Dummy
♡ 9 8 6 4

Declarer
♡ A 4 3

Declarer
♡ 9 4 2

Declarer
♡ A K

In the first example, you have three cards in your hand and only two in the dummy, so there is an opportunity to trump a loser in the dummy. In the second example, there are again more hearts in your hand than there are in the dummy, so you have the chance to trump losers in the dummy. In the third example, however, there are more hearts in the dummy than there are in your hand. This is not the pattern that gives you a chance to trump losers in the dummy.

Handling the trumps in the dummy

It seems obvious, but the only way you can trump losers in the dummy is to have some trumps in the dummy to do the job. If you have a lot of trumps in the dummy, this will usually not present a problem. On many hands, however, your trumps have to be carefully handled in order to preserve the number of the dummy's trumps you need to take care of the losers in your hand. Consider the following example. We'll focus on only two suits: the trump suit, spades, and a side suit, hearts.

Dummy
♠ 4 3
♡ –
♦ x x x x x
♣ x x x x x x

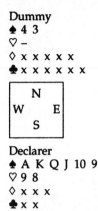

Declarer
♠ A K Q J 10 9
♡ 9 8
♦ x x x
♣ x x

Count the losers in hearts and spades, concentrating on your hand. There are no losers in spades and there are two losers in hearts. Since the dummy has no hearts, the small trump cards can be used to take care of your heart losers. Now, decide how many trumps you will need to take care of your losers. In this example, you need both of the trumps in the dummy. You cannot draw even one round of trumps. Your first priority has to be to get rid of your heart losers.

You plan to play a heart from your hand and trump it in the dummy. That will eliminate one heart loser and use up one of dummy's trump cards. You then need to get back to your hand to repeat the process, but you cannot do it with a spade. The remaining spade in the dummy is needed to take care of your second heart loser. You can't have your cake and eat it too. You will have to find another way to get back into your hand. Let's assume that you have an entry in another suit enabling you to get back to your hand. You can then play your remaining heart and trump it in the dummy.

By using your trump cards in the dummy separately, you get rid of both losers. You end up taking eight tricks – the six high spades in your hand will all take tricks and you get two tricks with the small spades in the dummy. Notice that you trumped losers in the dummy, not in your hand, in order to get the extra tricks. How many trumps would you need in the dummy to take care of the losers in your hand in each of the following side suits?

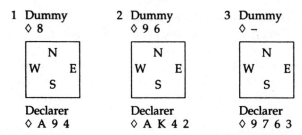

1 **Dummy**
◊ 8

2 **Dummy**
◊ 9 6

3 **Dummy**
◊ –

Declarer
◊ A 9 4

Declarer
◊ A K 4 2

Declarer
◊ 9 7 6 3

In the first example, you have two more cards in the diamond suit in your hand than you have in the dummy so you would need two of dummy's trumps to take care of the losers. In the next example, you have two more cards in your hand than in the dummy and so again you would need two of the dummy's trumps to take care of the losers. In the final example, you would need four of the dummy's trumps to take care of all four of your losers. You can see that you may not always have enough trumps to do the job. In the next chapter, we'll look at another way of getting rid of losers in case you can't trump them in the dummy.

Trumping in the declarer's hand

Let's change the layout of the suits from our earlier example:

Dummy
♠ 4 3
♡ 7 6 5
◊ x x x x
♣ x x x x

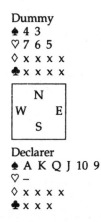

Declarer
♠ A K Q J 10 9
♡ –
◊ x x x x
♣ x x x

In your hand, you have no losers in spades or hearts. If you were to play a heart from the dummy and trump it in your hand, you would gain nothing since you would be using a trump which would be a winner in any case. You only gain tricks when you are able to trump losers in the hand with the shorter trumps, which are usually in the dummy. You can avoid thinking you are getting extra tricks by trumping in the long side, in this case in your hand, by focusing on the hand pattern. Since you do not have more cards in the heart suit in your hand than are in the dummy, this is not the pattern you are looking for. Look for hand patterns in which the declarer has more cards in a side suit than there are in the dummy.

Getting ready to trump losers in the dummy

It is convenient to have a void in the dummy when you are planning to trump losers, but this won't always be the case. Sometimes you have to do a little work to create the void in dummy. Again, let's focus on a hand where spades are trumps and hearts are one of your side suits:

Dummy
♠ 4 3 2
♡ 7
◊ x x x x
♣ x x x x x

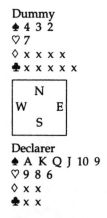

Declarer
♠ A K Q J 10 9
♡ 9 8 6
◊ x x
♣ x x

You have no spade losers and three heart losers. When you look to the dummy, you can see an opportunity to get rid of two, not three, of your heart losers by trumping them. You will need two spades in the dummy to trump your losing hearts. You will also have to lose a heart trick before the dummy has a heart void and you are in a position to trump your losers.

What are your priorities? How are you going to handle your trumps? Should you draw one round of trumps? You only need two spades to take care of your losing hearts. Look at what might happen if you decide to draw one round of trumps. You are still left with two spades in the dummy, which may seem to be enough . . . if you didn't have opponents. When you give up a heart trick to the opponents, they may lead a spade, leaving you with only one spade in the dummy and two heart losers in your hand.

Don't take that chance. Your first consideration is to get rid of your heart losers, so first play the heart suit right away. The opponents may lead a spade but you can win the trick and still have two spades left in the dummy. Play a heart and trump it. Come back to your hand in another suit and play your third heart and trump it. You will take the six trump tricks in your hand and two trumps in the dummy which you used on your heart suit. Now, let's take this idea one step further.

Dummy
♠ 4 3 2
♡ 7 5
◊ x x x x
♣ x x x x

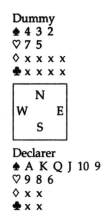

Declarer
♠ A K Q J 10 9
♡ 9 8 6
◊ x x
♣ x x

Again, you have three heart losers in your hand. Is there any opportunity to get rid of them? You could get rid of one heart loser after the two hearts have been played from the dummy. How many trumps do you need? Only one. Whenever you are in a trump contract, the priority of drawing the opponents' trump cards should be on your mind. Should this be a priority in this hand? After all, you need only one trump card this time to take care of the heart loser.

Consider what would happen if you drew even one round of trumps. You would have only two spades left in the dummy and you have to give up the lead twice before you are in a position to trump your heart loser. On both occasions when the opponents get the lead, they could play a trump, removing your last two trump cards before you could use one of them on your heart loser. It is important, then, to play a heart before touching the trumps, even once. If the defenders lead trumps each time they get the lead, they will only be able to take two rounds and you would still have one left to take care of your final heart.

The opportunity to trump a loser in the dummy exists whenever the declarer has more cards in the suit than the dummy. If the declarer has cards in the suit and the dummy has a void, there is an immediate opportunity to trump losers. Most of the time, however, the declarer has to play the suit, once, twice or more, in order to create the void so that one of the dummy's small trumps can be used. Let's look at a complete hand. You are in a part-score contract of 2 ♠ and the opening lead is the ♡4.

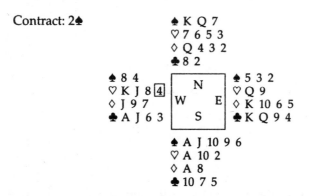

Contract: 2♠

♠ K Q 7
♡ 7 6 5 3
◇ Q 4 3 2
♣ 8 2

♠ 8 4   ♠ 5 3 2
♡ K J 8 4   ♡ Q 9
◇ J 9 7   ◇ K 10 6 5
♣ A J 6 3   ♣ K Q 9 4

♠ A J 10 9 6
♡ A 10 2
◇ A 8
♣ 10 7 5

Let's go through the plan. First our goal. In a contract of 2 ♠, we can afford five losers. We tally our losers. There is none in spades, two in hearts, one in diamonds and three in clubs. That totals six losers, one too many. The next step is to consider how we can eliminate one of our losers. The ♡4 is led and after our ♡A is gone, we have two losers. There does not seem to be the opportunity to get rid of a heart loser. Consider the diamonds. There are only two in our hand. Perhaps the queen in the dummy could win a trick but, as you can see on the actual layout of the cards, the ◊K could be held by East. It would do no good to trump one of the dummy's diamonds in our hand since that would not eliminate any losers. The pattern we are looking for is to have more cards in a side suit in our hand than we do in the dummy. In the diamond suit we have more cards in the dummy than we do in our hand. That leads us, finally, to the club suit.

Since there are more clubs in your hand than there are in the dummy, there is the opportunity to trump a club. First, however, you have to play two rounds of the suit so that there is a void in the dummy. Each time you give up the lead to the opponents while you are creating this void in the dummy, they can lead a spade. Since you have to give up the lead twice, they are able to play spades twice, leaving you with one left in the dummy. Notice that if you drew even one round of spades, you would run out of the trumps in the dummy needed to take care of the club loser. On this hand, your first priority is to play the clubs after winning the ♡A.

Preserving your entries

On to the last step to consider when trumping losers. You have seen that, in order to trump a loser in the dummy, you have to be in your hand to lead the loser that you plan to trump. This means that you may have to preserve entries back to your hand. First, look at the layout of this side suit:

Dummy
♣ K 4

Declarer
♣ A 6 3

You have more cards in the suit in your hand than in the dummy, so you have recognized the pattern for trumping losers in the dummy. You need one trump to take care of your losing club. You first have to play the clubs twice in order to get ready to trump in the dummy. Ask yourself which hand you would like to end up in after you have played two rounds of clubs. You want to end up in your hand, so that you can lead the third club and trump it in the dummy. So, win the first trick with the ♣K in the dummy and play the ♣4 back to your ♣A. Now you are in the right hand to play a third round of clubs.

Sometimes, the suit containing the losers may not provide the entry and you will have to look for an entry in another suit. You usually have a lot of high cards in the trump suit but you may not be able to use the trump suit since you need your trumps. Suppose you are planning to trump a loser in this suit:

Dummy
♣ 8 4

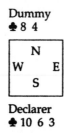

Declarer
♣ 10 6 3

The first two times you play this suit, it does not matter which side of the table you are on. After the suit has been played twice, however, you want to be in your hand to play the third round. You have to be careful to keep a high card in another side suit in your hand as a means of transport back to your hand.

Summary

The opportunity to trump losers in the dummy exists when the declarer has more cards in his hand in a side suit than in the dummy. You need to keep the appropriate number of trumps in the dummy to do the job. Sometimes the dummy has a void and the opportunity to trump a loser immediately exists. At other times, the declarer has to play the side suit once or twice until dummy has a void in the suit. The declarer has to keep an eye on the entries back to his hand and make sure there are enough to be able to get there so that he can lead the suit he wants to trump in the dummy.

Over Zia's shoulder

Hand 1 Dealer: South

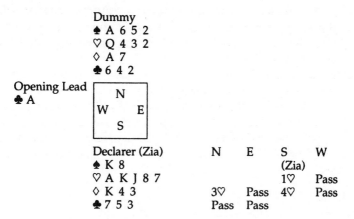

Dummy
♠ A 6 5 2
♡ Q 4 3 2
◊ A 7
♣ 6 4 2

Opening Lead
♣ A

Declarer (Zia)	N	E	S	W
♠ K 8			(Zia)	
♡ A K J 8 7			1♡	Pass
◊ K 4 3	3♡	Pass	4♡	Pass
♣ 7 5 3	Pass	Pass		

This time we are going to STOP and make our plan with the focus on the losers, since we are playing in a suit contract.

Solution to Hand 1:

Contract: 4♡

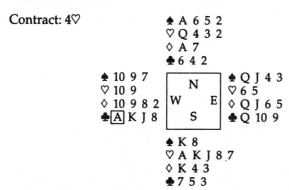

```
                ♠ A 6 5 2
                ♡ Q 4 3 2
                ◊ A 7
                ♣ 6 4 2
♠ 10 9 7                        ♠ Q J 4 3
♡ 10 9          N              ♡ 6 5
◊ 10 9 8 2   W     E           ◊ Q J 6 5
♣ A K J 8       S              ♣ Q 10 9
                ♠ K 8
                ♡ A K J 8 7
                ◊ K 4 3
                ♣ 7 5 3
```

S We can afford only three losers.
T We tally our losers and see that we could lose three club tricks – probably the first three tricks since the opponents have led a club – and a diamond trick.
O Let's organize a plan to get rid of the diamond loser. We know

our partner will not appreciate it if we don't make this contract after we accepted his invitation. The diamond loser could be eliminated by trumping the third diamond in the dummy. We will need one heart left after we draw trumps. If at all possible, drawing trumps is a priority. In this hand we have complete control since we don't have to give up the lead while accomplishing our task.

P Let's put the plan into action. After the opponents get the first three club tricks they have to give us the lead. Now we draw the trumps, and on this hand that requires only two rounds of the suit since the opponents' trumps are divided 2–2. Then we play the diamonds by taking the ◇A, ◇K and trumping the third in the dummy. There's no problem left in taking the rest of the tricks.

Hand 2 Dealer: West

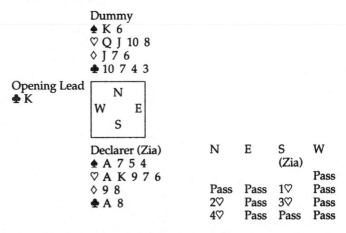

Dummy
♠ K 6
♡ Q J 10 8
◇ J 7 6
♣ 10 7 4 3

Opening Lead
♣ K

Declarer (Zia)	N	E	S	W
♠ A 7 5 4			(Zia)	
♡ A K 9 7 6				Pass
◇ 9 8	Pass	Pass	1♡	Pass
♣ A 8	2♡	Pass	3♡	Pass
	4♡	Pass	Pass	Pass

We have been bidding in our usual aggressive manner, but considering we haven't gone down yet on any hand, let's continue with that style. This hand looks a bit harder, and West always seems to have an honour to lead!

Solution to Hand 2:

Contract: 4♡

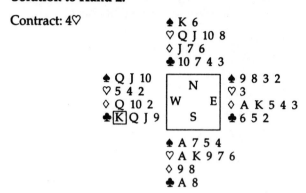

           ♠ K 6
           ♡ Q J 10 8
           ◊ J 7 6
           ♣ 10 7 4 3

♠ Q J 10   ♠ 9 8 3 2
♡ 5 4 2   N   ♡ 3
◊ Q 10 2 W   E ◊ A K 5 4 3
♣K Q J 9   S   ♣ 6 5 2

           ♠ A 7 5 4
           ♡ A K 9 7 6
           ◊ 9 8
           ♣ A 8

We STOP before playing the first card; this hand isn't so easy.

S We can afford three losers.

T Our tally tells us that we have two spade losers, two diamond losers and a club loser – two too many.

O We can plan to get rid of the two spade losers by trumping them in the dummy. Normally, after winning the first trick with the ♣A, we might consider drawing the trumps. If they are divided 2–2, this would be fine. We could keep two trumps in the dummy to take care of the spade losers and could use our hearts to get back to our hand by trumping clubs. However, if the trumps are divided 3–1 or 4–0, we can't draw all of them. We cannot even afford to draw two rounds of trumps. Once our ♣A is driven out, we will have no way to get back quickly to our hand to trump the fourth spade. The opponents can lead a third round of trumps and down we go. We can only draw one round of trumps and must then start to trump our losers.

P We win the ♣A and play one round of trumps, winning with the dummy's ♡Q. Then, we play the ♠K from the dummy which will win the trick and a small spade to the ♠A in our hand. We are in the right hand to trump our first spade loser. With two trumps left in dummy, we can use one of them to come back to our hand and now we can trump the second spade loser. We'll draw the opponent's remaining trump when we are next back in our hand. Task accomplished. Put the cards out and try drawing two rounds of trumps to see what happens.

Hand 3 Dealer: South

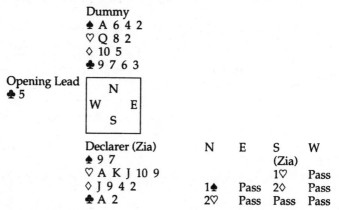

Dummy
♠ A 6 4 2
♡ Q 8 2
◇ 10 5
♣ 9 7 6 3

Opening Lead
♣ 5

Declarer (Zia)
♠ 9 7
♡ A K J 10 9
◇ J 9 4 2
♣ A 2

N	E	S	W
		(Zia)	
		1♡	Pass
1♠	Pass	2◇	Pass
2♡	Pass	Pass	Pass

This is not an unwelcome dummy in a modest 2 ♡ contract – but that doesn't mean we shouldn't give it our best. But just what is our best?

Solution to Hand 3:

Contract: 2♡

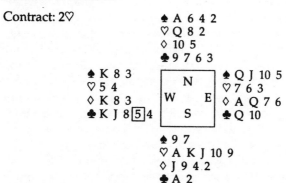

♠ A 6 4 2
♡ Q 8 2
◇ 10 5
♣ 9 7 6 3

♠ K 8 3
♡ 5 4
◇ K 8 3
♣ K J 8 5 4

♠ Q J 10 5
♡ 7 6 3
◇ A Q 7 6
♣ Q 10

♠ 9 7
♡ A K J 10 9
◇ J 9 4 2
♣ A 2

S We can afford five losers.

T Our tally tells us we have a spade loser, four diamond losers and a club loser – a total of six, one too many.

O Pausing after the opening lead (you did, didn't you?) and making a plan tells us that by simply playing on diamonds before the trumps, we can *ruff* (trump) at least one of our losing diamonds in the dummy. This is another case of delaying drawing trumps when there is something more urgent to do.

P Win the ♣A and lead a diamond. Even if the opponents win and lead a trump, we can win and lead another diamond. They can lead a second trump but we win the race and can trump one of our diamond losers in the dummy.

CHAPTER 23

Discarding Losers

The Acol system, popular in Britain, got the name Acol because it was first developed in a house in Acol Road, London.

In the last chapter, we saw that the declarer could get rid of losers by trumping them in the dummy. In this chapter, we are going to consider another way for the declarer to get rid of his losers. This time the extra strength in the dummy, rather than the shortness, is used to eliminate some of the losers in the declarer's hand. You can go through four steps when thinking about using the dummy's strength to get rid of your losers. First, you again have to recognize the hand patterns where the opportunity exists. Second, you may have to play a side suit several times before you can use it for throwing away a loser. Third, you may have to look for opportunities to create extra winners in the dummy through promotion, length in a suit or the finesse. Finally, you may have to arrange transport, or entries, to the dummy so that you are in a position to put the plan into action. Let's look at each of these steps in turn.

Recognising hand patterns

It is important to spot the characteristics in your hand and in the dummy that afford the opportunity to throw away losers from your hand on the dummy's extra strength. Look for a side suit in which there are more cards in the dummy than there are in your hand. This is the reverse of the pattern you wanted when you were trumping losers in the dummy, where you wanted more cards in your hand than in the dummy. After you have located a suit that is longer in the dummy, look to see whether there is enough strength in the suit to enable the dummy to win a trick while you are throwing away a loser from your hand. Consider this hand where spades are trumps.

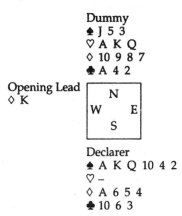

Dummy
♠ J 5 3
♡ A K Q
◊ 10 9 8 7
♣ A 4 2

Opening Lead
◊ K

Declarer
♠ A K Q 10 4 2
♡ —
◊ A 6 5 4
♣ 10 6 3

Find the suit with more cards in the dummy than in the declarer's hand. There are three hearts in the dummy and none in your hand. Next consider the strength of the heart suit. Since there are three winners, you can use this extra strength to get rid of three losers in your hand. After the opponents' trumps are drawn, you can cross to the dummy's ♣A and discard three of your losers on the hearts.

Here are three other possible layouts for the heart suit. Which ones offer a chance to throw away a loser from your hand on the dummy's extra strength?

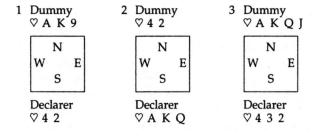

1 Dummy
   ♡ A K 9

   Declarer
   ♡ 4 2

2 Dummy
   ♡ 4 2

   Declarer
   ♡ A K Q

3 Dummy
   ♡ A K Q J

   Declarer
   ♡ 4 3 2

The pattern in the first example is worth looking at since there are more cards in the dummy than there are in your hand. There is not, however, the extra strength needed to throw away a loser. After the ♡A and ♡K are played, the opponents have the remaining winners in the suit. In the second example, there is the strength in the suit and the suit is unevenly divided, but you cannot throw away a loser in your hand. The pattern you are looking for is one that has more cards in the dummy. The third example offers an opportunity to get rid of a loser from your hand. After the suit has been played three times, you have none left and can throw a card, a loser, from another suit. (Since the side suit has to be played so many times before you are in a position to get rid of a loser, it would be a good idea to first draw the trumps.)

Taking advantage of the dummy's extra winners

You are the declarer in a contract of 4 ♡ and count your losers in these two suits:

Dummy
◊ A K Q
♣ 7 6 5

Declarer
◊ 4
♣ A 8 3

In diamonds, you look to have one loser in your hand but a glance at the dummy shows that there is plenty of strength there to take care of it. You have two club losers. When you look to dummy's clubs, there is no help in the club suit. The diamonds, however, offer an opportunity for you to eliminate your club losers by throwing them on the second and third diamond trick.

You have taken advantage of a side suit that is unevenly divided between your hand and the dummy. When you were trumping a loser in the dummy, you wanted to work to eliminate all of dummy's cards in the side suit. When you are throwing away losers, you want to work toward getting rid of the declarer's cards in the suit. Here is another example:

Dummy
◊ A K Q
♣ A 4 3

```
┌─────────┐
│    N    │
│ W     E │
│    S    │
└─────────┘
```

Declarer
◊ 4 3
♣ K 8 7

You have two diamond losers in your hand but look to the dummy to see that the ◊A and ◊K can take care of them. The dummy's ♣A in combination with your ♣K eliminate two of the losers in that suit, but there is still one left. The diamonds offer a chance to eliminate your club loser. Play the three top diamonds and, on the third round, discard a club from your hand.

Whenever you are in a trump contract, look for opportunities to get rid of losers. Your first step is to identify side suits which are unevenly divided between your hand and the dummy. In the example above, the diamonds were unevenly divided. On the third round, because you had no diamonds left in your hand, you had an opportunity to discard a club, a loser in another suit.

Look at the effect this has. Now your clubs are no longer 3–3 and, when the third round is played, you are able to trump it, resulting in no losers in the club suit.

Developing extra winners in the dummy

There are times when there are more cards in the dummy than in your hand and, although there are not immediate winners, the suit offers possibilities. You can develop extra tricks in the dummy through promotion, length in a suit or by using the finesse.

Developing extra tricks through promotion

Let's look again at two side suits, clubs and diamonds. Hearts are trumps.

Dummy
◊ K Q J
♣ A 4 3

```
      N
  W       E
      S
```

Declarer
◊ 4 3
♣ K 8 7

You have one diamond loser and one club loser. Consider what these two suits will look like if you lead a diamond to the dummy's ◊J to drive out the opponents' ◊A:

Dummy
◊ K Q
♣ A 4 3

```
      N
  W       E
      S
```

Declarer
◊ 4
♣ K 8 7

Look for your unevenly divided side suit. There is an extra diamond in the dummy. Therefore when you play the suit for the third time, there will be a chance to discard a loser from another suit, your small club. Now, you end up with only one loser, the ◊A. This time, you had to promote your winners before they could be used to get rid of a loser.

Establishing a winner through length

We saw earlier on, when playing in no-trump contracts, that small cards can be turned into winners when they are part of a long suit.

Consider this layout:

Dummy
◊ A 8 7 6 5

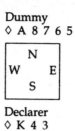

Declarer
◊ K 4 3

There are eight combined cards in the suit and the odds favour them being divided 3–2. This means that, after three rounds of the suit have been played, the dummy's remaining two small cards will be winners and the declarer will have no cards left in the suit.

There are other considerations when you are looking to your small cards for winners in the above layout. Because you can only throw away a loser on the fourth round of the suit, you would have to draw the opponents' small trumps so that they do not use them to win a trick by trumping an established winner. You also have to be able to get to the winners in the dummy. You might have an entry you can use in another suit or you may have to give up a trick early, keeping one of your high cards in the suit as an entry, as discussed in Chapter 17. Nevertheless, if you can turn those two small diamonds into winners, it is worth going through all those steps. Look at this idea in a complete hand. You are in a contract of 4 ♠ and the lead is the ♡Q:

Dummy
♠ 8 4 2
♡ A 4 2
◊ 10 7
♣ A 5 4 3 2

Opening Lead
♡ Q

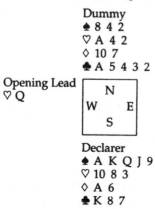

Declarer
♠ A K Q J 9
♡ 10 8 3
◊ A 6
♣ K 8 7

Go through the plan. You can afford three losers in a contract of 4
♠. You have no spade losers, two heart losers, a diamond loser and
a club loser. You want to eliminate one of your losers. What are
your options? You don't have more cards in your hand than you
do in the dummy in any side suit, so you cannot trump any losers
in the dummy. Instead, look for the pattern to throw away losers.
You have more clubs in the dummy than you do in your hand.
Since there are two more clubs, you have a chance to throw away
two losers.

After winning the first trick with the ♡A, draw the opponents'
trumps. Next, take the ♣K and give up a club trick, leaving the ♣A
in the dummy. What can the opponents do? They can take their
two heart tricks but, whatever they lead next, you can win the
trick. You can play your remaining club and win the trick with
your carefully preserved ♣A. You are in the dummy and, if the
suit has split the way you expect, 3–2, you are in a position to play
one of your club winners and throw away your diamond loser.

Establishing a winner through the finesse

Another way of establishing an extra winner is through the
finesse. Consider this example. Hearts are trumps and we are
looking at two side suits, clubs and diamonds:

Dummy
◊ A Q
♣ K 8 7

Declarer
◊ 4
♣ A 4 2

You have a small diamond in your hand but the ◊A in the dummy
will take care of that. You have one club loser after the ♣A and ♣K
have been played. Where could you get rid of the club loser? Look
to the diamonds, your unevenly divided suit. Although you don't
have a sure winner, there is a possible winner with the ◊Q. Play

your ◊4 towards the ace-queen combination. If your finesse against the ◊K is successful and the ◊Q wins the trick, you can play your ◊A and throw away a small club. Now you have only two clubs in your hand and when the suit is played a third time, you can trump.

It is important to look not only at the immediate chance to discard losers on the dummy's extra winners but also down the road to see what winners could be developed through promotion, length or the finesse.

Getting to the dummy

If you are planning on throwing away a loser on an extra winner in the dummy, you have to be sure to have an entry to the dummy. Let's look at one side suit, this time the spades, since hearts are trumps:

Dummy
♠ K Q J

Declarer
♠ 4

Once the ♠A has been played, you have two extra winners in the dummy, if you can get to them. You have to look to your other suits and try to preserve an entry so that, after the ♠A has been played, you have transport to your promoted ♠Q and ♠J.

Summary

One way to get rid of a loser in a declarer's hand is to throw it on a winner in the dummy. You can recognize this opportunity by:

- Looking for a suit that has more cards in the dummy than in your hand.
- Realising that you will probably have to play the side suit more

than once before you are ready to throw a loser away. Whenever possible, you will want to draw the opponents' trumps first.

- Looking for opportunities to establish extra winners in the dummy through promotion, establishing small cards in long suits or the finesse.
- Looking ahead so that you have an entry in the dummy to get to the winners when you are ready to discard your losers.

Over Zia's shoulder

Hand 1 Dealer: North

Dummy
♠ A 6 5 4
♡ 9 7 5
◇ 7 6 5
♣ K Q 8

Opening Lead
♡ J

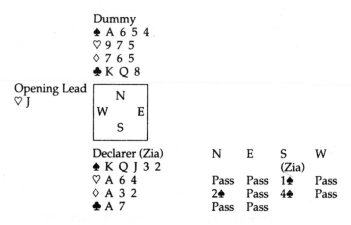

Declarer (Zia)
♠ K Q J 3 2
♡ A 6 4
◇ A 3 2
♣ A 7

N	E	S	W
		(Zia)	
Pass	Pass	1♠	Pass
2♠	Pass	4♠	Pass
Pass	Pass		

We can only afford three losers. Let's work together to see if we can hold ourselves to that number.

Solution to Hand 1:

Contract: 4♠

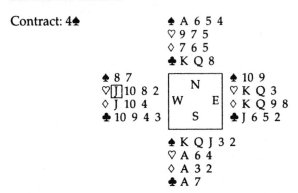

        ♠ A 6 5 4
        ♡ 9 7 5
        ◇ 7 6 5
        ♣ K Q 8

♠ 8 7   ♠ 10 9
♡ J 10 8 2   ♡ K Q 3
◇ J 10 4   ◇ K Q 9 8
♣ 10 9 4 3   ♣ J 6 5 2

        ♠ K Q J 3 2
        ♡ A 6 4
        ◇ A 3 2
        ♣ A 7

S Well, we decided we needed to lose no more than three tricks.

T Our tally tells us that we could possibly lose two hearts and two diamonds.

O What can we do? Is there any extra strength in the dummy that can be used? To recognize these opportunities we have to look for a side suit that has more cards in the dummy than it does in our hand. The clubs fit that description. First, we plan to draw the trumps; we have nothing to lose by doing that since we don't give up the lead and we don't need the trump suit for entries or to trump any losers from our hand.

P Let's play the clubs carefully; first the ♣A, the high card from the short side, then the ♣7 over to the ♣K and ♣Q in the dummy. On the third round of clubs we can throw one of our losers, either a diamond or a heart. You choose, and we make yet another contract.

Hand 2 Dealer: East

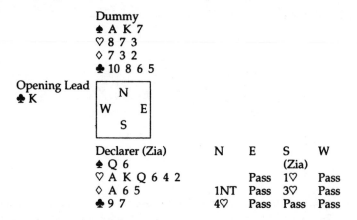

Dummy
♠ A K 7
♡ 8 7 3
◇ 7 3 2
♣ 10 8 6 5

Opening Lead
♣ K

Declarer (Zia)
♠ Q 6
♡ A K Q 6 4 2
◇ A 6 5
♣ 9 7

	N	E	S	W
			(Zia)	
		Pass	1♡	Pass
	1NT	Pass	3♡	Pass
	4♡	Pass	Pass	Pass

Our partner has bid aggressively but we have reached a good contract. West always seems to have an easy lead! Let's play the hand.

Solution to Hand 2:

Contract: 4♡

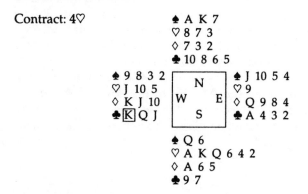

♠ A K 7
♡ 8 7 3
◇ 7 3 2
♣ 10 8 6 5

♠ 9 8 3 2   ♠ J 10 5 4
♡ J 10 5   ♡ 9
◇ K J 10   ◇ Q 9 8 4
♣ K Q J   ♣ A 4 3 2

♠ Q 6
♡ A K Q 6 4 2
◇ A 6 5
♣ 9 7

My immediate reaction is that I like the contract and expect to make it. So let's stop to make our plan.

S We can afford three losers.

T We have two diamond and two club losers, one too many.

O Do we have any extra strength in the dummy? The ♠K will be an extra trick and can provide a good chance to discard a loser.

Should we draw trumps first? A good idea. We don't have to give up the lead to the opponents, so they can't take any of their winners before we have a chance to get rid of our losers. Also we don't need the trumps in dummy on this hand.

P There is one catch. Look at the spades. What would happen if you first lead the ♠A and play the ♠6 from declarer's hand and then play the ♠7 from the dummy and win the trick with the ♠Q from declarer's hand? Not pleasant, is it? In order to make the best of those spades, we have to play the high card from the short side and win the first trick with the ♠Q in declarer's hand and then play a small spade to our winners in the dummy.

Hand 3 Dealer: East

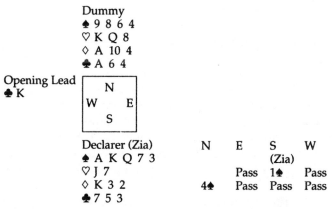

Dummy
♠ 9 8 6 4
♡ K Q 8
◊ A 10 4
♣ A 6 4

Opening Lead
♣ K

Declarer (Zia)
♠ A K Q 7 3
♡ J 7
◊ K 3 2
♣ 7 5 3

N	E	S	W
		(Zia)	
	Pass	1♠	Pass
4♠	Pass	Pass	Pass

The bidding is natural, simple and to the point. Can the play be similar?

Solution to Hand 3:

Contract: 4♠

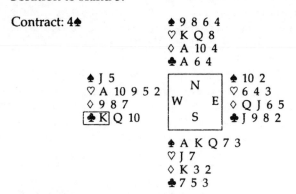

```
                    ♠ 9 8 6 4
                    ♡ K Q 8
                    ◇ A 10 4
                    ♣ A 6 4
   ♠ J 5                            ♠ 10 2
   ♡ A 10 9 5 2       N             ♡ 6 4 3
   ◇ 9 8 7        W       E         ◇ Q J 6 5
   ♣ K Q 10           S             ♣ J 9 8 2
                    ♠ A K Q 7 3
                    ♡ J 7
                    ◇ K 3 2
                    ♣ 7 5 3
```

S We can afford only three losers.

T Our tally tells us that we have a heart loser, a diamond loser and two club losers. One too many.

O Before we go any further, look at the side suits that are unevenly divided. There are more hearts in the dummy than in our hand. Remember, it doesn't do much good to trump in our hand since we are trumping with a card we had already counted as a winner. To be effective, we should be trumping in the short hand. So, when there are more cards in the dummy than in our hand we are looking for an opportunity to throw away a loser. Does the heart suit offer that possibility? Maybe not on the first trick but, if we drive out the ♡A, we have two winners in the dummy and we could throw a loser on one of them, either a diamond or a club.

P That's a good plan. So, we draw the trumps – since there is no reason not to – and play the ♡J, starting with the high card from the short side. After the ♡A is driven out and we regain the lead, we can throw a loser on the promoted heart winner in the dummy – and we are fresh for a new challenge.

CHAPTER 24

Managing Trumps

Martina Navratilova says that no matter where she goes she can always make new friends at the bridge table.

There is a story that goes back to the days of playing whist, a forerunner of bridge. Whist was a gambling game, and the rumour was that there were hundreds of players who walked the streets of London, penniless, without food or lodging, because they failed to draw trumps. Apparently the story goes on to say that even the children of these players had to beg for a cup of coffee, all because their parents lost so much money at the gambling table due to their failure to draw trumps. When you first start to play bridge, one piece of advice that is often given is always to *draw trumps* before you do anything else.

One thing is certain. When you are playing in a suit contract, whether or not to lead trumps at your first opportunity is one of the decisions you have to make. You have several choices. You can lead trumps right away, extracting all of the opponents' cards in the suit; you can avoid drawing them altogether; you can compromise and play some trumps, then another suit; or, vice-versa, play another suit and then play trumps.

The guideline for drawing trumps does not come from an isolated rule like 'always draw trumps at your first chance' or 'save your trumps until you need them'. Instead, it comes as a result of making your plan. Before we go any further, let's consider what drawing trumps is all about.

Drawing trumps

Although the trump suit is more powerful than the other suits, and therefore unique, it also resembles the other suits. You go about playing the trump suit in much the same way that you would a side suit. You look for ways of promoting winners, you establish tricks in your long suit, you try finesses.

Usually your side has eight cards or more in the trump suit. If you have an eight-card fit, the opponents, therefore, have five cards in the suit, an odd number. You can expect them to be divided evenly between your opponents' hands, three on one side and two on the other, or 3–2. You would have to play the trump suit three times in order to get all the opponents' trump cards. If you have a nine-card fit, the opponents would have four cards, an even number. You expect them to be divided not 2–2 but 3–1. You still expect to have to draw trumps three times to remove the opponents' trump cards. Of course, there are no guarantees. When you have an eight-card fit, the opponents' cards could be divided 4–1 or 5–0, although that would be against the odds.

Sometimes, you can draw trumps without giving up the lead to the opponents and sometimes you have to give them the lead. Look at the difference between these two holdings in the trump suit:

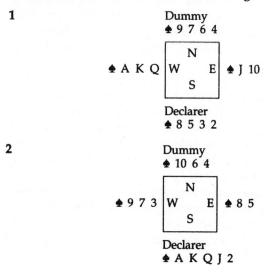

1

Dummy
♠ 9 7 6 4

♠ A K Q   W   E   ♠ J 10

Declarer
♠ 8 5 3 2

2

Dummy
♠ 10 6 4

♠ 9 7 3   W   E   ♠ 8 5

Declarer
♠ A K Q J 2

In each case you have eight trump cards. In the first example, they are divided 4–4 between your hand and the dummy. If you were going to draw trumps you would have to play the suit three times and would lose the lead three times. In the second example, you would have to play the trumps three times also, but you would not have to give up the lead even once to do so.

There are times when the trump suit is *solid*, as in the second example above, but, more frequently, your trump tricks have to be established through length as in the first example. You may also have to use the finesse when playing your trump suit. Consider this layout:

Dummy
♡ Q 6 4

```
  +-------+
  |   N   |
  | W   E |
  |   S   |
  +-------+
```

Declarer
♡ A 8 7 5 2

You have an eight-card fit and expect the opponents' cards to be divided 3–2. You plan to play the suit three times to draw all their trumps. You have a winner with the ♡A. You can also hope to win a trick with the ♡Q. To finesse against the ♡K, lead towards the card you hope will take a trick. Lead from your hand towards the dummy's ♡Q.

Since the advice to draw trumps at your first opportunity is so often given, before we look at the exceptions let's consider why this advice is so popular. If a player cannot follow suit, a small trump card has more power than an honour card in the side suit led. Because of this, the declarer generally wants to get rid of the opponents' trump cards so that they will not be used against his winners.

Let's look at two hands where drawing trumps is a good idea. In the first hand, you are in a contract of 4 ♡. The opening lead is the ♠K.

Contract: 4♡

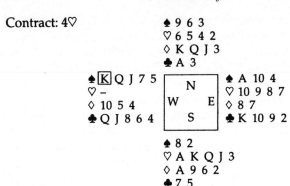

```
                    ♠ 9 6 3
                    ♡ 6 5 4 2
                    ◊ K Q J 3
                    ♣ A 3
        ♠ K Q J 7 5           ♠ A 10 4
        ♡ -          N        ♡ 10 9 8 7
        ◊ 10 5 4   W   E      ◊ 8 7
        ♣ Q J 8 6 4  S        ♣ K 10 9 2
                    ♠ 8 2
                    ♡ A K Q J 3
                    ◊ A 9 6 2
                    ♣ 7 5
```

You can afford three losers and have two spade losers and one club loser. When you organize your plan, you want to play the cards in an order that does not put you in a position to create an extra loser. Look at what would happen if you did not draw the trumps. If you were to play diamonds, for example, the third round could be trumped by East – a loser you didn't count on.

You might think that using two of your trumps to draw out one of the opponents' trumps is not a good bargain. The alternative, however, is to let East enjoy a winner with one of his hearts. By drawing all his trumps, you prevent this.

Let's look at another example. This time you are in a part-score contract of 3 ♡. The lead is the ♣K.

Contract: 3♡

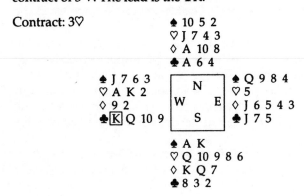

```
                    ♠ 10 5 2
                    ♡ J 7 4 3
                    ◊ A 10 8
                    ♣ A 6 4
        ♠ J 7 6 3            ♠ Q 9 8 4
        ♡ A K 2     N        ♡ 5
        ◊ 9 2     W   E      ◊ J 6 5 4 3
        ♣ K Q 10 9   S       ♣ J 7 5
                    ♠ A K
                    ♡ Q 10 9 8 6
                    ◊ K Q 7
                    ♣ 8 3 2
```

This time you can afford four losers and so you aren't too concerned when the opponents drive out your ♣A, leaving you with two club losers. You are also missing the ♡A and the ♡K. You have no losers in either spades or diamonds so you should be able to make the contract. When you organize your plan, don't create an extra loser for yourself. Where could an extra loser be created? Look at the diamonds. If you try to take three rounds of diamonds before drawing trumps, West will score not only the ♡A and ♡K but the ♡2 as well. To avoid this, draw the trumps, even though you have to give up the lead twice to do this.

You don't mind giving West the trump tricks he has coming to him, the ♡A and ♡K, but you want to avoid an unnecessary loser in the trump suit. After winning the ♣A, play a heart. West will win the trick and the defenders can take their club tricks. They might then lead a diamond, which you will win. Lead another heart and again give West the lead. Now what can West do? Whatever he leads, you can win the tricks and draw his remaining trump. Now, you can take your diamond winners in comfort.

It might seem as if the only time you draw trumps is when you have the number of losers you can afford. So as not to leave that impression, let's look at one more hand where drawing trumps is a priority. You are in a part-score contract of 3 ♠ with the opening lead of the ♡Q.

Contract: 3♠

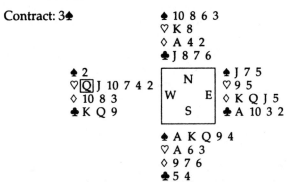

```
                    ♠ 10 8 6 3
                    ♡ K 8
                    ◇ A 4 2
                    ♣ J 8 7 6
   ♠ 2                           ♠ J 7 5
   ♡ Q J 10 7 4 2       N        ♡ 9 5
   ◇ 10 8 3          W     E     ◇ K Q J 5
   ♣ K Q 9              S        ♣ A 10 3 2
                    ♠ A K Q 9 4
                    ♡ A 6 3
                    ◇ 9 7 6
                    ♣ 5 4
```

You can afford four losers in your 3 ♠ contract. You have no spade losers, one heart loser, two diamond losers and two club losers. You need to get rid of one loser. Look for unevenly divided suits between your hand and the dummy to see if there is either the opportunity to trump a loser in the dummy or to get rid of a loser on one of the dummy's winners. When you look at the two hands for opportunities to get rid of losers, you see that there are more hearts in your hand than in the dummy and that there is an opportunity to trump a loser in the dummy. Unlike the first two examples, where you had the number of losers you could afford, this time you have to trump a loser in the dummy.

Does it matter whether you draw trumps first or trump a heart in the dummy first? Look at all four hands. If you try to trump a heart before getting rid of the trumps in the opponents' hands, East will be able to *overtrump* anything you can contribute in the dummy with his ♠J. You only need one trump to get rid of your heart loser. You do not have to give up the lead to draw trumps. Therefore, the best plan is to draw the trumps and then get rid of your loser.

You cannot conclude that it is always the best idea to draw trumps before you go about trumping losers in the dummy. Each hand is different and you have to look at it in the context of your plan. As we have seen in previous chapters, on many hands where you are going to trump a loser in the dummy, you cannot afford to draw the trumps. How can you know when playing trumps is right? Make your plan and use it to look ahead a few tricks. In the hand we just looked at, you knew you needed only one trump left in the dummy to take care of the heart loser in your hand, and you had four trumps. You could also see that drawing trumps would not give up the lead. You still had control of the hand. In this situation you had nothing to lose by drawing trumps before trumping your loser. The opponents could not get the lead and interrupt your plan.

Delaying drawing trumps

Let's look at two situations where you should delay drawing trumps. Remember, the reason you count losers when you are in a trump contract is that you have the opportunity, because of the power of the trumps, to get rid of those losers. You can either trump them in the dummy or you can throw away losers from your hand on the extra strength in the dummy. Both ways of getting rid of losers are closely connected to the trump suit.

First, if you are going to trump losers in the dummy, you have to make sure you have enough trumps in the dummy to do the job. In the last hand, we could comfortably draw trumps and still have a trump in dummy to take care of our loser. But that is not always, or normally, the case. More often, you have to guard your trumps carefully.

There is another important aspect of managing your trumps so that you have enough in the dummy to take care of the declarer's losers, and that is to remember that you have opponents. You are not the only player at the table who can draw trumps. You have first to decide how many trumps in the dummy you are going to need to take care of the losers in your hand. Then you have to consider how many times you have to give up the lead to the opponents before you are in a position to trump your losers. Before you go about drawing even a single round of trumps, consider what will happen if your opponents draw them for you. Let's look at a hand. You are in a contract of 2 ◊ and the opening lead is the ♣3.

Contract: 2◊

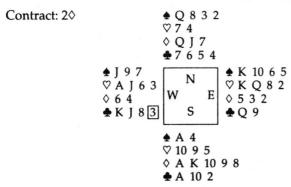

```
                  ♠ Q 8 3 2
                  ♡ 7 4
                  ◊ Q J 7
                  ♣ 7 6 5 4
   ♠ J 9 7          ┌─────┐        ♠ K 10 6 5
   ♡ A J 6 3        │  N  │        ♡ K Q 8 2
   ◊ 6 4          W │     │ E      ◊ 5 3 2
   ♣ K J 8 ③        │  S  │        ♣ Q 9
                  └─────┘
                  ♠ A 4
                  ♡ 10 9 5
                  ◊ A K 10 9 8
                  ♣ A 10 2
```

You can afford five losers but it looks as if you have six: one spade, three hearts and two clubs. You have to get rid of one loser. What are the possibilities? You can't get rid of a spade loser since there are fewer cards in your hand than in the dummy and there is no extra strength in the suit in the dummy. The heart suit, if you look closely, has the right pattern to trump a loser in the dummy. You have three hearts in your hand and only two in the dummy. You need only one trump to take care of your heart loser and so you have to manage your trumps so that there is one left in the dummy.

The next observation to make is that you have to give the opponents the lead twice before you are in a position to trump your loser in the dummy. That means that the opponents could draw your trumps twice, leaving you with only one in the dummy. That you can afford. But, if you also draw a round of trumps, then you will be left with no diamonds to trump your losing heart trick and will be left with your original six losers. One occasion to avoid drawing trumps, then, is when you need to keep your trumps in the dummy to take care of a loser or losers in your hand.

The second way of getting rid of an extra loser is to throw it on one of the dummy's strong side suits. Should you draw the trumps before you do this? After all, you are not really counting on the dummy's trumps this time.

One consideration here is whether drawing the trumps would give up the lead. When you have to get rid of a loser, you may have to do it quickly, before you give the opponents the lead, because once they get in they might be able to take enough tricks to defeat the contract.

This is best seen by looking at a complete hand. The contract is 4 ♡ and the opening lead is the ◊Q.

Contract: 4♡

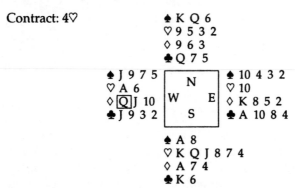

♠ K Q 6
♡ 9 5 3 2
◊ 9 6 3
♣ Q 7 5

♠ J 9 7 5
♡ A 6
◊ Q J 10
♣ J 9 3 2

♠ 10 4 3 2
♡ 10
◊ K 8 5 2
♣ A 10 8 4

♠ A 8
♡ K Q J 8 7 4
◊ A 7 4
♣ K 6

You can afford three losers. You have no spade losers, one heart loser, two diamond losers and one club loser, one too many. You need to get rid of one of your losers. Is there the opportunity to do this? Look for your unevenly divided side suits. There are more spades in the dummy than there are in your hand so this suit offers a good opportunity to get rid of a loser from your hand. A closer look shows that it is an excellent opportunity, since you have the first three tricks in the suit.

Are you going to draw the trumps before you try to get rid of your loser in the spade suit? Look ahead. What would happen if you started to draw the trumps? The opponents could take a trick with the ♡A. Now what would you expect them to do? They would take their two diamond winners and would probably be able to figure out to take the ♣A. You would have lost four tricks and would be defeated in your contract of 4 ♡.

You cannot give up the lead to the opponents before you get rid of a loser. So, suppose that instead of drawing trumps after you win the first trick with the ♢A, you play the spades and throw a diamond loser on the third round. Then you draw the trumps. Again, the opponents get the lead and try to take two diamond tricks. However, since you threw a diamond away, you can trump on the third round. You are successful in holding yourself to only three losers, enough to make the contract.

Summary

It is generally a good idea to draw the opponents' trumps as quickly as possible to prevent the opponents from playing a trump on one of your winners. Draw trumps in the following situations:

- When you have the winners you can afford – even if you have to give up the lead a couple of times in the process.
- When you don't have enough tricks but you don't have to give up the lead, and don't need all your trumps to trump losers in the dummy.

Delay drawing trumps in two situations:

- When you are going to need trumps in the dummy to take care of one or more losers in your hand, and you will not have enough left if you, or the opponents, draw trumps.

- When you would have to give up the lead to the opponents by drawing trumps and they can then take enough tricks to defeat your contract.

Over Zia's shoulder

Hand 1 Dealer: East

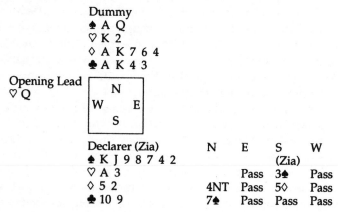

Dummy
♠ A Q
♡ K 2
◇ A K 7 6 4
♣ A K 4 3

Opening Lead
♡ Q

Declarer (Zia)
♠ K J 9 8 7 4 2
♡ A 3
◇ 5 2
♣ 10 9

	N	E	S	W
			(Zia)	
		Pass	3♠	Pass
	4NT	Pass	5◇	Pass
	7♠	Pass	Pass	Pass

Our first hand in this chapter is a grand slam. It seems easy enough, doesn't it? This hand will be fun to play together.

Solution to Hand 1:

Contract: 7♠

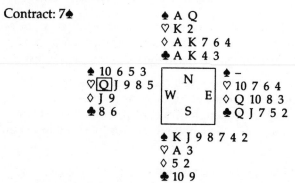

♠ A Q
♡ K 2
◇ A K 7 6 4
♣ A K 4 3

♠ 10 6 5 3
♡ Q J 9 8 5
◇ J 9
♣ 8 6

♠ –
♡ 10 7 6 4
◇ Q 10 8 3
♣ Q J 7 5 2

♠ K J 9 8 7 4 2
♡ A 3
◇ 5 2
♣ 10 9

S We can afford no losers.

T We have no losers in spades, hearts, diamonds or clubs. That's good news.

O Where could extra losers come from? Well, there is a possibility that if we don't draw the opponents' trump cards we could have an unexpected loser. This hand seems straightforward enough. There is one careless mistake we could make. Suppose we take the first heart trick with the ♡A in our hand. Does it really matter where we win the first heart? Let's follow through. We have to draw four rounds of trumps before the opponents' spades are exhausted because they are unfortunately divided 4–0. This should be no problem since we have the four top honours. So we are in our hand. We play the trumps and get stuck in the dummy. We can't afford to overtake the ♠Q with the ♠K or we would establish West's ♠10 as a trick. We have to find another way to get back to our hand to draw the trump. How can we get back to our hand? We could trump either a club or a diamond, but if we trump with a small card West will overtrump with his ♠10. If we trump with the ♠K or the ♠J to avoid this, West will later win a trick with the ♠10 by force. Once we make the mistake of putting the ♡A on the first trick we can no longer make the contract.

P Instead, we have to play the ♡K on the first trick. Now we play the two top trumps from the dummy and come over to our hand with the ♡A and draw the rest of West's trumps. Now, we can enjoy the winners in the other suits. On this hand it was necessary to draw the trumps in order to avoid an extra loser in the trump suit. To do this we had to be able to get to our long trumps and had to keep the high card with our long suit.

Hand 2 Dealer: South

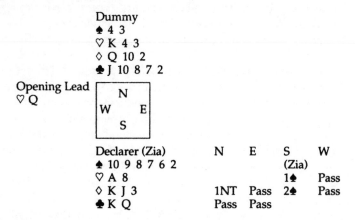

Dummy
♠ 4 3
♡ K 4 3
◊ Q 10 2
♣ J 10 8 7 2

Opening Lead
♡ Q

```
      N
   W     E
      S
```

Declarer (Zia)	N	E	S	W
♠ 10 9 8 7 6 2			(Zia)	
♡ A 8			1♠	Pass
◊ K J 3	1NT	Pass	2♠	Pass
♣ K Q	Pass	Pass		

When you first look at this hand there seems to be too much to do. Where do we start?

Solution to Hand 2:

Contract: 2♠

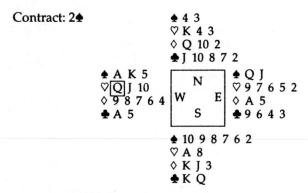

```
          ♠ 4 3
          ♡ K 4 3
          ◊ Q 10 2
          ♣ J 10 8 7 2
♠ A K 5                    ♠ Q J
♡ Q J 10      N            ♡ 9 7 6 5 2
◊ 9 8 7 6 4  W   E         ◊ A 5
♣ A 5          S           ♣ 9 6 4 3
          ♠ 10 9 8 7 6 2
          ♡ A 8
          ◊ K J 3
          ♣ K Q
```

S We can afford five losers.

T Our loser count tells us that we have at least three spade losers – assuming they are divided 3–2 – one diamond loser and one club loser.

O We can afford five losers. Are there any dangers in the hand? Yes. If we don't start by getting the opponents' trumps out of the way we are liable to find that they use their high trumps separately. We have enough length in the trumps not to worry. There is nothing to ruff in the dummy so we have no reason to delay drawing the trumps, even if it means giving them the lead three times.

P So, we win the first heart trick and immediately lead a trump. When we next get the lead, we lead another trump. Once all their trumps are gone, we have no more worries. If we didn't decide on this plan, they will probably get an extra trick in the trump suit, which they don't deserve.

Hand 3 Dealer: South

Dummy
♠ 8 4 2
♡ A Q 9 7
◊ 9 8 7
♣ Q J 3

Opening Lead
◊ Q

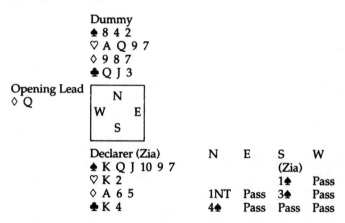

		N		
W				E
		S		

Declarer (Zia)
♠ K Q J 10 9 7
♡ K 2
◊ A 6 5
♣ K 4

N	E	S	W
		(Zia)	
		1♠	Pass
1NT	Pass	3♠	Pass
4♠	Pass	Pass	Pass

It is annoying, but West has again found the best lead. On any other lead we would be waltzing. Well, never say die.

Solution to Hand 3:

Contract: 4♠

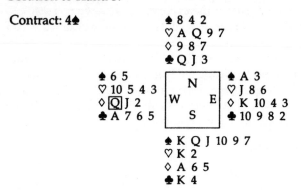

S We can afford three losers.

T It looks as if there is a spade loser, two diamond losers and a
club loser. We have to get rid of one.

O Normally, in a suit contract, we like to go after the trumps as
soon as possible. That is a pretty useful guideline, but only
when there is no more urgent job. Here, if we win the diamond
lead and start our trumps, the nasty opponents – opponents are
nearly always nasty! – might take two diamond tricks and the
♠A and the ♣A. That won't do! We'll have to delay drawing
trumps until we first discard one of our losing diamonds on the
♡Q.

P After winning the ◊A, we'll start playing the hearts with the
♡K, the high card from the short side. After a diamond loser has
been discarded on the extra heart winner in the dummy, we can
go about drawing the trumps.

CHAPTER 25

The Plan's the Thing

No matter where you travel, there is a game of bridge and therefore new friends nearby.

We have come full circle. In the first chapter, we asked whether you should play the ace or the queen on the first trick of a hand. Before you could answer, you had to consider the question in the context of the whole hand. As you have seen throughout the book, on every hand, before you can decide whether to develop tricks by promotion, or length or through the finesse or, in fact, whether you need to develop tricks at all, you have to consult your plan. The plan's the thing.

Before you make a decision on how to play a particular suit, or whether or not to play a suit, you need to consult your plan. You need to know how many tricks you need or how many losers you can afford, and what options you have. In organising your plan, choose the option that gives you the best chance of making the contract, trying to combine options whenever possible. Take a look at what may happen if you have to give up the lead to the opponents. Only then are you ready to put the plan into action and play your first card.

Over Zia's shoulder

Hand 1 Dealer: West

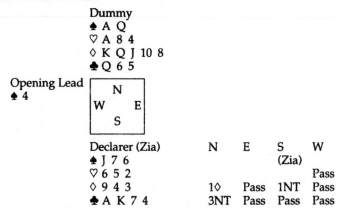

Dummy
♠ A Q
♡ A 8 4
◊ K Q J 10 8
♣ Q 6 5

Opening Lead
♠ 4

Declarer (Zia)
♠ J 7 6
♡ 6 5 2
◊ 9 4 3
♣ A K 7 4

	N	E	S	W
			(Zia)	
				Pass
	1◊	Pass	1NT	Pass
	3NT	Pass	Pass	Pass

Here we are, ending our journey together, talking about whether to finesse or not. Let's make our plan.

Solution to Hand 1:

Contract: 3NT

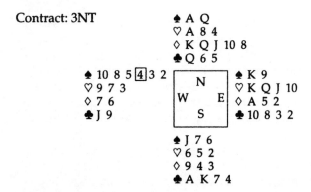

♠ A Q
♡ A 8 4
◊ K Q J 10 8
♣ Q 6 5

♠ 10 8 5 4 3 2
♡ 9 7 3
◊ 7 6
♣ J 9

♠ K 9
♡ K Q J 10
◊ A 5 2
♣ 10 8 3 2

♠ J 7 6
♡ 6 5 2
◊ 9 4 3
♣ A K 7 4

Well, we're not going to be so quick as to play the ♠Q without a little thought.

S We have to take nine tricks.

T We have one spade, one heart and three club tricks, a total of five.

O There are three places where we might think about getting extra tricks. We might consider playing the ♠Q to gain an extra trick. If West has the ♠K, we gain a trick immediately. If East has the ♠K, our ♠J will be promoted to a winner. We can promote four winners in diamonds by driving out the ◊A. We also might get an extra trick from the club suit if the missing clubs are divided 3–3. Since the diamonds will provide all the tricks we need, this is the suit we want to focus on.

P Since our plan tells us that we don't need an extra trick from the spade suit, we should win the ♠A and go about our business of developing the diamond suit. What would have happened if we took the spade finesse? East would win and lead back a heart, driving out our ♡A. The opponents would end up with five tricks: the ♠K, three heart tricks and the ◊A. Instead, we have to be quicker at promoting our diamonds while we have control. After we take the ♠A and play a diamond, East can take the ◊A and also the ♠K but must then give us back the lead since we still have the ♠J left. Timing is everything.

Hand 2 Dealer: East

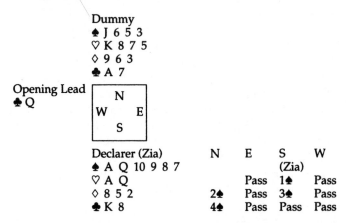

```
                Dummy
                ♠ J 6 5 3
                ♡ K 8 7 5
                ◊ 9 6 3
                ♣ A 7
Opening Lead    ┌──────────┐
♣ Q             │    N     │
                │ W     E  │
                │    S     │
                └──────────┘
                Declarer (Zia)    N     E      S      W
                ♠ A Q 10 9 8 7          (Zia)
                ♡ A Q                    Pass   1♠     Pass
                ◊ 8 5 2            2♣    Pass   3♠     Pass
                ♣ K 8             4♠    Pass   Pass   Pass
```

Contracts in the spade suit always remind me of a lion – a king of the jungle. But what dangers lurk in the forest? I wonder.

Solution to Hand 2:

Contract: 4♠

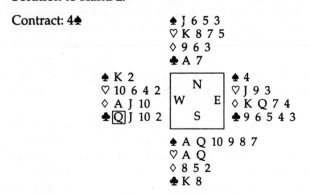

```
              ♠ J 6 5 3
              ♡ K 8 7 5
              ◊ 9 6 3
              ♣ A 7
♠ K 2                        ♠ 4
♡ 10 6 4 2      N           ♡ J 9 3
◊ A J 10     W     E        ◊ K Q 7 4
♣ Q J 10 2      S           ♣ 9 6 5 4 3
              ♠ A Q 10 9 8 7
              ♡ A Q
              ◊ 8 5 2
              ♣ K 8
```

S We can afford to lose three tricks in our 4 ♠ contract.

T We have one potential spade loser and three diamond losers, one too many.

O It is tempting to take the first trick with the ♣A and take the spade finesse, trying to get rid of our extra loser that way. We should examine all the possibilities, however, before deciding on our plan. The dummy has an extra heart winner and we could use it to discard one of our diamond losers. This is a better alternative than taking the spade finesse right away. If it does not work – perhaps one of the opponents will trump our heart winner – we can fall back on the spade finesse later.

P One more thought before we play to the first trick. We will need the ♣A as an entry to the dummy, so we should win the first trick with the ♣K in our hand. Then we play the ♡A and ♡Q. Now it is time for the ♣A so that we can get to the dummy to play the ♡K and discard a diamond loser. When this works successfully, we can turn our attention to the spade suit. We no longer mind that the finesse loses. Lucky for us that West did not find a diamond opening lead!

Hand 3 Dealer: West

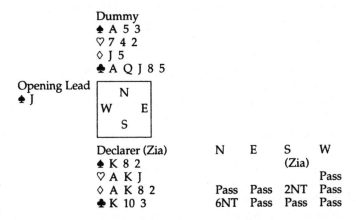

Dummy
♠ A 5 3
♡ 7 4 2
◊ J 5
♣ A Q J 8 5

Opening Lead
♠ J

	N	
W		E
	S	

Declarer (Zia)
♠ K 8 2
♡ A K J
◊ A K 8 2
♣ K 10 3

N	E	S (Zia)	W
			Pass
Pass	Pass	2NT	Pass
6NT	Pass	Pass	Pass

It's nice to finish off with a slam contract. We've got eleven sure tricks and it looks as if there are good chances for a twelfth trick but, before we decide what to do, let's go through the steps of the plan.

Solution to Hand 3:

Contract: 6NT

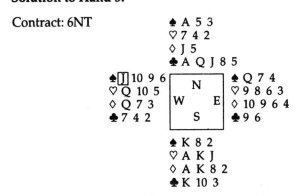

♠ A 5 3
♡ 7 4 2
◊ J 5
♣ A Q J 8 5

♠ J 10 9 6   ♠ Q 7 4
♡ Q 10 5   ♡ 9 8 6 3
◊ Q 7 3   ◊ 10 9 6 4
♣ 7 4 2   ♣ 9 6

♠ K 8 2
♡ A K J
◊ A K 8 2
♣ K 10 3

S We need to come up with twelve winners to make our slam.

T We have two sure spade tricks, two sure heart tricks, two sure diamond tricks and five sure club tricks. That's eleven tricks and we need only one more.

O The obvious place for our extra trick appears to be in the heart suit. If East has the ♡Q, a successful finesse will see us home. Before staking everything on the location of the ♡Q, however, we want to look for other options. The dummy's ◊J gives us a second chance. If West has the ◊Q, we can get a trick by leading towards the dummy's ◊J. Since there are two choices, we'd like to combine them if possible. Does it matter which we try first? Suppose we try the heart finesse first and it loses to West's ♡Q. Now, it is too late to try leading towards the dummy's ◊J. Even if West has the ◊Q, he will win a trick with it and the defence will have two tricks, defeating the contract. Let's try it the other way. If we lead toward the ◊J first and it turns out that East has the ◊Q, we can still fall back on our second chance of the heart finesse. That sounds like a better approach.

P Having gone through our plan, we now know to win the first trick with the ♠K in our hand and lead a diamond towards the dummy's ◊J. When West wins this trick with the ◊Q, the dummy's ◊J has become our twelfth trick. Careful play has brought in our slam contract, along with the substantial scoring bonus for making it. A nice way to finish. Thank goodness we took time to make our plan before playing to the first trick.

PART THREE: DEFENCE

CHAPTER 26

General Principles

Investing in a new sport can be costly. When you decide to take up bridge all the equipment you need is a pack of cards, a table, and four people. Already you are as well-prepared as a world champion.

Defence has been labelled the most difficult part of the game of bridge. That is certainly true, but it is as intriguing and exciting as it is difficult. You defend contracts twice as often as you end up being *declarer* since, when your side is playing the contract, you are the *dummy* half the time, whereas a defender is involved in every hand and has to be constantly alert.

Becoming a good *defender*, therefore, can double your effectiveness at the bridge table. In addition, when you take the opportunity to think about the defence of a hand, the game becomes much more interesting. Rather than waiting for those occasions when you are declarer, you find yourself looking forward to every hand.

The defenders are interested in preventing the declarer from making his contract. They work as a team, but the catch is, unlike the declarer, they don't have the benefit of being able to see each other's cards. This is quite a test because they are dealing with the unknown. In the game of bridge, your relationship with your partner is as important as luck and skill, and this is constantly tested when you have to use your imagination and work as a team to defeat the declarer's contract. In this book, we will let you in on some of the secrets of the experts and show you how they make magic from their cards when they are defending. In this book, the declarer will always be in the South position and the dummy in the North position. You will sometimes be West, and sometimes East.

Making a plan

Most bridge books traditionally start teaching defence by concentrating on rules for making the opening lead. A typical example would be for a beginner to be shown a hand like the following and asked what he would lead against a no-trump contract:

♠ A K
♡ 8 4
◊ Q J 10 6 5
♣ 6 5 3 2

The most crucial point of the defence, however, and the concept that will make you more effective, is to understand that it is necessary to look at the big picture before you are ever able to select an opening lead. What no-trump contract are you defending against? 1NT, 3NT or 6NT?

The defenders, in the same manner as the declarer, get their best results through making a plan. Always take a moment to think about how you are going to defeat the contract before playing a card. The letters S T O P can be used to help you remember the steps to go through in defence as in declarer play. **STOP** stands for:

S – stop to consider your goal
T – tally your winners
O – organize your plan
P – put your plan into operation

Defence has two parts, so you will sometimes have to STOP twice. First, before the opening lead when all you have to go on is the bidding and your hand; then, after the dummy goes down and you have more information.

Stop to consider your goal

The first step when defending is to consider your goal. How many tricks do you and your partner need to defeat the contract? This might seem an elementary point and yet, whether you are a world champion or a beginner, the process is the same. If the opponents are playing in a contract of 3NT, you need five tricks to defeat the contract. If they are playing in 6NT, you need only two tricks. The goal affects each card played by the partnership, starting with the opening lead.

Tally your winners

After you have considered the partnership's goal, the next step is to see how close you are to getting there. Tally your winners. A *winner*, or a *sure trick*, is a trick you can take without giving up the lead to the declarer. For example, look at the following hand and consider how many winners you have:

♠ 10 7 2
♡ A 8 6 5 4
◇ K Q
♣ 8 3 2

You have one winner, the ♡A. Although there is good potential for an extra trick in the diamond suit, there is no sure trick. If declarer has the ◇A, you would have to give up the lead before you could take a trick in the diamond suit. Now, consider this hand:

♠ 7 4
♡ Q 9 6 5 4
◇ A K Q
♣ A 5 3

Here, you have four sure tricks: the ◇A, ◇K, ◇Q and ♣A. One final example:

♠ 3
♡ J 8 4 3 2
◇ K J 10
♣ A Q 4 3

There is only one winner. You have lots of potential for taking more tricks, but the only trick you can take for sure is the ♣A.

There is an interesting difference between counting sure tricks when you are the declarer and counting them when you are a defender. Take a look at this layout of cards from the declarer's point of view:

Dummy
♡ Q 10 4

Declarer
♡ A K 2

When you are the declarer, you can see that there are three sure tricks in the heart suit. Now let's look at a similar holding from the defender's point of view:

You   Partner
◇ Q 10 4   ◇ A K 2

Your ◇Q is a winner against a no-trump contract (and against a suit contract, unless the declarer is void), but you are unlikely to be sure that it is a winner since you cannot see your partner's cards.

A defender, therefore, must be more flexible than a declarer when it comes to counting winners. You have to be prepared to recognize the potential for tricks by making assumptions about your partner's hand. As we shall see, the bidding and any cards that have already been played will often give you clues as to where your side's winners lie.

Organize your plan

Having considered your goal and counted your sure tricks, you can see how close you are to reaching your objective. You now look at the options available to get you to your target. Let's bring back our first hand:

♠ A K
♡ 8 4
◇ Q J 10 6 5
♣ 6 5 3 2

Let's first suppose you are defending against a contract of 6NT. The first step of the plan tells you that your goal is to take two tricks in order to defeat the contract. The second step tells you that you have two winners. When you come to the third step, you don't need to think of any ways of developing additional tricks, since you already have enough winners to defeat the contract. You can move on to putting your plan into action.

Suppose, however, that you are defending against a contract of 3NT. Now you need five tricks to defeat the contract but have only two sure winners. At the third step of your plan, you are going to have to look for ways to develop the extra tricks you need. After examining the options, you will have to organize them to give your side the best chance of defeating the contract.

Your focus would shift from the spade suit to the diamond suit, since it appears to have the potential to develop the extra tricks you need. If your partner had bid hearts or clubs during the auction, you would consider the option of leading his suit to try and establish the winners you need. With more than one choice, you will have to decide which approach gives you the best chance of defeating the contract. Sometimes, you may even be able to combine your chances. The remaining chapters in this book will focus on the options the defenders have for developing the additional winners they need.

Put your plan into operation

Only after you have gone through the first three steps of your plan are you ready to choose a card to play. Even though you have decided on the suit you are going to play, there may be a consideration as to which card you should play in the suit. By choosing the card carefully, you may be able to give information to your partner.

In our example hand above, having decided that you should

lead a diamond against a contract of 3NT, most players would lead the ◊Q, top of a *sequence*. As we shall see in later chapters, there are technical reasons for selecting a specific card from your holding in a suit.

You do not simply make a plan before choosing the opening lead. Both partners must be formulating a plan on every hand. Often, your plan will have to change as you acquire additional information.

For example, suppose your partner has led the ♣5 against a contract of 3NT and, after seeing the dummy, you (East) have to choose what to do on the following hand:

Contract: 3NT

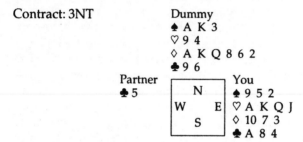

Dummy
♠ A K 3
♡ 9 4
◊ A K Q 8 6 2
♣ 9 6

Partner
♣ 5

You
♠ 9 5 2
♡ A K Q J
◊ 10 7 3
♣ A 8 4

Stop to consider your goal
You are defending against a contract of 3NT and so you need to take five tricks. That is your goal.

Tally your winners
A winner is a trick you can take without giving up the lead to the opponents. Look at the cards you hold in each suit and count the sure tricks:

Spades: 0 winners
Hearts   4 winners
Diamonds: 0 winners
Clubs: 1 winner

The total is five sure tricks. This is enough to reach your goal.

Organize your plan

You have the option of winning the first trick with the ♣A or play-ing one of your other clubs. If you win the ♣A, you have the option of *returning your partner's suit*, by leading another club, or switch-ing to a different suit. Since the first two steps of your plan have told you that you have enough sure tricks to defeat the contract, you do not have to look further.

Put your plan into operation

This hand is quite straightforward. Win the first trick with the ♣A and take your four heart tricks, defeating the contract. You can then lead another club and see if your partner has any more tricks for the defence.

Looking at the complete hand, you can see that doing anything else would be fatal:

Contract: 3NT

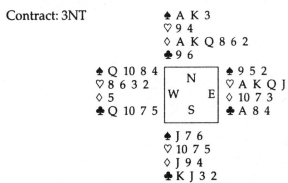

```
                    ♠ A K 3
                    ♡ 9 4
                    ◇ A K Q 8 6 2
                    ♣ 9 6
   ♠ Q 10 8 4                      ♠ 9 5 2
   ♡ 8 6 3 2         N             ♡ A K Q J
   ◇ 5            W     E          ◇ 10 7 3
   ♣ Q 10 7 5        S             ♣ A 8 4
                    ♠ J 7 6
                    ♡ 10 7 5
                    ◇ J 9 4
                    ♣ K J 3 2
```

If you did not win the first trick with the ♣A, the declarer would win the first trick and quickly scamper home, taking two spade tricks and six diamond tricks in addition to the first trick. The same thing would happen if, after winning the ♣A, you do anything except take your four heart tricks.

Let's change your hand slightly from the previous example:

Contract: 3NT

Dummy

♠ A K
♡ A 4
◊ A K Q 8 6 2
♣ 9 6 4

Partner
♣ 5

You
♠ 9 5 2
♡ K Q J 10 9
◊ 10 7 3
♣ A 8

Stop to consider your goal
You again need to take five tricks to defeat the contract.

Tally your winners
Look at your sure tricks in each suit:

Spades: 0 winners
Hearts: 0 winners
Diamonds: 0 winners
Clubs: 1 winner

Although you have a strong-looking heart suit, you do not have sure winners in that suit since you will have to *drive out* the dummy's ♡A first.

Organize your plan
Again you have a couple of options. You can win the ♣A and lead another club, returning your partner's suit. Alternatively, you can win the ♣A and lead a heart, planning to drive out the ♡A and establish four heart tricks, enough to defeat the contract if you can regain the lead. It is certainly not a good idea to let the declarer win the first club trick, since he will immediately be able to take two spade tricks, a heart trick and six diamond tricks to make the contract.

Should you switch to hearts or lead back a club? This is the type of situation you will often encounter when defending. It would help if you could see your partner's cards, but you cannot. You will have to try to visualize a holding in your partner's hand that would allow you to defeat the contract. If you switch to a heart, the declarer will be able to win the ♡A and take enough tricks to make the contract. Instead, you will have to hope that your partner has a good enough club suit to let the defence take the first five tricks.

Put your plan into operation
Having gone through your plan, you come down to your only option of winning the ♣A and leading back your remaining club. The rest is up to your partner. Let's take a look at the complete hand:

Contract: 3NT

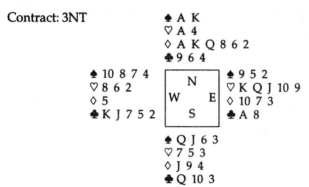

As you can see, your club return traps the declarer's ♣Q and allows your partner to take four more club tricks to defeat the contract. By always making a plan first, you will find yourself making the right decisions in defence.

Summary

Before deciding what card to lead or what card to play on a particular trick, STOP to consider the total picture. What is your goal? How close are you to reaching it? Organize a plan: either take your winners if you have enough on your own to defeat the contract or develop a way of getting the extra tricks your partnership needs. Only after you have gone through the plan are you ready to put it into operation.

The defenders have more of a challenge because they cannot see each other's hands. They each have to keep very open minds when making their plan and must be ready to adjust as they see the cards played by their partner and the declarer.

Over Zia's shoulder

Now we are going to watch Zia in action to see how even a world-class player has to STOP to make a plan before deciding on what card to play in a specific suit. We are going to look over Zia's shoulder. Sometimes Zia will be in the position of making the opening lead and will be sitting West; at other times he will be sitting East and his partner will have made the opening lead.

In each example, we will give the auction first and then you can see how Zia endeavours to defeat the opponents.

Here's our first hand:

Hand 1 Dealer: South

North	East	South	West (Zia)
		1◊	Pass
1♡	Pass	2NT	Pass
6NT	Pass	Pass	Pass

```
          (Zia)
          ♠ 9 6              ┌───────────┐
          ♡ 10 9 8 6 2       │     N     │
          ◊ K 7 3           │ W       E │
          ♣ K Q 10         │     S     │
                            └───────────┘
```

The very first hand and I find myself on lead against a slam. I hope the opponents aren't going to have such good hands all the time. Against no-trump contracts, I usually lead my longest suit, hoping to develop as many tricks as I can for our side. Before leading a card, however, I'm going to STOP and go through the steps of my plan. How are we going to defeat this slam contract?

Solution to Hand 1:

Contract: 6NT

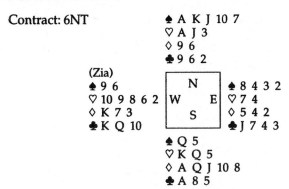

```
                        ♠ A K J 10 7
                        ♡ A J 3
                        ◊ 9 6
                        ♣ 9 6 2
        (Zia)
        ♠ 9 6                          ♠ 8 4 3 2
        ♡ 10 9 8 6 2   W       E       ♡ 7 4
        ◊ K 7 3                         ◊ 5 4 2
        ♣ K Q 10                        ♣ J 7 4 3
                        ♠ Q 5
                        ♡ K Q 5
                        ◊ A Q J 10 8
                        ♣ A 8 5
```

S Stop to consider the goal. We need two tricks to defeat 6NT.
T Tally the winners. We look to see how many sure tricks we have in each suit and can't find any. Not a good start for the defence. I always like to have a couple of aces to lead against a slam.
O Organize the plan. We won't get any tricks in spades or hearts unless my partner has a high card in one of the suits. Since the opponents have bid a slam, that is unlikely. I might get a trick with the ◊K, since the opponent on my right bid diamonds. I can also develop a trick by leading the ♣K to drive out the ♣A and establish my ♣Q. That looks like the best chance for two tricks.
P Put the plan into operation. I lead the ♣K and the declarer wins the ♣A. After he takes some spade tricks, he leads a diamond from the dummy and plays the ◊Q. I win the trick with the ◊K and quickly take the ♣Q to defeat the contract.

In fact, we can take three more tricks – the ♣Q, partner's ♣J and the thirteenth club in the East hand. Three down in a slam contract that would have been made had we not taken time to make a plan! If I had led a heart, instead of the ♣K, the declarer would have won the trick and played on the diamond suit. Although he would lose a trick to my ◊K, he would have the rest of the tricks no matter what I led back. I'll bet that my partner was happy to see us defeat the contract with his pathetic collection of cards!

Hand 2 Dealer: North

North	East (Zia)	South	West
1♣	Pass	1♡	Pass
4♡	Pass	Pass	Pass

Dummy
♠ Q 3
♡ K Q 7 5
◇ Q 6
♣ A K Q J 3

Partner
♠ 10

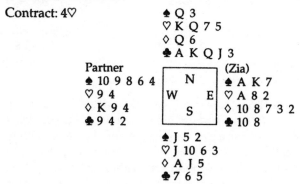

(Zia)
♠ A K 7
♡ A 8 2
◇ 10 8 7 3 2
♣ 10 8

This time, they've only bid to a game contract. Let's try and keep our record intact by defeating this contract as well. Partner seems to have found a good lead since it looks as though I'm going to get two sure spade tricks. That won't be enough to defeat the contract, however, so I'd better STOP and make a plan.

Solution to Hand 2:

Contract: 4♡

                 ♠ Q 3
                 ♡ K Q 7 5
                 ◇ Q 6
                 ♣ A K Q J 3

Partner
♠ 10 9 8 6 4   (Zia)
♡ 9 4   ♠ A K 7
◇ K 9 4   ♡ A 8 2
♣ 9 4 2   ◇ 10 8 7 3 2
                       ♣ 10 8

                 ♠ J 5 2
                 ♡ J 10 6 3
                 ◇ A J 5
                 ♣ 7 6 5

S We need four tricks

T We tally our sure tricks:

Spades:	2 winners: the ♠A and ♠K
Hearts:	1 winner: the ♡A
Diamonds:	0 winners
Clubs:	0 winners

O We organize our plan.

Since we have only three tricks, we'll need to use our imagination to see where we can find one more. It doesn't look as if we can get any more tricks from spades, hearts or clubs, so it will have to be the diamond suit. It should be possible if my partner has either the ◊A or ◊K, as long as we don't wait too long. Otherwise, the declarer may be able to discard his diamond losers.

P We put the plan into operation.

We win the first trick with the ♠K and lead a diamond. There is no need to take the ♠A right away. My partner will realize that we have the ♠A when our ♠K wins the first trick. On the actual hand, my partner wins with the ◊K and then leads another spade. Our ♡A defeats the contract.

If we had taken both our spade tricks before making a plan, the declarer could make the contract. When we then led a diamond, the declarer could win the ◊A and discard the dummy's remaining diamond on his established ♠J. Oops!

CHAPTER 27

Sure Tricks in Defence

Bridge is luck, skill and your relationship with your partner. Never underestimate the importance of the power of this connection with the person sitting opposite you.

The defenders may sometimes have enough sure tricks to defeat the contract, but taking them may not be so easy.

Taking your sure tricks

Consider the following suit that you and your partner hold when defending against a no-trump contract:

You
♡ Q 8 3

```
     N
  W     E
     S
```

Partner
♡ A K J 10 2

If you were the declarer, you would have no trouble seeing that you have five sure tricks in this suit. You would also have no difficulty in taking the tricks. You could start by playing the *high card* from the *short side*, the queen and then playing a small card to your partner's remaining high cards.

As a defender, the situation is much more complex. First, you cannot see your partner's hand. Looking at only your cards, it is impossible to know that your side has five tricks in the suit. You might choose to lead a completely different suit. Even if you choose to lead the suit, you may not get all the tricks you are entitled to. Suppose you lead a small card and your partner wins the first two tricks with the ace and king and then leads a small card back to your queen. Now you are on lead and your partner's remaining winners are *stranded* unless he has an *entry* (a winner in another suit).

If you are defending against a suit contract, there are additional difficulties. Even if you could see your partner's cards, you would not know how many sure tricks you had without some additional information. After all, the declarer could have a singleton, or even a void. You may have no sure tricks in the suit.

The situation is far from hopeless, however. You can get clues from the auction – both from the bids made by your side and those made by your opponents. This will help you plan the defence and decide which cards to play during the hand. Next, there are a number of guidelines to help you when you have no other information to go on. Finally, you and your partner can help each other through the use of *signals*. You can give information through the specific card you choose to play in a suit.

In this chapter, we'll look at some examples of how the defenders co-operate to make sure they get the tricks to which they are entitled. In later chapters, we'll develop these concepts in more detail. The most important thing to remember is that you have to use your imagination. To compensate for the declarer's advantage of being able to see both his hand and the dummy, you will have to try to visualize the layout of the missing cards. With a little practice, you'll soon find yourself defending as though you could see right through the backs of the cards.

Leading your partner's suit

Where are you going to start looking for your side's sure tricks when they are not staring you in the face? If your partner has bid a suit during the auction, perhaps when opening the bidding or making an overcall, a good place to start looking is your partner's suit. In fact, unless you have a clearly better alternative, a good guideline is: **lead your partner's suit.**

To make sure that you get the sure tricks you are entitled to, you have to be careful in choosing the card you lead. Suppose this is

the layout:

```
        ┌─────┐
You     │   N │  Partner
♡ A 4   │ W   E│  ♡ K Q J 10 2
        │   S │
        └─────┘
```

If you lead the ♡4, your partner can win the first trick and lead another heart which you win with the ♡A. You have taken the first two tricks but you are now on lead. Your partner cannot take the rest of his sure tricks in the suit. Instead, you want to use the same principle that the declarer uses in this situation. You start by leading the ♡A, the high card from the short side. Now you can play the ♡4 over to your partner and he can take the rest of his sure tricks in the suit. For a full explanation of this principle, refer back to Chapter 16, General Principles of declarer play.

Notice that you cannot actually see your partner's cards when you lead the ♡A. Instead, you are visualizing the potential layout of the missing cards that will allow you to take your side's sure tricks in the suit. As a general rule, always lead the **top of a doubleton in your partner's suit**. Let's see how this works out when you have to make an opening lead from the following hand:

♠ 8 7 3
♡ J 7
♢ 10 9 8 7 2
♣ 9 6 5

The opponents have reached a contract of 3NT after your partner opened the bidding with 1♡. You should lead your partner's suit. With a doubleton, you follow the guideline of leading the top card, the ♡J. Here is the complete hand:

Contract: 3NT

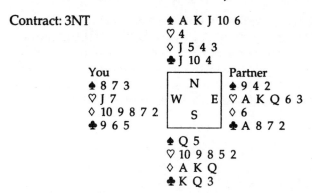

♠ A K J 10 6
♡ 4
◊ J 5 4 3
♣ J 10 4

You
♠ 8 7 3
♡ J 7
◊ 10 9 8 7 2
♣ 9 6 5

Partner
♠ 9 4 2
♡ A K Q 6 3
◊ 6
♣ A 8 7 2

♠ Q 5
♡ 10 9 8 5 2
◊ A K Q
♣ K Q 3

Your ♡J wins the first trick and, when you lead another heart, your partner takes the ♡A, ♡K, ♡Q, ♡6 and ♣A to defeat the contract by two tricks. If you had led a diamond, the declarer would make the contract, taking five spade tricks and four diamond tricks. If you had led the ♡7 instead of the ♡J, your partner would have won the first trick – but look what happens now! If he returns a small heart, you can win with the ♡J but have no more hearts to lead to your partner's hand. And if your partner instead leads the ♡A or ♡K to the second trick, your ♡J will crash underneath it and establish a winner for declarer's ♡10. Remember – in order to follow the principle of playing the high card from the *short side* in our side's long suits, we must lead the top card from a doubleton in partner's bid suit.

Leading your own suit

Suppose you end up defending against a no-trump contract and your partner has not bid a suit. Now, you might have to look for sure tricks from one of your own suits. It is not difficult to see where the sure tricks are coming from if you have a suit headed by the ace, king and queen, for example, but what if your suit looks like this:

♠ A Q 8 4 2

This is where you are going to have to use your imagination. If you need to get a lot of tricks from this suit, you will have to visualize that your partner holds the ♠K. If that is the case, how should you

Defence

go about taking your tricks in the suit? You want to play the high card from the short side first, so you should start by leading a small spade. When your partner wins the first trick with his (hoped for) ♠K, he will be able to lead a small spade back to you so that you can take the rest of your sure tricks. You hope the complete layout of the suit is something like this:

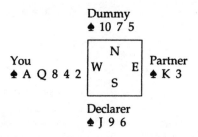

Note that if you started by leading the ♠A and then a spade to your partner's ♠K, your partner would have no spade left to lead back to your ♠Q. Of course your partner may not have the ♠K but, as we shall see later, it may still be a good idea to start off by leading a low spade when you are going to need some help from your partner in the suit.

Sometimes, you cannot afford to lead a low card, even when you are missing one or more high cards. Suppose you have this suit:

◊ K Q J 10 2

If you were sure that your partner held the ◊A, you could lead a small diamond and your partner could lead a diamond back so that you would get five sure tricks in the suit. Unfortunately, you cannot see your partner's cards and it is unlikely that you can be certain that your partner holds the ◊A. If the declarer holds the ◊A and you lead a small diamond, the declarer may win the trick with the ◊9 and still have the ◊A. As we shall see in the next chapter, in situations where you have a strong sequence of cards, it is usually best to lead one of your high cards. In the above example, if the declarer does hold the ◊A, you will at least prevent him from winning a trick with a smaller diamond and holding on to his ◊A for later.

When you lead from a strong sequence of cards, you lead the top of your *touching cards*, the ◊K in the above example. Why? Remember our earlier comment about giving information to your partner. By always leading the top card of a sequence, you tell your partner that you do not have the next higher card, but you do have the next lower card. In the above example, leading the ◊K tells your partner that you do not have the ◊A, the next higher card, but you do have the ◊Q, the next lower card. All of a sudden your partner has information about the location of three cards.

Leading the top of a sequence can help the partnership take its sure tricks in this type of situation:

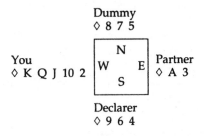

```
                    Dummy
                    ◊ 8 7 5
                   ┌─────────┐
                   │    N    │
    You            │ W     E │  Partner
    ◊ K Q J 10 2   │    S    │  ◊ A 3
                   └─────────┘
                    Declarer
                    ◊ 9 6 4
```

You can see that you have five sure tricks in the diamond suit but actually taking them at the table might not be so easy. If you start by leading the ◊K and your partner lets you win the first trick, you can lead a second diamond to his ◊A. Once again, however, you have ended in the wrong hand at the wrong time.

How can this be prevented? By leading the ◊K, you are telling your partner that you have the ◊Q and possibly the ◊J as well, since you are leading the top of a strong sequence, rather than leading a low card. Now it is your partner's turn to use his imagination. He can visualize your holding in the suit and he knows that the defence wants to start by winning with the high card from the short side. Instead of letting you win the first trick with the ◊K, he can *overtake* it with his ◊A and then lead back the ◊3 to the rest of your sure tricks. The technical term for this type of play is *unblocking the suit* since the suit would be blocked if your partner had only the ◊A left with no small card to lead to your winners.

The declarer would have had an easy time taking five tricks with the above combination of cards. But the defenders can accomplish the same task with the use of a little imagination and ingenuity.

Summary

The defenders take their sure tricks in the same way that the declarer does. Whenever possible, they want to start by leading the high card(s) from the short side so that they can then lead a small card over to the remaining winners on the long side. Unfortunately, since they cannot see each other's cards, it is more difficult for the defenders to determine whether or not they have sure tricks in a suit and, even then, they may have to be careful to ensure that they get all their tricks.

The defenders have to use their imagination to help visualize where sure tricks are coming from. They get their clues from the auction, from the cards their partner leads and from the cards their partner plays during the hand. In the end, you will often find that two heads are better than one!

Over Zia's shoulder

Hand 1 Dealer: North

North	East	South	West
			(Zia)
1◊	1♡	1♠	Pass
2♣	Pass	2NT	Pass
3NT	Pass	Pass	Pass

(Zia)
♠ J 10 9 6 2
♡ K 6
◊ 7 6
♣ J 10 9 7

```
        N
   W         E
        S
```

Here I am on lead against 3NT and my best suit appears to be spades. I also have a nice-looking sequence in clubs. Should I start by leading a spade, or are there other things I should be thinking about? I'd better STOP and make my plan before I do the wrong thing.

Solution to Hand 1:

Contract: 3NT

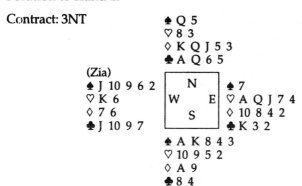

♠ Q 5
♡ 8 3
◇ K Q J 5 3
♣ A Q 6 5

(Zia)
♠ J 10 9 6 2
♡ K 6
◇ 7 6
♣ J 10 9 7

♠ 7
♡ A Q J 7 4
◇ 10 8 4 2
♣ K 3 2

♠ A K 8 4 3
♡ 10 9 5 2
◇ A 9
♣ 8 4

S Stop to consider the goal. We are going to need five tricks to defeat 3NT.

T Tally the winners. We don't have any sure tricks in our hand.

O Organize the plan. With no winners in our hand, we are going to have to find some. I'm going to need help from my partner, so which suit offers the most promise? Although spades is our best suit, we must remember to listen to the auction. My partner overcalled in hearts, so that is where his length and strength is likely to be. With no clearly better alternative, I should lead my partner's suit, hearts.

P Put the plan into operation. With a doubleton in my partner's suit, I lead the top card, the ♡K. On the actual hand, this works very nicely. My partner lets us win this trick and I continue with the ♡6 over to my partner's remaining winners. We get the first five tricks and defeat the contract.

If I had not led a heart, the declarer would make the contract, taking three spade tricks, five diamond tricks and a club trick. It is always important to listen to what your partner has said during the auction. Also, if I had led a small heart, my partner could win the trick and lead a heart back to my ♡K, but we would be in the wrong hand to take the rest of our winners. By leading the ♡K, we tackle the suit by playing the high card from the short side first.

Hand 2 Dealer: East

North	East (Zia)	South	West
	Pass	1♡	Pass
3♡	Pass	4♡	Pass
Pass	Pass		

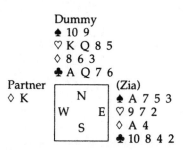

Dummy
♠ 10 9
♡ K Q 8 5
◇ 8 6 3
♣ A Q 7 6

Partner
◇ K

(Zia)
♠ A 7 5 3
♡ 9 7 2
◇ A 4
♣ 10 8 4 2

It looks as though my partner has made a good lead. If the declarer has no singletons or voids, we should have two sure tricks in diamonds and one in spades. But where is the *setting trick* (by 'setting trick' I mean the trick that will defeat, or *set*, the contract) going to come from?

Solution to Hand 2:

Contract: 4♡

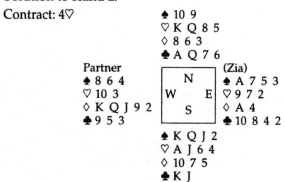

♠ 10 9
♡ K Q 8 5
◇ 8 6 3
♣ A Q 7 6

Partner
♠ 8 6 4
♡ 10 3
◇ K Q J 9 2
♣ 9 5 3

(Zia)
♠ A 7 5 3
♡ 9 7 2
◇ A 4
♣ 10 8 4 2

♠ K Q J 2
♡ A J 6 4
◇ 10 7 5
♣ K J

S We need four tricks to defeat 4♡.

T Tally the sure tricks:

Spades: 1 winner (the ♠A)

Hearts: 0 winners

Diamonds: 2 winners: (the ◊A and my partner's ◊K)

Clubs: 0 winners

O Organize the plan. Since we have only three tricks, we must use our imagination to see where we can find one more. My partner's lead of the ◊K has given a clue. Since he leads the top of touching high cards when he has a sequence, he should have the ◊Q and, perhaps, the ◊J as well. If the declarer has three diamonds in his hand, we are entitled to three sure tricks in the suit to go along with our ♠A.

P Put the plan into operation. We have to be careful to ensure that we get all our diamond tricks. On my partner's ◊K, I will have to play the ◊A, so that I will have a small diamond left to lead back to my partner's winners. Otherwise, the suit will be blocked. On the actual hand, this lets us take the first three diamond tricks and then a spade trick.

If I let my partner's ◊K win the first trick, the declarer makes the contract. My partner can lead a diamond to my ◊A, but we have no way to get our other diamond trick. The declarer will eventually discard his remaining diamond on one of the dummy's club winners.

CHAPTER 28

Promoting High Cards

Staring at either your partner or the opponents should be avoided.

As we saw in the previous chapter, the defenders sometimes have enough sure tricks to defeat the contract. All they have to do is be careful to take them. More often, however, they will need to develop some of the winners they will need in order to defeat the contract. When a declarer needs extra tricks, one of his most straightforward options is to develop them through *promotion*. There is nothing to stop the defenders from using the same technique.

Promoting winners

When you have a series, or *sequence*, of touching high cards, you have a good opportunity to promote winners. Consider this suit:

♠ K Q J 10 9

If the declarer has the ♠A, you do not have a single sure trick. There is, however, a lot of potential to develop winners. You can lead the ♠K – remember, you lead the top of your touching high cards to help tell your partner what you have – and drive out the ♠A. You will end up promoting your remaining cards in the suit into four winners.

You will not always be dealt such a powerful sequence. Nevertheless, promoting winners when you have a sequence is an excellent source of tricks. Look at this holding:

♡ Q J 10 9 8

Even if the other side has both the ♡A and ♡K, your side has the potential to enjoy three tricks from this suit. You would have to give the lead up twice but, with a little patience, you will eventually develop some winners. Notice that you will have to give up the lead to the declarer when you are trying to promote tricks. You have no choice, however, if that is the only way you can get enough winners to defeat the contract. Don't be afraid to give up the lead, if it will help you reach your objective.

There may be times when you have to give up the lead as many as three times in order to promote the winners you need. For example, suppose you are on lead against a contract of 3NT with the following hand:

♠ J 10 9 8 7
♡ A 6 3
♢ A 5
♣ A 8 5

You need five tricks to defeat the contract but you only have three sure tricks. Where can the extra winners come from? It may seem like a lot of work, but you should be able to promote the winners you need in the spade suit. Let's look at the complete hand and see what happens if you start off by leading the top of your sequence, the ♠J:

Contract: 3NT

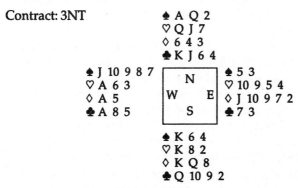

```
                    ♠ A Q 2
                    ♡ Q J 7
                    ♢ 6 4 3
                    ♣ K J 6 4
  ♠ J 10 9 8 7                        ♠ 5 3
  ♡ A 6 3          ┌─────────┐        ♡ 10 9 5 4
  ♢ A 5            │    N    │        ♢ J 10 9 7 2
  ♣ A 8 5         W│         │E       ♣ 7 3
                   │    S    │
                   └─────────┘
                    ♠ K 6 4
                    ♡ K 8 2
                    ♢ K Q 8
                    ♣ Q 10 9 2
```

The declarer has the top three cards in the spade suit but, if you are persistent, you can prevail. The declarer can win the first trick but he also needs to promote some winners to make the contract. Suppose he leads a club. You win with the ♣A and lead another spade, driving out his second winner in the suit. When the declarer leads a heart, to develop winners in that suit, you win and lead a spade once more. This drives out the declarer's remaining high card in the suit. He still does not have enough winners to make the contract. When he finally leads a diamond, you win with the ◊A and take your two promoted spade winners to set the contract.

Many hands are similar to this. It is a race between the declarer and the defenders to see which side can develop the tricks they need first. The defenders will not always win the race. They do, however, have the advantage of the opening lead. They can strike the first blow.

Preserving entries

In the above hand, it was important that you led spades every time you had the lead and that you held on to your aces in the other suits. Each ace was an *entry* to your hand, a winner that let you get the lead. Entries are important to the defenders, especially when they are trying to promote winners. To promote winners, you have to give up the lead to the declarer. You will need entries, therefore, to regain the lead and let you take your winners once they are established.

On the above hand, look what would happen if you had started by taking your three aces before you led spades. You would get the first three tricks but the declarer would now be able to take the rest. By taking your aces, you would be promoting winners for the declarer, rather than helping the defence.

How do you know when to take your winners and when to hold on to them as entries? After all, in the previous chapter we saw that the defenders must sometimes take their sure tricks in order to defeat the contract. The secret is always to make your plan. Your plan will tell you how many winners you need to defeat the contract. If you have enough winners, go ahead and take them. If you do not, your priority is to develop the extra winners you need, not to take your sure tricks.

Getting help from your partner

When promoting tricks, you do not need all the high cards in the same hand. Consider this layout when defending against a no-trump contract:

The only high card missing is the ♣A, so you should be able to develop four sure tricks through promotion. The difficulty, of course, is that you cannot see your partner's hand. How do you know that he has the ♣Q and ♣10? You cannot be sure. This is where you have to rely on your imagination once again. You have to visualize the high clubs in your partner's hand. Once you have done that, how do you actually go about promoting the tricks? Remembering the principle of playing the high card from the short side first, you want to use your partner's high card(s) first, so that he will have a small card left to lead back to your winners. You do this by leading a low card initially. This is the same way that a declarer would tackle the suit.

Although you cannot see your partner's cards, leading a low card from a suit in which you do not have a strong sequence will work well against a no-trump contract in a number of situations. For example, the complete layout of the suit might actually be something like this:

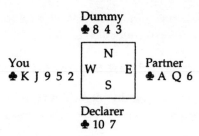

Dummy
♣ 8 4 3

You
♣ K J 9 5 2

Partner
♣ A Q 6

Declarer
♣ 10 7

In this case, you are not actually promoting tricks. Instead, you are taking your sure tricks. You could not tell, when you led your low card, which would be the case. In fact, your partner might have neither the ♣A nor the ♣Q. Even so, as we shall see in later chapters, leading a low club may work out well.

In promoting winners in a suit when the high cards are divided between the two hands, the partners must co-operate. If one partner starts leading a suit, trying to promote winners, and the other partner gains the lead, he should return his partner's suit unless he has a clearly better alternative. Otherwise, the partnership will be working at cross-purposes. The partnership does not usually have the time or resources for each partner to promote his own suit. The partner making the opening lead has set the direction and, unless it becomes clear that things have got off on the wrong foot, both partners should work together on the same plan for defeating the contract. Here is an example in a complete hand:

Contract: 3NT

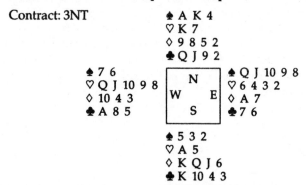

♠ A K 4
♡ K 7
◊ 9 8 5 2
♣ Q J 9 2

♠ 7 6
♡ Q J 10 9 8
◊ 10 4 3
♣ A 8 5

♠ Q J 10 9 8
♡ 6 4 3 2
◊ A 7
♣ 7 6

♠ 5 3 2
♡ A 5
◊ K Q J 6
♣ K 10 4 3

West gets off to the opening lead of the ♡Q, top of a sequence, planning to promote winners in the suit. The declarer wins the first trick with the ♡A and leads the ◊K, trying to promote his own winners in order to make the contract. What does East do when he wins the ◊A? East has his own spade suit in which he would like to promote winners, but it is too late for that. If East leads a spade, the declarer wins the trick and drives out West's ♣A. Whether West leads a heart or a spade, the declarer can win and take enough tricks to make the contract.

Instead, East must work with West to finish promoting the heart suit. After winning the ◊A, East leads another heart, driving out the dummy's ♡A. When the declarer leads a club, West can now win the ♣A and take his three promoted heart tricks to defeat the contract.

Putting it into practice

Having seen some of the ways you can go about developing tricks through promotion, let's see how you would choose the card to lead against a contract of 3NT with each of the following hands. We will assume that you have chosen to lead a spade. In later chapters, we will look further at the reasons you might choose a spade rather than one of the other suits.

1	♠ QJ1096	2	♠ Q10863	3	♠ QJ863
	♡ K72		♡ K72		♡ K72
	◊ 84		◊ 84		◊ 84
	♣ A95		♣ A95		♣ A95

In the first hand, lead the ♠Q, top of the touching cards in your strong sequence. Even if your partner has neither the ♠A nor ♠K, you should eventually be able to promote some winners in the suit. You do not want to lead your ♠6 in case the declarer can win the first trick with the ♠8 and still have the ♠A and ♠K left.

In the second hand, you do not have a strong sequence. You are going to need some help from your partner to promote tricks in the suit. Start by leading a low spade. With luck, your partner will have the ♠A, ♠K or ♠J and will be able to help you out. He may even hold two of these cards, making your task easier.

In the last hand, you have two touching cards but it is not really a strong sequence. It looks as though you are going to need some help from your partner to promote winners in the suit. Lead a low card. You are hoping that your partner holds the ♠A, ♠K or ♠10 to help you promote winners in the suit.

Summary

Promotion is one of the techniques the defenders can use to develop the tricks they need to defeat a contract. With a strong sequence of high cards, you generally lead the top of your touching cards. This helps to give your partner the information he needs to co-operate in promoting the tricks. Without a strong sequence, you will need help from your partner. In this case, you can lead a low card. The idea is to ensure that you get the (hoped for) high card(s) from the short side played first.

You will usually have to help when your partner is trying to promote winners. An important guideline to keep in mind is to return your partner's suit, unless you clearly have something better to do. This avoids the problem of working at cross-purposes with your partner's plan.

Over Zia's shoulder

Hand 1 Dealer: East

North	*East*	*South*	*West*
			(Zia)
	Pass	1♠	Double
2♠	Pass	3♠	Pass
4♠	Pass	Pass	Pass

(Zia)
♠ A K
♡ 8 6 4 2
◇ Q J 10
♣ A 7 6 3

Despite my *takeout double*, the opponents have bid on to game. How can I teach them to have a little more respect when I come into the auction? (For an explanation of the takeout double refer back to Chapter 15 on Doubles.)

Solution to Hand 1:

Contract 4♠

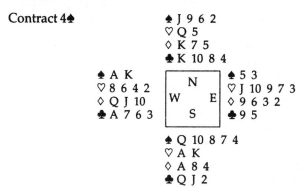

```
                    ♠ J 9 6 2
                    ♡ Q 5
                    ◊ K 7 5
                    ♣ K 10 8 4
   ♠ A K                          ♠ 5 3
   ♡ 8 6 4 2         N            ♡ J 10 9 7 3
   ◊ Q J 10      W     E          ◊ 9 6 3 2
   ♣ A 7 6 3         S            ♣ 9 5
                    ♠ Q 10 8 7 4
                    ♡ A K
                    ◊ A 8 4
                    ♣ Q J 2
```

S Stop to consider the goal. We need four tricks to defeat the 4♠ contract.

T Tally the winners. We have two sure tricks in spades and one in clubs.

O Organize the plan. We are going to have to find one more winner. Looking at the diamond suit, there is the possibility for promoting a trick in the suit, even if the declarer has both the ◊A and ◊K. This looks like our best choice. Developing a trick in another suit would require my partner to hold some strength, unlikely when the opponents have bid a game and we hold as much as we do.

P Put the plan into operation. When promoting tricks, it is best to get started as soon as possible, keeping our other high cards as entries. I start by leading the ◊Q, top of my sequence. The declarer can win the first trick and start to draw trumps. I'll win a spade trick and play another diamond, promoting my remaining diamond into a winner. When we regain the lead, we can take our diamond trick to defeat the contract.

If we had not gone about promoting a diamond trick, the declarer would make the contract. He would eventually discard one of his diamond losers on the dummy's extra club winners once our ♣A had been driven out.

Hand 2 Dealer: South

North	East	South	West
			(Zia)
		1NT	Pass
3NT	Pass	Pass	Pass

(Zia)
♠ K J 9 6 2
♡ 10 8 2
◇ 9 5
♣ A 8 3

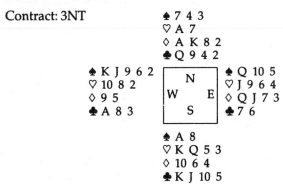

Here I am defending another game. I've only got one sure trick to take. I'd better STOP and make a plan to decide how best to go about defeating this contract.

Solution to Hand 2:

Contract: 3NT

```
                    ♠ 7 4 3
                    ♡ A 7
                    ◇ A K 8 2
                    ♣ Q 9 4 2
  ♠ K J 9 6 2                      ♠ Q 10 5
  ♡ 10 8 2          N              ♡ J 9 6 4
  ◇ 9 5         W       E          ◇ Q J 7 3
  ♣ A 8 3           S              ♣ 7 6
                    ♠ A 8
                    ♡ K Q 5 3
                    ◇ 10 6 4
                    ♣ K J 10 5
```

S Stop to consider the goal. We will need five sure tricks to defeat the 3NT contract.

T Tally the winners. We have only one sure trick, the ♣A.

O Organize the plan. I do not have a suit in which I can promote the winners we need all by myself. It looks as though I will need some help from my partner. Putting our imagination to work, we should be able to promote some tricks in the spade suit if my partner has one or more of the missing high spades. That suit offers the best possibility since any other suit will require a lot more help from my partner.

P Putting the plan into action, I lead a low spade. If my partner does have the help I need, I want to start by playing the high card from the short side, which should be my partner's side when we have length in the suit. On the actual hand, this works like a charm. My partner has the ♠Q, enough to help us drive out the declarer's ♠A. When we regain the lead with the ♣A, we can take our four promoted tricks in the spade suit.

If I was afraid to lead a spade on this hand, in case my partner did not have any help in the suit, we would never have defeated the contract. The declarer would drive out our ♣A and have an easy time taking nine tricks.

CHAPTER 29

Establishing Small Cards

Remember at the bridge table you want to meet old friends and make new ones ... not lose friends.

There are five *honours* in each suit – the ace, king, queen, jack and ten – and eight small cards – the nine down to the two. It is not often that the defenders have enough combined strength to defeat the contract with their high cards alone. It is important to remember, however, that a small card can have the same power as an honour if it can be established as a winner. This is especially valuable in a no-trump contract, since the declarer will have no trump suit to prevent you from taking a winner once it is established. Let's consider how you can defend by making the best use of the small cards.

Establishing tricks in long suits

Consider the layout of the following suit:

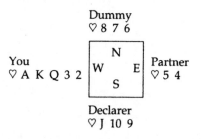

Dummy
♡ 8 7 6

You
♡ A K Q 3 2

Partner
♡ 5 4

Declarer
♡ J 10 9

You initially have only three sure tricks, the ♡A, the ♡K and the ♡Q. After you have played the suit three times, however, none of the other players has any hearts left. If the contract is in no trumps, you can now take two more tricks, the ♡3 and the lowly ♡2. The small cards in your long suit have become established as winners.

As we have seen in previous chapters, the high cards do not all have to be in the same hand for the defenders to have the opportunity to establish their small cards. Look at this layout:

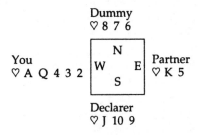

The situation is virtually identical. This time, however, you will have to start by leading a small card to your partner's ♡K and he can then return his small card back to your winners. We have seen in earlier chapters that leading a small heart from your holding is not unusual. It is the same thing you have to do when taking sure tricks or promoting winners, in order to get the high card played from the short side first.

Giving up the lead

You do not necessarily need any high cards in a suit in order to develop tricks through length. Look at this example:

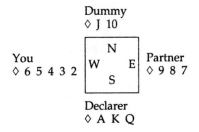

Although the declarer has all the honours in the suit, you can still develop two winners in the suit by leading it three times. Each time you lead the suit, one of the declarer's high cards disappears until, finally, no one has any diamonds left and your remaining two diamonds are winners.

To develop winners in this manner takes some patience and some luck. You must keep leading the suit at every opportunity. You must also be fortunate enough to have high cards in other suits with which to regain the lead each time you give it up. You don't always have to do all the work by yourself. If your partner has high cards in other suits he can help you out by leading diamonds every time he gets the opportunity to lead.

The moral, however, is not to be afraid to give up the lead if it will get you where you want to be. The declarer will frequently have to give you back the lead. Don't forget that the declarer is also trying to develop the tricks he needs and this will occasionally involve losing the lead to the defenders.

Considering the division of the missing cards

How many tricks can you expect to get from your small cards? That depends on how the missing cards are *divided* among the remaining hands. Suppose we return to an earlier example:

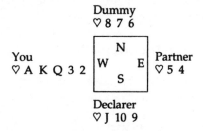

In this layout, you end up with five tricks – two from small cards – because the opponents' hearts are divided 3-3 (three in one hand, three in the other). Suppose we change the layout slightly:

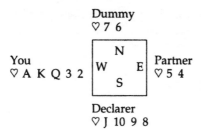

Dummy
♡ 7 6

You
♡ A K Q 3 2

Partner
♡ 5 4

Declarer
♡ J 10 9 8

With the opponents' hearts divided 4-2, you can only take the first three sure tricks before the declarer will have a winner left in the suit. You can still establish one trick through length by leading the suit again to drive out the declarer's winner. Now, let's change the distribution a bit more:

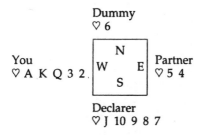

Dummy
♡ 6

You
♡ A K Q 3 2

Partner
♡ 5 4

Declarer
♡ J 10 9 8 7

If this is the layout of the heart suit, you never get more than your three sure tricks. You cannot get any tricks with your small cards.

In general, what can you expect? Will the missing cards be divided as they are in the first case, the second, or the third? You would like to have some idea of what to expect so that you will know whether or not there is a reasonable chance of developing the tricks you need from a particular suit.

If you know how many cards the opponents hold in a suit, you can determine their most likely division using the following chart:

Expected Division of Opponents' Cards

Number of cards held	Most likely distribution
3	2-1
4	3-1
5	3-2
6	4-2
7	4-3
8	5-3

You don't need to memorize the chart. It is enough to notice the general concept: an even number of cards tend to divide unevenly, an uneven number of cards tend to divide evenly.

It is much more straightforward for a declarer to make use of such a chart than for a defender. After all, a declarer can see both his hand and the dummy. A defender will usually be uncertain how many cards his partner has in a suit and will, therefore, be uncertain how many cards are held by the opponents.

On the other hand, a defender sometimes has an advantage over a declarer in this respect. If he can determine how many cards his partner has, he can determine exactly how many cards the declarer has by looking at the number of cards in the dummy. Sometimes, you can get a clue from the auction to how many cards your partner has in a suit. Later, when you look at the chapter on signals, you will see how the defenders can sometimes tell each other exactly how many cards they have in a suit.

Knowing about the likely division of the missing cards can help you decide which suit to lead when you have a choice. Suppose the auction proceeds as follows:

North	East	South	West
			(You)
		1NT	Pass
3NT	Pass	Pass	Pass

After this uninformative auction, you find yourself on lead with the following hand:

♠ A 8 6 3
♡ A 7 5 4 2
◊ 7 2
♣ 8 5

With only two sure tricks, you are going to have to find three extra tricks from somewhere. It looks as though both the spade suit and the heart suit have some potential for developing extra tricks through length, but which suit should you lead? Here is where you can put your imagination to work. You cannot see your partner's hand so you are going to have to visualize what he might hold. Let's make a reasonable assumption that he holds three or four small cards in both suits. Now, which suit presents the better potential?

If your partner has three spades, the opponents have six spades between them. The most likely division is for an even number of missing cards to divide unevenly, 4-2, so one of the opponents is likely to have four spades. This makes it unlikely that you can get an extra trick through length. Even if your partner has four spades, there is only potential for one extra trick through length.

Turning our attention to the heart suit, the potential for extra tricks through length is much better. Now, even if your partner has only three small cards, there is a good chance for two extra tricks in the suit. The complete layout of the suit might look something like this:

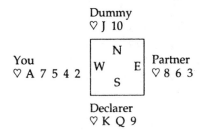

Dummy
♡ J 10

You
♡ A 7 5 4 2

N
W   E
S

Partner
♡ 8 6 3

Declarer
♡ K Q 9

You have one sure trick and, by leading the suit twice more, can develop two extra tricks from length.

The conclusion is that the longer the suit, the more potential for developing tricks through length. Given two suits of equal strength, you should lead your longer suit if you are planning to develop tricks from length. This applies most often when you are defending against a no-trump contract. Against a suit contract, developing extra winners in a long suit is often not very useful, since the declarer will be able to trump them.

Getting to your winners

In order to enjoy the winners you have developed in a suit, you have to regain the lead so that you can take them. You need an entry to your winners. One reason why established small cards sometimes do not end up taking tricks is that they become stranded – the defender who has the entry is not the defender who holds the winners. How can the defenders avoid this problem?

Once again, the answer lies in using a lot of imagination. Let's suppose you are on lead with the following hand against a contract of 3NT:

♠ A 8 7 6 3
♡ 7 4
◇ 9 6 2
♣ 8 7 5

In making your plan, you know that your side has to take five tricks in order to defeat the contract. You have only one sure trick, the ♠A. Somehow, your side has to take four more tricks. Where can they come from? You are not sure how the missing spades are divided but, if you assume that your partner has three and that the opponents' cards are divided 3-2, you could end up with two winners from your small cards after the suit has been played three times. That's fine, but in order to make use of these winners you have to be able to get to them. Let's suppose that this is the layout of the spade suit:

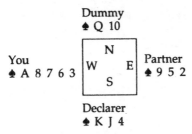

To establish your small cards as winners, the suit will have to be played three times. Suppose you start off by leading the ♠A and another spade. The declarer will win the second trick and go about his business. If he has to give up a trick to East, your partner can lead another spade to drive out the declarer's last spade and establish your two remaining spades as winners. But they are stranded. You have no entry with which to regain the lead. Even if your partner manages to regain the lead, he has no spades left to lead to your winners.

To get round this problem you must start by leading a *low* spade, giving the first trick up to the opponents. If your partner wins a trick and leads another spade, you still must not take your ♠A. Instead, you must *duck* – let the opponents win a trick which you could have won. Now the situation is completely different. If your partner regains the lead, he still has a spade left to lead to your ♠A. Your small cards are established and you can take your winners.

You have preserved your ♠A as an entry to your winners. Essentially, you have merely changed the order in which you gave up the spade tricks. Instead of playing the ♠A and then giving up two spade tricks, you have given up two spade tricks and then taken the ♠A. This little change in order makes all the difference. As a defender, you should keep the following principle in mind: if you have to lose one or more tricks to the declarer when establishing long cards in a suit, it is usually best to lose the tricks as early as possible.

Let's see how this principle can be applied when the auction has proceeded:

North	East	South	West
			(You)
		2NT	Pass
3NT	Pass	Pass	Pass

and you have to lead with the following hand:

♠ A K 9 8 4
♡ J 4 2
◇ 9 4
♣ 9 7 5

With only two sure tricks, the best hope for developing additional tricks appears to be in the spade suit. Your partner could hold the ♠Q, or may hold some length. In either case, you can give your side the best chance to defeat the contract by leading a small spade. If your partner has the ♠Q, so much the better. If not, you are losing the trick you have to lose as early as possible. Here is the complete hand:

Contract: 3NT

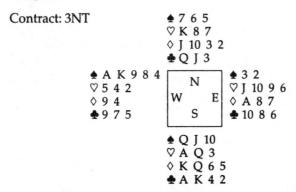

```
                    ♠ 7 6 5
                    ♡ K 8 7
                    ◇ J 10 3 2
                    ♣ Q J 3
    ♠ A K 9 8 4   ┌─────────┐   ♠ 3 2
    ♡ 5 4 2       │    N    │   ♡ J 10 9 6
    ◇ 9 4         │ W     E │   ◇ A 8 7
    ♣ 9 7 5       │    S    │   ♣ 10 8 6
                  └─────────┘
                    ♠ Q J 10
                    ♡ A Q 3
                    ◇ K Q 6 5
                    ♣ A K 4 2
```

Your partner has a rather disappointing holding in the spade suit and, when you lead a small spade, the declarer can win the first trick with the ♠10. All is not over, however. The declarer, needing to establish winners in the diamond suit, leads a diamond and your partner takes the trick with the ◇A. He has a spade left to lead back and you can take the ♠A and ♠K. No one else has any spades left and you can now take your remaining two small spades to defeat the contract.

What if you had started off by leading the ♠A and ♠K? You could still establish your remaining small spades as winners by leading the suit again, but it would not do you any good. When the declarer leads a diamond and your partner takes his ◇A, your partner has no spade left to lead back to you. You have no entry left to your hand. Whatever suit your partner leads, the declarer can win and take the rest of the tricks, making the contract.

Summary

When you are looking for ways to develop the additional winners needed to defeat a contract, consider the possibility of developing winners from the small cards in your long suits. The longer your suit, the more potential for developing winners.

When developing cards in long suits, always consider the division of the missing cards in the opponents' hands. In general, an odd number of missing cards will tend to divide as evenly as possible and an even number of missing cards will tend to divide unevenly. For example, five missing cards will tend to be divided 3-2, rather than 4-1 or 5-0; six missing cards will tend to be divided 4-2, rather than 3-3, 5-1 or 6-0.

You will usually have to give up tricks to the declarer in order to establish your small cards in a suit. Consider how you are going to get to your winners once they are established. You will need an entry. If you have to give up tricks to the declarer, it is usually best to lose the tricks as early as possible, holding on to your high cards as entries.

Over Zia's shoulder

Hand 1 Dealer: South

North	East	South	West
			(Zia)
		1NT	Pass
3NT	Pass	Pass	Pass

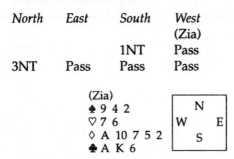

(Zia)
♠ 9 4 2
♡ 7 6
◊ A 10 7 5 2
♣ A K 6

I can see three sure tricks against the opponents' 3NT contract. Where are tricks four and five going to come from?

Solution to Hand 1:

Contract: 3NT

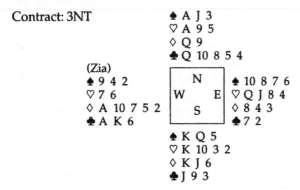

♠ A J 3
♡ A 9 5
◊ Q 9
♣ Q 10 8 5 4

(Zia)
♠ 9 4 2
♡ 7 6
◊ A 10 7 5 2
♣ A K 6

♠ 10 8 7 6
♡ Q J 8 4
◊ 8 4 3
♣ 7 2

♠ K Q 5
♡ K 10 3 2
◊ K J 6
♣ J 9 3

S Stop to consider the goal. We need five tricks to defeat the 3NT contract.

T Tally the winners. We have one sure trick in diamonds and two in clubs.

O Organize the plan. We are going to have to find two more winners. Although our high cards in clubs are attractive, our long diamond suit offers the better potential to develop tricks from length, without too much help from our partner. I think we should start by leading a small diamond.

P Put the plan into operation. On the actual layout, the declarer wins the first diamond trick and, needing to develop some club tricks make the contract, leads a club. We win the club trick and lead diamonds again. Holding the ♣A as an entry, we can afford to lead the ◇A and another diamond to establish our remaining small diamonds as winners. The declarer is helpless. When he leads another club, we win and take our diamonds to defeat the contract.

Notice how important it was to keep our ♣A and ♣K as entries. If we had taken them early, we would be doing the declarer's work for him – establishing winners in the club suit. Instead, we go about our business of setting up some extra diamond winners.

Hand 2 Dealer: East

North	East	South	West
			(Zia)
	Pass	1NT	Pass
3NT	Pass	Pass	Pass

Dummy
♠ K 5
♡ 9 8 6
◇ K Q J 10 5
♣ Q J 10

(Zia)
♠ 10 9 8
♡ J 7 5 3
◇ 2
♣ A 9 8 5 4

	N	
W		E
	S	

After making my plan, I decide to lead a small club, hoping to develop some extra tricks in my club suit from the small cards. Of course, I'll need a little help from my partner ... but that is what partners are for! After I lead a club, the dummy comes down and my partner wins the first trick with the ♣K and, being a good partner, returns my suit by leading another club. Well, now I can see two sure tricks for the defence but it looks as though the dummy is going to get a club trick. Where are the rest of our tricks going to come from?

Solution to Hand 2:

Contract: 3NT

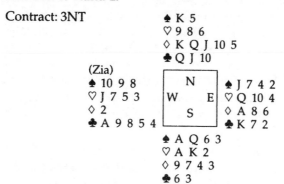

```
                        ♠ K 5
                        ♡ 9 8 6
                        ◇ K Q J 10 5
                        ♣ Q J 10
(Zia)
♠ 10 9 8          N          ♠ J 7 4 2
♡ J 7 5 3    W       E       ♡ Q 10 4
◇ 2               S          ◇ A 8 6
♣ A 9 8 5 4                  ♣ K 7 2
                        ♠ A Q 6 3
                        ♡ A K 2
                        ◇ 9 7 4 3
                        ♣ 6 3
```

S Stop to consider the goal. We need five sure tricks to defeat the 3NT contract.

T Tally the winners. We have only one sure trick, the ♣A.

O Organize the plan. Looking at my hand, the best chance to develop extra tricks appears to be in the club suit. Since I have five clubs, I may be able to develop some tricks through length if my partner has three or four clubs.

P Put the plan into operation. Putting our plan into action, I lead a small club and my partner wins the first trick with the ♣K and returns a club. Things have got off to a good start but this is where we must be careful. If we win this trick and lead another club, we will drive out the dummy's last club and establish our remaining two clubs as winners. But how will we regain the lead to take our winners? We have no entry. Instead of winning the second trick, we must play a small card, letting the dummy win the trick and keeping our ♣A as an entry. On the actual hand, the declarer wins the second club trick and has to lead a diamond to establish the winners he needs. Fortunately, our partner can win this trick with the ◇A and has a small club left to lead to our ♣A and we can now take our two established winners to defeat the contract.

We needed a little luck to defeat the contract – my partner held the ◇A and three clubs. But, without our careful play, we would have had no chance at all.

CHAPTER 30

The Finesse in Defence

At the bridge table, the president of a company and the mail clerk are equal.

A *finesse* is an attempt to take a trick with a card when the opponents hold a higher card. For example, you may want to try to win a trick with the king when the opponents hold the ace, or win a trick with the queen when the opponents hold the ace or king or both, or even win a trick with the jack when the opponents have the ace, king or queen. Instead of focusing on how the number of missing cards are divided, as you did when looking for tricks through length, you have to focus on the location of the missing high cards when trying to get extra tricks from finesses. Let's start by considering a simple finesse: when the missing high card is in the dummy and both you and your partner can see it.

Finessing against a high card in the dummy

Once the dummy has been put down on the table, the defenders can see the location of some of the high cards that their side is missing. In some respects, this can make it easier for the defenders than for the declarer when it comes to taking a finesse. Consider this situation, where your partner has led the ♠3 against the declarer's contract:

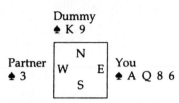

If the declarer plays the ♠9 from the dummy, you can see that you only need to play the ♠Q to win the trick. The dummy's ♠K is *trapped* by your ♠A and ♠Q. There are many similar types of situations that will arise in defence. For example, let's change the cards in the dummy and your hand slightly:

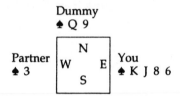

You do not really care where the ♠A is. Suppose the declarer has it. If the declarer plays the dummy's ♠Q, you will play your ♠K and, if the declarer wins the trick with the ♠A, your ♠J has become a winner. If the declarer plays the ♠9 from the dummy, you will finesse the ♠J, forcing him to win the trick with the ♠A and making your ♠K a winner.

Repeating a finesse

Just as a declarer can repeat a finesse, so can the defenders. Take a look at this layout where your partner has led the ♡2:

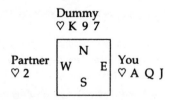

If the declarer plays the dummy's ♡K, you can win the ♡A and take tricks with your ♡Q and ♡J. But suppose the declarer plays a small heart from the dummy. You can take a finesse, which you know will work, by playing the ♡J.

Although you could play the ♡Q rather than the ♡J, you should generally win the trick by playing only as high a card as necessary in order to give information to your partner. When your ♡J wins the trick your partner will know that you hold the ♡Q as well since otherwise the declarer would have won the trick with that card. On the other hand, if you win the first trick with the ♡Q, your partner will probably think that the declarer holds the missing ♡J.

Once you win the first trick, what do you do next? If you play the ♡A, you will establish the declarer's ♡K as a winner. Unless you are sure that only two heart tricks will be enough to defeat the contract, you will probably want to get three heart tricks from this layout. That means that you want to repeat the finesse. You can only repeat the finesse by switching to another suit and waiting until your partner (or the declarer) leads hearts again. You can see the advantage of winning the first trick with the ♡J. When your partner regains the lead, he will know that you still have the ♡A and ♡Q left and he can lead another heart.

Let's put this idea into action on a complete hand after the auction has gone:

North	East	South	West
(Dummy)	(You)	(Declarer)	(Partner)
1◇	1♡	1♠	Pass
3♠	Pass	4♠	Pass
Pass	Pass		

Your partner leads the ♡4, the suit you bid, and the dummy comes down:

Contract: 4♠

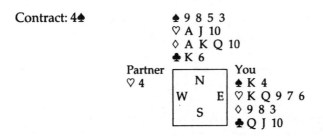

```
                    ♠ 9 8 5 3
                    ♡ A J 10
                    ◇ A K Q 10
                    ♣ K 6
        Partner    ┌───────┐    You
        ♡ 4        │   N   │    ♠ K 4
                   │ W   E │    ♡ K Q 9 7 6
                   │   S   │    ◇ 9 8 3
                   └───────┘    ♣ Q J 10
```

The declarer plays the ♡10 from the dummy on the first trick and what do you do? It's time to STOP and make your plan. You need four tricks to defeat the contract and it looks as though you are going to win the first heart trick. Where are the other tricks going to come from? You might be able to get a second heart trick, but you cannot lead another heart from your side of the table since the ♡A and ♡J are still left in the dummy. It looks as though you are going to need your partner to have a high card in spades or clubs to help you out. To put your plan into action, you must win the first trick with the ♡Q so that your partner will know that you also have the ♡K and, when he regains the lead, he can co-operate with your plan for defeating the contract.

After winning the first trick with the ♡Q, you lead back a club, hoping that your partner has the ♣A and can win and lead another heart through the dummy. A club is probably a better choice than a spade since, if your partner has a trick in the trump suit, he will get it anyway, as soon as the declarer starts *drawing trumps*. Let's look at the complete hand:

Contract: 4♠

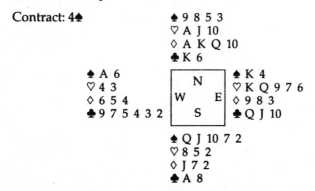

```
                    ♠ 9 8 5 3
                    ♡ A J 10
                    ◇ A K Q 10
                    ♣ K 6
    ♠ A 6          ┌─────────┐        ♠ K 4
    ♡ 4 3          │    N    │        ♡ K Q 9 7 6
    ◇ 6 5 4        │ W     E │        ◇ 9 8 3
    ♣ 9 7 5 4 3 2  │    S    │        ♣ Q J 10
                   └─────────┘
                    ♠ Q J 10 7 2
                    ♡ 8 5 2
                    ◇ J 7 2
                    ♣ A 8
```

It turns out that your partner does not have the ♣A but has the ♠A instead. That is still good enough to defeat the contract. The declarer wins the club trick and starts drawing trumps by leading a spade. Your partner wins the ♠A and, visualizing the situation in the heart suit, leads his remaining small heart through the dummy. The declarer is helpless. If he plays the dummy's ♡J, you will win the ♡K and, if he plays the dummy's ♡A, your ♡K is established as a winner which you can take when you win a trick with the ♠K. It does the declarer no good to win the dummy's ♡A and start playing diamonds before giving you a trick with the ♠K, hoping to discard his heart loser on the dummy's fourth diamond. Your partner will be able to trump the last diamond with the ♠6 and the contract will still be defeated.

Leading a high card through the dummy

The defender's high cards do not all need to be in one hand in order to trap a missing high card. Consider this situation:

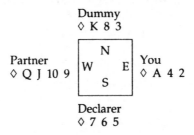

Your partner can lead the ◊Q, top of a sequence, and the dummy's ◊K is trapped. If the declarer plays the dummy's ◊K, you can win the trick with the ◊A and the defenders have the rest of the tricks in the suit. If the declarer plays a small card from the dummy, you can play one of your small cards, letting your partner's ◊Q win the trick.

The importance to the defenders of always leading the top of touching high cards can be illustrated by making the situation a little more complicated. Let's look at this layout of the cards where your partner leads the ◊J:

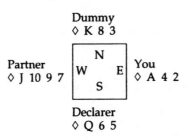

There is no problem for the defenders if the declarer plays the ◊K from the dummy. You can win the ◊A and lead the suit back, restricting the declarer to one diamond trick, the ◊Q. What if the declarer plays a small diamond from the dummy, rather than the ◊K? You know from your partner's lead of the ◊J that the declarer holds the ◊Q, since your partner always leads the top of his touching cards. Does that mean you should take the ◊A to prevent the declarer from winning the first trick with the ◊Q?

Look at what happens if you do play the ◊A on the first trick. The declarer will play a small diamond from his hand and will end up with two tricks in the suit, the ◊K and the ◊Q. Instead, suppose you do not play the ◊A on the first trick. The declarer wins with the ◊Q but now has only one trick in the suit since the remaining cards look like this:

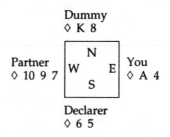

The dummy's ◊K is now trapped. When your partner regains the lead, he can lead the ◊10 or ◊9 and the declarer cannot get any more diamond tricks. If he plays the ◊K, you win the ◊A and if he plays a low diamond, you let your partner's high diamond win the trick. Here is a similar example in a complete hand where the auction has gone:

North	East	South	West
(Dummy)	(You)	(Declarer)	(Partner)
		1♡	Pass
4♡	Pass	Pass	Pass

Your partner leads the ♠J and this is the complete layout:

Contract: 4♡

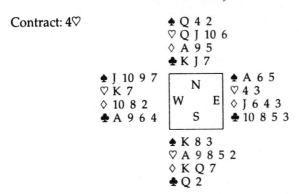

When the declarer plays a small spade from the dummy on the first trick, you must be careful not to play the ♠A. The declarer will win the first trick with the ♠K, but now you have the dummy's ♠Q trapped. When the declarer leads a club, your partner can take the ♣A and lead another high spade. Whether the declarer plays the dummy's ♠Q or a small card, the defenders get two spade tricks. Eventually, your partner also gets a trick with the ♡K and the contract is defeated. If you play the ♠A on the first trick, the declarer ends up making the contract, losing only one spade trick, one heart trick and one club trick.

Trapping the declarer's high cards

The defenders, of course, can trap high cards in the declarer's hand as well as those in dummy. The difficulty in this situation, however, is that they cannot actually see the high card(s) in the declarer's hand and, instead, must try to visualize them. Sometimes it is easy. Consider the following layout of the club suit when defending against a no-trump contract:

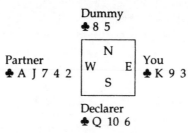

Dummy
♣ 8 5

Partner
♣ A J 7 4 2

You
♣ K 9 3

Declarer
♣ Q 10 6

We have seen in earlier chapters that it is a good idea when defending against a no-trump contract to lead a low card from a long suit, rather than a high card, when you do not have a strong sequence. This is to allow the high card to be won from the short side first when taking sure tricks and to preserve an entry to your long suit when trying to establish winners through length. It also works well in this type of situation, when the defenders need to take a finesse.

Your partner leads a small club and you win the first trick with the ♣K. When you lead a club back, the declarer's ♣Q is trapped. Whether he plays the ♣Q or ♣10, your partner gets the rest of the tricks in the suit. If your partner had started by leading the ♣A, he could continue by leading a small club to your ♣K, but now you could no longer trap the declarer's ♣Q.

In the above situation, you did not consciously have to think about trapping a high card in the declarer's hand. After all, you were merely returning your partner's suit. Your partner might have held both the ♣A and ♣Q, in which case you would be helping to take your side's sure tricks. Your partner might have held the ♣Q, and the declarer the ♣A, in which case you would be helping to promote tricks in your partner's hand by driving out the declarer's ♣A. Or your partner might have held neither the ♣A nor ♣Q, in which case you would be helping your partner develop tricks from his length in the suit.

Nevertheless, there are times when you must visualize how you might be able to trap the unseen high cards in the declarer's hand. Since you can only see the high cards in the dummy, you usually follow the guideline of *leading through strength and up to weakness* in such situations. That is, you try to lead through the declarer's (assumed) strength and up to the weak holding in the dummy. For example, your partner leads the ♡J after the following auction:

North	East	South	West
(Dummy)	(You)	(Declarer)	(Partner)
1◊	Pass	1♠	Pass
3♠	Pass	4♠	Pass
Pass	Pass		

Contract: 4♠

```
                      ♠ A J 6 5
                      ♡ K Q
                      ◊ K Q 10 8
                      ♣ J 7 6
          Partner         ┌─────────┐   You
          ♡ J             │    N    │   ♠ 10
                          │ W     E │   ♡ A 6 5 4
                          │    S    │   ◊ 7 5 4 3
                          └─────────┘   ♣ 10 9 8 2
```

The declarer plays the ♡Q from the dummy and you must STOP to figure out what your plan is. You need four tricks and have only one sure trick yourself, so it looks as though your partner is going to have to provide the others. Where can they come from? Whatever tricks your partner may have in the trump suit he is sure to get eventually. There is not much future in the heart suit, since the dummy has the ♡K and will be able to trump hearts, even if you drive out that card. It looks as though the tricks will have to come from diamonds or clubs. Which suit should you lead? Here is where you have to try to visualize the high cards in the declarer's hand. If he has a high card in diamonds, there is not much you can do, but if he has a high card in clubs, you might be able to trap it by leading through his (supposed) strength and up to the club weakness in the dummy.

Following your plan, you win the ♡A and lead back a club. This is the complete hand:

Contract: 4♠

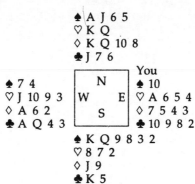

♠ A J 6 5
♡ K Q
◊ K Q 10 8
♣ J 7 6

♠ 7 4
♡ J 10 9 3
◊ A 6 2
♣ A Q 4 3

You
♠ 10
♡ A 6 5 4
◊ 7 5 4 3
♣ 10 9 8 2

♠ K Q 9 8 3 2
♡ 8 7 2
◊ J 9
♣ K 5

When you return a club, the declarer's ♣K is trapped. Whether the declarer plays the ♣K or ♣5, your partner gets two tricks in the suit. He also takes the ◊A, to defeat the contract. What if you had not led back a club but had led another heart instead? The declarer would win the trick, draw trumps and lead a diamond to drive out your partner's ◊A. Your partner could no longer trap the declarer's ♣K. If he took the ♣A, the declarer's ♣K would be promoted. If he did not take the ♣A, the declarer would be able to discard his club losers on the dummy's extra diamond winners. To defeat the hand, you had to lead through the declarer's strength.

Summary

A finesse is an attempt to win a trick with a high card when the opponents hold a higher card in the suit. In order to do this, you usually need to lead towards the card you hope will take the trick. With a strong sequence, you can sometimes lead the top of your touching cards to help your partner trap the opponents' high cards. Both defenders need to keep their eyes open for opportunities to trap the opponents' high cards.

It is easier to trap a high card which you can see in the dummy rather than an unseen high card in the declarer's hand. The defenders can use the principle of *leading through strength and up to weakness* to help guide them when it is difficult to visualize the exact layout of the missing cards.

Over Zia's shoulder

Hand 1 Dealer: East

North	East (Zia)	South	West
	Pass	Pass	Pass
1NT	Pass	2♡	Pass
Pass	Pass		

Dummy
♠ A Q J 6
♡ 10 9 7
◇ A K 8
♣ 9 5 4

Partner
♠ 2

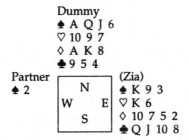

(Zia)
♠ K 9 3
♡ K 6
◇ 10 7 5 2
♣ Q J 10 8

Finally, my opponents have stopped in a partscore contract. That doesn't mean I plan to relax. Every hand is important. It hurts my pride – and, sometimes my wallet – whenever I fail to defeat a contract that can be beaten. The declarer plays the ♠J on the first trick. What's my plan going to be?

Solution to Hand 1:

Contract: 2♡

♠ A Q J 6
♡ 10 9 7
◇ A K 8
♣ 9 5 4

Partner
♠ 10 8 7 2
♡ A 5
◇ Q 6 4 3
♣ A 7 3

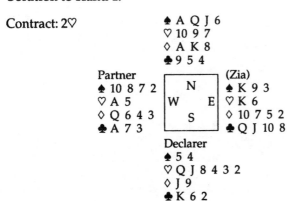

(Zia)
♠ K 9 3
♡ K 6
◇ 10 7 5 2
♣ Q J 10 8

Declarer
♠ 5 4
♡ Q J 8 4 3 2
◇ J 9
♣ K 6 2

S We need six tricks to defeat 2♡.

T When the declarer plays the dummy's ♠J on the first trick, we can see one sure trick in spades.

O I am going to need some help from my partner if we are to develop enough tricks to defeat the contract. He might have a trump trick or two, but he will get them no matter what I do. I am going to have to find some tricks from the club suit. I cannot see the high cards in the declarer's hand but I can use the idea of leading through strength to try to trap a high card in his hand.

P Having decided where our tricks might come from, we win the first trick with the ♠K and lead back the ♣Q, top of our sequence, hoping to trap the ♣K in the declarer's hand. On the actual layout of the cards, this works well. We are able to take three club tricks and eventually get the ♡A and ♡K as well, enough to defeat the contract.

If I had not visualized the possibility of trapping a high card in the declarer's hand, we would not have defeated the contract. If we lead back a spade or a diamond, the declarer can win the trick and discard one of his small clubs on the dummy's extra spade winner. Now it is too late for the defence to get all three of its club tricks.

Hand 2 Dealer: West

North	East (Zia)	South	West
			Pass
1♣	Pass	1♡	Pass
4♡	Pass	Pass	Pass

Dummy
♠ Q 8 4
♡ A Q 6 5
◇ 9
♣ A K Q 10 2

Partner
◇ J

```
        N
    W       E
        S
```

(Zia)
♠ K J 5 3
♡ 10 3
◇ A 7 5 2
♣ 9 5 4

The opponents are back to normal, bidding all the way to a game contract. That's a pretty nice-looking dummy. Do we have a chance?

Solution to Hand 2:

Contract: 4♡

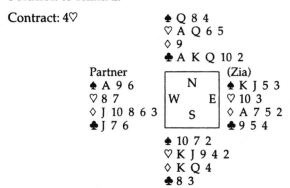

```
                  ♠ Q 8 4
                  ♡ A Q 6 5
                  ◊ 9
                  ♣ A K Q 10 2
      Partner                    (Zia)
      ♠ A 9 6           N        ♠ K J 5 3
      ♡ 8 7        W        E    ♡ 10 3
      ◊ J 10 8 6 3       S       ◊ A 7 5 2
      ♣ J 7 6                    ♣ 9 5 4
                  ♠ 10 7 2
                  ♡ K J 9 4 2
                  ◊ K Q 4
                  ♣ 8 3
```

S We are going to have to find four tricks to defeat 4♡.

T The only sure trick we have is the ◊A.

O Since my partner has led the top of his touching high cards, I know that the declarer will be able to win the first trick with the ◊Q unless we take the first trick with the ◊A. After that, the declarer will be able to trump any losing diamonds in the dummy. It doesn't look as though we are going to get any tricks from hearts or clubs, so our best hope must be in the spade suit. Perhaps my partner holds the ♠A. In that case, I should be able to trap the dummy's ♠Q if my partner helps me out.

P Putting the plan into operation, I win the first trick with the ◊A and lead back a small spade to my partner's (hoped for) ace. When my partner wins the ♠A on the actual hand, he too will have to visualize the finesse situation and lead back a spade so that I can take two more spade tricks by trapping the dummy's ♠Q.

This is the only defence to beat the contract. If I had led back anything else but a small spade, the declarer would have had no trouble taking the rest of the tricks.

CHAPTER 31

The Opening Lead against No-Trumps

Bridge is a sport that you can start as a child and be playing with as much enthusiasm and skill when you are ninety.

Now that we have seen some of the ways in which the defenders can get tricks, it is time to turn our attention to the specific task of selecting an opening lead. The opening lead must be chosen before the dummy is seen, reducing the amount of information the defender has available. Once the opening lead has been made and dummy has gone down, the defenders are in a better position to make a complete plan for defeating the contract.

For this reason, we sometimes modify our STOP mnemonic to think in these terms when we are making an opening lead:

S – stop to review the bidding
T – think about the best lead
O – organize your plan
P – put your plan into operation

In this chapter, we'll use this approach to see how we go about selecting the best lead against a no-trump contract. In a later chapter, we'll look at the differences when we have to make the opening lead against a suit contract.

Reviewing the bidding

Before choosing your opening lead, you should always STOP and review the bidding. It is amazing how much information about the other players' hands you can get from the auction, even before you see the dummy. Taking the time to try to visualize the hands will help you throughout the defence. As you see more and more cards, you can update your mental picture until it is as though you are seeing through the backs of the hidden cards.

For example, if one of the other players has bid a suit during the auction, he will usually have at least four cards in the suit. If your partner has overcalled in a suit, you can expect him to have at least five cards in the suit. If an opponent has bid and rebid a suit, without support from his partner, he will have at least a five-card suit and probably more. If his partner fails to support the suit, especially in the case of a major suit, it is probably because he has only one or two cards in the suit. If a player describes a balanced hand, perhaps by opening or rebidding in no trumps, you can be certain that he has no singletons or voids, and probably only one doubleton.

Similarly, when someone opens the bidding at the one level, he probably has a hand of 12 or more points. If he subsequently makes a minimum raise of his partner's response or rebids his suit at the lowest available level, he probably has a hand of about 12–15 points. If he makes a jump raise of the responder's suit or jumps to the three level in his own suit, he probably has a medium-strength hand of about 16–18 points. If the opener jumps in a new suit or takes the responder right to game after a one-level response, he probably has a maximum hand of about 19–21 points.

You can also draw information from what the opponents do not do during the auction. If they stop in a partscore contract, they likely have fewer than 26 combined points. If they stop in a game contract, they probably have fewer than the combined 33 points required for a small slam. If an opponent passes originally and then bids strongly thereafter, he probably has 10–11 points, not quite enough to open the bidding.

Let's look at some examples of the type of picture you can draw. Suppose you are West and the auction proceeds as follows:

North	East	South	West
			(You)
1◊	Pass	1♡	Pass
2◊	Pass	2NT	Pass
3NT	Pass	Pass	Pass

What do we know about North's hand? He must have four diamonds and 12 or more points to open the bidding 1◊ and, since he bid them again without support, he must have at least five of them. He did not support his partner's heart suit at any point in the auction so he must have three or fewer hearts. He did not bid 1♠ or 2♣ at his second opportunity, so he is unlikely to have four cards in either of these suits. He also did not open 1NT or rebid 1NT, so he does not have a balanced hand. What about his strength? He made a minimum rebid at his first opportunity, so we can expect about 12–15 points. He did, however, accept his partner's invitational bid of 2NT by raising to game. So North should be at the top of his range, 14 or 15 points, counting points for his long suit. We might expect the dummy to come down looking something like this:

♠ A 4 3
♡ Q 5
◊ A K 10 9 4 2
♣ 9 7

What about the declarer's (South's) hand? He will have at least four hearts for his 1♡ response, but is very unlikely to have as many as six of them, since he did not try to suggest that suit as trumps once his partner failed to show support at the first opportunity. His no-trump rebid suggests a balanced hand. With an unbalanced hand, he might have bid another suit or supported the opener's diamond suit. As far as his strength is concerned, he did not pass the opener's minimum rebid but also did not go all the way to game, choosing an invitational rebid of 2NT instead. This implies that he has about 11–12 points, enough to invite the opener to carry on to game. A hand consistent with South's bidding would be something like this:

♠ K J 5
♡ K 9 8 3
◊ 7 5
♣ A 8 6 4

We even know something about our partner's hand! He does not have a good enough suit or enough points to enter the auction with an overcall or takeout double after the 1◊ bid. Negative inferences such as this can sometimes be as important as the positive ones gained from the bids made.

Thinking about the best lead

Let's review the earlier auction when the opponents reached 3NT:

North	East	South	West
			(You)
1◊	Pass	1♡	Pass
2◊	Pass	2NT	Pass
3NT	Pass	Pass	Pass

Forming a mental picture of the missing hands helps you decide what to lead when you have a hand such as the following:

♠ 10 6 2
♡ A J 2
◊ Q 8 3
♣ Q 10 5 2

The picture you have constructed from the bidding steers you away from considering a heart or diamond lead, since those are the suits bid by the opponents. It comes down to a choice between the black suits. You need less help from your partner in the club suit than the spade suit, especially since he did not have enough to make an overcall in spades. You reach the conclusion that a club would be the best lead. You are rewarded when the complete hand turns out to be:

Contract: 3NT

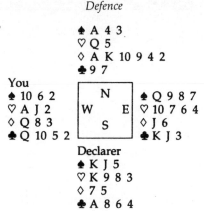

```
              ♠ A 4 3
              ♡ Q 5
              ◊ A K 10 9 4 2
              ♣ 9 7
You
♠ 10 6 2        N        ♠ Q 9 8 7
♡ A J 2      W     E     ♡ 10 7 6 4
◊ Q 8 3         S        ◊ J 6
♣ Q 10 5 2               ♣ K J 3
              Declarer
              ♠ K J 5
              ♡ K 9 8 3
              ◊ 7 5
              ♣ A 8 6 4
```

On a club lead, the defenders are able to promote three club tricks by driving out the declarer's ♣A. The declarer has to give up a diamond trick in order to develop the tricks he needs and the defence ends up with a heart trick, a diamond trick and three club tricks. Did you see through the backs of the cards? Not quite, but you defended as though you had. If you had led any other suit, the declarer would have had no trouble making the contract.

When choosing the suit to lead against a no-trump contract, you usually want to try to find the longest combined suit in the partnership hands. The longer the suit, the more potential for establishing the tricks you need to defeat the contract.

To help find the best suit to lead, consider the following guidelines:

• **Lead your partner's suit** – if your partner has opened the bidding or overcalled, unless you clearly have a better alternative. The reason for this is that your partner will have some length in the suit he bid and is likely to have more high cards than you. His high cards will serve as entries to help develop tricks in his long suit.

• **Avoid leading a suit bid by the opponents.** It is unlikely that you are going to find much help in your partner's hand if the opponents have bid a suit you are considering leading. Unless you have a very strong sequence to lead from, you are more likely to help the declarer by leading one of his suits. After all, the declarer may also need to get tricks from that suit to make his contract. It cannot be right for both sides to want to attack the same suit.

- **Lead your longest suit if there is nothing else to go on.** Your longest suit has the best chance of being the longest combined suit in the partnership hands and, therefore, of having the best potential for developing the number of tricks you need.
- **Lead the stronger suit if there is a choice of equally long suits** – since you will need less help from your partner to develop winners in the suit.

Let's look at a practical example by considering the following hand from which you have to make a lead against the opponents' 3NT contract:

♠ 9 6
♡ K 10 8 5 2
◊ 6
♣ J 10 6 3 2

If your partner has opened the bidding 1♠, or overcalled in spades during the auction, you should lead your spade since you do not have a clearly better alternative. You are hoping to develop tricks in your partner's suit and that he will have an entry so that he can take them once they are established.

If the opponents had bid hearts during the auction, you should avoid leading that suit and, instead, pick the longer of your remaining suits, clubs. If the opponents did not bid anything during the auction, you would choose the stronger of your two five-card suits and lead hearts.

As you can see from this example, you cannot choose the suit to lead until you have first reviewed the auction.

Choosing the card to lead

Once you have selected the suit you are going to lead, you must choose the specific card in the suit that you are going to lead. From the discussions in previous chapters, we can draw up the following guidelines for leading against no-trump contracts:

When leading partner's suit:
- Lead the top of a doubleton (<u>9</u> 2, Q 3)
- Lead the top of touching high cards (Q J 10, J 10 9)
- Otherwise, lead low (Q 7 <u>2</u>, K 8 4 <u>3</u>)

When leading your own suit:
- Lead the top of a three-card or longer sequence (<u>K</u> Q J 7, Q J 10 8 2)
- Lead the top of an *interior sequence* (K J 10 9, A <u>10</u> 9 8 5)
- Lead the top of a *broken sequence* (<u>K</u> Q 10 8, Q J 9 6 2)
- Otherwise, lead low (fourth best) (K J 8 <u>5</u>, A 10 8 <u>4</u> 3)

Let's review the reason for each of these leads in turn. You lead the top of a doubleton in your partner's suit to avoid blocking the suit. You want to make sure that the high card gets played from the short side first. For example:

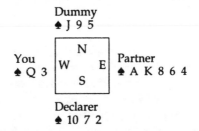

Dummy
♠ J 9 5

You
♠ Q 3

Partner
♠ A K 8 6 4

Declarer
♠ 10 7 2

By leading the ♠Q, the defence can take the first five tricks. The situation would be similar if you were promoting tricks, rather than taking sure tricks:

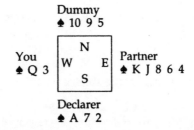

Dummy
♠ 10 9 5

You
♠ Q 3

Partner
♠ K J 8 6 4

Declarer
♠ A 7 2

If you were to lead a low spade first and your partner's ♠K drove out the declarer's ♠A, your partner could lead a small spade back to your ♠Q when he regained the lead. But your partner's remaining winners would be stranded unless he has an entry in another suit.

You lead low from three or more cards for two reasons. It helps your partner distinguish between the case where you hold a doubleton and where you hold three or more cards, since you would lead the top card from a doubleton, rather than a low card. It may also help the defenders trap cards in the declarer's hand. For example:

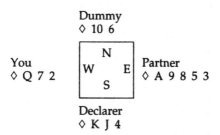

When you lead the ◊2, your partner can win the first trick with the ◊A and lead a diamond back, trapping the declarer's ◊J. On the other hand, if you had led the ◊Q, the declarer would end up with two tricks in the suit.

When leading your own suit, you lead the top of a three-card or longer sequence to prevent the declarer from winning a cheap trick in the suit. For example:

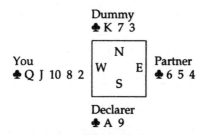

If you were to lead a low club, the ♣2 or ♣8, the declarer would win the first trick with the ♣9 and still have the ♣A and ♣K left for two more tricks. By leading the ♣Q, you force the declarer to win the trick with one of his high cards. You can subsequently lead the

♣J or ♣10 to drive out the declarer's other high card and establish the remainder of your clubs as winners.

Another reason for leading the top of your touching cards is to give your partner information. He knows you have the next lower card but not the next higher card. You tell him about the location of three cards all at the same time.

An interior sequence is one in which you have two or more touching cards and you also have a higher card in the suit. Leading the top of your touching cards helps trap cards in either the declarer or the dummy's hand. For example:

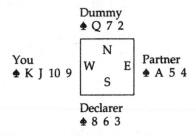

Dummy
♠ Q 7 2

You
♠ K J 10 9

Partner
♠ A 5 4

Declarer
♠ 8 6 3

When you lead the ♠J, the dummy's ♠Q is trapped. If the declarer plays the ♠Q, your partner wins the ♠A and you get four tricks in the suit. If the declarer plays a small spade from the dummy, your partner can let your ♠J win the trick and you still end up taking the first four tricks. We can now complete the rule regarding the lead of an honour card thus:

When we lead an honour card, we promise the honour immediately below it and deny the honour immediately above it. For example, the lead of the ♠Q promises the ♠J but denies the ♠K. If the honour led is the queen, jack or ten, then we may or may not have a higher card in the suit. For example, we would lead the ♠Q from both ♠ Q J 10 and ♠ A Q J. We would lead the ♠J from both ♠ J 10 9 and ♠ K J 10. We would lead the ♠10 from both ♠ 10 9 8 and ♠ Q 10 9 or ♣K 10 9.

Leading the top of an interior sequence also works well in this type of layout:

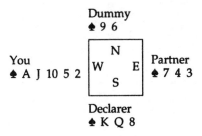

You lead the ♠J and the declarer wins the first trick with the ♠Q. If your partner gets the lead, he can lead back a spade trapping the declarer's remaining ♠K. The defence ends up with four spade tricks.

A broken sequence is one in which you are missing the second or third card in what would otherwise be a four-card or longer sequence. You lead the top of the touching cards to prevent the declarer from getting a cheap trick. You hope that if the declarer has the missing card in the sequence, you will be able to trap it. For example:

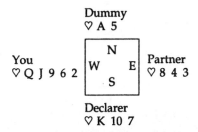

If you were to lead a small heart, the declarer would win the first trick with the ♡10 and end up with three tricks in the suit. By leading the ♡Q, you retain the option to trap the declarer's ♡10 in the above situation. The declarer can win the first trick with the dummy's ♡A, keeping the ♡K and ♡10 in his hand but if your partner gets the lead for the defence, he can lead a heart through the declarer's strength, trapping the ♡10.

Finally, let's review why you lead a low card when you do not have a strong sequence. One reason is to ensure that, if your partner has a high card, you start by playing the high card from the short side first:

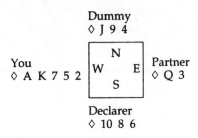

Leading a low diamond lets the defenders take the first four tricks. If you start with a high diamond, the suit becomes blocked. Worse, if you play both the ◊A and ◊K, your partner's ◊Q never takes a trick and the declarer gets an undeserved trick with the ◊J.

Leading low also helps to preserve communications between the defenders' hands in this type of layout:

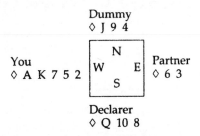

By leading a low diamond, you ensure that you have an entry back to your winners if your partner subsequently wins a trick. If you started with your high diamonds and then another diamond to establish your small cards, your remaining winners would be stranded since your partner has no diamonds left.

You might hear bridge players giving the advice: "Lead the fourth highest of your longest and strongest suit against a no-trump contract."

For example, from a suit such as ♡ A Q 8 6 2, you would lead the ♡6, fourth down from the top, rather than the ♡2. This is a conventional way to convey some information to your partner about your length in the suit. It is more important, however, that you understand why you lead a low card, rather than a high card, from such suits.

Putting it into practice

Let's put everything together and see what you would lead from the following hands after the auction has gone:

North	East	South	West (You)
	1◊	1NT	Pass
3NT	Pass	Pass	Pass

1	♠ Q J 8 5	2	♠ 9 6 3	3	♠ Q 9 5
	♡ 9 8 4 2		♡ Q 8 5		♡ 8 4 2
	◊ J 6		◊ Q J 4		◊ K 3 2
	♣ 10 5 3		♣ 10 6 5 3		♣ 9 8 6 4

Your partner has bid diamonds so, with nothing better to do, you should lead his suit on each of the hands. On the first hand, you lead the ◊J, top of your doubleton. On the second hand, lead the ◊Q, top of your touching high cards. On the last hand, lead the ◊2, low from three or more cards with no touching high cards.

Now, let's see what you would lead in each of the following hands after the auction has gone:

North	East	South	West (You)
	Pass	1NT	Pass
3NT	Pass	Pass	Pass

1	♠ Q J 10 7	2	♠ K 4	3	♠ 9 5 2
	♡ J 8 6 3		♡ 9 8 3		♡ A J 8 5 3
	◊ A 7		◊ A 10 9 8 5		◊ J 7 2
	♣ 10 8 4		♣ 7 4 2		♣ 9 4

This time, you have nothing much to go on from the auction, so you will have to look toward your own long suits. On the first hand, you have four cards in both spades and hearts. With a choice, pick the stronger suit. Since you have a sequence, lead the top card, the ♠Q. With the second hand, the diamond suit clearly represents your best chance to develop tricks. Start with the ◊10, top of your interior sequence. On the last hand, you are going to try to develop tricks from your long heart suit. With no sequence to lead from, start with a low heart. Traditionally, you would lead the ♡5, fourth highest.

Summary

When leading against a no-trump contract, always stop to review the bidding before choosing the suit to lead. Use the following guidelines:

- Lead your partner's suit
- Avoid leading a suit bid by the opponents
- Lead your longest suit. With a choice of suits, lead the stronger suit

Having chosen the suit, you must think about the best card to lead. Use the following guidelines:

When leading your partner's suit:
- Lead the top of a doubleton (<u>9</u> 2, Q 3)
- Lead the top of touching high cards (<u>Q</u> J 8, <u>J</u> 10 9)
- Otherwise, lead low (Q 7 <u>2</u>, K 8 4 <u>3</u>)

When leading your own suit:
- Lead the top of a three-card or longer sequence (<u>K</u> Q J 7, <u>Q</u> J 10 8 2)
- Lead the top of an interior sequence (K <u>J</u> 10 9, A <u>10</u> 9 8 5)
- Lead the top of a broken sequence (<u>K</u> Q 10 8, <u>Q</u> J 9 6 2)
- Otherwise, lead low (fourth best) (K J 8 <u>5</u>, A 10 8 <u>4</u> 3)

Over Zia's shoulder

Hand 1 Dealer: West

North	East	South	West
			(Zia)
			Pass
Pass	1♠	1NT	Pass
2NT	Pass	3NT	Pass
Pass	Pass		

(Zia)
♠ 9 2
♡ Q 10 9 8 7 3
◊ 5 2
♣ 10 9 8

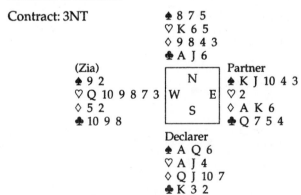

Luckily, my partner had enough strength to open the bidding. With this motley collection of cards, I was expecting the opponents to reach slam. Looking at the nice interior sequence in hearts, what am I going to lead?

Solution to Hand 1:

Contract: 3NT

```
                ♠ 8 7 5
                ♡ K 6 5
                ◊ 9 8 4 3
                ♣ A J 6
  (Zia)                      Partner
  ♠ 9 2         ┌─────┐      ♠ K J 10 4 3
  ♡ Q 10 9 8 7 3│  N  │      ♡ 2
  ◊ 5 2         │W   E│      ◊ A K 6
  ♣ 10 9 8      │  S  │      ♣ Q 7 5 4
                └─────┘
                Declarer
                ♠ A Q 6
                ♡ A J 4
                ◊ Q J 10 7
                ♣ K 3 2
```

S It's time to stop and review the bidding. My partner has given us a clue what to do by opening the bidding 1♠.

T In thinking about the best card to lead, I am tempted to start with my long heart suit. My partner's suit takes preference,

Defence

however. I have no reason to believe that my suit is any better than my partner's and, even if I can promote some winners, I have no entry back to my hand to help me take them.

O There's no time to waste. I have to lead my partner's suit right away to avoid giving the declarer the opportunity to establish his suits. Since I am leading my partner's suit, I start with the ♠9, top of a doubleton.

P The defenders' plan springs into action. Leading a spade helps my partner drive out one of the declarer's high spades. When the declarer leads a diamond to try to establish the tricks he needs, my partner wins and leads another spade to drive out the declarer's remaining high card in the suit. The declarer leads another diamond to establish his suit, but he loses the race. My partner wins and takes his three established spade winners to defeat the contract.

If we had led our own suit, we would not have defeated the contract. Apart from being successful, leading my partner's suit had other advantages. If it worked out badly, at least we have a reasonable excuse. If I had led my own suit and it worked out badly, my partner would have been likely to lose a little of his love for me.

Hand 2 Dealer: North

North	East	South	West
			(Zia)
Pass	Pass	2NT	Pass
3NT	Pass	Pass	Pass

(Zia)
♠ A Q 9 8 4
♡ J 4 2
◇ 9 4
♣ 9 7 5

```
        N
    W       E
        S
```

At least I know which suit I'm going to lead against this contract, but which card should I lead? A high spade or a small one?

Solution to Hand 2:

Contract: 3NT

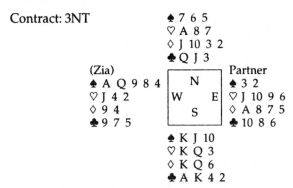

♠ 7 6 5
♡ A 8 7
◊ J 10 3 2
♣ Q J 3

(Zia)
♠ A Q 9 8 4
♡ J 4 2
◊ 9 4
♣ 9 7 5

Partner
♠ 3 2
♡ J 10 9 6
◊ A 8 7 5
♣ 10 8 6

♠ K J 10
♡ K Q 3
◊ K Q 6
♣ A K 4 2

S The auction has not given us much to go on, but we are going to have to find five tricks to defeat it.

T With only one sure trick in spades, we'll have to try to establish some tricks through length.

O We may have to give up a spade trick or two to the declarer in order to establish the suit. Is it better to take the ♠A and then drive out the declarer's remaining spade(s), or should we start with a low spade? With no other entries to our hand outside the spade suit, we should start with a low spade. We need to have a strong sequence to lead a high spade.

P We lead the ♣8, fourth highest, and the declarer wins the first trick with the ♣10. This looks a little discouraging, but it's not all over yet. He can take three heart tricks and four club tricks but, sooner or later, he is going to have to lead a diamond to establish his ninth trick. When he does, our partner wins the ◊A and leads back to a spade, trapping the declarer's ♠K and allowing us to take four spade tricks to defeat the contract.

Leading a small spade is the only thing that works on this hand. If we lead another suit, or start with the ♠A, the declarer has an easy time making the contract.

CHAPTER 32

The Use of Trumps in Defence

We often wonder what it would be like to play a sport against the best in the world. At a bridge tournament, you often get the privilege of that experience. There are events which are open and if you want the challenge, you can play a few hands against a player like Omar Sharif.

Defending against a suit contract is, in many ways, similar to defending against a no-trump contract. Against no-trump contracts you can get the extra tricks you need through promotion, through establishing your small cards in long suits and through the finesse. All of these methods can also be used when defending against a trump contract but, because of the trump suit, there are some additional considerations.

Promoting tricks

Promoting winners by driving out a declarer's higher cards is still an excellent source of extra tricks when defending a trump contract, but you may find that you cannot establish as many tricks as you would like because of the declarer's ability to use his trumps once he becomes void in a suit. For example, consider this layout of the spade suit when defending a contract in which hearts are trumps:

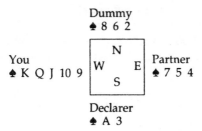

Dummy
♠ 8 6 2

You
♠ K Q J 10 9

Partner
♠ 7 5 4

Declarer
♠ A 3

You lead the ♠K and drive out the declarer's ♠A. If you were defending a no trumps contract, you would now have established four sure tricks for the defence once you regain the lead. In a heart contract, however, you have only established one sure trick since, when you lead the suit a third time, the declarer will be able to *ruff* (trump) with a small trump.

On top of that, you cannot even see how many spades the declarer has left when he wins the first trick with the ♠A. He might have started with only the singleton ♠A, in which case you have no sure tricks to take, or he might have started with three spades, in which case you have two sure tricks to take. The only thing you have to guide you is the bidding and, as we shall discuss in a later chapter, your partner's signals. For example, if the opener has described a balanced hand during the auction, he is unlikely to have a singleton spade. You can be more confident of the number of tricks you have to take when you see the shortness in the dummy.

Using length

Establishing your small cards in a suit suffers from the same problem. Consider this layout of the heart suit when diamonds are trumps:

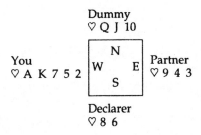

Dummy
♡ Q J 10

You
♡ A K 7 5 2

Partner
♡ 9 4 3

Declarer
♡ 8 6

Defending a no-trump contract, you would probably start by leading a small heart. The dummy would win the first trick but the defence is now poised to take four tricks in the suit when they regain the lead: the ♡A and ♡K and the remaining two long hearts in your hand. This would not work well against a diamond contract, however. Even if you establish your little hearts as winners, the declarer will be able to ruff them with diamonds unless he has run out of trumps. Worse, if you start off by leading a low heart, the declarer will win the first trick and you will not even get both your ♡A and ♡K because the declarer can trump the third round of the suit.

Such considerations mean that you may have to consider different tactics when you lead against a suit contract from those when you lead against a no-trump contract. That is not to say that developing tricks in a long suit is never of any use against a trump contract. After all, the declarer may run out of trumps; then you will be able to take your winners when you regain the lead. In that type of situation, the declarer is said to have *lost control of the hand*. That is, he is no longer capable of stopping you from taking all your winners. We shall see an example of this later in the chapter.

Using the finesse

The defensive finesse works in a suit contract in the same manner as in a no-trump contract. Once again, however, the presence of the trump suit may limit the number of tricks you can get through this technique. Consider this layout of the diamond suit when spades are trumps:

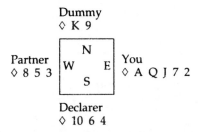

Dummy
◊ K 9

Partner
◊ 8 5 3

N
W   E
S

You
◊ A Q J 7 2

Declarer
◊ 10 6 4

Your partner leads a diamond and you have the dummy's ◊K trapped. That would be great in a no-trump contract, since you would get five tricks in the suit. With spades as trumps, however, the dummy will be able to trump the third round of the suit, limiting you to two tricks. Even if the dummy has no trumps left, the declarer will be able to trump the fourth round of the suit.

Limiting the numbers of winners the defence can take in such suits is, of course, the major reason why your opponents have chosen to play in a trump contract, rather than no trumps. That does not mean that the defence is powerless, however. The declarer's weapon of the trump suit can often be turned against him through resourceful defence.

Giving your partner a ruff

While the declarer can ruff your winners when he runs out of the suit, the defenders can also trump the declarer's winners when they are short in a suit. That is the reason that the declarer usually wants to draw trumps when he has the opportunity, but the defenders may not always give him that chance. Let's look at the following hand where the declarer is in a contract of 4♠ and you start off by leading the ◊A:

Contract: 4♠

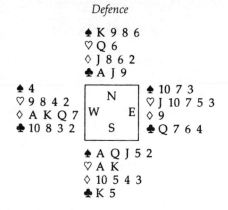

You start off winning the ◊A and, seeing no reason to switch, continue with the ◊K on which your partner discards a small heart. The way to defeat the contract becomes clear. Since there are exactly thirteen cards in the diamond suit, you can work out that the declarer started with four of them when your partner *shows out* (discards) on the second round. You continue by leading the ◊Q. This would not be such a good idea against a no-trump contract, since it establishes the dummy's ◊J as a winner. Against a suit contract, however, that is only temporary. Following your plan, you lead yet another diamond and your partner is able to defeat the contract by trumping with a small spade.

Defending this contract, it turned out to the defenders' advantage that spades were the trump suit. The declarer was unfortunate that the diamonds were so badly divided but, as a defender, you have to take advantage of such opportunities.

Although the declarer can use his trumps when he becomes void in a suit, that may do him no good if one of the defenders is also void in the suit. Look at how the defenders can co-operate on this hand, defending a contract of 4♠:

Contract: 4♠

```
                    ♠ 9 6 5 2
                    ♡ 8 4
                    ◊ A J 3 2
                    ♣ K 6 4
   You
   ♠ 7 3           N          ♠ J 8
   ♡ K Q J 9 2  W    E        ♡ A 7
   ◊ 10 8          S          ◊ 9 7 6 5 4
   ♣ 10 9 3 2                 ♣ A 8 7 5
                    ♠ A K Q 10 4
                    ♡ 10 6 5 3
                    ◊ K Q
                    ♣ Q J
```

As West, you start off by leading the ♡K, hoping to promote winners in the suit. When the dummy comes down, however, you see
that there are only two hearts and that limits the number of tricks
you can take in the suit. All is not lost, though, because your partner also has only two hearts. Remembering the earlier discussions
about unblocking suits, your partner carefully overtakes your ♡K
with the ♡A and returns the suit. When you win the second heart
trick, you have to ask yourself the meaning of this sequence of
plays by your partner. When you draw the conclusion that your
partner must also have a doubleton heart, the defence becomes
clearer. You lead another heart. Although the declarer can trump
with one of dummy's spades, your partner can *overtrump* with a
higher spade. Your partner now takes the ♣A to defeat the contract.

Getting a ruff

Besides looking for opportunities for helping your partner use his
trumps against the declarer, you can deliberately set out to try
to obtain a ruff. You do this by leading a *short suit*, a singleton or
doubleton. Let's see how this works when the auction has gone:

North	East	South	West
			(You)
1NT	Pass	3♠	Pass
4♠	Pass	Pass	Pass

You find yourself on lead with the following hand:

♠ A 8 2
♡ 3
◊ A 6 5 4
♣ J 6 4 3 2

You need four tricks to defeat the contract and can see only two, the ♠A and ◊A (assuming the declarer is not void in diamonds). You might find your partner with two high cards that can win tricks, but a better chance is to lead your singleton heart. You are hoping for one of two things. Either that your partner may be able to win the first heart trick and lead another heart for you to ruff. Or that the declarer will win the first trick but, when you regain the lead with the ♠A, that you will be able to find an entry to your partner's hand, perhaps the ◊K or ♣A, and he can lead a heart for you to trump. Here's the complete layout:

Contract: 4♠

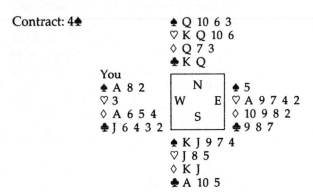

```
                        ♠ Q 10 6 3
                        ♡ K Q 10 6
                        ◊ Q 7 3
                        ♣ K Q
         You
         ♠ A 8 2          N          ♠ 5
         ♡ 3         W         E     ♡ A 9 7 4 2
         ◊ A 6 5 4        S          ◊ 10 9 8 2
         ♣ J 6 4 3 2                 ♣ 9 8 7
                        ♠ K J 9 7 4
                        ♡ J 8 5
                        ◊ K J
                        ♣ A 10 5
```

Your heart lead defeats the contract right away. Your partner wins the first trick with the ♡A and leads one back for you to trump. The ♠A and ◊A provide the setting tricks.

Of course, there is a big assumption implicit in the above defence. Your partner must co-operate with your plan by winning the first trick and leading back the suit, even though he can see the heart winners in the dummy. That means that your partner (or you, if you were in partner's place) must be aware of the possibility that you have led a short suit in such a situation. In Chapter 33 we will look at additional ways in which the defenders can help each other when trying to get ruffs.

Running the declarer out of trumps

Earlier in the chapter, we mentioned the possibility of the declarer losing control of the hand, that is, running out of trumps. The defenders can often help bring about the declarer's demise. Look at this hand where you are West:

Contract: 4♠

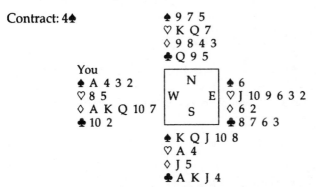

```
                    ♠ 9 7 5
                    ♡ K Q 7
                    ◊ 9 8 4 3
                    ♣ Q 9 5
You
♠ A 4 3 2         N         ♠ 6
♡ 8 5         W       E     ♡ J 10 9 6 3 2
◊ A K Q 10 7      S         ◊ 6 2
♣ 10 2                      ♣ 8 7 6 3
                    ♠ K Q J 10 8
                    ♡ A 4
                    ◊ J 5
                    ♣ A K J 4
```

Looking at the ♠A and potentially three sure tricks in diamonds, you start off by leading the ◊A, ◊K and ◊Q. Unfortunately, the declarer has only a doubleton diamond and is able to trump the third round. The declarer now starts to draw trumps. He has to do this, otherwise you will be able to ruff one of his winners with a small trump. When you win the ♠A, you will have to reconsider your original plan.

Although the declarer was able to trump the third diamond, that brought him down to four trumps, the same number you have. By leading another of your diamond winners, even though you know that the declarer can trump it, you can defeat the contract. When the declarer trumps, he now has fewer trumps left than you do. If he plays the rest of his trumps, he will lose control since you will still have a trump left, along with another diamond winner to take. If the declarer does not draw your trumps but starts playing his winners instead, you will be able to trump one of them and again defeat the contract.

As a general guideline, it does not usually do the defence any harm to make the declarer ruff with the trumps in the longer hand, that is, the hand which holds most of the trumps (usually the declarer's hand). The declarer will probably get tricks with these trumps anyway and you may make him use up his trumps before he is ready. On the other hand, it does not usually do the defence much good to make the declarer trump in the shorter hand (usually the dummy), since the declarer will still have trumps left in the long hand with which to draw trumps and keep control of the hand.

Promoting a trump trick

Occasionally, the defenders will be in a position actually to promote one of their trumps as a winner. Take a look at the following hand where you are defending a contract of 4♡ after your partner has overcalled in spades:

Contract: 4♡

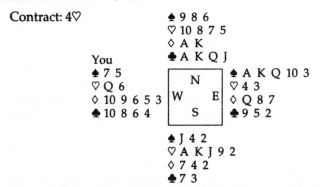

You dutifully lead your partner's suit and he takes the first three tricks with the ♠A, ♠K and ♠Q. Where is the defenders' fourth trick going to come from? Your partner can see that there is no hope in the diamond or club suits and he knows that there are no more tricks coming from the spade suit, since everyone else is void. The only hope is in the trump suit. If you have the ♠A or ♠K, you will get a trump trick no matter what your partner does at this point but what if you do not have a natural trump trick, as on the actual hand? Left to his own devices, the declarer will probably play the ♡A and ♡K and you will never get a trick with the ♡Q.

Your partner can help you out by leading another spade, even though he knows that both the declarer and the dummy are void. In most circumstances, it would be a poor idea to lead a suit again when both the declarer and the dummy are void. When the declarer has no losers to get rid of, however, as in the above hand, such a play can sometimes generate a trick for the defence out of thin air.

Look what happens on the actual hand when your partner leads a fourth round of spades. The declarer is lost. If he discards, or trumps with a low heart, you will overruff with your ♡Q to defeat the contract. If he trumps with the ♡A or ♡K, you will discard another suit and your ♡Q has been promoted into the setting trick. This tactic of promoting a trump trick by the defence is called an *uppercut*, since you are effectively delivering a blow to the jaw of the declarer to promote a trump trick for your side. You could not use such a tactic when defending against a no-trump contract so, once again, the defenders do have some special opportunities for creating tricks when the declarer is in a trump contract.

Summary

When defending against a trump contract, the defenders can still use the techniques of promotion, establishing long suits and finessing to develop the extra winners they need. Due to the power of the trump suit, however, they cannot always take all their winners since the declarer can trump them when he runs out of the suit. They will have to take this into consideration when making their plan and when choosing an opening lead.

On the other hand, the defenders have new opportunities when the declarer is playing in a trump suit. They can take advantage of their own shortness in a suit to ruff a declarer's winners. They may also be able to promote winners in the trump suit by running the declarer out of trumps or making use of an *uppercut*.

Over Zia's shoulder

Hand 1 Dealer: South

North	East	South	West
			(Zia)
		1♡	Pass
4♡	Pass	Pass	Pass

West (Zia)
♠ J 6 5 4
♡ K 6 2
◇ 9 8 5 3 2
♣ 4

The opponents have bounced into a game again and I'm going to have to find a lead to set them back on their heels. Where does my best chance lie?

Solution to Hand 1:

Contract: 4♡

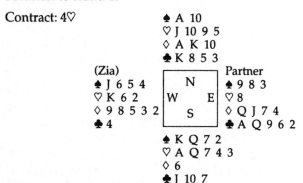

```
                        ♠ A 10
                        ♡ J 10 9 5
                        ◇ A K 10
                        ♣ K 8 5 3
         (Zia)                          Partner
         ♠ J 6 5 4        N             ♠ 9 8 3
         ♡ K 6 2      W       E         ♡ 8
         ◇ 9 8 5 3 2      S             ◇ Q J 7 4
         ♣ 4                            ♣ A Q 9 6 2
                        ♠ K Q 7 2
                        ♡ A Q 7 4 3
                        ◇ 6
                        ♣ J 10 7
```

S We need four tricks to defeat the opponents' 4♡ contract.

T We do not appear to have any sure tricks in our hand.

O Perhaps I will get a trick with my ♡K if the declarer holds the ♡A, but I will require some help from my partner if we are to defeat the contract. I don't want to ask for any more help than I need, so perhaps I can spot some further potential in my own hand. Since this is a trump contract, I can try leading my single-ton club. If my partner can get the lead, I should be able to get a ruff with one of my little trumps. That way I'll only need a couple of tricks from my partner's hand.

P Leading my singleton club quickly puts paid to the declarer's chances of making the contract. On the actual hand, our lead traps the dummy's ♣K, and my partner is able to win the first two club tricks. When I show out on the second round, discarding one of my small diamonds, my partner has no trouble leading a third round of clubs for me to ruff. I then sit back and wait for my trick with the ♡K.

Perhaps I was lucky to find that my partner had such a nice club holding. Nonetheless, I did help make a little of my own luck by seizing the opportunity to lead a singleton against a trump contract.

Hand 2 Dealer: South

North	East	South	West (Zia)
		3♠	4♡
4♠	Pass	Pass	Pass

```
                          Dummy
                          ♠ A K
                          ♡ 6 5
                          ◊ A Q J 3 2
                          ♣ K 5 4 3
          (Zia)          ┌─────────┐
          ♠ Q 2          │    N    │
          ♡ A K Q J 4    │ W     E │
          ◊ 9 7 5        │    S    │
          ♣ A 7 6        └─────────┘
```

South's pre-emptive opening bid has got the auction up high pretty quickly. This time, things look a bit better even before I make my opening lead, since it looks as though I have at least three sure tricks and there must be some potential for a trick with my ♠Q. After leading the ♡A, the dummy comes down and I am in a better position to adjust my plan. The declarer plays a small heart from the dummy and both my partner and the declarer follow with small hearts. Where do I go from here?

Solution to Hand 2:

Contract: 4♠

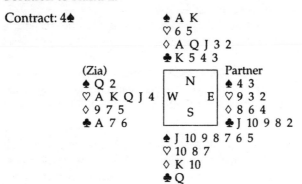

        ♠ A K
        ♡ 6 5
        ◇ A Q J 3 2
        ♣ K 5 4 3

(Zia)
♠ Q 2
♡ A K Q J 4
◇ 9 7 5
♣ A 7 6

Partner
♠ 4 3
♡ 9 3 2
◇ 8 6 4
♣ J 10 9 8 2

♠ J 10 9 8 7 6 5
♡ 10 8 7
◇ K 10
♣ Q

S We are going to have to find four tricks to defeat 4♠.

T It looks as though we have three sure tricks, the ♡A, ♡K and ♣A.

O Where can our fourth trick come from? There is some possibility that my partner has the ◇K but, even then, the declarer might have a singleton. If the declarer has three hearts, however, I can promote my ♠Q by forcing him to trump in the dummy.

P Putting my plan into action, I take the ♡A and ♡K and then take my ♣A. I do not want to give the declarer the opportunity to discard a club loser on the dummy's diamonds. Now I apply the coup de grâce and lead the ♡Q. The declarer has no choice. To win the trick, he must ruff with the dummy's ♠K. When he plays the ♠A, my ♠Q has become a winner.

CHAPTER 33

The Opening Lead against a Trump Contract

Even if you don't like cards, bridge may be your game. It is the Rolls-Royce of card games.

Some things do not change regardless of whether you are leading against a trump contract or a no-trump contract. You still want to take enough tricks to defeat the contract. If your partner bids a suit during the auction, it is usually a good idea to lead it. As we saw in Chapter 32, however, the trump suit does have an effect on where the defenders' tricks can come from and we must take this into account when deciding on the best opening lead.

Reviewing the bidding

The first step in selecting an opening lead is to STOP and review the bidding. There are always some clues to be found. Consider the following auction:

North	East	South	West
			(You)
1♣	Pass	1♠	Pass
1NT	Pass	3♡	Pass
4♡	Pass	Pass	Pass

What do we know about North's hand? He should have four clubs for his opening bid of 1♣. His 1NT rebid showed a balanced hand of 15–17 points and, since he did not support his partner's spade suit, he cannot have four of them. On the other hand, he did support the responder's second suit, so he is likely to have four hearts. We can expect the dummy to come down looking something like this:

♠ J 4
♡ A J 6 5
◊ A 9 2
♣ K Q 9 7

What about the declarer's (South's) hand? His first response was 1♠, so he must have at least four of them, and he later bid hearts, so he has at least four of them as well. If he had four hearts and only four spades, he would have responded 1♡, bidding the lower-ranking suit first to make it easier to find a fit in either major suit. Since he bid spades first, the inference is that his spades are longer than his hearts, so he has at least five of them.

South made a forcing rebid by jumping to 3♡, so he must have enough strength to want to be in a game contract opposite the opener's 1NT rebid. The declarer's hand might look something like this:

♠ A Q 10 6 2
♡ K Q 10 8
◊ 8 6 5
♣ J

Thinking about the best lead

Reviewing the above bidding gives us the help we need to find the best lead with the following hand:

♠ K 9 5
♡ 7 3
◊ Q 10 4 3
♣ 10 6 4 2

The picture constructed from the bidding steers us towards the diamond suit. Leading a spade is likely to help the declarer rather than the defenders. Hearts is the trump suit, and leading one is likely to help the declarer by starting to draw trumps. The declarer will then have the time to establish his suits. North has bid clubs, so is likely to have some of his high cards there. Leading a club may help the declarer promote winners in the suit. Everything points to leading a diamond. When you lead one, you are amply rewarded when the complete hand turns out to be:

Contract: 4♡

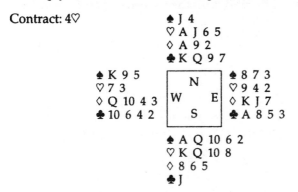

♠ J 4
♡ A J 6 5
◇ A 9 2
♣ K Q 9 7

♠ K 9 5
♡ 7 3
◇ Q 10 4 3
♣ 10 6 4 2

♠ 8 7 3
♡ 9 4 2
◇ K J 7
♣ A 8 5 3

♠ A Q 10 6 2
♡ K Q 10 8
◇ 8 6 5
♣ J

On a diamond lead, the defenders are able to promote sure tricks in the suit by driving out the dummy's ◇A. When the declarer plays a club, your partner can win the ♣A and the defenders can take their two diamond tricks. Eventually, you also get a spade trick when the declarer's spade finesse loses. Once again, you have found the only lead to defeat a contract.

Choosing the suit to lead

Against no-trump contracts you were usually looking towards developing tricks in the partnership's longest combined suit. As we saw in Chapter 32, however, establishing winners in a long suit may not do much good when defending against a suit contract because of the declarer's ability to trump once he runs out of a suit. To compensate, you may be able to get tricks from shortness, using your side's trumps to ruff the declarer's winners.

As when leading against no-trump contracts, you should give priority to leading your partner's suit. Your partner is likely to have some strength in the suit he bid and that may be a good source of tricks for the defenders. For example, suppose the auction proceeds this way:

North	East	South	West (You)
1NT	2◊	4♠	Pass
Pass	Pass		

You find yourself on lead with the following hand against the declarer's 4♠ contract:

♠ 10 7
♡ 8 7 5 4
◊ J 3 2
♣ J 10 9 8

With no clearly better choice, give priority to leading your partner's suit. This works out well when the complete hand is:

Contract: 4♠

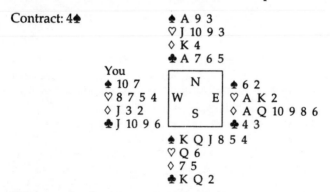

When you lead a diamond, the dummy's ◊K is trapped. Your partner can take the first two diamond tricks and also the ♡A and ♡K to defeat the contract. If you were to lead another suit, the top of your club sequence perhaps, the declarer would make the contract. The declarer can win the club lead and, after drawing trumps, can promote the dummy's hearts into winners by driving out your partner's high hearts. Each time your partner wins a heart trick, he cannot lead diamonds without giving a trick to the dummy's ◊K. Eventually, the declarer will be able to discard one or both of his small diamonds on the dummy's extra heart winners.

As when leading against no-trump contracts, you generally want to avoid leading a suit bid by one of the opponents. They are likely to have some strength in the suit and you will probably be helping the declarer, rather than hurting him. For example, consider this suit layout where the declarer has bid diamonds during the auction:

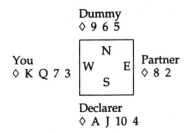

Dummy
◊ 9 6 5

You
◊ K Q 7 3

Partner
◊ 8 2

Declarer
◊ A J 10 4

Leading the ◊K will promote your ◊Q as a trick for the defence but, after the declarer has drawn trumps, he will be able to promote the rest of his diamond suit into winners. If you left the declarer to play the suit himself, you would end up with two tricks instead of one.

When choosing one of your own suits to lead, prefer a suit in which you have a strong sequence to leading a low card from a suit in which you have one or two high cards. For example, consider this layout of the club suit in a contract in which diamonds are trumps:

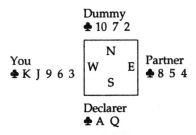

Dummy
♣ 10 7 2

You
♣ K J 9 6 3

Partner
♣ 8 5 4

Declarer
♣ A Q

Against a no-trump contract, it might be a good idea to lead a small card from this suit. Although the declarer can win the first trick with the ♣Q, you can lead the suit again when you regain the lead to drive out the declarer's ♣A and establish three winners in the suit. Against a suit contract, however, a small club lead might prove fatal. The declarer wins the first trick with the ♣Q and the second with the ♣A. You now have some winners in the suit but, when you lead one, the declarer will be able to trump it. Instead of getting three tricks in the suit, you end up with none. It is better to lead another suit and wait until your partner or the declarer leads a club. That way, at least you get one trick with your ♣K.

Here is an example in a complete hand. The auction is as follows:

North	East	South	West
			(You)
Pass	Pass	1♡	Pass
2♡	Pass	4♡	Pass
Pass	Pass		

You have to lead from this hand:

♠ K Q J
♡ 9 7
♢ K J 9 8 2
♣ 6 5 4

With a choice of suits to lead and no help from your partner, the ♠K is a better choice than a diamond or one of the other suits. You can see that leading the ♠K is likely to promote two winners for the defence. Who knows what will happen if you lead a diamond? Here is the complete hand:

Contract: 4♡

```
                      ♠ 6 4 2
                      ♡ K J 10 8
                      ♢ 4 3
                      ♣ K 10 8 3
        ♠ K Q J                      ♠ 8 7 5 3
        ♡ 9 7           N            ♡ 5 2
        ♢ K J 9 8 2  W     E         ♢ 10 7 6
        ♣ 6 5 4         S            ♣ A J 9 7
                      ♠ A 10 9
                      ♡ A Q 6 4 3
                      ♢ A Q 5
                      ♣ Q 2
```

When you lead the ♠K, the defence has no trouble defeating the contract. You promote two sure tricks and eventually get tricks from your partner's ♣A and your ◇K. If you had led a diamond, the declarer would never have to lose a trick in the suit. He would win the first trick with his ◇Q, take the ◇A and trump his remaining small diamond with one of the dummy's trumps.

It is especially dangerous to lead a low card when you hold the ace of a suit. Consider this layout of the diamond suit when hearts are trumps:

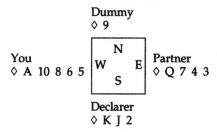

                Dummy
                ◇ 9

You   Partner
◇ A 10 8 6 5   ◇ Q 7 4 3

                Declarer
                ◇ K J 2

Leading a low diamond might work well against a no-trump contract. After the declarer wins the first trick, your partner may get the lead and lead a diamond through the declarer trapping the declarer's remaining high card. Against a suit contract, it is unlikely to work very well. The declarer will win the first trick and be able to trump his remaining diamonds in the dummy. You do not even take a trick with your ◇A. If you do decide to lead a suit in which you have the ace, you are usually better off leading the ace than leading a small card.

As we saw in Chapter 32, leading a short suit is an alternative worth considering against a trump contract. Your partner may be able to win a trick and give you a ruff. Here is an example in a complete hand where you have to find an opening lead against a 4♠ contract:

Contract: 4♠

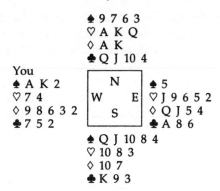

```
                    ♠ 9 7 6 3
                    ♡ A K Q
                    ◇ A K
                    ♣ Q J 10 4
    You
    ♠ A K 2           N          ♠ 5
    ♡ 7 4        W         E     ♡ J 9 6 5 2
    ◇ 9 8 6 3 2       S          ◇ Q J 5 4
    ♣ 7 5 2                      ♣ A 8 6
                    ♠ Q J 10 8 4
                    ♡ 10 8 3
                    ◇ 10 7
                    ♣ K 9 3
```

With nothing much in any of the side suits, you visualize the possibility of getting an extra trick with your small spade. To do this, you start by leading a heart. The declarer wins and starts to draw trumps. Winning the first trick with the ♠K, you continue with your plan and lead another heart, making yourself void. The declarer wins and continues to lead trumps. Winning the next trick with the ♠A, you now have one more problem to overcome. You have to get to your partner's hand. The only option appears to be in clubs and, when you lead one, you are fortunate to find your partner with the ♣A. With luck, your partner has been watching your efforts in the heart suit and, realizing what you are up to, leads another heart to give you a ruff and defeat the contract.

Leading a trump

There is one other consideration when defending a trump contract and that is to lead a trump! This may seem to violate the earlier caution about avoiding leading a suit bid by the opponents, but there are a couple of times when, after reviewing the bidding, you can come to the conclusion that it represents the best chance to defeat the contract.

A declarer will often make use of the dummy's trumps to ruff some of the losers in his hand when the dummy is short in a suit. When the auction indicates that this might be the case, leading trumps at every opportunity may thwart the declarer's plan. We will look at an example of preventing the declarer from using the dummy's trumps in Chapter 34.

The other time to lead a trump is when it appears dangerous to lead anything else. This is called a *passive defence*. You try not to give up a trick on the opening lead and you leave the declarer to fend for himself. For example, consider the following auction:

North	East	South	West
			(You)
1♣	Pass	1♡	Pass
2NT	Pass	3♠	Pass
4♠	Pass	Pass	Pass

You are on lead with this hand:

♠ 7 6 4
♡ Q 10 9 6
◊ A 9 5
♣ Q 10 7

Everything looks dangerous. The opponents have bid spades, hearts and clubs and you want to avoid leading the ◊A since it may promote the ◊K in either the declarer or the dummy's hand. This is the time to go passive and lead a spade. Here is the complete hand:

Contract: 4♠

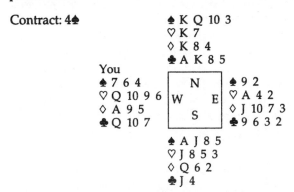

```
                        ♠ K Q 10 3
                        ♡ K 7
                        ◊ K 8 4
                        ♣ A K 8 5
   You
   ♠ 7 6 4          N          ♠ 9 2
   ♡ Q 10 9 6   W     E        ♡ A 4 2
   ◊ A 9 5          S          ◊ J 10 7 3
   ♣ Q 10 7                    ♣ 9 6 3 2
                        ♠ A J 8 5
                        ♡ J 8 5 3
                        ◊ Q 6 2
                        ♣ J 4
```

The trump lead gives nothing away. Left to his own devices, the declarer loses two heart tricks and two diamond tricks. If you had led a heart, the declarer might make the contract by playing a small heart from the dummy, forcing your partner to win with the ♡A and establishing the dummy's ♡K as a trick. If you had led the

$\Diamond$A, you would have promoted both the $\Diamond$K and $\Diamond$Q into tricks. If you had led a club, the declarer could play a small club from the dummy and win the first trick with the $\clubsuit$J, then use the dummy's extra club winner to discard one of his diamond losers.

Choosing the card to lead

Having selected the suit you are going to lead, you must choose the specific card in the suit. The guidelines are virtually identical to those when leading a suit against a no-trump contract:

When leading partner's suit:
- Lead the top of a doubleton (9 2, Q 3)
- Lead the top of touching high cards (Q J 8, J 10 9)
- Otherwise, lead low* (Q 7 2, K 8 4 3)

When leading your own suit:
- Lead the top of a two-card or longer sequence (K Q 8 7, Q J 10 2)
- Lead the top of an interior sequence* (K J 10 9, Q 10 9 5)
- Lead the top of a broken sequence (K Q 10 8, Q J 9 6 2)
- Otherwise, lead low* (fourth best) (K J 8 5, Q 10 8 4 3)

We have already discussed the reason why you avoid leading a low card against a trump contract when you hold the ace of the suit you are leading. There is a danger that you will never get a trick with your ace if the declarer or the dummy holds a singleton.

Let's look at the reasoning behind the other small change. That is, that you would usually lead the top of two touching cards when leading your own suit against a trump contract, whereas you would tend to lead low from a similar holding against a no-trump contract. Consider this layout of the heart suit in a contract where spades are the trump suit:

---

* Except when holding the ace, in which case you should lead it.

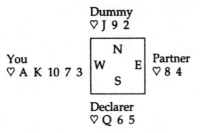

Dummy
♡ J 9 2

You
♡ A K 10 7 3

Partner
♡ 8 4

Declarer
♡ Q 6 5

You would lead a low heart against a no-trump contract so that your partner would have a heart left as an entry back to your hand if he gets the lead. That gives you the best chance of taking four tricks in the suit. If spades are trumps, however, it is unlikely to do much good to try to develop your small hearts into winners. By leading the ♡A and ♡K, you guarantee two tricks in the suit and, on the actual layout, you can lead the suit again and your partner will be able to trump the declarer's winner with a small spade, giving the defence a third trick.

Here is another possible layout for the heart suit when defending against a trump contract:

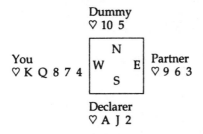

Dummy
♡ 10 5

You
♡ K Q 8 7 4

Partner
♡ 9 6 3

Declarer
♡ A J 2

If you lead a small heart, the declarer will end up with no losers in the suit. He can win the first trick with the ♡10 or ♡J, play the ♡A and ruff his remaining heart with one of the dummy's trumps. By leading the ♡K, at least you are sure of promoting one winner in the suit.

Putting it into practice

Let's put the choice of suit and the choice of card together to see what you would lead from the following hands after the auction has gone:

North	East	South	West
			(You)
	1◊	1♡	Pass
3♡	Pass	Pass	Pass

1	♠ QJ85	2	♠ 963	3	♠ J95
	♡ 9842		♡ Q85		♡ 842
	◊ Q3		◊ J104		◊ A32
	♣ 1053		♣ 10653		♣ 9864

Your partner has bid diamonds so, with nothing clearly better to do, you should lead his suit on each hand.

On the first hand, lead the ◊Q, top of your doubleton.

On the second hand, you would lead the ◊J, top of your touching high cards.

On the last hand, you would lead the ◊2, low from three or more cards against a no-trump contract. Against a suit contract, however, you should not usually lead a small card when you have the ace. Lead the ◊A.

Now, let's see what you would lead on the following hands after the auction has gone:

North	East	South	West
			(You)
	Pass	1♠	Pass
3♠	Pass	4♠	Pass
Pass	Pass		

1	♠ Q107	2	♠ 842	3	♠ 952
	♡ KJ83		♡ 98632		♡ AQ53
	◊ QJ107		◊ 8		◊ K72
	♣ J8		♣ J432		♣ Q94

This time, you do not have any help from your partner, so you will have to look towards your own suits.

On the first hand, you have a strong sequence in diamonds and that is preferable to your heart suit, in which you are missing the ♡A and ♡Q. Lead the ◊Q, top of the touching cards.

On the second hand, you are going to need to find tricks somewhere and the only feature of your hand is the singleton diamond.

Lead it and hope you can get one or more ruffs with your small trumps.

On the last hand, every suit looks dangerous. Lead a low trump, trying not to give anything away with the lead. You might even be able to get rid of enough of the dummy's trumps to stop the declarer from ruffing some of his losers.

Summary

When leading against a trump contract, always stop to review the bidding before choosing the suit to lead. Use the following guidelines:

- Lead your partner's suit
- Avoid leading a suit bid by the opponents
- Lead from a strong sequence, if possible, rather than a suit with only one or two high cards
- Lead from a short suit if you think you can get a ruff
- Lead a trump if everything else looks dangerous. Lead a trump if you think that you can prevent declarer from trumping his losing cards with the dummy's small trumps.

Having chosen the suit, you must think about the best card to lead. Use the following guidelines:

When leading partner's suit:
- Lead the top of a doubleton (9 2, Q 3)
- Lead the top of touching high cards (Q J 8, J 10 9)
- Otherwise, lead low* (Q 7 2, K 8 4 3)

When leading your own suit:
- Lead the top of a two-card or longer sequence (K Q 8 7, Q J 10 2)
- Lead the top of an interior sequence* (K J 10 9, Q 10 9 5)
- Lead the top of a broken sequence (K Q 10 8, Q J 9 6 2)
- Otherwise, lead low* (fourth best) (K J 8 5, Q 10 8 4 3)

---

* Except when holding the ace, in which case you should lead it.

Over Zia's shoulder

Hand 1 Dealer: South

North	East	South	West
			(Zia)
		1◊	Pass
1♡	Pass	2♣	Pass
3◊	Pass	4♣	Pass
4♡	Pass	5◊	Pass
Pass	Pass		

(Zia)
♠ K J 9 8 6
♡ A 2
◊ 4 3
♣ Q J 10 8

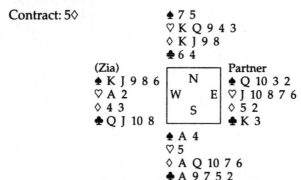

That was quite an auction by the opponents. I have a strong sequence in clubs and a club lead looks less dangerous than a spade – but is it?

Solution to Hand 1:

Contract: 5◊

♠ 7 5
♡ K Q 9 4 3
◊ K J 9 8
♣ 6 4

(Zia)
♠ K J 9 8 6
♡ A 2
◊ 4 3
♣ Q J 10 8

Partner
♠ Q 10 3 2
♡ J 10 8 7 6
◊ 5 2
♣ K 3

♠ A 4
♡ 5
◊ A Q 10 7 6
♣ A 9 7 5 2

S Stop and review the bidding. The opponents have spoken to each other during the bidding conversation, describing their hands. The declarer bid clubs twice, likely showing a five-card suit, so we are more likely to be helping him by leading a club. On the other hand, they avoided playing in 3NT, choosing to play in a minor suit instead. From the auction, it sounds as though they were afraid of the spade suit, since they bid all the other suits. Let's use that information to our advantage and choose a spade.

T Think about the best card to lead. Without touching high cards, we should lead a small spade, traditionally, fourth best. We'll lead the ♠8.

O When the dummy comes down, we can work further on organizing our plan of defence. My partner's (hoped for) ♠Q drives out the declarer's ♠A, promoting my ♠K into a winner. Since the declarer has bid clubs and diamonds and never supported hearts, we expect him to have a singleton. If he leads a heart, we plan to take the ♡A and take our ♠K before the rats get at it. We'll have to hope we can get one more trick from clubs or diamonds.

P Once we put our plan into action, the declarer has no chance. When he wins the first trick with the ♠A and leads his singleton heart towards the dummy, we take the ♡A and the ♠K before the declarer can discard his losing spade on the dummy's hearts. Later in the hand, we get a club trick since the declarer cannot discard all his club losers on the dummy's hearts.

If we had led anything else, the declarer would be able to establish a heart winner in the dummy on which to discard his losing spade.

Hand 2 Dealer: East

North	East	South	West (Zia)
	Pass	1♠	Pass
4♠	Pass	4NT	Pass
5♡	Pass	6♠	Pass
Pass	Pass		

(Zia)
♠ 5 4 2
♡ 9
◊ 9 6 5 4
♣ Q 10 8 4 3

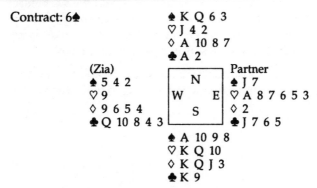

If you played as much rubber bridge as I do, you would get used to being on lead with a large amount of money at stake. It hurts when you do the wrong thing – but we won't, will we?

Solution to Hand 2:

Contract: 6♠

♠ K Q 6 3
♡ J 4 2
◊ A 10 8 7
♣ A 2

(Zia)
♠ 5 4 2
♡ 9
◊ 9 6 5 4
♣ Q 10 8 4 3

Partner
♠ J 7
♡ A 8 7 6 5 3
◊ 2
♣ J 7 6 5

♠ A 10 9 8
♡ K Q 10
◊ K Q J 3
♣ K 9

S We need two tricks and the opponents' direct and rapid auction has not given us much to go on. They have bid a slam, however, so I cannot expect too much from my partner.

T In thinking about the best card to lead, I have the option of leading my singleton heart, hoping my partner has the ♡A and can give me a ruff, or leading a club, hoping my partner has the ♣K and I can promote a trick with my ♣Q.

O My partner will need two high cards to defeat the contract if we lead a club (or a diamond). That is, he will need the ♣K to promote my ♣Q to winning rank, and he will also need another high card to take the second trick for the defence. If I lead a heart, though, I need him to have only one good card – the ♡A or the ♠A. It is a good principle of defence that when you have a choice of plans, you should follow the one which requires least help from your partner. So the best choice appears to to be my singleton heart.

P Putting our plan into action, I lead the ♡9 and find my partner with the one card we need. He wins with the ♡A and has little difficulty figuring out what we are up to. He returns a heart and we take the setting trick with the lowly ♠2.

This hand reminds me of David and Goliath. The opponents had almost all the strength, but our carefully aimed blow defeated the contract.

CHAPTER 34

After Partner Leads

Bridge is the only sport where the participants pay at a tournament and the spectators get in free.

When it is your partner who has made the opening lead, you are able to see his first card and the dummy before you have to STOP and make your plan. You have additional information. You should review the bidding to see what clues you have about the cards in the declarer's hand. Your partner's lead has also told you more about his hand than just the card he chose to lead. For example, if he has led the top of a sequence, you can expect him to have the next lower card but not the next higher card, and so on. Even the first card the declarer plays from the dummy will provide you with a further clue as to your best plan.

Since you will be the third person to play to the first trick, your position is sometimes referred to as *third hand* and this chapter looks at some guidelines for third-hand play. Of course, any time your partner leads to a trick throughout the hand, you will be in the position of third hand and can use the same principles discussed here.

Playing third hand high

As third hand, you are the last player to contribute a card to the trick for your side. Unless your partner's card is clearly going to win the trick, the card you choose to play will be vital in determining which side wins the trick. In general, you want to make your best effort to win the trick for your side, although, as we shall see, sometimes there is more to gain by letting the declarer win the first trick.

When your partner leads a low card that is obviously not going to win the trick, the general principle you follow is *third hand high*. That is, you tend to play as high a card as necessary to try to win the trick. Let's look at an example where your partner has led the ♠2 against a no trumps contract:

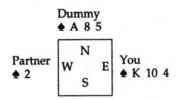

Dummy
♠ A 8 5

Partner
♠ 2

N
W   E
S

You
♠ K 10 4

If the declarer plays the dummy's ♠A on this trick, then there is nothing you can play to win the trick. That does not mean that the card you play is unimportant. As you will see in Chapter 11, the card you choose can convey important information to your partner. For now, let's suppose that the declarer plays the dummy's ♠5. Which card do you play? Being in third hand, you want to try to win the trick for your side and you can do this by playing the ♠K, third hand high. What about playing the ♠10 instead of the ♠K, saving the ♠K for later? The problem with making such a half-hearted effort is that it may cost your side a trick. For example, here is the complete layout of the suit:

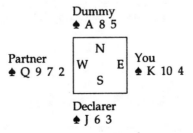

Dummy
♠ A 8 5

Partner
♠ Q 9 7 2

N
W   E
S

You
♠ K 10 4

Declarer
♠ J 6 3

If you play the ♠10, the declarer will win with the ♠J and still have the ♠A left as a second trick in the suit. If you play the ♠K, the declarer only gets one trick. His ♠J is trapped when you return the suit.

Let's change the layout slightly:

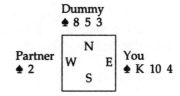

Dummy
♠ 8 5 3

Partner
♠ 2

You
♠ K 10 4

Now it is not so clear that playing the ♠K will win the trick. What if the declarer has the ♠A? Nonetheless, you should put the guideline to work and play the ♠K, third hand high, making your best effort to win the trick. There are a number of possible ways in which the missing high cards might be distributed. Let's start with an example where your partner holds the ♠A:

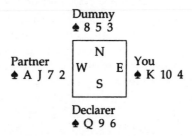

Dummy
♠ 8 5 3

Partner
♠ A J 7 2

You
♠ K 10 4

Declarer
♠ Q 9 6

If you feebly play the ♠10, the declarer will win a trick with the ♠Q. Whereas, if you play the ♠K, you will win the trick and can lead back a spade to trap the declarer's ♠Q. The declarer ends up with no tricks in the suit. Now let's give the declarer the ♠A:

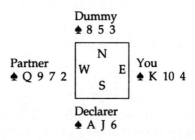

Dummy
♠ 8 5 3

Partner
♠ Q 9 7 2

You
♠ K 10 4

Declarer
♠ A J 6

If you play the ♠10, the declarer wins the ♠J and ends up with two tricks in the suit. Playing the ♠K does not actually win the trick, but it drives out the declarer's ♠A, promoting your partner's ♠Q into a winner. Better still, if you regain the lead, you can lead another spade, trapping the declarer's ♠J and giving your side three tricks in the suit.

Playing only as high as necessary

You do not have to play your highest card in third hand, only as high as necessary to make your best effort to win the trick. Look at this layout where your partner has led the ♡3:

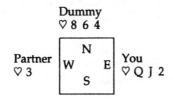

Dummy
♡ 8 6 4

Partner
♡ 3

You
♡ Q J 2

When the declarer plays a small heart from the dummy, your ♡Q and ♡J have equal value. Either one of them could be used to drive out any high card the declarer might hold. In such situations, you should play the *lower* card, the ♡J. What difference does it make? Let's look at the complete layout from your partner's perspective:

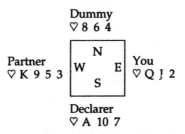

Dummy
♡ 8 6 4

Partner
♡ K 9 5 3

You
♡ Q J 2

Declarer
♡ A 10 7

When your ♡J drives out the declarer's ♡A, your partner is able to work out that you must hold the ♡Q as well. If the declarer held the ♡Q, he would have won the first trick with it, keeping his ♡A as a second trick in the suit. If your partner regains the lead, he can confidently lead another small heart to your ♡Q and you could lead your last heart back to his remaining winners.

If you were to play the ♡Q, your partner will assume that the complete layout is something like this:

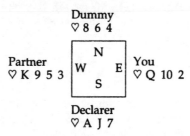

Dummy
♡ 8 6 4

Partner
♡ K 9 5 3

You
♡ Q 10 2

Declarer
♡ A J 7

If he regains the lead, he will not want to lead another small heart since he would expect that the declarer would be able to win it with the ♡J.

Playing the lower of touching cards when playing third hand high has a similar effect to leading the top of touching cards. It can help your partner to visualize the location of cards he cannot actually see.

Finessing against the dummy

Suppose your partner leads the ◊4 in this layout:

Dummy
◊ Q 8 3

Partner
◊ 4

You
◊ K J 2

When the declarer plays a small diamond from the dummy, you would play the ◊J, not the ◊K, since the ◊J is as high as necessary to try to win the trick. The complete layout might be:

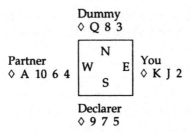

Playing the ◊J allows the defenders to take the first four tricks in the suit. If you were to play the ◊K on the first trick, the declarer would eventually get a trick with the dummy's ◊Q. Playing only as high a card as necessary in third hand is not always straightforward. Let's change the situation slightly:

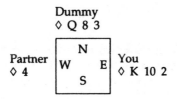

When your partner leads the ◊4 and the declarer plays the ◊3 from the dummy, should you play the ◊K or the ◊10? How high is it necessary to play? The situation is essentially equivalent to the previous layout but it is much more difficult to visualize when you do not have the ◊J. Let's look at the complete layout:

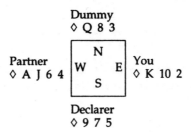

If you play the ◊10, it will win the trick and the defenders can take the rest of the tricks in the suit. On the other hand, if you were to play the ◊K, the declarer would end up taking a trick with the dummy's ◊Q.

Playing the ◊10 in the above example is referred to as *taking a finesse against the dummy* since you are essentially doing exactly that – taking a finesse.

Many similar situations arise in third hand play and you will have to try to visualize the layout of the missing cards to decide exactly what to do. As a general principle, however, you want to keep the dummy's high card trapped whenever possible. By playing the ◊10 in the above layout, you are keeping your ◊K to trap the dummy's ◊Q. Here is a similar situation:

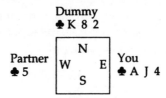

If the declarer plays a low club from the dummy on your partner's lead of the ♣5, you should finesse the ♣J, keeping your ♣A to trap the dummy's ♣K. The layout you are visualizing is something like this:

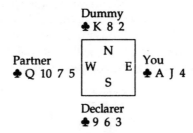

Playing the ♣A would give the declarer an unnecessary trick with the ♣K. What if the declarer rather than your partner held the ♣Q? For example:

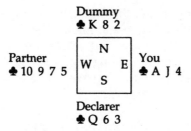

Dummy
♣ K 8 2

Partner
♣ 10 9 7 5

You
♣ A J 4

Declarer
♣ Q 6 3

The declarer would win your ♣J with his ♣Q, but that is the only trick he gets since the dummy's ♣K remains trapped. If you were to play the ♣A on the first trick, the declarer would get tricks with both the ♣K and ♣Q. This type of situation is similar to that on the following hand. The auction proceeds:

North	East	South	West
(Dummy)	(You)	(Declarer)	(Partner)
1◇	1♡	1♠	Pass
3♣	Pass	4♠	Pass
Pass	Pass		

Your partner leads the ♡7, top of a doubleton in your suit and this is the complete hand:

Contract: 4♠

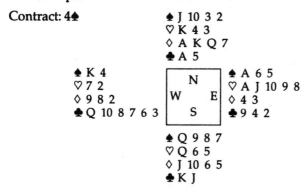

♠ J 10 3 2
♡ K 4 3
◇ A K Q 7
♣ A 5

♠ K 4
♡ 7 2
◇ 9 8 2
♣ Q 10 8 7 6 3

♠ A 6 5
♡ A J 10 9 8
◇ 4 3
♣ 9 4 2

♠ Q 9 8 7
♡ Q 6 5
◇ J 10 6 5
♣ K J

When the declarer plays a low heart from the dummy, your play as third hand becomes critical to the success or failure of the defence. If you win the trick with the ♡A, the declarer loses only one heart trick and two trump tricks and makes the contract.

Instead, you must visualize the situation and insert the ♡8, taking a finesse against the dummy and forcing the declarer to win the first trick with the ♡Q. When your partner regains the lead with the ♠K, he can lead his remaining heart and the dummy's ♡K is trapped. Whatever the declarer plays, you win two heart tricks and end up defeating the contract.

Playing after your partner leads a high card

The same principles are used when your partner leads a high card, rather than a low card, and you have to decide what to do in third hand. The difference here is that your partner's high card may be high enough to win the trick. For example, your partner leads the ♠J against a no trumps contract and this is the layout you see:

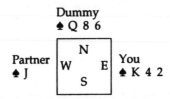

If the declarer plays a small spade from the dummy, there is no need to play the ♠K. Your partner's ♠J will be high enough to force out the ♠A if the declarer holds it, and will win the trick if he is leading the top of an interior sequence. For example, the complete layout might be:

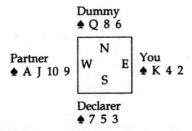

On the other hand, you will have to defend differently if your partner leads the ♠J and this is what you see:

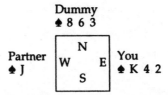

Dummy
♠ 8 6 3

Partner
♠ J

You
♠ K 4 2

Your partner's lead of the ♠J tells you that he does not hold the ♠Q and, since it is not in the dummy, the declarer must have it. If you play a low spade, the declarer will be able to win the trick. Instead, you must play the ♠K on top of your partner's ♠J, visualizing the layout as something like this:

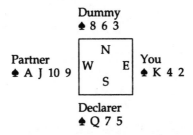

Dummy
♠ 8 6 3

Partner
♠ A J 10 9

You
♠ K 4 2

Declarer
♠ Q 7 5

You can lead back another spade, trapping the declarer's ♠Q and taking all four tricks in the suit. What if the declarer, rather than your partner, holds the ♠A? After all, the complete layout might be something like this:

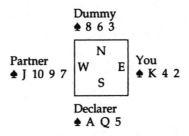

Dummy
♠ 8 6 3

Partner
♠ J 10 9 7

You
♠ K 4 2

Declarer
♠ A Q 5

Playing the ♠K does no harm. The declarer was entitled to two tricks in the suit anyway.

You still follow the principle of keeping the dummy's high cards trapped whenever possible. For example:

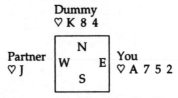

Dummy
♡ K 8 4

Partner   N   You
♡ J   W   E   ♡ A 7 5 2
                 S

Although your partner's lead of the ♡J tells you that the declarer
has the ♡Q, you should not play your ♡A when a small heart is
played from the dummy. You want to keep the dummy's ♡K
trapped if the layout is something like this:

Dummy
♡ K 8 4

                 N
Partner   W   E   You
♡ J 10 9 6   ♡ A 7 5 2
                 S

Declarer
♡ Q 3

Playing the ♡A would give the declarer two tricks in the suit.

Unblocking

We have looked earlier at the importance of playing the high card
from the short side when the defenders are taking sure tricks or
trying to promote high cards. Here is a situation in which you
must be careful to do the right thing in third hand. Suppose your
partner leads the ◊Q against a no trumps contract and the declarer plays the ◊A from the dummy in this situation:

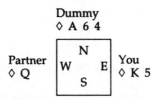

Dummy
◊ A 6 4

                 N
Partner   W   E   You
◊ Q   ◊ K 5
                 S

You should *unblock the suit* by playing the ◊K on the dummy's ◊A!
The situation you visualize is something like this:

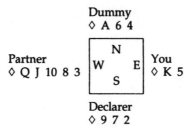

Dummy
◇ A 6 4

Partner
◇ Q J 10 8 3

You
◇ K 5

Declarer
◇ 9 7 2

If you hold on to the ◇K, you have no small card left to lead back to your partner's winners. You should play the ◇K even if the declarer plays a small diamond from the dummy on the first trick. That way, you can lead your ◇5 back to your partner's hand to help him promote the rest of his winners.

Returning your partner's suit

If you win the first trick and are planning to return your partner's suit, which of your remaining cards should you lead when you have a choice? In general, follow the same principle as when leading your partner's suit originally. That is:

- Lead the top of a doubleton (9̲ 2, Q 3)
- Lead the top of touching high cards (Q J 8, J̲ 10 9)
- Otherwise, lead low (Q 7 2̲, K 8 4 3̲)

In this case, we are talking about the lead you make from the remaining cards in your hand after you have played to the first trick. For example, suppose this is the situation:

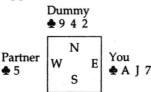

Dummy
♣ 9 4 2

Partner
♣ 5

You
♣ A J 7

Your partner leads the ♣5 and you play third hand high, winning the trick with the ♣A. Lead back the ♣J, top of your remaining doubleton. The complete layout might be something like this:

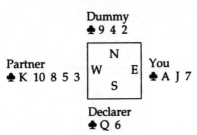

Dummy
♣ 9 4 2

Partner   N   You
♣ K 10 8 5 3   W   E   ♣ A J 7
                 S

Declarer
♣ Q 6

If you lead back the ♣7, rather than the ♣J, your partner will win the declarer's ♣Q with his ♣K and can lead the suit again back to your ♣J, but now his remaining winners are stranded. Returning the ♣J from your doubleton is following the principle of playing the high card from the short side to avoid blocking the suit.

Summary

When your partner leads to a trick and you are third to play, keep the principle of third hand high in mind. Only play as high a card as necessary to try to win the trick and, whenever possible, try to keep any high cards in the dummy trapped with your higher cards by finessing against the dummy.

When returning your partner's suit, lead back the same card from your remaining cards that you would if you were originally leading your partner's suit.

Over Zia's shoulder

Hand 1 Dealer: South

North	East (Zia)	South	West
		2NT	Pass
3NT	Pass	Pass	Pass

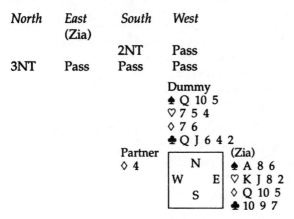

Dummy
♠ Q 10 5
♡ 7 5 4
♢ 7 6
♣ Q J 6 4 2

Partner
♢ 4

(Zia)
♠ A 8 6
♡ K J 8 2
♢ Q 10 5
♣ 10 9 7

Once again, South seems to hold most of the high cards. I have a few myself, however. How do I plan to put them to use after my partner's lead of ♢4?

Solution to Hand 1:

Contract: 3NT

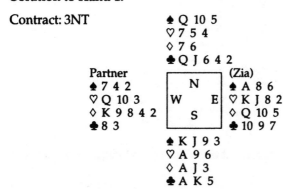

♠ Q 10 5
♡ 7 5 4
♢ 7 6
♣ Q J 6 4 2

Partner
♠ 7 4 2
♡ Q 10 3
♢ K 9 8 4 2
♣ 8 3

(Zia)
♠ A 8 6
♡ K J 8 2
♢ Q 10 5
♣ 10 9 7

♠ K J 9 3
♡ A 9 6
♢ A J 3
♣ A K 5

S We are going to have to come up with five tricks to put this contract down.

T The only sure trick we have is the ♠A.

O My partner has chosen the suit in which he wants to develop tricks and, with nothing clearly better in sight, it is up to me to help him out as best I can. It looks as though our plan is to try to establish diamond winners, using our high cards in other suits as entries.

P To help put the plan into operation we must start by playing the ◊Q, following the principle of third hand high. Our work is not done yet, however. The declarer takes the first trick with the ◊A, and then takes his five sure club tricks. When he eventually leads a spade, I must hop up with our ♠A and lead back my partner's suit. I return the ◊10, top of my remaining doubleton.

Had we played the ◊10 or ◊5 on the first trick, the declarer would win with the ◊J and have an easy time making the contract after driving out my ♠A. The principle of third hand high made our task easy on this hand.

Hand 2 Dealer: East

North	East	South	West
	(Zia)		
	Pass	1♣	Pass
1◊	Pass	1NT	Pass
3NT	Pass	Pass	Pass

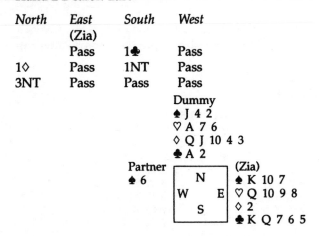

Dummy
♠ J 4 2
♡ A 7 6
◊ Q J 10 4 3
♣ A 2

Partner
♠ 6

(Zia)
♠ K 10 7
♡ Q 10 9 8
◊ 2
♣ K Q 7 6 5

My partner leads the ♣6, the declarer plays dummy's ♣2 and I play ... ?

Solution to Hand 2:

Contract: 3NT

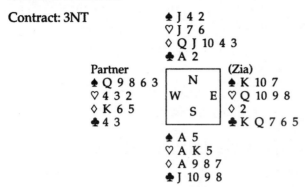

```
                    ♠ J 4 2
                    ♡ J 7 6
                    ◊ Q J 10 4 3
                    ♣ A 2
   Partner                            (Zia)
   ♠ Q 9 8 6 3      ┌─────────┐      ♠ K 10 7
   ♡ 4 3 2          │    N    │      ♡ Q 10 9 8
   ◊ K 6 5          │ W     E │      ◊ 2
   ♣ 4 3            │    S    │      ♣ K Q 7 6 5
                    └─────────┘
                    ♠ A 5
                    ♡ A K 5
                    ◊ A 9 8 7
                    ♣ J 10 9 8
```

S We need to find five tricks to defeat the contract.

T In our hand, there do not appear to be any sure tricks.

O We might be able to establish tricks in hearts, if my partner has a high card, or in clubs by driving out the dummy's ♣A. But that is not our priority. My partner has chosen the suit to attack and I have no reason to doubt his judgement. Let's concern ourselves with helping my partner to establish tricks in the spade suit. I want to play third hand high, but only as high as necessary. Should I play the ♠K or ♠10 on the first trick? Relying on the principle of keeping the dummy's high cards trapped whenever possible, I should play the ♠10, keeping the ♠K to take care of the dummy's ♠J.

P Putting the plan into action, I insert the ♠10 and this drives out the declarer's ♠A. When the declarer tries an unsuccessful diamond finesse, my partner wins the ◊K and leads a spade to my ♠K. I lead a spade back to my partner's ♠Q and he takes two more spade tricks to defeat the contract.

Had we played the ♠K on the first trick, the defence would have had no chance. The declarer would win with the ♠A and drive out my partner's ◊K. The dummy's ♠J would prevent my partner from taking more than one spade trick and the declarer would make the contract. Thank goodness for those general principles of third hand play!

CHAPTER 35

Signals in Defence

Tennis champion Martina Navratilova says that when Wimbledon was rained out she spent her time playing bridge to keep her sharp and on her toes.

Each defender tries to form a mental picture of the unseen hands when making his plan to defeat the contract. The defenders have many opportunities to help each other throughout the hand. We have already seen examples of how the defenders can pass information through the card that they lead. Leading the top of a sequence, for example, gives your partner information about more than the actual card played. It tells him something about the next higher card and the next lower card. Playing the lower of touching cards when playing third hand high can also give him information, as we saw in Chapter 32.

When you are playing to a trick that you are not going to win, you sometimes have a choice of cards to play. The specific card you choose can be used as a *signal* to your partner to give him some useful information about your hand. In this chapter, we will look at how you can use such signals to tell your partner your attitude towards a suit, how many cards you have in a suit and what you would like him to do next. Of course, signalling is a two-sided affair. Not only will you have to give the appropriate signal when an opportunity arises but you will also have to watch for the signals he gives you during the hand, so that you can form a better picture of the hidden cards and amend your plan accordingly.

Giving an attitude signal

One of the most useful pieces of information you can give a partner is whether or not you would like him to lead, or continue leading, a particular suit when he has the opportunity. This is referred to as an *attitude signal*. The principle is quite simple: *a high card is an encouraging signal, a low card is a discouraging signal*. Let's look at an example where your partner has led the ♡3 against a no-trump contract:

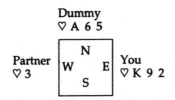

If the declarer were to play a low heart from the dummy, you would have no choice about what to play. You would have to play the ♡K, third hand high, in order to win the trick for your side. If the declarer plays the dummy's ♡A on the first trick, however, you have a choice of cards to play. Since you like the suit your partner has led, you should play the ♡9, an encouraging card. If your partner regains the lead, he will know that you would like him to lead the suit again. Contrast the above layout with this one:

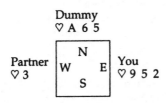

This time, you are not enamoured with your partner's lead so you would play the ♡2, a discouraging card, if the ♡A is played from the dummy. This will suggest to your partner that he find some other suit to lead at the next opportunity. Let's look at some examples in complete hands. On the first, the auction has gone:

North	East	South	West
(Dummy)	(Partner)	(Declarer)	(You)
	Pass	1♠	Pass
3♠	Pass	4♠	Pass
Pass	Pass		

Contract: 4♠

```
                        ♠ 8 7 4 2
                        ♡ J 9 7 6
                        ◊ A K 4
                        ♣ K 2
        You
        ♠ K 3              N          ♠ A Q 6
        ♡ 10 8 5      W       E       ♡ 4 3 2
        ◊ J 10 9 3         S          ◊ Q 8 5
        ♣ 9 8 7 6                     ♣ Q J 10 3
                        ♠ J 10 9 5
                        ♡ A K Q
                        ◊ 7 6 2
                        ♣ A 5 4
```

Against the declarer's 4♠ contract, you start off by leading the ◊J, top of your sequence, and the declarer wins the ◊K in dummy. The declarer then leads a small spade to his ♠J and you win with the ♠K. What do you do now?

Without the help of signals, this type of situation would be almost impossible for a defender. The opponents' auction has not given you much information and anything might be right. Your partner may have the ♡A and ♡K, and be hoping that you lead a heart, or he may have the ♣A and ♣Q and this is your last chance to trap the dummy's ♣K. Using attitude signals, however, makes the defence much easier. When the declarer wins the first trick with the ◊K, your partner should play the ◊8, an encouraging signal. Your partner, looking at the ◊Q, wants you to continue leading the suit to promote his ◊Q as a winner. If you have watched his signal, you will lead another diamond to defeat the contract. The defence ends up with a diamond trick and three spade tricks.

It does the declarer no good to try to discard his diamond loser on the dummy's extra heart winner before the trumps are drawn, since you will be able to ruff the dummy's ♡J. If you had not continued diamonds, however, the declarer would have been able to draw your small trump and then discard his diamond loser, making the contract.

You can sometimes use attitude signals to help get a ruff on defence. This time, we will put you in the East seat after the auction has gone:

North	East	South	West
(Dummy)	(You)	(Declarer)	(Partner)
		1♡	Pass
3♡	Pass	4♡	Pass
Pass	Pass		

Your partner starts off by leading the ♠A, top of his touching high cards and here is the complete hand:

Contract: 4♡

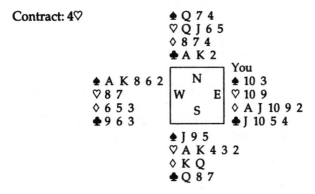

```
                        ♠ Q 7 4
                        ♡ Q J 6 5
                        ◊ 8 7 4
                        ♣ A K 2
                                    You
        ♠ A K 8 6 2    ┌─────┐     ♠ 10 3
        ♡ 8 7          │  N  │     ♡ 10 9
        ◊ 6 5 3        │W   E│     ◊ A J 10 9 2
        ♣ 9 6 3        │  S  │     ♣ J 10 5 4
                       └─────┘
                        ♠ J 9 5
                        ♡ A K 4 3 2
                        ◊ K Q
                        ♣ Q 8 7
```

Which card do you play on the first trick? Again, this is an opportunity to use an attitude signal. Although you do not have a high card in the suit, you do have a shortness and would like your partner to continue leading the suit and give you a ruff. Your ◊A will then be enough to defeat the contract. To encourage your partner to continue, you must play the ♠10, not the ♠3. If you play the ♠3, a discouraging signal, your partner will not lead the suit again, being afraid to establish the ♠Q in the dummy as a winner.

Playing the ♠10 gives your partner the clue he needs about what to do next. He will realize that you must be encouraging him to continue leading the suit because you can trump the third round and so will continue by leading the ♠K and another spade.

You ruff this, take your ◊A and can now congratulate each other on your fine defence.

Let's look at one more example. This time, the auction goes:

North	East	South	West
(Dummy)	(Partner)	(Declarer)	(You)
1♠	Pass	2♡	Pass
3♡	Pass	Pass	Pass

```
                    ♠ A K 7 5 3
                    ♡ J 8 4
                    ◊ 8 7 2
                    ♣ A 3
   You                            Partner
   ♠ 4 2           ┌─────────┐    ◊ 3
   ♡ K 9 7 3       │    N    │
   ◊ A K 5         │ W     E │
   ♣ J 9 4 2       │    S    │
                   └─────────┘
```

You lead the ◊A, top of your touching high cards, and your partner plays the ◊3 on the first trick. What now?

Your partner's ◊3 is a discouraging signal, asking you not to continue leading the suit. What should you do instead? Neither hearts nor spades looks too appealing, so you try leading a small club. You are amply rewarded when this turns out to be the full hand:

Contract: 3♡

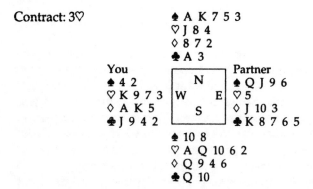

```
                    ♠ A K 7 5 3
                    ♡ J 8 4
                    ◊ 8 7 2
                    ♣ A 3
   You                            Partner
   ♠ 4 2           ┌─────────┐    ♠ Q J 9 6
   ♡ K 9 7 3       │    N    │    ♡ 5
   ◊ A K 5         │ W     E │    ◊ J 10 3
   ♣ J 9 4 2       │    S    │    ♣ K 8 7 6 5
                   └─────────┘
                    ♠ 10 8
                    ♡ A Q 10 6 2
                    ◊ Q 9 4 6
                    ♣ Q 10
```

The club switch defeats the contract. When the declarer plays a low club from the dummy, your partner wins the trick with the

♣K and leads back the ◊J to trap the declarer's ◊Q. In addition to your three diamond tricks and club trick, you eventually get a trick with the ♡K. What if you had ignored your partner's signal and continued by leading the ◊K? You would have established the declarer's ◊Q as a trick and the declarer would make the contract.

Giving a count signal

Sometimes, it will be clear to your partner whether or not you like a suit. In these situations, it is usually more important to tell him how many cards you have in the suit. This is referred to as giving a *count signal*. The method for giving a count signal is quite simple: a high card followed by a low card shows an even number of cards; a low card followed by a high card shows an odd number of cards.

Of course, it is not quite so straightforward in practice. You need to recognize the situations that call for a count signal rather than an attitude signal. If you play a low card, your partner needs to know whether this is a discouraging signal or the start of a count signal. Also, you will not always have the luxury of being able to play two cards in the suit before your partner has to make a decision. He may have to assume that the high card you played on the first trick is the start of a signal to show an even number of cards, or that the low card you played on the first trick is to show an odd number of cards. In addition, you may want to start a low-high signal to show an odd number of cards but your lowest card is a seven or an eight. You will have to do the best you can with the cards you were dealt.

It is easier to see how a count signal can be put to use by looking at a complete hand. One common situation in which it is used is when the declarer is trying to establish a long suit in the dummy and has no entry outside the suit. Here is an example:

Contract: 3NT

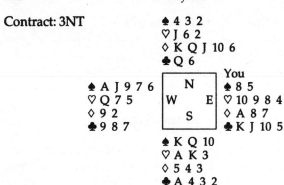

```
                    ♠ 4 3 2
                    ♡ J 6 2
                    ◊ K Q J 10 6
                    ♣ Q 6
                                  You
  ♠ A J 9 7 6   ┌─────────┐   ♠ 8 5
  ♡ Q 7 5       │   N     │   ♡ 10 9 8 4
  ◊ 9 2         │ W     E │   ◊ A 8 7
  ♣ 9 8 7       │   S     │   ♣ K J 10 5
                └─────────┘
                    ♠ K Q 10
                    ♡ A K 3
                    ◊ 5 4 3
                    ♣ A 4 3 2
```

The opponents reach 3NT and your partner leads the ♠7. The declarer wins the first trick with the ♠10 and goes about trying to promote the winners he needs to make the contract by leading a diamond. Look at what happens if you win the first or second diamond trick with the ◊A. When you lead back your partner's suit, the declarer plays the ♣Q and your partner wins the ♣A and drives out the declarer's ♣K to establish two more winners in the suit. But it does no good. On winning the ♣K, the declarer still has a diamond left to lead to the dummy's winners. He ends up taking two spade tricks, two heart tricks, four diamond tricks and a club trick to make the contract.

How could you have prevented this? Because the declarer started with three diamonds, you cannot afford to win the ◊A on the first or second round. You must wait until the third round. The dummy's diamond winners are now stranded. Try as he might, the declarer cannot get to them and he ends up with only two diamond tricks instead of four. This is called a *hold-up play* and the declarer often uses the same technique to try to strand the defenders' winners.

How are you to know that the declarer started with three diamonds? After all, if he only had two diamonds, you could win the second trick and the dummy's diamonds would be stranded. You could restrict the declarer to one trick in the suit. The answer, of course, is to make use of a count signal. When the declarer starts leading diamonds, it is obvious to both you and your partner that you are not interested in attitude towards the diamond suit – neither of you likes it. Instead, your partner can give a count signal by playing the ◊9 on the first trick and the ◊2 on the second trick, high-low to show an even number. Since the declarer has shown up with a couple of diamonds, you know that your partner has two, rather than four, and that leaves the declarer with exactly three. This lets you know that you must hold up your ◊A until the third round of the suit. Had your partner played low-high in diamonds, to show three, you would have been able to win the second diamond trick in the knowledge that the declarer started with only two diamonds.

Giving a suit preference signal

The third type of signal that the defenders can use is a *suit preference signal*. This arises when you want to tell your partner which of two suits you would prefer him to lead, while you are playing a card in a third suit. The opportunity for this type of signal does not arise very often. It is only used when you clearly do not want to give an attitude signal or a count signal and when your partner is going to have to decide between one of two suits.

When the situation does arise, the basic principle is the following: a low card shows preference for the lower-ranking suit. As you can see, the situation for a suit preference signal must be very clear. Otherwise your partner will interpret a low card as a discouraging card or the start of a low-high count signal, and a high card as an encouraging card or the start of a high-low count signal. Nonetheless, a suit preference signal can be very useful when the opportunity arises.

Here is an example of the use of a suit preference signal when giving your partner a ruff:

Contract: 2♡

```
              ♠ Q 8 6 4
              ♡ Q 4 3 2
              ◇ K 6 3
              ♣ K 2
Partner                      You
♠ 3          ┌──────────┐   ♠ A K 10 2
♡ 10 8 7     │    N     │   ♡ 6 5
◇ Q J 8 7 4  │ W     E  │   ◇ 9 5 2
♣ J 10 6 5   │    S     │   ♣ A Q 8 7
             └──────────┘
              ♠ J 9 7 5
              ♡ A K J 9
              ◇ A 10
              ♣ 9 4 3
```

Against the opponents' partscore contract of 2♡, your partner decides to lead his singleton spade. You win the ♠K and ♠A and, when your partner shows out, lead another spade for him to ruff. So far so good, but what does your partner do next? Should he lead a diamond or a club? Without suit preference signals, he would have no way of knowing what to do. If he leads a diamond, the declarer wins, draws the remaining trumps and eventually loses two club tricks, just making the contract.

This is a hand where the suit preference signal can be put to use. After playing the ♠A and ♠K, you have a choice of leading the ♠10 or ♠2 for your partner to ruff. Since the spade you chose is clearly not useful as an attitude or count signal in the spade suit, it can be used to give a suit preference signal. Your partner is not going to be interested in leading back a heart, so his choice will be between diamonds and clubs. You would lead back the ♠2, your lowest spade, as a suit preference signal for the lower-ranking suit, clubs. When your partner ruffs this, he can use your signal to lead a club. The dummy's ♣K is trapped and you get two club tricks. You can then lead your remaining spade for your partner to ruff, defeating the contract. Had your clubs and diamonds been reversed, you would lead back the ♠10, your highest spade, as a suit preference signal for diamonds, the higher-ranking suit.

Summary

When a defender has a choice of cards to play in a suit, he can use the card he plays as a signal to his partner. The three types of signal he can give are:

- **Attitude signal** – a high card is an encouraging signal; a low card is a discouraging signal.
- **Count signal** – a high card followed by a low card shows an even number of cards; a low card followed by a high card shows an odd number of cards.
- **Suit preference signal** – a high card shows preference for a higher-ranking suit; a low card shows preference for a lower-ranking suit.

Both defenders need to be aware of what type of signal the situation calls for. In general, an attitude signal takes preference, followed by a count signal and then a suit preference signal.

Over Zia's shoulder

Hand 1 Dealer: South

North	East	South	West (Zia)
			1♡
2◊	Pass	2NT	Pass
3NT	Pass	Pass	Pass

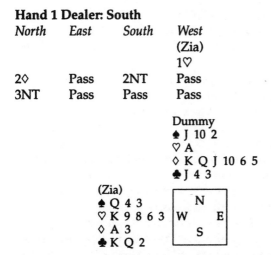

Dummy
♠ J 10 2
♡ A
◊ K Q J 10 6 5
♣ J 4 3

(Zia)
♠ Q 4 3
♡ K 9 8 6 3
◊ A 3
♣ K Q 2

Against the opponents' 3NT contract, I start with the ♡6, fourth highest of my long suit. The dummy's ♡A wins the trick as my

partner plays the ♡10 and the declarer the ♡4. The declarer now
goes about promoting some diamond winners by leading the ◇K,
on which my partner plays the ◇9 and the declarer the ◇4. I hold
up my ◇A on the first round, hoping to strand the dummy's diamond winners, but I have to take it on the next round as my partner follows suit with the ◇2 and the declarer with the ◇7. What do
I do now?

Solution to Hand 1:

Contract 3NT

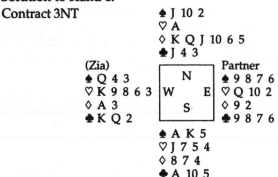

```
                         ♠ J 10 2
                         ♡ A
                         ◇ K Q J 10 6 5
                         ♣ J 4 3
    (Zia)                                   Partner
    ♠ Q 4 3          ┌─────────────┐        ♠ 9 8 7 6
    ♡ K 9 8 6 3      │      N      │        ♡ Q 10 2
    ◇ A 3            │ W         E │        ◇ 9 2
    ♣ K Q 2          │      S      │        ♣ 9 8 7 6
                     └─────────────┘
                         ♠ A K 5
                         ♡ J 7 5 4
                         ◇ 8 7 4
                         ♣ A 10 5
```

S We need five tricks to defeat 3NT.

T Initially, we only have the ◇A as a sure trick but, once the
dummy's ♡A is driven out, our ♡K has become a second sure
trick.

O Needing three more tricks, I will have to hope that my partner
has either the ♡Q or ♣A. It is too much to expect him to have
enough high cards in spades to help defeat the contract. Before
deciding whether to lead another heart of the ♣K, I should
review what is happening with the diamond suit. I was hoping
that the declarer had only a doubleton but my partner's high-
low shows an even number so the declarer must have one left.
I'll have to make the right decision on what to lead now, otherwise the declarer will probably manage to take at least nine
tricks with all those diamond winners in the dummy.

My partner has given me the clue I need by playing the ♡10 on
the first trick, an encouraging card. My best bet is to hope that
he has the ♡Q.

P In putting our final plan into operation, I must be careful, at this point, to lead a low heart to my partner's ♡Q so that he can lead another one back to my ♡K. If I lead the ♡K first, the suit will become blocked when my partner wins the next trick with the ♡Q. There is no entry back to my hand.

As you see in the actual layout, leading a low heart after winning the ◇A is the only way to defeat the contract. It's nice to have a partner who knows how to signal!

Hand 2 Dealer: East

North	East (Zia)	South	West
	Pass	1♣	1♠
2◇	Pass	3NT	Pass
Pass	Pass		

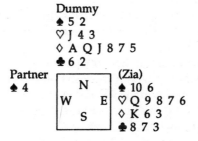

Dummy
♠ 5 2
♡ J 4 3
◇ A Q J 8 7 5
♣ 6 2

Partner
♠ 4

(Zia)
♠ 10 6
♡ Q 9 8 7 6
◇ K 6 3
♣ 8 7 3

My partner leads the ♠4 against the 3NT contract and I play the ♠10 on the first trick, third hand high. The declarer wins the trick with the ♠Q and plays the ◇10. My partner plays the ◇9 and the declarer plays a small diamond from the dummy. What do I do now?

Solution to Hand 2:

Contract 3NT

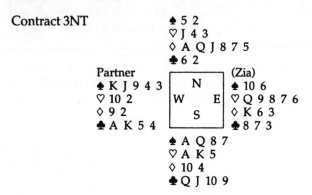

```
              ♠ 5 2
              ♡ J 4 3
              ◊ A Q J 8 7 5
              ♣ 6 2
Partner                     (Zia)
♠ K J 9 4 3      N          ♠ 10 6
♡ 10 2       W       E      ♡ Q 9 8 7 6
◊ 9 2            S          ◊ K 6 3
♣ A K 5 4                   ♣ 8 7 3
              ♠ A Q 8 7
              ♡ A K 5
              ◊ 10 4
              ♣ Q J 10 9
```

S Once again we need five tricks.

T We don't start with any sure tricks but, when the declarer takes the diamond finesse, we have an opportunity to get one trick with the ◊K.

O My general plan is to help my partner establish his spade tricks and hope that he has an entry so that he can take them. It looks as if we should win the ◊K and lead another spade to drive out any remaining high cards in the declarer's hand, or perhaps trap a high card there. I must not be so busy planning to return my partner's suit that I ignore what the declarer is up to, however. The declarer is trying to establish the dummy's diamonds as winners. If we win this trick with the ◊K, he will be successful. My partner's ◊9 looks like the start of a high-low count signal to show an even number. If my partner has two diamonds, the declarer has only two diamonds and, by holding up our ◊K, we can strand the dummy's winners.

P We let the declarer win the trick with the ◊10 and there is nothing he can do. If he repeats the finesse, hoping my partner holds the ◊K, he will never get more than one diamond trick. If he switches to his club suit, he only ends up with two tricks in each suit, one too few.

CHAPTER 36

Thwarting the Declarer's Plan

Avoid detaching a card from your hand, ready to play, before it is your turn. This implies that you know what your opponents or partner intend to do before they do.

Although the defenders' objective is to develop the tricks they need to defeat the contract, they can also help themselves by preventing the declarer from taking the tricks he needs. We saw an example of this in the last chapter. By making use of the hold-up play, the defenders can sometimes strand some of the declarer's winners. Also, by holding on to the right cards when discarding, the defenders can prevent the declarer from taking an undeserved trick in a suit.

In this final chapter, we will take a look at other things the defenders can do to ensure that the declarer's tricks are kept to a minimum. We will concentrate on the defensive play by *second hand*. That is, when declarer leads a card from his hand or the dummy and you are next to play.

Playing second hand low

When you are the second player to a trick, there is not as much need for you to try to win the trick for your side. It is often to your advantage to wait and make the declarer commit himself first, since your partner will play last to the trick. For this reason, the common guideline for second-hand play is *second hand low*.

That is, when you have a choice of playing a high card to try to win the trick, or a low card to let the declarer or your partner win the trick, you should play the low card if you have nothing better to guide you.

Let's see why this is so. Look at the following layout of the heart suit:

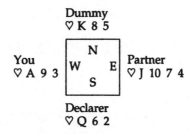

Suppose the declarer leads the ♡2 toward the dummy's ♡K. You can see that if you play a small heart, the dummy will win the trick with the ♡K. This might tempt you to play the ♡A. If you do, however, the declarer gets two tricks in the suit, one with the ♡K and one with his ♡Q. If you follow the guideline and play second hand low, letting the declarer win the first trick with the dummy's ♡K, that is the only trick he gets. The declarer's ♡Q remains trapped by your ♡A.

You should not always play low, of course. If you can see that taking your ♡A will certainly defeat the contract, then you should take it. It might be dangerous to play low and end up letting the declarer make the contract. Nonetheless, the guideline remains useful whenever you are uncertain what to do.

Here is an example in a complete hand:

Contract: 4♡

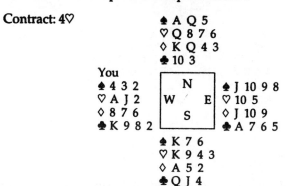

```
                        ♠ A Q 5
                        ♡ Q 8 7 6
                        ◊ K Q 4 3
                        ♣ 10 3
        You
        ♠ 4 3 2                           ♠ J 10 9 8
        ♡ A J 2         N                 ♡ 10 5
        ◊ 8 7 6     W       E             ◊ J 10 9
        ♣ K 9 8 2        S                ♣ A 7 6 5
                        ♠ K 7 6
                        ♡ K 9 4 3
                        ◊ A 5 2
                        ♣ Q J 4
```

You decide to make the aggressive lead of the ♣2, hoping that your partner will be able to help you in that suit. This works well when he wins the ♣A and returns a club to your ♣K for the second defensive trick. You now lead a spade, hoping to find that your partner has the ♠K, but the declarer wins the trick in his hand and starts to draw trumps by leading a small heart. There is no hurry to take your ♡A. You simply follow the principle of playing second hand low. The declarer has to play the dummy's ♡Q to win the trick, otherwise your partner would win the trick with the ♡10. When the declarer leads another heart, he finds that his ♡K is trapped by your ♡A and ♡J. Down he goes.

Keeping the declarer guessing

Apart from the technical merit of playing second hand low, there is another good reason behind the principle. The declarer often has to guess what to do and the more often you can make him guess, the more chance you have that he will go wrong. Look at this hand:

Contract: 4♡

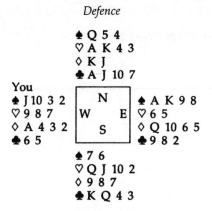

                          ♠ Q 5 4
                          ♡ A K 4 3
                          ◊ K J
                          ♣ A J 10 7

    You
    ♠ J 10 3 2   ┌─────────┐   ♠ A K 9 8
    ♡ 9 8 7   │   N   │   ♡ 6 5
    ◊ A 4 3 2   W │   E │   ◊ Q 10 6 5
    ♣ 6 5   │   S   │   ♣ 9 8 2
                      └─────────┘
                          ♠ 7 6
                          ♡ Q J 10 2
                          ◊ 9 8 7
                          ♣ K Q 4 3

Against the 4♡ contract, you start off with the ♠J, top of your touching high cards. This works well when the dummy's ♠Q is trapped by your partner's ♠A and ♠K. Unfortunately, the declarer trumps the third round of the suit and proceeds to draw three rounds of trumps and then takes his four club tricks, ending up in his hand. Finally, he leads a small diamond towards the dummy and you ... ?

If you have been watching everything that has been going on, you should play a small diamond without any hesitation. When you play low, the declarer has to guess whether to play the dummy's ◊K or ◊J to make the contract. If he plays the ◊K, he makes the contract, since you have the ◊A, but if he plays the ◊J, he loses two diamond tricks.

If you play the ◊A, or even think a long time about whether or not to take it, you make the declarer's task easy. When you play a small diamond, the declarer may decide to play the dummy's ◊J, hoping that you have the ◊Q and that it is your partner who holds the ◊A. At least you have given the defence a 50-50 chance.

Covering an honour

One difficult decision that arises for a defender is when the declarer leads a high card, rather than a low card, from his hand or the dummy. If you hold a higher card, you have to decide whether to play it, *covering the honour*, or whether to follow the principle of second hand low. In such situations, there is a second guideline that says you should cover an honour with an honour if you are uncertain what to do.

Let's see where this rather contradictory piece of advice comes from. Suppose this is the layout of the diamond suit and the declarer leads the ◊J from the dummy:

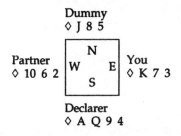

Dummy
◊ J 8 5

Partner
◊ 10 6 2

You
◊ K 7 3

Declarer
◊ A Q 9 4

If you play second hand low, the dummy's ◊J will win the trick. The declarer can then lead another diamond from the dummy and your ◊K is trapped. Whether you play it now or not, the declarer ends up with all four tricks in the diamond suit. By following the principle of covering an honour with an honour, you can end up promoting a trick for your side. When the ◊J is led, you play the ◊K and force the declarer to win with the ◊A. The declarer can take a trick with the ◊Q, but now your partner's ◊10 has been promoted as a trick.

That is the idea of covering an honour with an honour. You hope to make the declarer use two of his high cards to capture one of yours and thereby end up promoting one or more tricks for your side. There is no point in covering an honour if you can see that there is nothing to promote for your side. For example, consider this hand where the auction has gone:

North	East	South	West
(Dummy)	(You)	(Declarer)	(Partner)
	Pass	2NT	Pass
3NT	Pass	Pass	Pass

Your partner leads the ♠5 and this is the complete hand:

Contract: 3NT

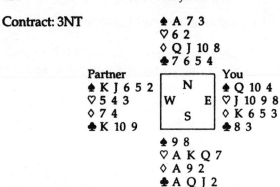

♠ A 7 3
♡ 6 2
◊ Q J 10 8
♣ 7 6 5 4

Partner
♠ K J 6 5 2
♡ 5 4 3
◊ 7 4
♣ K 10 9

You
♠ Q 10 4
♡ J 10 9 8
◊ K 6 5 3
♣ 8 3

♠ 9 8
♡ A K Q 7
◊ A 9 2
♣ A Q J 2

The declarer plays a low spade from the dummy and you win the trick with the ♠Q and lead back the ♠10. The declarer plays low from the dummy again – the declarer also knows about the hold-up play – but has to win the ♠A on the third round. He now leads the dummy's ◊Q. Should you cover with the ◊K or not? Looking at all the high cards in the dummy's diamond suit, you can see that there is nothing to promote for your side by covering the ◊Q. You should play a low diamond. The declarer takes the finesse and leads the ◊J from the dummy. Again, you should play low. The declarer can win a trick with the ◊A, but only gets three tricks in the suit. He ends up with a spade trick, three heart tricks, three diamond tricks and a club trick. When your partner wins a trick with the ♣K, he takes his spade tricks to defeat the contract.

If you had covered either the ◊Q or ◊J, the declarer would capture your ◊K with the ◊A and end up taking four diamond tricks. Only cover an honour when there is the possibility of promoting a trick for your side.

Summary

As well as trying to take their own tricks, the defenders should look for ways to prevent the declarer from getting his tricks. In addition to making sure they hold on to the right cards during the hand, they can use tactics such as the hold-up play to strand the declarer's winners.

An important consideration in avoiding giving extra tricks to the declarer is second-hand play. In general, you should follow the guideline of playing second hand low when the declarer leads a small card from his hand or from the dummy. If the declarer leads a high card, you should cover an honour with an honour if there is the possibility of promoting a trick for your side. Otherwise, you should generally play low.

Over Zia's shoulder

Hand 1 Dealer: South

North	East (Zia)	South	West
		2♣	Pass
2◊	Pass	2NT	Pass
3NT	Pass	Pass	Pass

```
                        Dummy
                        ♠ K 8 7
                        ♡ 9 4 3
                        ◊ 10 6 5
                        ♣ 8 6 4 2
        Partner                      (Zia)
        ♠ Q         ┌──────────┐     ♠ 9 3
                    │    N     │     ♡ J 10 6
                    │ W     E  │     ◊ Q 9 8 7 4
                    │    S     │     ♣ A J 3
                    └──────────┘
```

South holds a big hand once again and North carries on to game with his meagre values. My partner leads the ♠Q and that wins the first trick. He continues with another spade but the declarer wins this with the dummy's ♠K. The declarer now leads a small club from the dummy. What should I do?

Solution to Hand 1:

Contract: 3NT

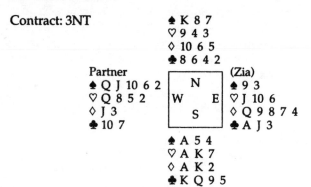

           ♠ K 8 7
           ♡ 9 4 3
           ◇ 10 6 5
           ♣ 8 6 4 2

Partner   (Zia)
♠ Q J 10 6 2   N   ♠ 9 3
♡ Q 8 5 2   W   E   ♡ J 10 6
◇ J 3   S   ◇ Q 9 8 7 4
♣ 10 7   ♣ A J 3

           ♠ A 5 4
           ♡ A K 7
           ◇ A K 2
           ♣ K Q 9 5

S We need five tricks to defeat 3NT.

T The only sure trick we have is the ◇A.

O It looks as though my partner knows what he is doing. He has led from a sequence and is trying to drive out the declarer's high cards to promote some winners. I'll have to hope he has an entry. When the declarer leads a club from the dummy, there is no need to panic and take my ♣A. I cannot see all the missing cards, so I should follow the general principle of playing second hand low.

P When I play the ♣3, the declarer wins the trick with the ♣Q. Unluckily for him, there is no other entry to the dummy which would enable him to lead towards his ♣K. He has to play a small club from his hand and hope that I started with a doubleton ♣A. When this is not the case, he ends up with the only two club tricks to go along with his two tricks in each of the other suits. That's only eight tricks.

If I had played the ♣A right away, I would have solved the declarer's problem of the lack of entries to the dummy. Playing low left him helpless. Notice that I couldn't afford the half measure of playing the ♣J. The declarer might win the ♣Q and lead the ♣K, felling my partner's ♣10 and promoting his ♣9 into a winner. If we are going to play low, we might as well play as low as possible.

Hand 2 Dealer: East

North	East (Zia)	South	West
	Pass	1NT	Pass
3NT	Pass	Pass	Pass

Dummy
♠ A 5 2
♡ 7 4 3
◊ J 5
♣ A K 8 6 2

Partner
♡ 5

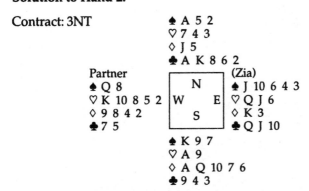

(Zia)
♠ J 10 6 4 3
♡ Q J 6
◊ K 3
♣ Q J 10

My partner leads the ♡5 against the 3NT contract and I play the ♡J, third hand high, but only as high as necessary. The declarer wins with the ♡A and plays a club to the dummy's ♣K. He then leads the ◊J from the dummy. Well, we have gone this far without letting the declarer make a contract. What do we have to do to defeat this one?

Solution to Hand 2:

Contract: 3NT

```
                      ♠ A 5 2
                      ♡ 7 4 3
                      ◊ J 5
                      ♣ A K 8 6 2
        Partner              (Zia)
        ♠ Q 8          N     ♠ J 10 6 4 3
        ♡ K 10 8 5 2  W   E  ♡ Q J 6
        ◊ 9 8 4 2      S     ◊ K 3
        ♣ 7 5                ♣ Q J 10
                      ♠ K 9 7
                      ♡ A 9
                      ◊ A Q 10 7 6
                      ♣ 9 4 3
```

S Once more we need to find five tricks.

T As usual, we don't have any to start with. I guess we'll have to work hard to get them.

O My partner has led a heart and my ♡J has driven out the declarer's ♡A, so there is some hope that we are on the right track. In the meantime, we do not want to give anything away. The declarer's lead of the ◊J from the dummy presents us with a problem. Is it time for second hand low or should I cover an honour with an honour? Although I cannot see anything to promote, there is the possibility that I might promote a trick in my partner's hand by covering. After all, we will be getting two of the declarer's high cards for one of ours.

P I play the ◊K on the ◊J and the declarer wins the ◊A. He takes the ◊Q and ◊10, but now my partner's ◊9 is promoted into a winner. When the declarer forces out my partner's ◊9, he leads a small heart over to my ♡Q and I return one to defeat the contract.

It's a good thing I played the ♡J on the first trick to help my partner determine who had the ♡Q. I also did well to cover the ◊J. Otherwise, the declarer would get five diamond tricks and make the contract. Fancy my partner's lowly ◊9 being promoted into a winner. Oh well, I had to keep my record intact. I can't have my opponents thinking they can slip something by me when I'm on defence. It's too hard on my wallet ... and my ego!

Glossary

Acol	A bidding system used extensively in Britain. It is named after the street on which the bridge club, where the system was first played, was located.
Acol Two Bid	An opening bid of 2♢, 2♡ or 2♠ which shows a powerful hand and forces the responder to bid at least once.
Approach bid	The style of bidding suits to search for a suitable trump suit before settling on the final contract.
Artificial bid	A bid made for reasons other than to suggest playing in the denomination mentioned in the bid. For example, the Stayman Convention uses an artificial bid of 2♣ response to a 1NT opening bid, to ask a partner about his major suits, not to suggest clubs as a trump suit.
Attitude (signal)	A signal by a defender which tells his partner whether or not he likes a particular suit. A high card is an encouraging signal, a low card is a discouraging signal.
Auction	A series of bids to determine the final contract.
Balanced hand	One of three hand patterns characterised by having no voids, no singletons and no more than one doubleton. The only three-hand patterns that fall into this category are the following:

xxxx	xxxx	xxxxx
xxx	xxxx	xxx
xxx	xxx	xxx
xxx	xx	xx

Bid	A number, from one to seven, combined with a word, either club(s), diamond(s), heart(s), spade(s) or no trump(s), which says something about the strength and distribution of your hand.

Bidding message	Every bid gives your partner one of three messages: bid again – a forcing message; pass – a sign-off message; make a choice whether to bid or pass – an invitational message.
Blackwood	A convention used to discover the combined number of aces held by the partnership when considering a slam contract.
Bonus	Extra points given to a partnership that either bids and makes a game or slam contract or defeats the opponents' contract.
Book	The first six tricks, which are assumed to be included in a bid for the contract.
Broken sequence	A sequence in which you are missing the third card in a four-card or longer sequence.
Buying the contract	Winning the auction.
Call	Any bid or pass, double, or redouble.
Captain	Usually the responder, although he can pass responsibility over to the opener by making a limited response.
Cash	To lead a card that is the highest in its suit and win a trick with it.
Combined hands	Both your hand and your partner's hand.
Competition	Both partnerships bidding to try to buy the contract.
Contract	The number of tricks and the denomination suggested by the bid. The number of tricks to be taken is arrived at by adding six (the book) to the number bid. For example, 4♡ is a contract to take 10(4 + 6) tricks with hearts as the trump suit.
Control	Having sufficient trumps or high cards to allow you to keep or get the lead before the opponents can take enough tricks to defeat the contract.

Convention	An artificial bid that carries a special message. For example, a 2♣ opening bid to show a very strong hand, unrelated to the club suit.
Count (signal)	A signal by a defender which tells his partner how many cards he holds in a suit. A high card followed by a low card shows an even number of cards; a low card followed by a high card shows an odd number of cards.
Cover (an honour)	Play a card higher than the previous (high) card played to a trick.
Cue bid	A forcing bid in a suit in which the bidder does not want to play; a bid in a suit bid by the opponents; a bid in another suit after the trump suit has already been agreed.
Cut (the pack)	Before the dealer deals out the cards, the player on his right takes the shuffled pack and removes four or more cards from the top and places them beside the remaining (bottom) cards. The dealer completes the cut by placing the bottom cards above the original top cards.
Dangerous opponent	An opponent who, if he gets the lead, will be able to defeat your contract.
Dealer	The player who deals out the cards at the start of the hand and who has the first opportunity to open the bidding.
Declarer	The player who first bid the denomination of the final contract. The declarer plays both his cards and the dummy's.
Declarer play	The play of the hand by the declarer, who chooses the cards to play from both his hand and from the dummy.
Defeat (contract)	Take enough tricks to prevent the declarer from making his contract.
Defence	The partnership that did not win the auction.

Defender	A member of the partnership which did not win the final contract. Both defenders co-operate to try to defeat the contract.
Denomination	The suit, or no trumps, in which a contract is played.
Describer	Usually the opener, who paints a picture of his hand for the responder.
Develop (tricks)	Play a suit until smaller cards are established or promoted into winners.
Discard	A card played to a trick from a suit other than the suit led or the trump suit.
Distribution	The shape or pattern of a hand, referring to the number of cards in each suit.
Division	The way a suit is distributed between the two hands of a partnership. For example, five cards in the defenders' hands might be divided 3-2, 4-1, or 5-0.
Double	A call that is used either to increase the size of the penalty if the opponents' contract is defeated (penalty double) or to ask a partner to bid a suit other than that bid by the opponents (takeout double).
Doubleton	A holding of only two cards in a suit.
Draw trumps	To play the trump suit until the opponents have none left.
Drive out	To play a suit until the opponents are forced to play a higher card than yours in order to win the trick.
Duck	To play a small card to a trick when you could play a higher card to try to win the trick.
Dummy	Declarer's partner. The dummy's hand is placed face up on the table with all the cards exposed and the declarer chooses the cards to be played from the dummy.

Entry	A high card, or trump, which allows the declarer, or the defenders, to get from one hand to another.
Establish (a suit)	Play a suit repeatedly, driving out the opponents' high cards, until your remaining small cards are established as winners.
Final contract	The final bid followed by three consecutive passes.
Finesse	An attempt to win a trick with a high card when a higher card is held by the opponents.
Fit	The partnership's combined holding in a suit, usually the trump suit.
Follow suit	Play a card of the same denomination as the suit led to a trick.
Forcing (bid)	A bid that compels a partner to bid. For example, an opening bid of 2♣, 2◊, 2♡ or 2♠.
Forcing for one round	A bid that compels a partner to bid at his next opportunity.
Forcing to game	A bid that compels a partner to keep bidding until the game zone has been reached.
Game contracts	The minimum contracts in each denomination that are awarded a special bonus in the scoring: 3NT, 4♡, 4♠, 5♣ and 5◊.
Gerber	A convention used to discover the combined number of aces held by the partnership when considering a slam contract.
Giving preference	Choosing one of two or more suits bid by a partner.
Go down	Be defeated in a contract.
Grand slam	A contract at the seven level, which commits to taking all the tricks.
Hand	The 13 cards held by one of the players. (The four hands held by the players are sometimes referred to as 'the hand'.)

Hand families	The set of balanced or unbalanced hand patterns (distributions).
Hand pattern	The number of cards held in each suit in a hand (see Distribution).
Hand valuation	The total points given to a hand. A combination of High Card Points – for aces, kings, queens and jacks – and distribution points – for long suits or short suits.
High card	One of the face cards – the ace, king, queen, or jack in a suit. (The ten is sometimes considered a high card.)
HCPs	Abbreviation for High Card Points, a strength valuation scheme where an ace is worth 4 points, a king 3 points, a queen 2 points and a jack 1 point.
Highest-ranking suit	The suits are ranked with spades as the highest, then hearts, then diamonds, then clubs.
Holding	The cards held by a player in a particular suit
Hold-up play	Delay taking the winner(s) in a suit led by the opponents with the objective of making it difficult for the opponents to develop and take their winners in the suit.
Honour (card)	The ace, king, queen, jack or ten in a suit.
Intermediate hand	A hand of mid-range strength, between a minimum strength hand and a maximum strength hand.
Interior sequence	A sequence in which you have two or more touching cards and you also have a higher card in the suit. An example is KJ10.
Invitational bid	A bid which asks a partner either to pass or bid again, depending on the strength of his hand.
Jump shift	A rebid in a new suit (shift), skipping (jumping) a level, used to describe a very strong hand.

Lead	The first card played to a trick. After the opening lead, the player who wins a trick leads to the subsequent trick.
Length points	Valuation points given for the length of a suit: 1 point for a five-card suit, 2 points for a six-card suit, and so on.
Limit (bid)	A bid which limits one's strength to a range of points. For example, a 1NT opening bid is a limit bid showing 12-14 points.
Location	The hand that contains a specific card.
Long side	The partnership hand containing the most cards in a particular suit.
Lose control	When the declarer has no trumps left and cannot prevent the opponents from taking all their winners.
Losers	Cards in the declarer's hand which may be taken by higher cards held by the opponents.
Lowest-ranking suit	Clubs are the lowest-ranking suit, followed by diamonds, hearts and then spades.
Major suits	Hearts and spades.
Make (the contract)	Take the number of tricks to which the partnership committed during the auction.
Minor suits	Clubs and diamonds.
Natural bid	A bid which suggests the denomination bid as a possible final contract.
Negative response	A conventional response to show a very weak hand.
No bid	Commonly used expression in Britain to mean 'Pass.'
No trumps	A contract played with no suit as trumps.
Offence	The partnership which wins the contract.
One of a suit	An opening bid, or overcall, of 1♣, 1♢, 1♡ or 1♠.

Opener	The player who makes the first bid in the auction.
Open the bidding	To make the first bid in the auction, other than 'Pass'.
Opening lead	The card led to the first trick. The player to the left of the declarer makes the opening lead.
Opponents	The players on the opposing side. If you are declarer, the two defenders.
Overcall	Make a bid after an opponent has opened the bidding.
Overtake	Play a card higher than the one already contributed by your side, even when the original card may win the trick.
Overtrump	Play on a trick a trump that is higher than one played previously.
Partscore	A contract below game level.
Pass	A call that indicates a player does not want to make a bid at this point in the auction. 'No bid' is an equivalent term.
Passive defence	Leading a suit which is unlikely to develop tricks for the defence but which is also unlikely to help the declarer make the contract.
Penalty	Points given to the opponents in the scoring if the declarer fails to make the contract.
Penalty double	A double used to increase the size of the penalty if the opponents are defeated.
Plan	Four steps – S T O P – which the declarer can use to guide his play of the hand.
Points	Values given for high cards and length to help determine the strength of a hand (see HCPs).
Positive response	A conventional response that indicates a hand of more than minimum strength.
Potential trick	A card that could take a trick after a higher card has been played or if a finesse is successful.

Pre-emptive bid	A bid made at a higher level than necessary to take bidding room away from the opponents during the auction.
Promote (winners)	Driving out the higher cards held by the opponents in a suit.
Quantitative raise	An invitational raise, limiting the strength of the hand to a range of points.
Raise	Bidding partner's suit at a higher level.
Rebid	The second bid made by either the opener or the responder.
Redouble	A bid made after an opponent's double that further increases the score for making the contract, and the penalty for being defeated in the contract.
Repeated finesse	A finesse taken more than once in the same suit.
Responder	Opener's partner.
Return a partner's suit	Lead the same suit that a partner led when you have the opportunity.
Reverse	A rebid at the two level, or higher, in a higher-ranking suit than that originally bid.
Revoke	Fail to follow suit when you could have done so.
Role	The part played by the opening bidder or responder during the auction. The opening bidder usually acts as the describer, while responder acts as the captain.
Rubber bridge	A form of bridge where the first side to make two games wins the match.
Ruff	Play a trump when you have no cards left in the suit led.
Ruff and discard	The lead of a suit in which both the declarer and the dummy are void while both still have trumps left. This allows the declarer to trump (ruff) in one hand and discard a loser from the other hand.

Second hand	The defender who has to play next when the declarer leads a card from his hand or the dummy.
Sequence	Series of touching high cards. For example, the king, queen and jack in a suit make up a sequence.
Shape	Distribution.
Short side	The partnership hand with the fewer number of cards in a particular suit.
Short suit	A holding of only one or two cards of a suit in a player's hand.
Show out	Discard when a suit is led.
Side suit	A suit other than the trump suit.
Signal	Information given by one defender to his partner through the specific card he chooses to play in a suit.
Sign-off bid	A bid that asks partner to pass.
Simple overcall	An overcall in a suit at the cheapest available level.
Singleton	An original holding of one card in a suit.
Slam	A commitment to take 12 tricks (small slam) or 13 tricks (grand slam).
Small cards	Cards below the ten in any suit.
Solid suit	Suit missing no high cards.
Stayman	A convention, developed by Sam Stayman, which is used after partner opens the bidding with 1NT or 2NT to discover whether or not he has a four-card major suit.
Stranded	Winner(s) left in a hand to which there is no entry.
Strength	An estimate of the value of a hand based on the high cards held: 4 points for an ace, 3 points for a king, 2 points for a queen and 1 point for a jack.

Suit	One of the four groups to which each card can belong: clubs, diamonds, hearts or spades.
Suit preference (signal)	A signal by a defender which tells his partner which of two suits he would prefer led, while he is playing a card in a third suit. A high card shows preference for a higher-ranking suit; a low card shows preference for a lower-ranking suit
Support	Three or more cards held in a suit bid by your partner.
Support points	Points given for a void, singleton or doubleton when you are supporting (raising) your partner's suit and will be the dummy.
Sure trick	A trick which can be taken without giving the lead to the opponents.
Takeout double	A double which asks a partner to bid his best suit.
Taking a finesse against the dummy	Playing a card other than your highest when your partner has led a low card and the declarer has not played the dummy's highest card. The objective is to try to keep the dummy's high card trapped by your higher card.
Third hand	The third person to play to a trick.
Touching suits	Two suits which are ranked next to each other. For example, diamonds and hearts.
Trap a (high card)	Capture an opponent's high card with the help of a finesse.
Trapped (card)	A card which can be captured by a higher card in the next opponent's hand when it is played.
Trick	The four cards played during one round of the play. One card is contributed by each player.

Trick score	The number of points given during the scoring for each trick bid and made by the declarer.
Trump suit	The suit named in the final contract. A trump played on a trick will win the trick if a higher trump is not played.
Unbalanced hand	A hand containing a void, a singleton or more than one doubleton.
Unbid suit	A suit which has not been mentioned during the auction.
Unblocking	Play the high card(s) in the short hand first so that the high cards in the opposite (long) hand can be promoted into winners.
Uppercut	Tactic by a defender of trumping with a high trump in order to promote a trump trick in his partner's hand.
Void	A suit in which no cards are held.
Weak no trump	An opening bid of 1NT used to show a balanced hand of 12-14 points.
Winner	A card which will win a trick when it is played.
Zone	The various levels on the bidding steps for which bonuses are awarded in the scoring: partscore, game and slam.

Rubber Bridge Scoring Table

A rubber bridge score sheet is divided into two columns: We and They. There is a line across the middle of the score sheet, and points are scored both above and below this line.

Only points for tricks 'bid and made' are scored below the line. All other points are scored above the line.

You can score points in three ways:
- By making the contract your side has bid
- By defeating the contract the enemy have bid
- By earning a bonus score.

Score for bidding and making a contract

If you make a contract, the number of points you score depends on the denomination of the contract. For each trick above six, you receive:

20 points if the contract was in a minor suit (♣ or ◊)

30 points if the contract was in a major suit (♡ or ♠)

40 points for the first trick at no trumps

30 points for each trick after the first at no trumps.

Remember, only points for tricks bid and made are scored below the line. So, for making a contract of three hearts, you score 90 below the line. For making five diamonds, you score 100. For making six no trumps, you score 190.

A score of 100 points or more below the line is a *game*. You can achieve a game with a single contract (3NT, four of a major, five of a minor) or by making two or more *partscore* contracts which add up to 100 points or more. When one side makes a game, a line is drawn underneath the game score and any partscores already achieved by the other side no longer count towards game. A side which has made a game is said to be *vulnerable*, a side which has not yet made a game is *not vulnerable*. The first side to win two games wins the *rubber* and is given a bonus for so doing.

If you make more tricks than your contract, you score points for the extra tricks, but they are scored above the line. So, if you play in three hearts but make 11 tricks, you score 90 below the line and 60 above it. You have not made game – you do not have 100 points below the line.

Score for defeating the enemy contract

If you defeat the enemy contract, the points you score depend on whether the enemy are vulnerable and whether the contract was doubled or redoubled. If the contract was not doubled, you receive:

50 points for each undertrick if the enemy are not vulnerable.

100 points for each undertrick if the enemy are vulnerable.

So, if the enemy play in four hearts and make eight tricks, you score 100 points if they are not vulnerable and 200 points if they are. These points are then scored above the line.

If the contract was doubled, the scoring is:

Number of undertricks	Not vulnerable	Vulnerable
1	100	200
2	300	500
3	500	800
4	800	1100
5	1100	1400
6	1400	1700

and each extra undertrick scores a further 300 points. If the contract was redoubled, the score is twice the score for a doubled contract.

If you are doubled and make the contract, the score for tricks bid and made is doubled (and if this brings the total above 100, you make game – so two hearts doubled is a game contract because it would score 120 if made). If you make overtricks, you score 100 points per trick if not vulnerable and 200 points per trick if vulnerable regardless of the denomination. You also score a bonus of 50 points for making a doubled contract and 100 points for making a redoubled contract. So, if you played in two no trumps doubled and made ten tricks not vulnerable, you would score 140 below the line (70x2) and 250 above the line (100 for each overtrick plus the 50 bonus).

Bonus scores

You can earn bonus scores for bidding and making a slam contract as follows:

	Not vulnerable	Vulnerable
Small slam	500	750
Grand slam	1000	1500

The side that wins the rubber also scores a bonus of 700 points if the enemy has not made a game, or 500 points if the enemy has made a game.

Finally, you can score a bonus for holding what are called *honours*. If you hold in your hand alone four of the five highest cards in the trump suit – four of the A, K, Q, J and 10 – you score 100 for honours. If you hold all five, you score 150 for honours. If you hold all four aces at no trumps you score 150 for honours. Declarer, dummy or either defender may score for honours. If you are declarer, you may claim your honours at any time, but if you are a defender you must wait till the end of the hand!

Index

BATSFORD BRIDGE BOOKS

Bread and Butter Bidding
Brian Senior
£9.99 216 pp
A basic grounding in correct bidding technique and standard meanings.

Bridge Adventures of Robin Hood
David Bird
£8.99 128 pp
After books on the bridge-playing monks, the scene shifts to Sherwood Forest.

Bridge: Basic Defence
Freddie North
£9.99 96 pp
This basic volume covers simple signalling and other basic themes.

Bridge for Beginners: A Complete Course
Zia Mahmood
£12.99 480 pp

Bridge in the Fourth Dimension
Victor Mollo
£8.99 144 pp
The brilliant sequel to Bridge in the Menagerie with the hilarious characters of the Griffins Club.

Bridge in the Menagerie
Victor Mollo
£8.99 144 pp
A long-overdue reprint of one of the great bridge books of all time.

Bridge: Learn from the Stars
Mark Horton and Tony Sowter
£9.99 128 pp
A collection of instructive hands of the last 10 years.

Bridge the Vital Principles
Freddie North
£8.99 128 pp
One of the game's top teachers explores common situations that confront any intermediate player.

Card Play Technique
Nico Gardener and Victor Mollo
£12.99 384 pp
An indispensable volume in every library.

Cards at Play
Freddie North
£8.99 144 pp
Describes a wide range of the major technques available to declarer.

Contract Killers
Phillip and Robert King
£8.99 144 pp
The Kings' first hilarious foray into bridge parody.

Conventional Bidding Explained
Freddie North
£8.99 144 pp
Over 30 common bidding conventions are thoroughly explained.

Defence in Depth
Martin Hoffman and Terence Reese
£9.99 176 pp

Expert Defence
Raymond Brock
£9.99   128 pp
Tough defensive problems for the reader.

Expert Tuition
Sally and Raymond Brock
£9.99   128 pp

Farewell, My Dummy
Phillip and Robert King
£8.99   144 pp
Five absorbing bridge novellas written in an entertaining and witty style.

First Principles of Card Play
Paul Marston
£6.99   128 pp
Equally suitable for club players and social rubber-bridge players.

Hand Evaluation in Bridge
Brian Senior
£9.99   128 pp

Hidden Side of Bridge, The
Terence Reese and David Bird
£8.99   128 pp
Intriguing hands are analysed by two of Britain's best bridge writers.

King's Tales, The
Phillip and Robert King
£8.99   144 pp
Scintillating pastiches in the best tradition of humorous bridge writing.

Learn Bridge in Five Days
Terence Reese
£6.99   112 pp
This quick introduction to the game covers all the essential aspects.

Masters & Monsters
Victor Mollo
£8.99   240 pp
A reissue of one of Mollo's classic menagerie series.

New Approach to Bidding, A
Jon Drabble
£8.99   144 pp
A Complete Hand Evaluation known as the Midmac System.

Over Your Shoulder: Learn from the Experts
Tony Forrester and Brian Senior
£8.99   144 pp
Unique insights into expert thinking in all areas of the game.

Play these hands with Brian Senior
Brian Senior
£8.99   128 pp
Brian Senior lets you follow his thought processes in both bidding and play.

Practical Bridge Endings
Chien-Hwa Wang
£9.99   128 pp
62 hands taken from actual play illustrate the range of possible endings.

Raising Partner
Brian Senior
£8.99   128 pp

Robin Hood's Bridge Memoirs
David Bird
£9.99   144 pp
David Bird is well-known for his hilarious stories. This features the outlaws of Sherwood Forest.

Secrets of Expert Card Play
Tony Forrester and David Bird
£9.99   144 pp
A major new work on the play of the cards by two top authors.

Secrets of Success
Tony Forrester
£9.99   160 pp
One of Europe's top players reveals his way of thinking.

Step-by-Step Card Play in No Trumps
Robert Berthe and Norbert Lébely
£8.99   144 pp

Step-by-Step Card Play in Suits
Brian Senior
£8.99   144 pp

Step-by-Step Competitive Bidding
Tony Sowter
£8.99   144 pp

Step-by-Step Constructive Bidding
Tony Sowter
£8.99   144 pp

Step-by-Step Deception in Defence
Barry Rigal
£8.99   128 pp

Step-by-Step Deceptive Declarer Play
Barry Rigal
£8.99   128 pp

Step-by-Step Overcalls
Sally Brock
£8.99   128 pp

Step-by-Step Planning the Defence
Raymond Brock
£8.99   144 pp

Step-by-Step Pre-empts
Alan Mould
£9.99   128 pp

Step-by-Step Signalling
Mark Horton
£8.99   144 pp

Step-by-Step Slam Bidding
Alan Mould
£8.99   128 pp

The Daily Telegraph Improve Your Bridge at Home
Tony Forrester
£8.99   128 pp
Aimed at all rubber-bridge enthusiasts, this book uses self-testing quizzes.

The Daily Telegraph Play Bridge at Home
Tony Forrester
£8.99   128 pp
A general introduction to the game.
